SIMON
SPURRIER

DYLAN
BURNETT

TRIONA
FARRELL

WEAVERS ™

BOOM!
STUDIOS

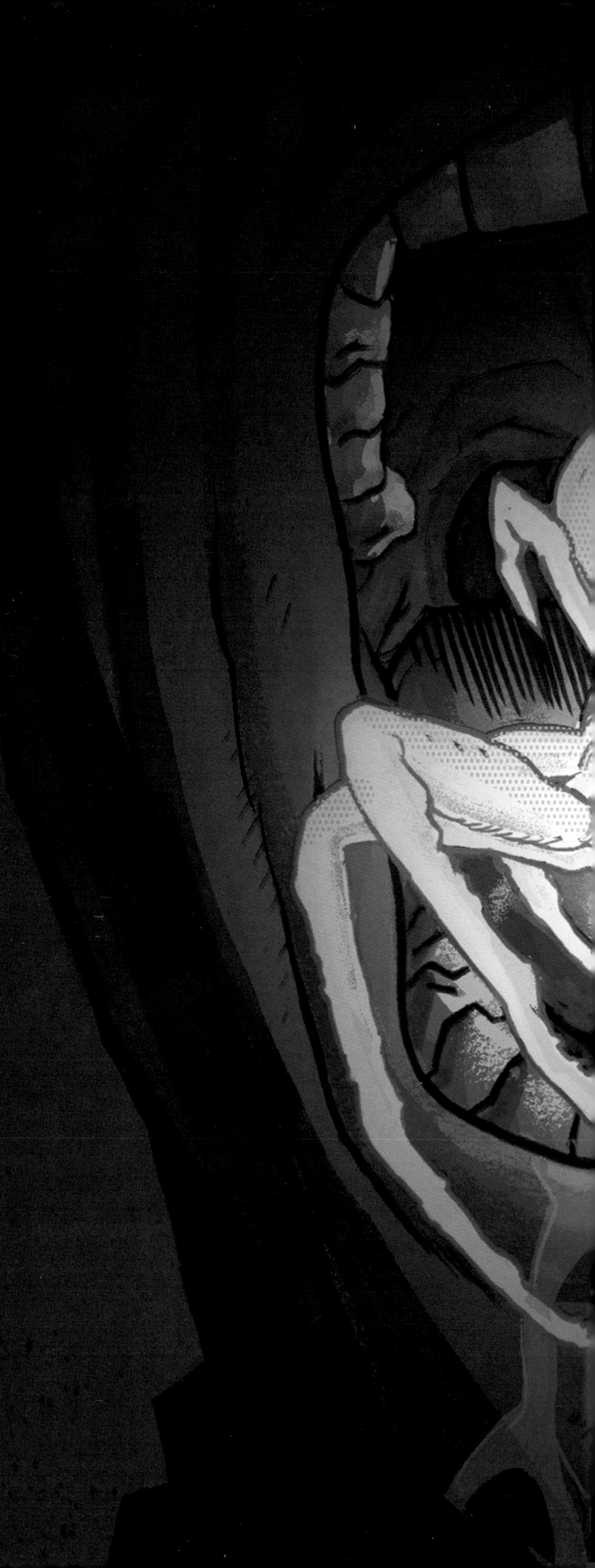

WEAVERS, May 2017. Published by BOOM! Studios, a division of Boom Entertainment, Inc. Weavers is ™ & © 2017 Simon Spurrier Ltd. Originally published in single magazine form as WEAVERS No. 1-6. ™ & © 2016 Simon Spurrier Ltd. All rights reserved. BOOM! Studios™ and the BOOM! Studios logo are trademarks of Boom Entertainment, Inc., registered in various countries and categories. All characters, events, and institutions depicted herein are fictional. Any similarity between any of the names, characters, persons, events, and/or institutions in this publication to actual names, characters, and persons, whether living or dead, events, and/or institutions is unintended and purely coincidental. BOOM! Studios does not read or accept unsolicited submissions of ideas, stories, or artwork.

A catalog record of this book is available from OCLC and from the BOOM! Studios website, www.boom-studios.com, on the Librarians Page.

BOOM! Studios, 5670 Wilshire Boulevard, Suite 450, Los Angeles, CA 90036-5679. Printed in China. First Printing.

ISBN: 978-1-60886-963-3, eISBN: 978-1-61398-634-9

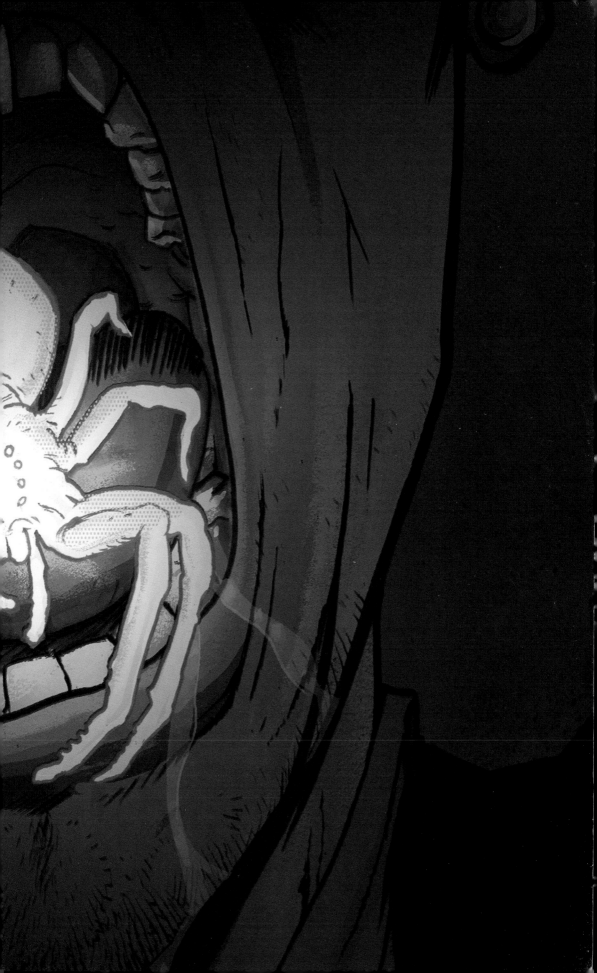

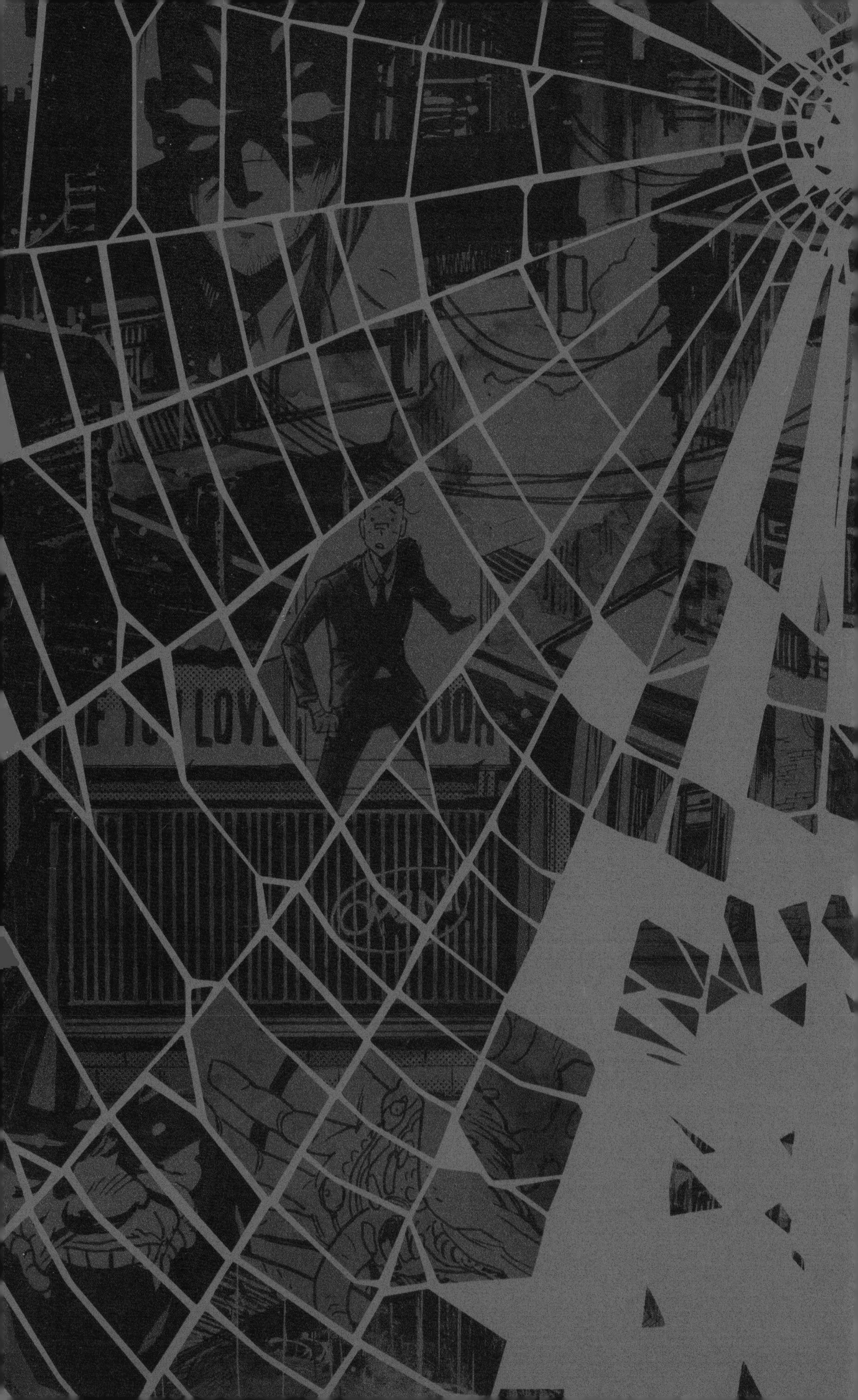
LOVE

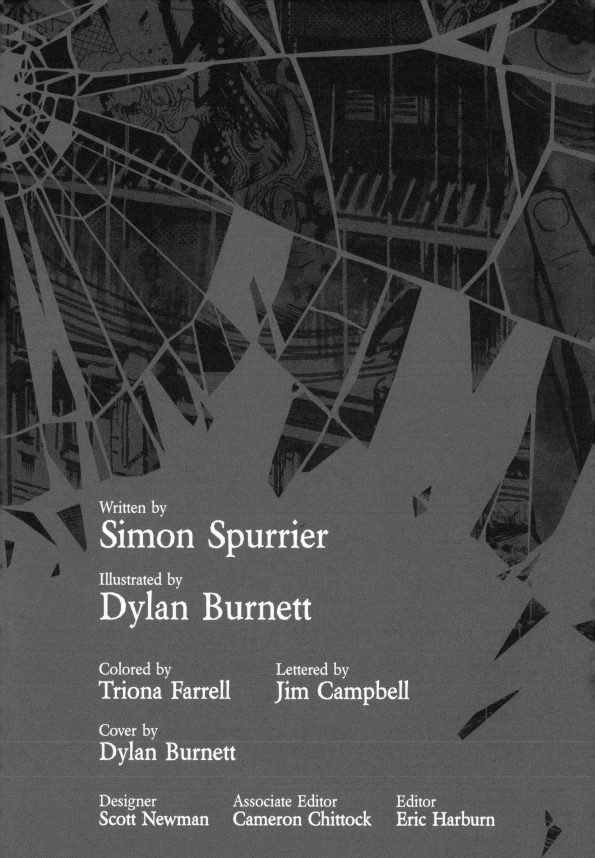

Written by
Simon Spurrier

Illustrated by
Dylan Burnett

Colored by
Triona Farrell

Lettered by
Jim Campbell

Cover by
Dylan Burnett

Designer
Scott Newman

Associate Editor
Cameron Chittock

Editor
Eric Harburn

WEAVERS ™

Created by **Simon Spurrier**

CHAPTER ONE

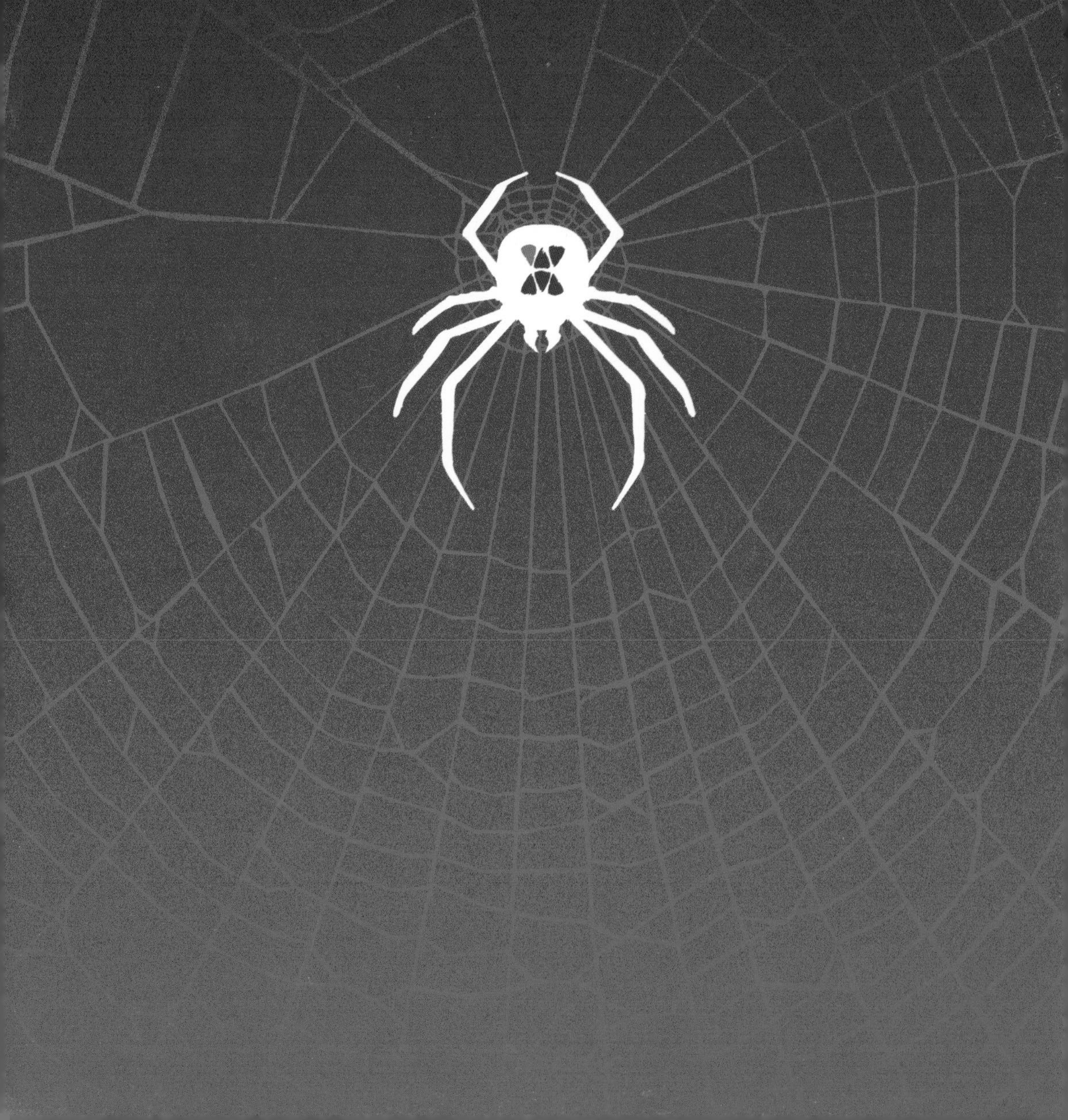

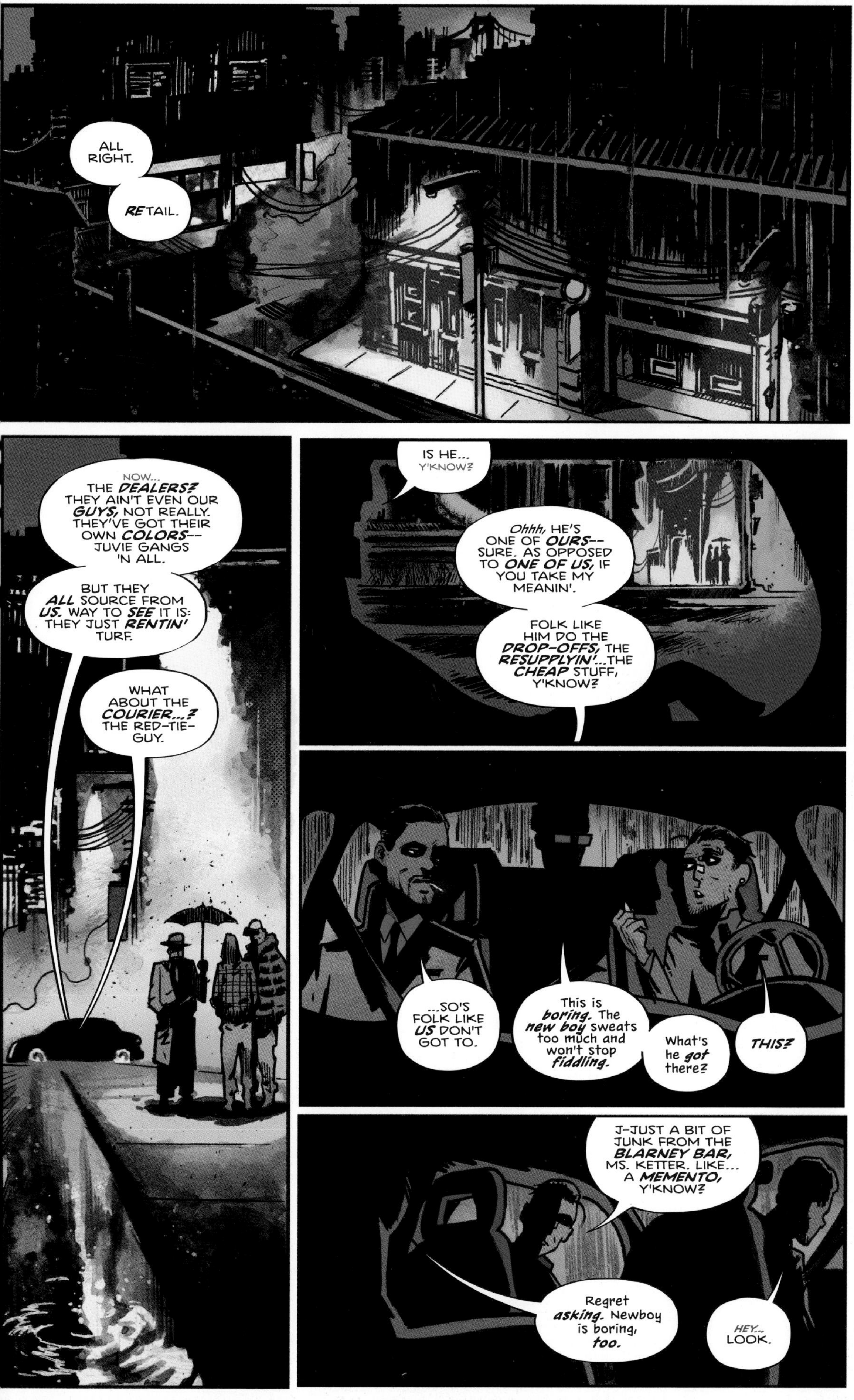

ALL RIGHT.
RETAIL.
NOW... THE DEALERS? THEY AIN'T EVEN OUR GUYS, NOT REALLY. THEY'VE GOT THEIR OWN COLORS-- JUVIE GANGS 'N ALL.
BUT THEY ALL SOURCE FROM US. WAY TO SEE IT IS: THEY JUST RENTIN' TURF.
WHAT ABOUT THE COURIER...? THE RED-TIE-GUY.
IS HE... Y'KNOW?
Ohhh, HE'S ONE OF OURS-- SURE. AS OPPOSED TO ONE OF US, IF YOU TAKE MY MEANIN'.
FOLK LIKE HIM DO THE DROP-OFFS, THE RESUPPLYIN'...THE CHEAP STUFF, Y'KNOW?
...SO'S FOLK LIKE US DON'T GOT TO.
This is boring. The new boy sweats too much and won't stop fiddling.
What's he got there?
THIS?
J-JUST A BIT OF JUNK FROM THE BLARNEY BAR, MS. KETTER. LIKE... A MEMENTO, Y'KNOW?
Regret asking. Newboy is boring, too.
HEY... LOOK.

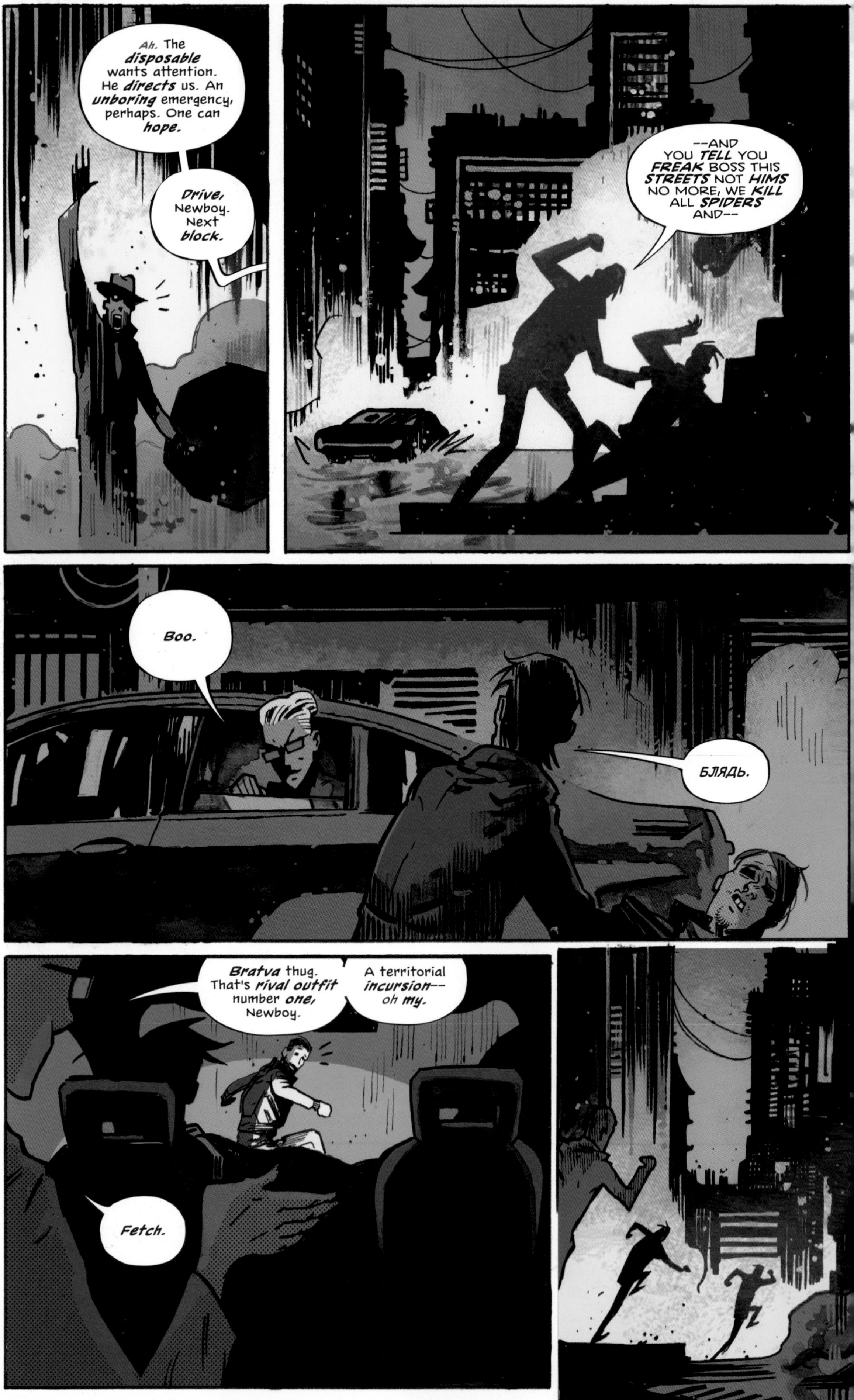
Ah. The disposable wants attention. He directs us. An unboring emergency, perhaps. One can hope.
Drive, Newboy. Next block.
--AND YOU TELL YOU FREAK BOSS THIS STREETS NOT HIMS NO MORE, WE KILL ALL SPIDERS AND--
Boo.
БЛЯДЬ.
Bratva thug. That's rival outfit number one, Newboy.
A territorial incursion-- oh my.
Fetch.

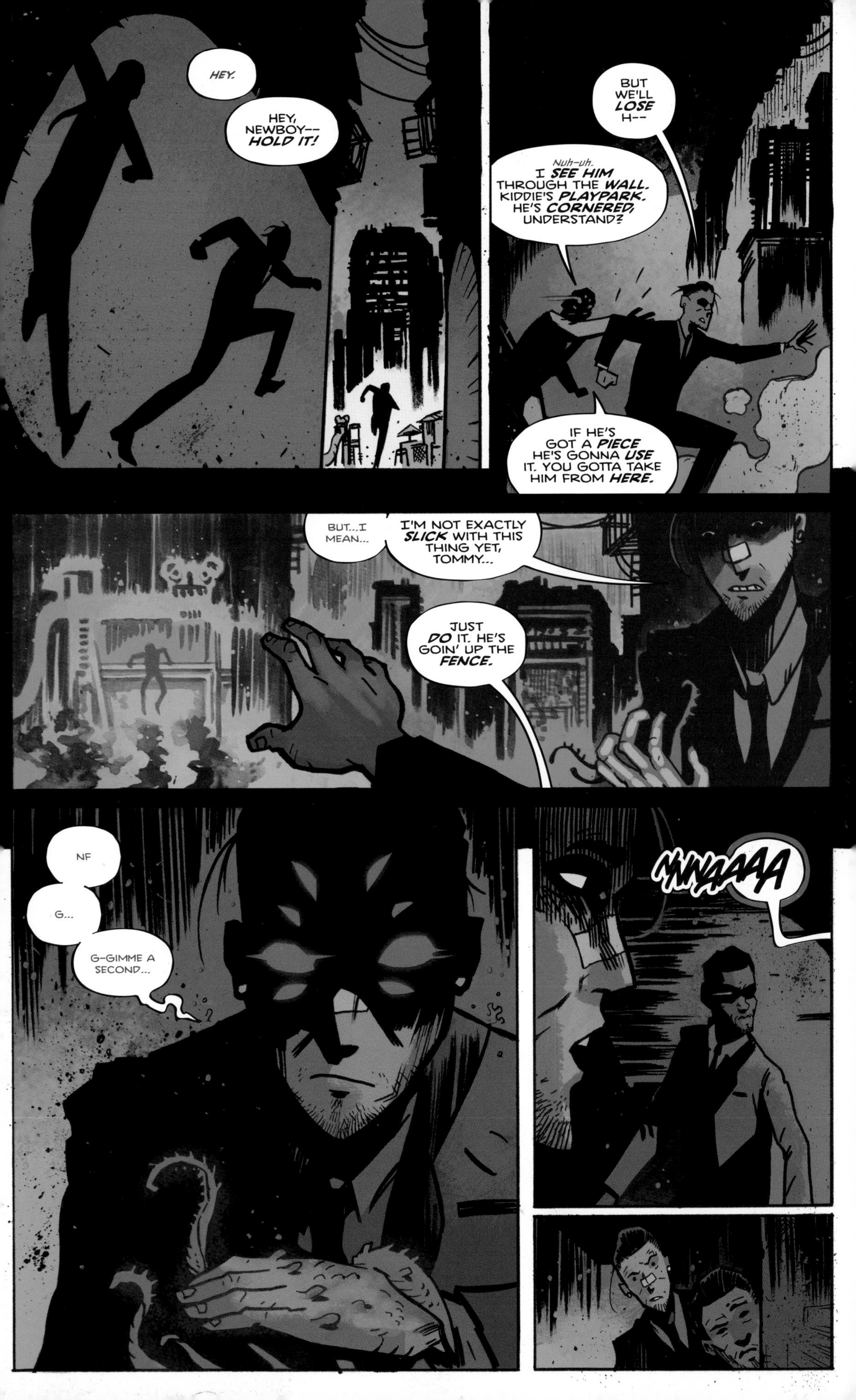
HEY.
HEY, NEWBOY-- HOLD IT!
BUT WE'LL LOSE H--
Nuh-uh. I SEE HIM THROUGH THE WALL. KIDDIE'S PLAYPARK. HE'S CORNERED, UNDERSTAND?
IF HE'S GOT A PIECE HE'S GONNA USE IT. YOU GOTTA TAKE HIM FROM HERE.
BUT...I MEAN...
I'M NOT EXACTLY SLICK WITH THIS THING YET, TOMMY...
JUST DO IT. HE'S GOIN' UP THE FENCE.
NF
G...
G-GIMME A SECOND...
MNNAAAA

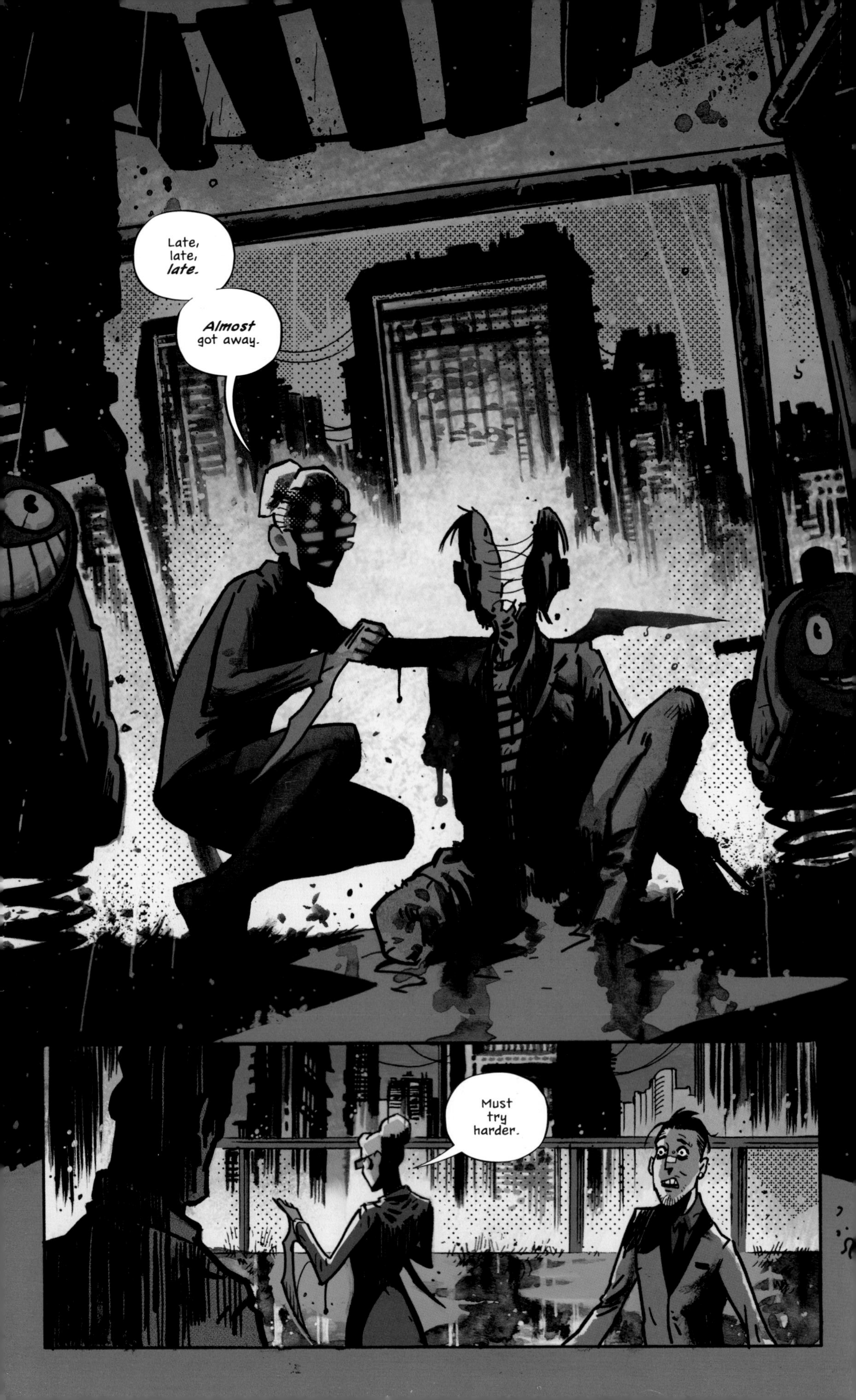
Late, late, *late.*
Almost got away.
Must try harder.

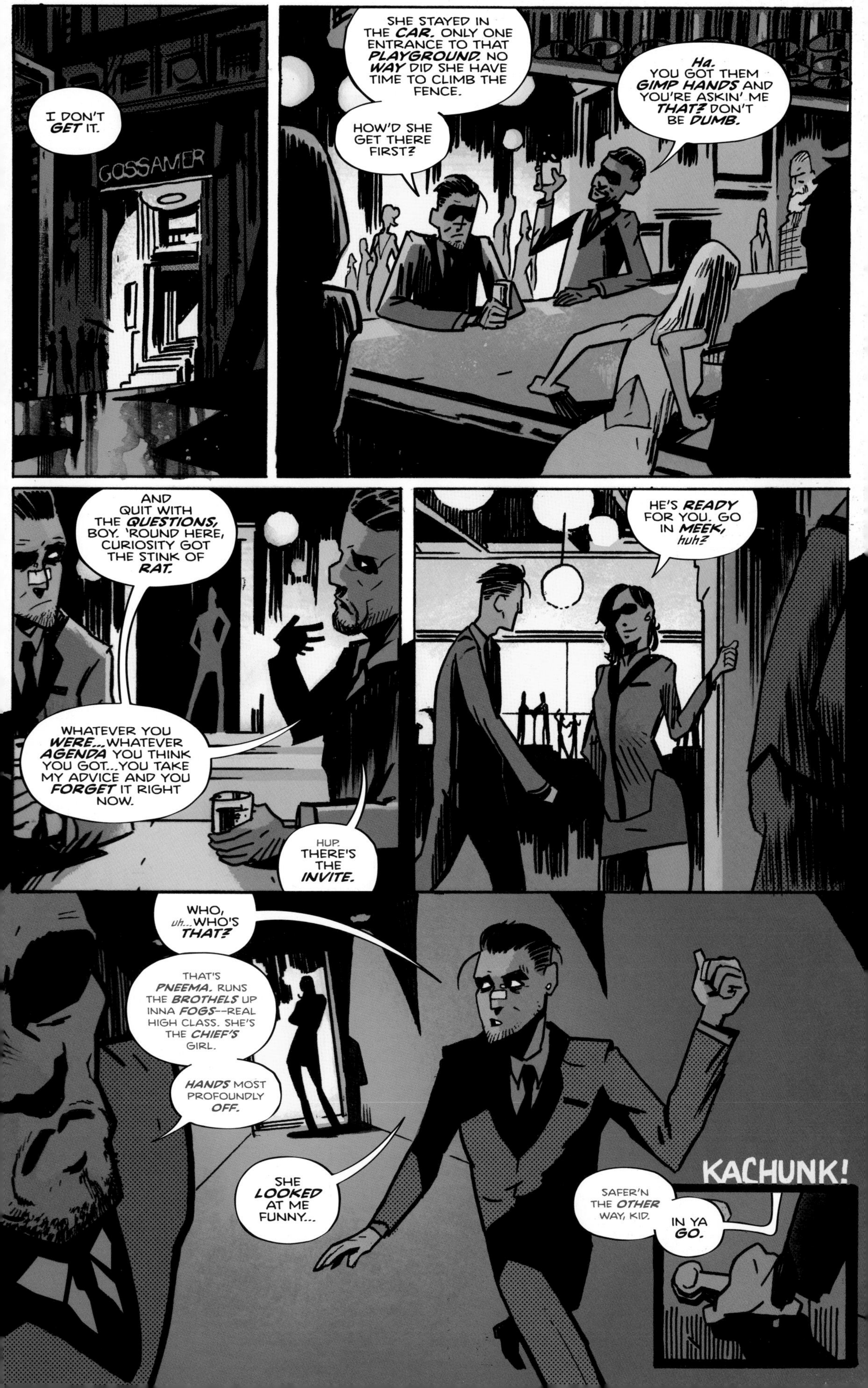
I DON'T GET IT.
GOSSAMER
SHE STAYED IN THE CAR. ONLY ONE ENTRANCE TO THAT PLAYGROUND. NO WAY DID SHE HAVE TIME TO CLIMB THE FENCE.
HOW'D SHE GET THERE FIRST?
Ha. YOU GOT THEM GIMP HANDS AND YOU'RE ASKIN' ME THAT? DON'T BE DUMB.
AND QUIT WITH THE QUESTIONS, BOY. 'ROUND HERE, CURIOSITY GOT THE STINK OF RAT.
WHATEVER YOU WERE...WHATEVER AGENDA YOU THINK YOU GOT...YOU TAKE MY ADVICE AND YOU FORGET IT RIGHT NOW.
HUP. THERE'S THE INVITE.
HE'S READY FOR YOU. GO IN MEEK, huh?
WHO, uh...WHO'S THAT?
THAT'S PNEEMA. RUNS THE BROTHELS UP INNA FOGS--REAL HIGH CLASS. SHE'S THE CHIEF'S GIRL.
HANDS MOST PROFOUNDLY OFF.
SHE LOOKED AT ME FUNNY...
KACHUNK!
SAFER'N THE OTHER WAY, KID.
IN YA GO.

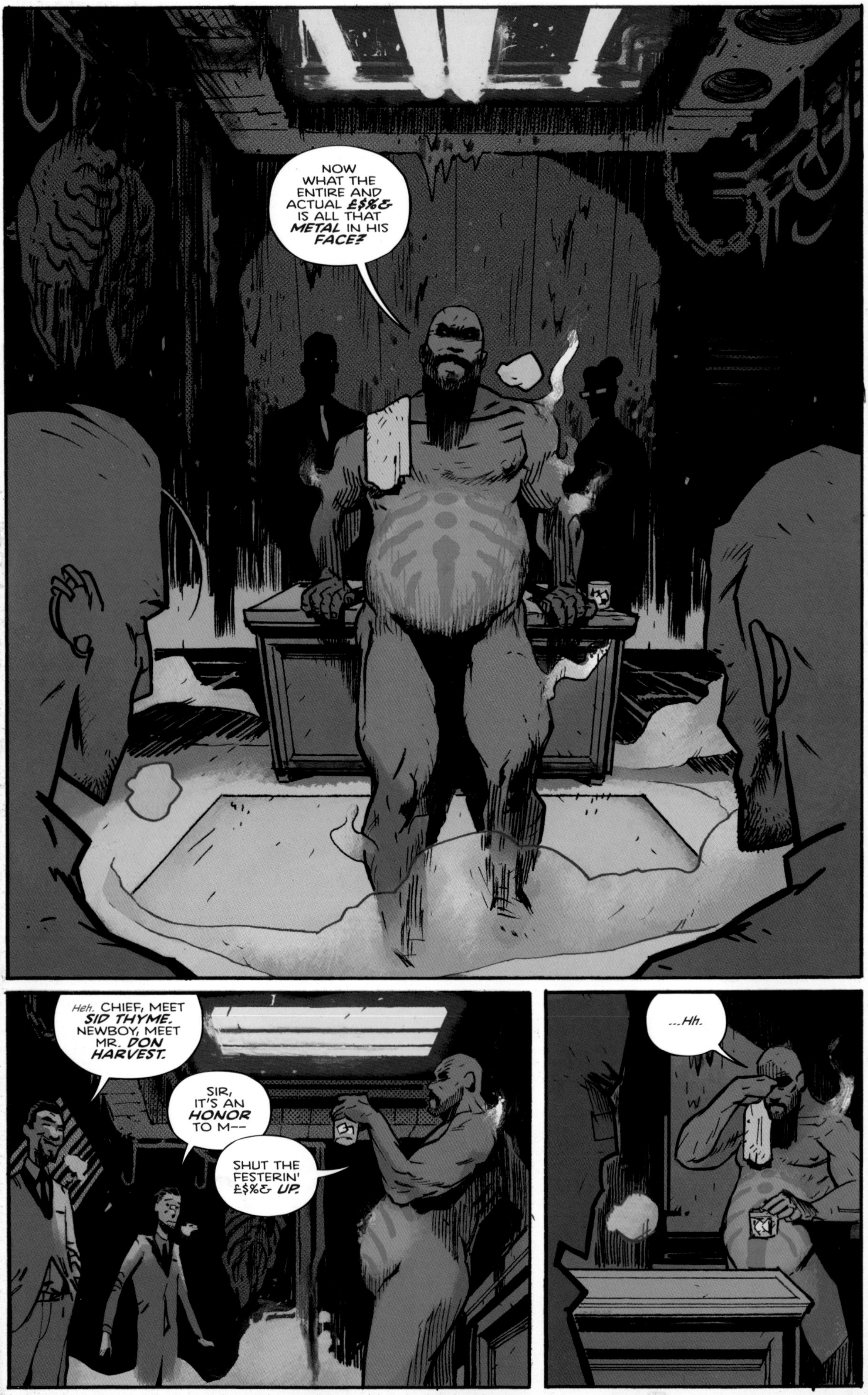
NOW WHAT THE ENTIRE AND ACTUAL £$%& IS ALL THAT METAL IN HIS FACE?
Heh. CHIEF, MEET SID THYME. NEWBOY, MEET MR. DON HARVEST.
SIR, IT'S AN HONOR TO M--
SHUT THE FESTERIN' £$%& UP.
...Hh.

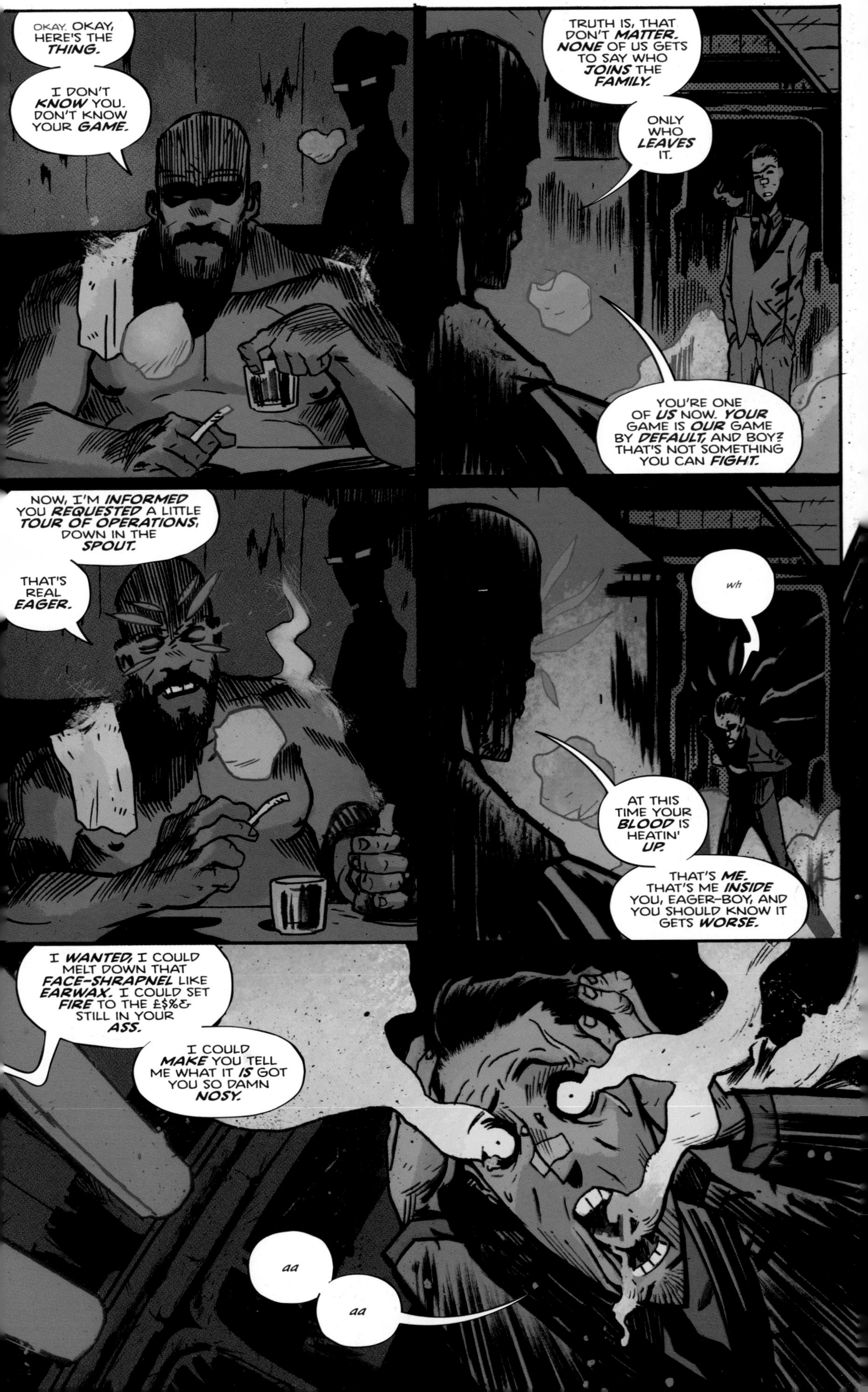
OKAY. OKAY, HERE'S THE THING.
I DON'T KNOW YOU. DON'T KNOW YOUR GAME.
TRUTH IS, THAT DON'T MATTER. NONE OF US GETS TO SAY WHO JOINS THE FAMILY.
ONLY WHO LEAVES IT.
YOU'RE ONE OF US NOW. YOUR GAME IS OUR GAME BY DEFAULT, AND BOY? THAT'S NOT SOMETHING YOU CAN FIGHT.
NOW, I'M INFORMED YOU REQUESTED A LITTLE TOUR OF OPERATIONS, DOWN IN THE SPOUT.
THAT'S REAL EAGER.
wh
AT THIS TIME YOUR BLOOD IS HEATIN' UP.
THAT'S ME. THAT'S ME INSIDE YOU, EAGER-BOY, AND YOU SHOULD KNOW IT GETS WORSE.
I WANTED, I COULD MELT DOWN THAT FACE-SHRAPNEL LIKE EARWAX. I COULD SET FIRE TO THE £$%& STILL IN YOUR ASS.
I COULD MAKE YOU TELL ME WHAT IT IS GOT YOU SO DAMN NOSY.
aa
aa

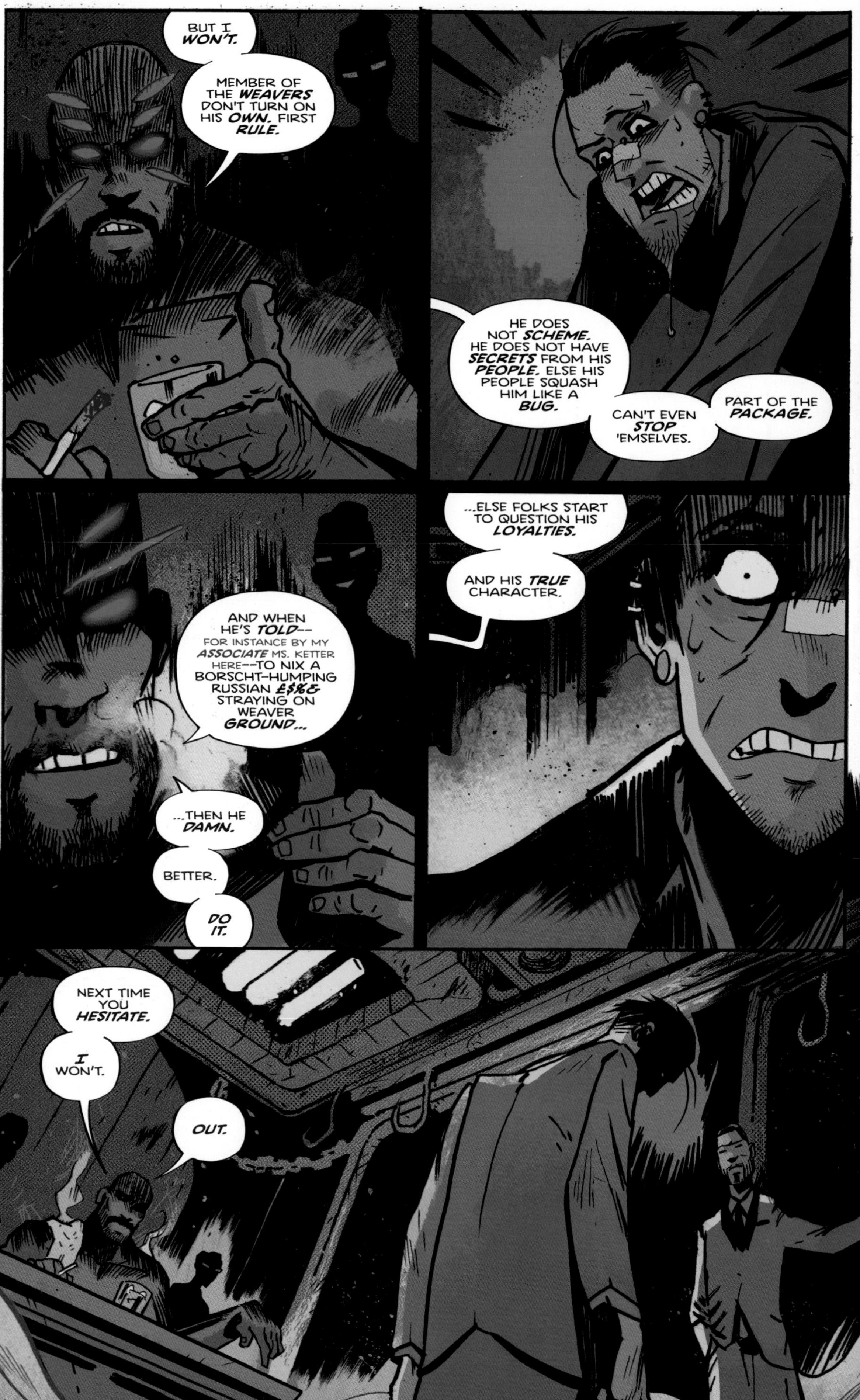
BUT I WON'T.
MEMBER OF THE WEAVERS DON'T TURN ON HIS OWN. FIRST RULE.
HE DOES NOT SCHEME. HE DOES NOT HAVE SECRETS FROM HIS PEOPLE. ELSE HIS PEOPLE SQUASH HIM LIKE A BUG.
CAN'T EVEN STOP 'EMSELVES.
PART OF THE PACKAGE.
AND WHEN HE'S TOLD-- FOR INSTANCE BY MY ASSOCIATE MS. KETTER HERE--TO NIX A BORSCHT-HUMPING RUSSIAN £$%& STRAYING ON WEAVER GROUND...
...THEN HE DAMN.
BETTER.
DO IT.
...ELSE FOLKS START TO QUESTION HIS LOYALTIES.
AND HIS TRUE CHARACTER.
NEXT TIME YOU HESITATE.
I WON'T.
OUT.

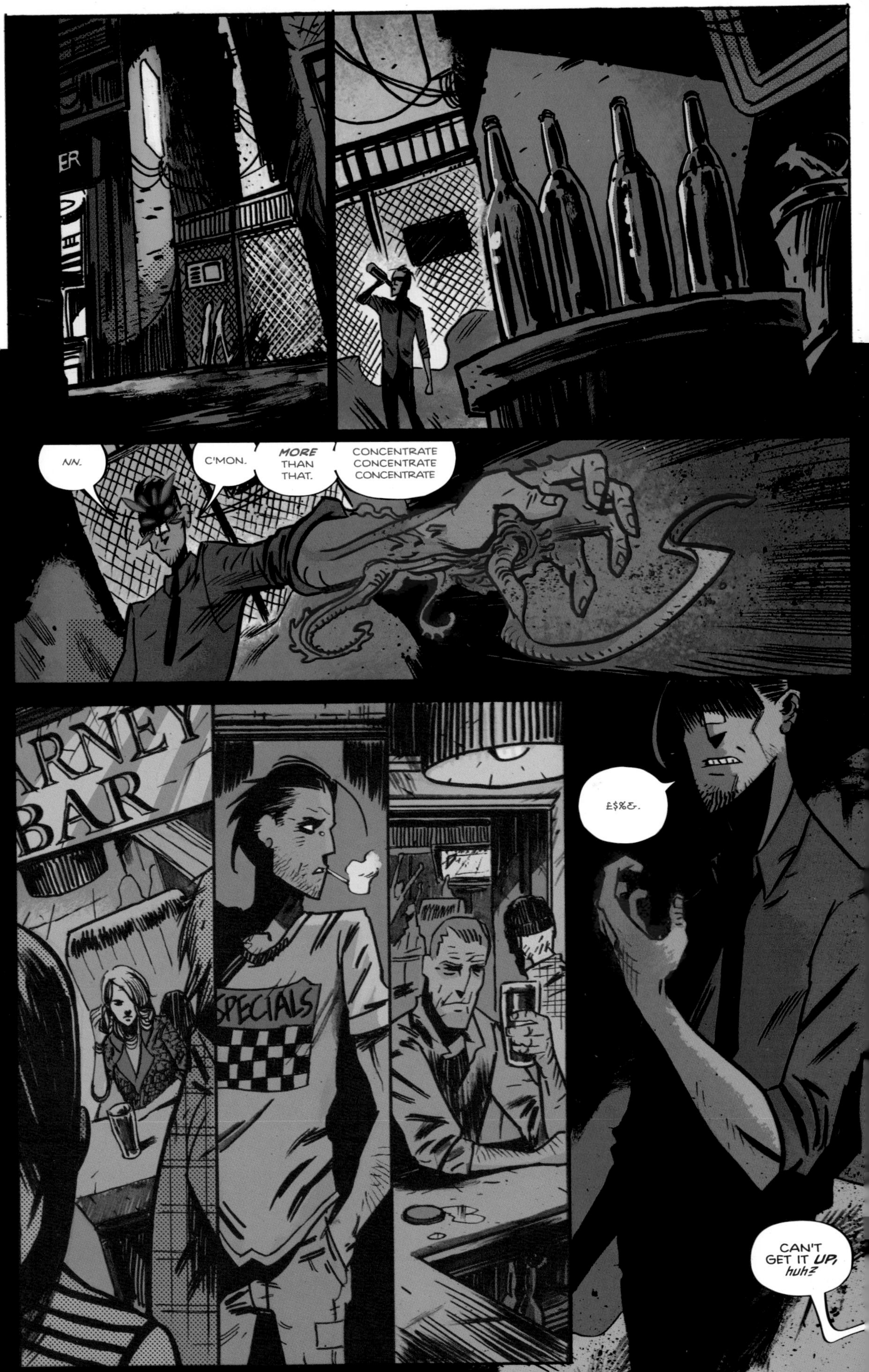
NN.
C'MON.
MORE THAN THAT.
CONCENTRATE CONCENTRATE CONCENTRATE
ARNEY BAR
SPECIALS
£$%&.
CAN'T GET IT UP, huh?

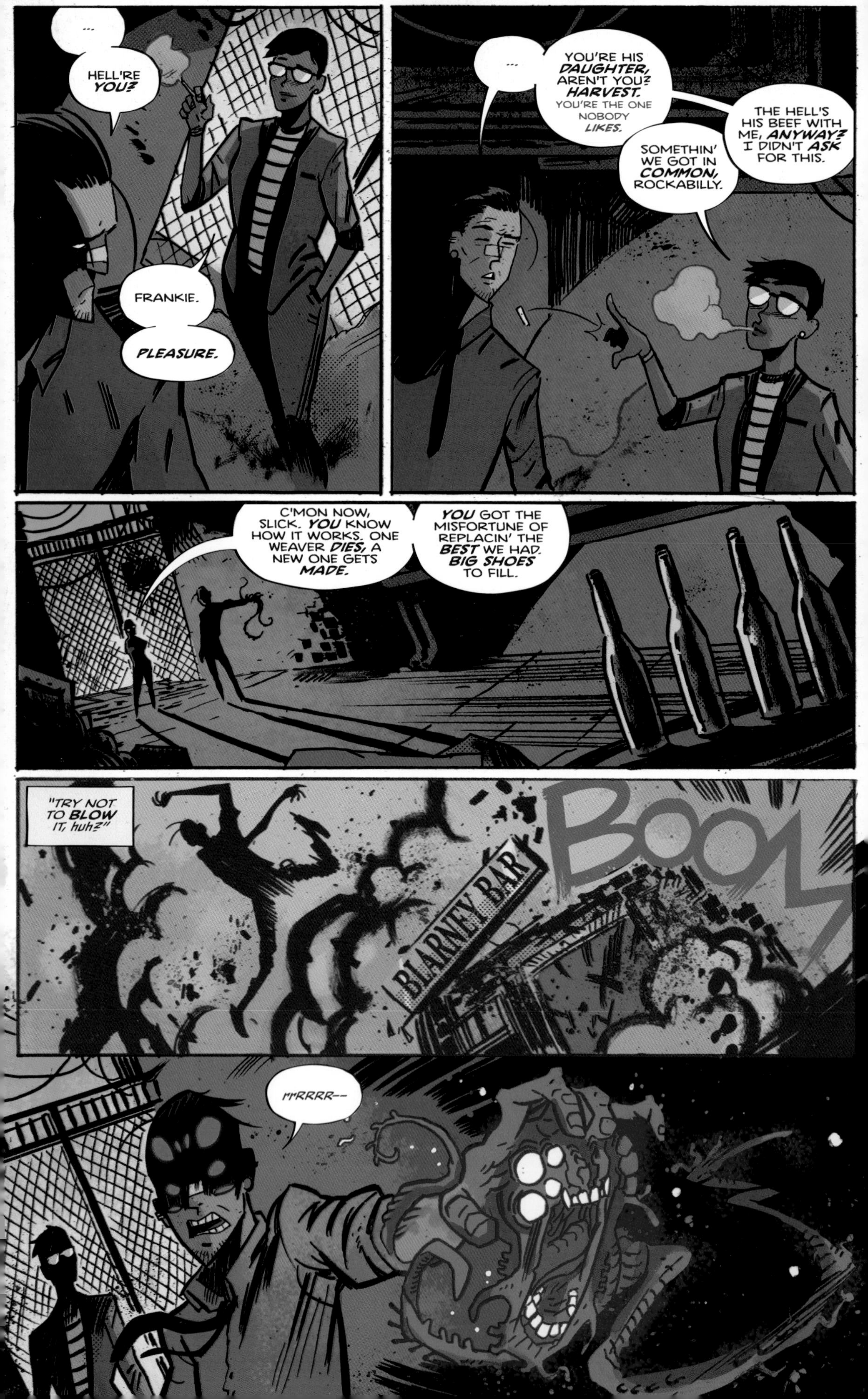
...
HELL'RE YOU?
FRANKIE.
PLEASURE.
...
YOU'RE HIS DAUGHTER, AREN'T YOU? HARVEST. YOU'RE THE ONE NOBODY LIKES.
THE HELL'S HIS BEEF WITH ME, ANYWAY? I DIDN'T ASK FOR THIS.
SOMETHIN' WE GOT IN COMMON, ROCKABILLY.
C'MON NOW, SLICK. YOU KNOW HOW IT WORKS. ONE WEAVER DIES, A NEW ONE GETS MADE.
YOU GOT THE MISFORTUNE OF REPLACIN' THE BEST WE HAD. BIG SHOES TO FILL.
"TRY NOT TO BLOW IT, huh?"
BLARNEY BAR
BOOM
rrrRRRR--

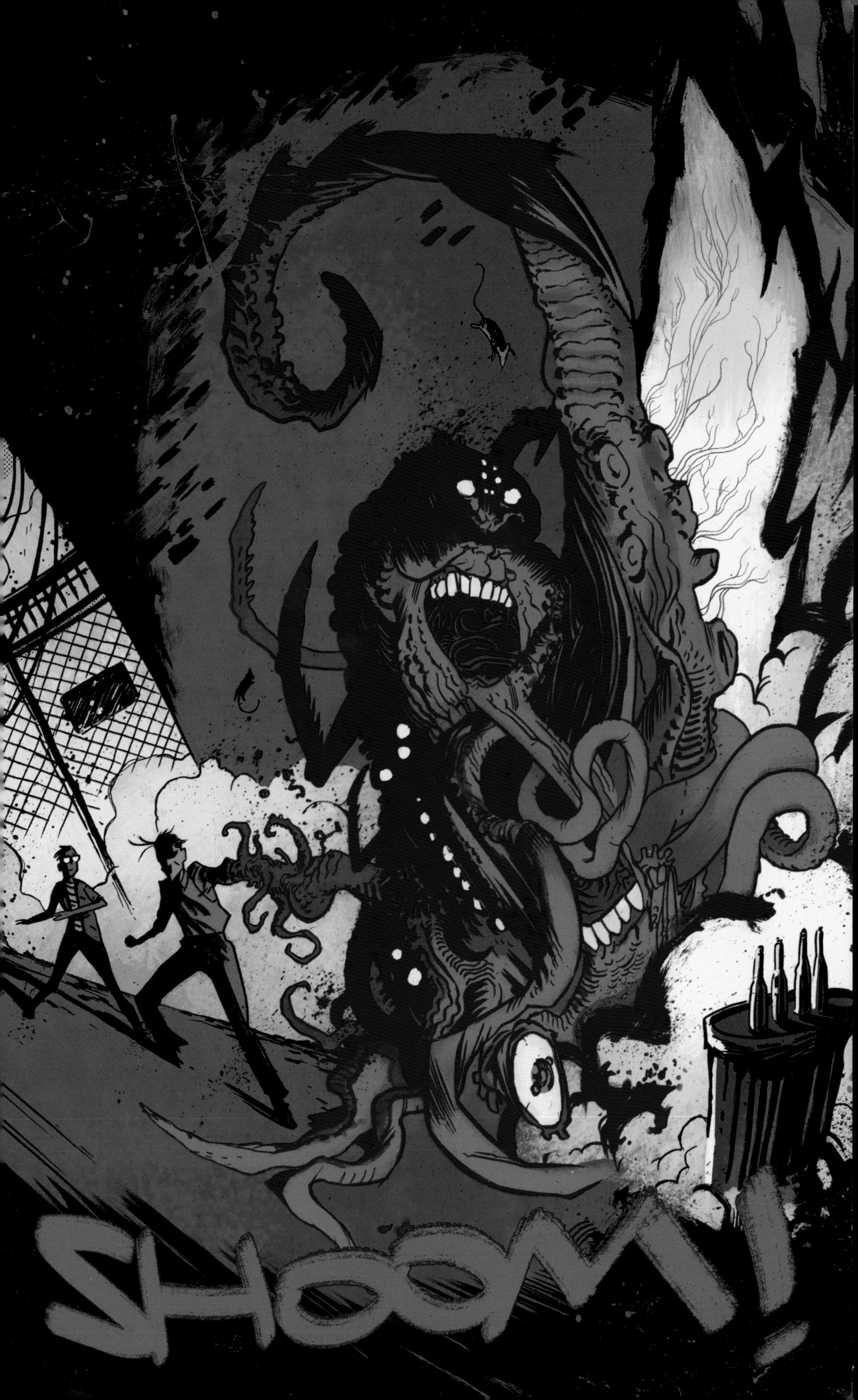
SHOOM!

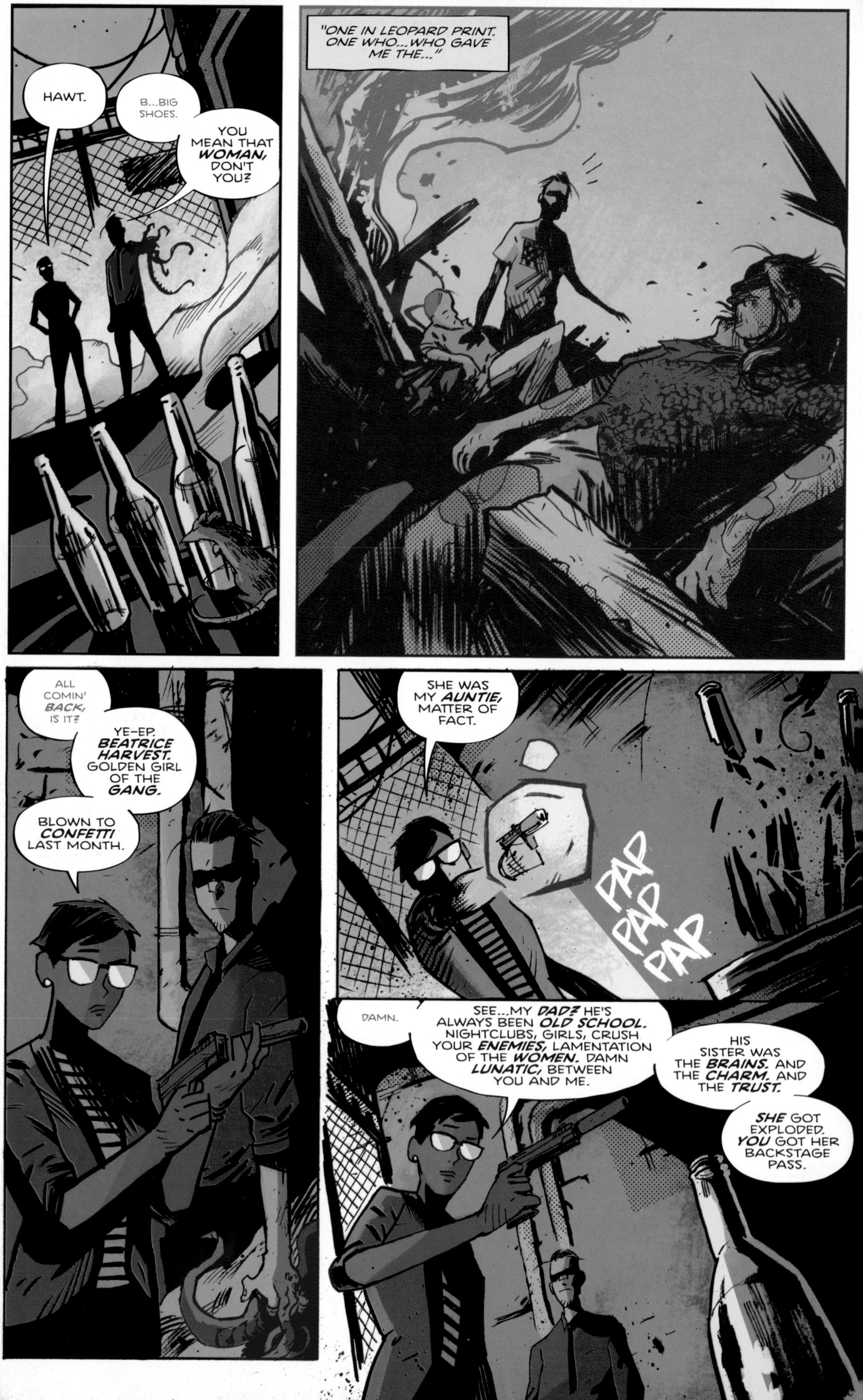
HAWT.
B...BIG SHOES.
YOU MEAN THAT WOMAN, DON'T YOU?
"ONE IN LEOPARD PRINT. ONE WHO...WHO GAVE ME THE..."
ALL COMIN' BACK, IS IT?
YE-EP. BEATRICE HARVEST. GOLDEN GIRL OF THE GANG.
BLOWN TO CONFETTI LAST MONTH.
SHE WAS MY AUNTIE, MATTER OF FACT.
PAP PAP PAP
DAMN.
SEE...MY DAD? HE'S ALWAYS BEEN OLD SCHOOL. NIGHTCLUBS, GIRLS, CRUSH YOUR ENEMIES, LAMENTATION OF THE WOMEN. DAMN LUNATIC, BETWEEN YOU AND ME.
HIS SISTER WAS THE BRAINS. AND THE CHARM. AND THE TRUST.
SHE GOT EXPLODED. YOU GOT HER BACKSTAGE PASS.

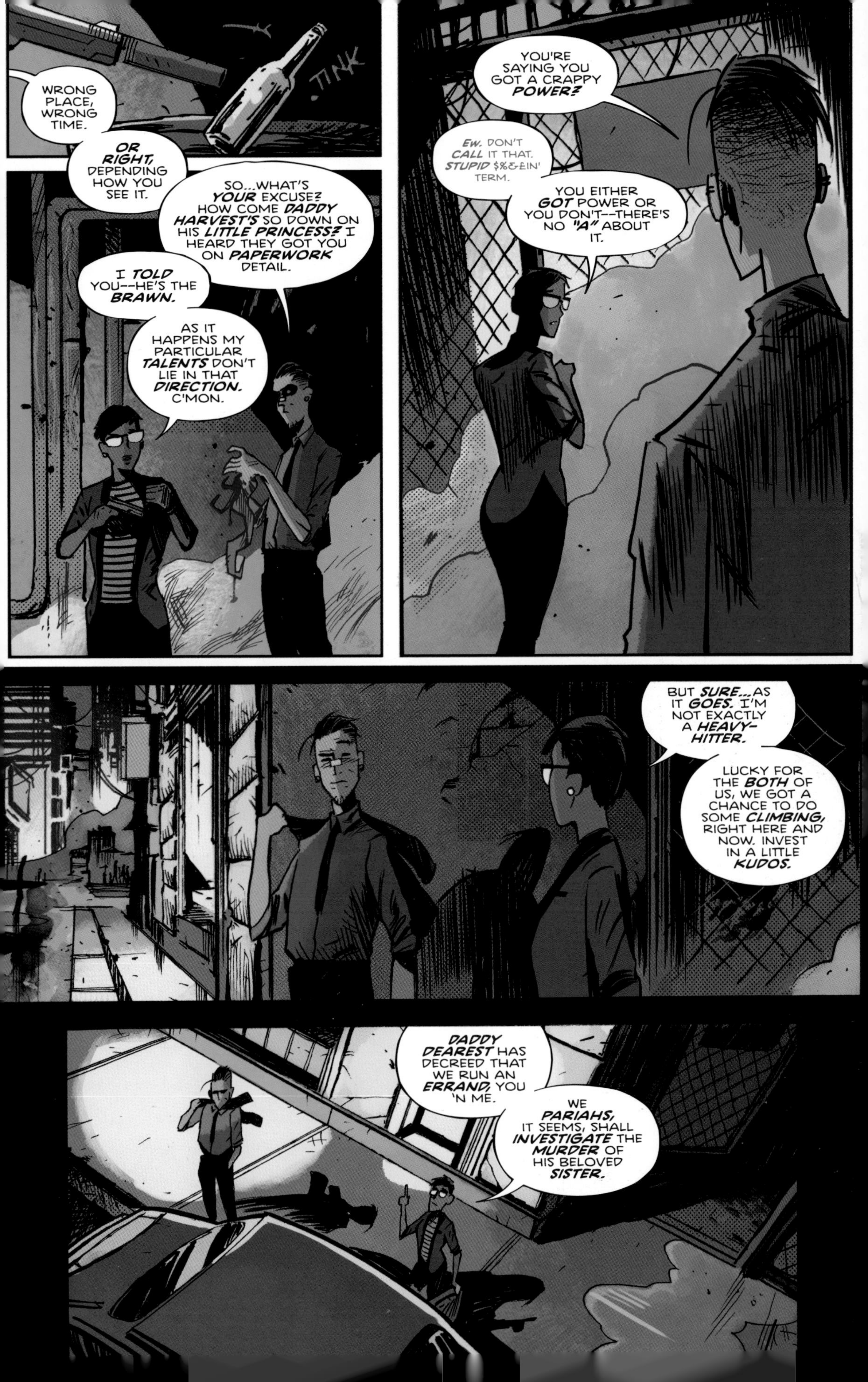
TINK
WRONG PLACE, WRONG TIME.
OR RIGHT, DEPENDING HOW YOU SEE IT.
SO...WHAT'S YOUR EXCUSE? HOW COME DADDY HARVEST'S SO DOWN ON HIS LITTLE PRINCESS? I HEARD THEY GOT YOU ON PAPERWORK DETAIL.
I TOLD YOU--HE'S THE BRAWN.
AS IT HAPPENS MY PARTICULAR TALENTS DON'T LIE IN THAT DIRECTION. C'MON.
YOU'RE SAYING YOU GOT A CRAPPY POWER?
Ew. DON'T CALL IT THAT. STUPID $%&£IN' TERM.
YOU EITHER GOT POWER OR YOU DON'T--THERE'S NO "A" ABOUT IT.
BUT SURE...AS IT GOES. I'M NOT EXACTLY A HEAVY-HITTER.
LUCKY FOR THE BOTH OF US, WE GOT A CHANCE TO DO SOME CLIMBING, RIGHT HERE AND NOW. INVEST IN A LITTLE KUDOS.
DADDY DEAREST HAS DECREED THAT WE RUN AN ERRAND, YOU 'N ME.
WE PARIAHS, IT SEEMS, SHALL INVESTIGATE THE MURDER OF HIS BELOVED SISTER.

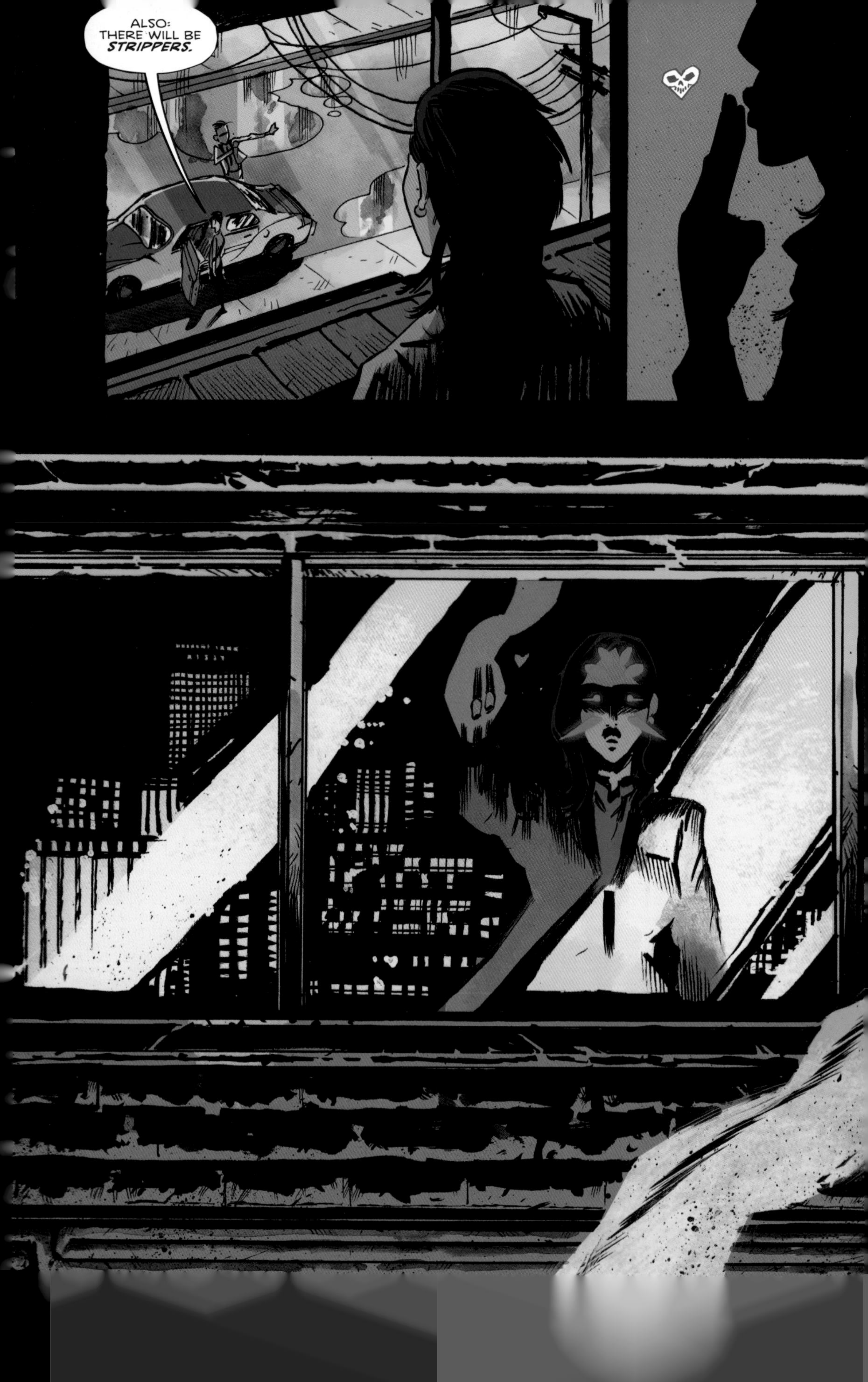
ALSO: THERE WILL BE STRIPPERS.

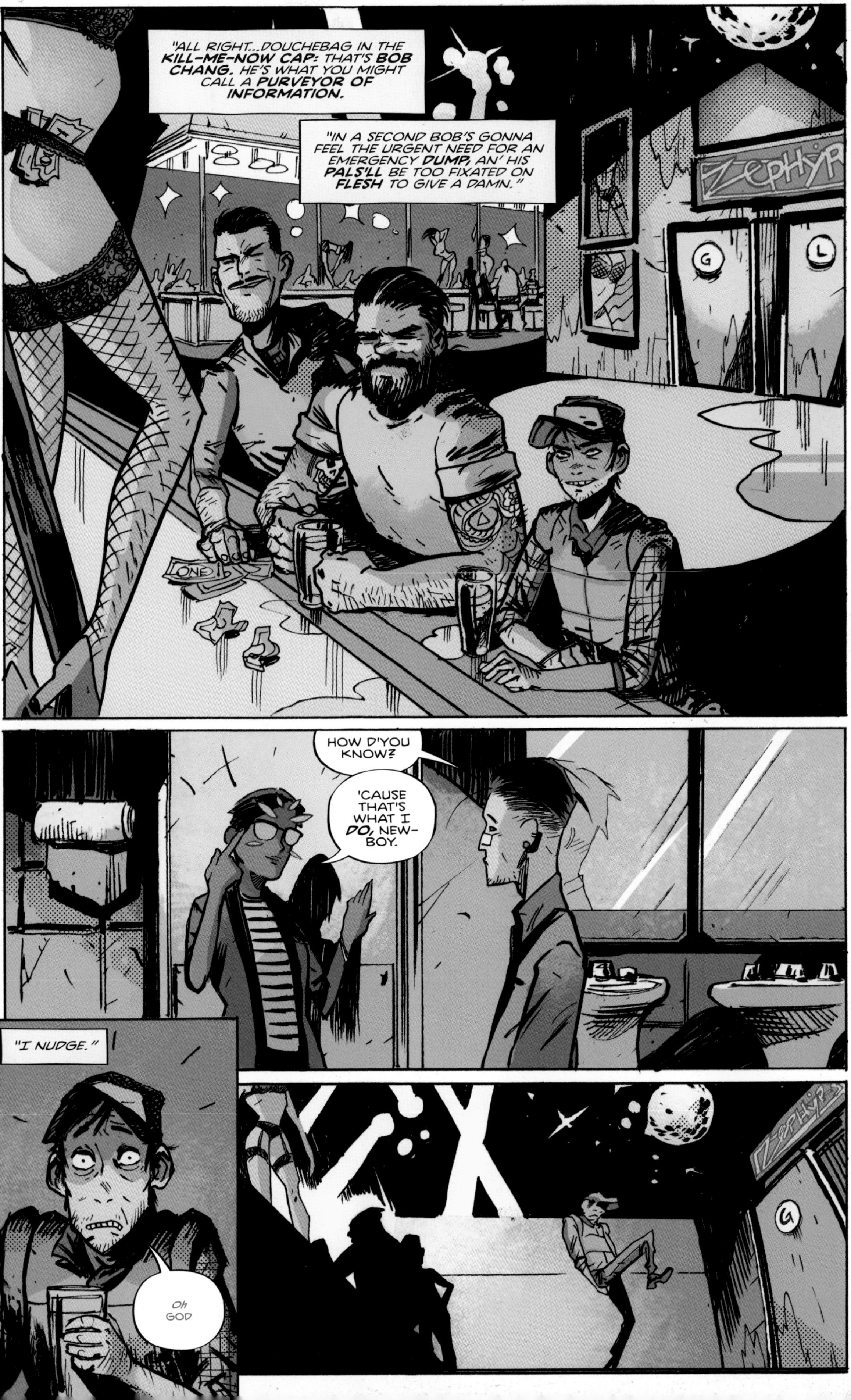
"ALL RIGHT...DOUCHEBAG IN THE KILL-ME-NOW CAP: THAT'S BOB CHANG. HE'S WHAT YOU MIGHT CALL A PURVEYOR OF INFORMATION.
"IN A SECOND BOB'S GONNA FEEL THE URGENT NEED FOR AN EMERGENCY DUMP, AN' HIS PALS'LL BE TOO FIXATED ON FLESH TO GIVE A DAMN."
ZEPHYR
G
L
ONE
HOW D'YOU KNOW?
'CAUSE THAT'S WHAT I DO, NEW-BOY.
"I NUDGE."
Oh GOD
ZEPHYR
G

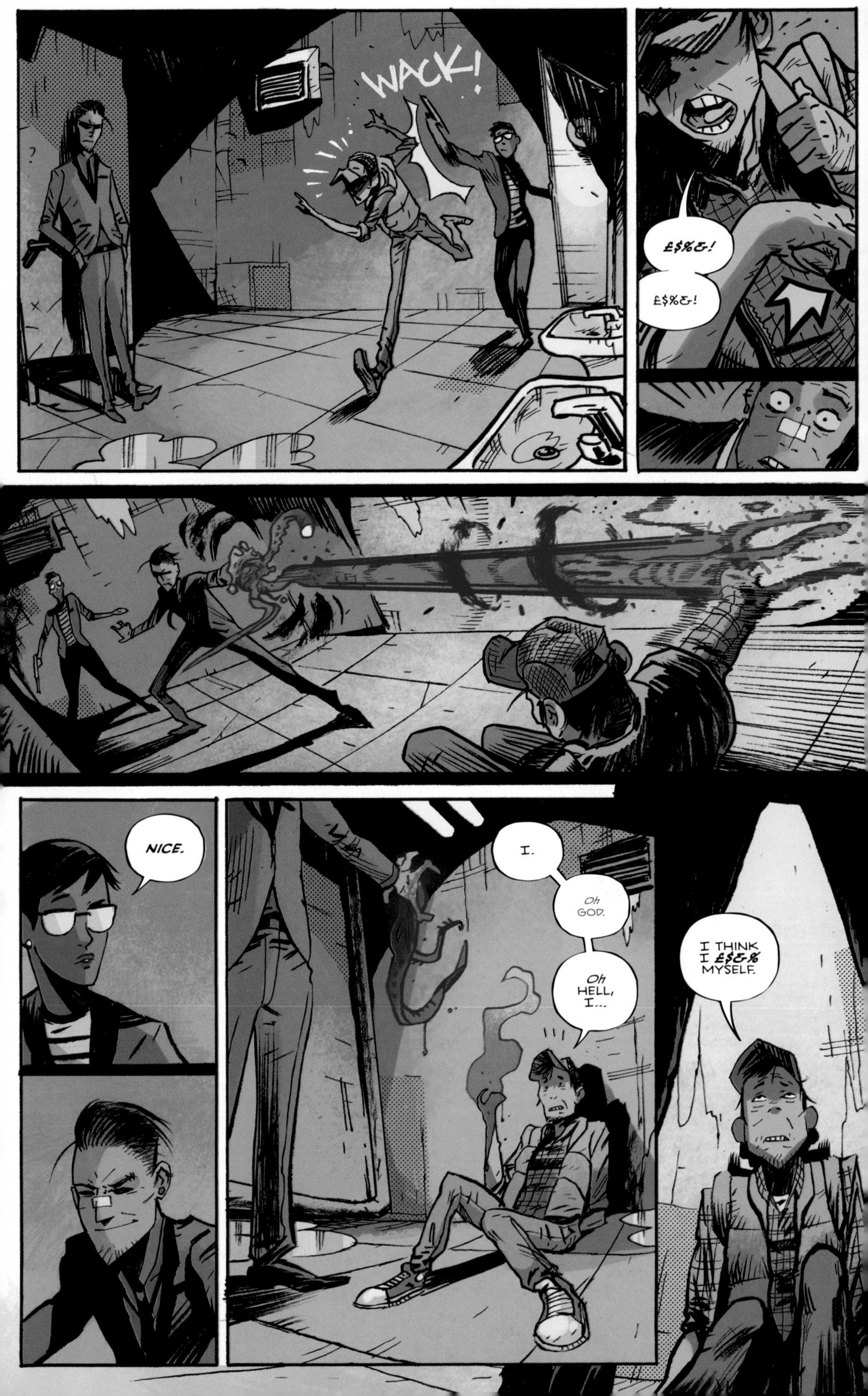
WACK!
£$%&!
£$%&!
NICE.
I.
Oh GOD.
Oh HELL, I...
I THINK I £$&% MYSELF.

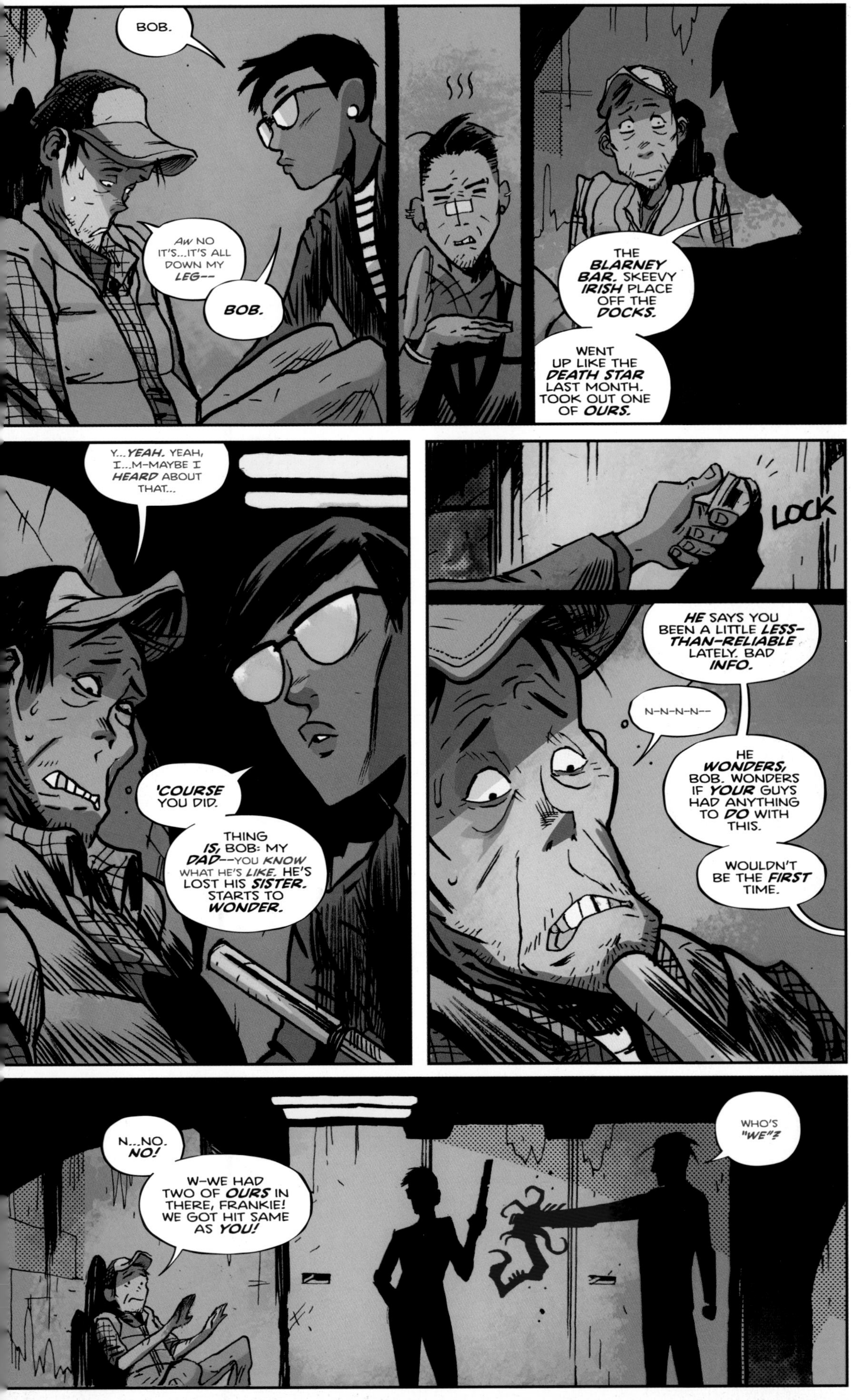
BOB.
AW NO IT'S...IT'S ALL DOWN MY LEG--
BOB.
THE BLARNEY BAR. SKEEVY IRISH PLACE OFF THE DOCKS.
WENT UP LIKE THE DEATH STAR LAST MONTH. TOOK OUT ONE OF OURS.
Y...YEAH. YEAH, I...M-MAYBE I HEARD ABOUT THAT...
'COURSE YOU DID.
THING IS, BOB: MY DAD--YOU KNOW WHAT HE'S LIKE. HE'S LOST HIS SISTER. STARTS TO WONDER.
LOCK
HE SAYS YOU BEEN A LITTLE LESS-THAN-RELIABLE LATELY. BAD INFO.
N-N-N-N--
HE WONDERS, BOB. WONDERS IF YOUR GUYS HAD ANYTHING TO DO WITH THIS.
WOULDN'T BE THE FIRST TIME.
N...NO. NO!
W-WE HAD TWO OF OURS IN THERE, FRANKIE! WE GOT HIT SAME AS YOU!
WHO'S "WE"?

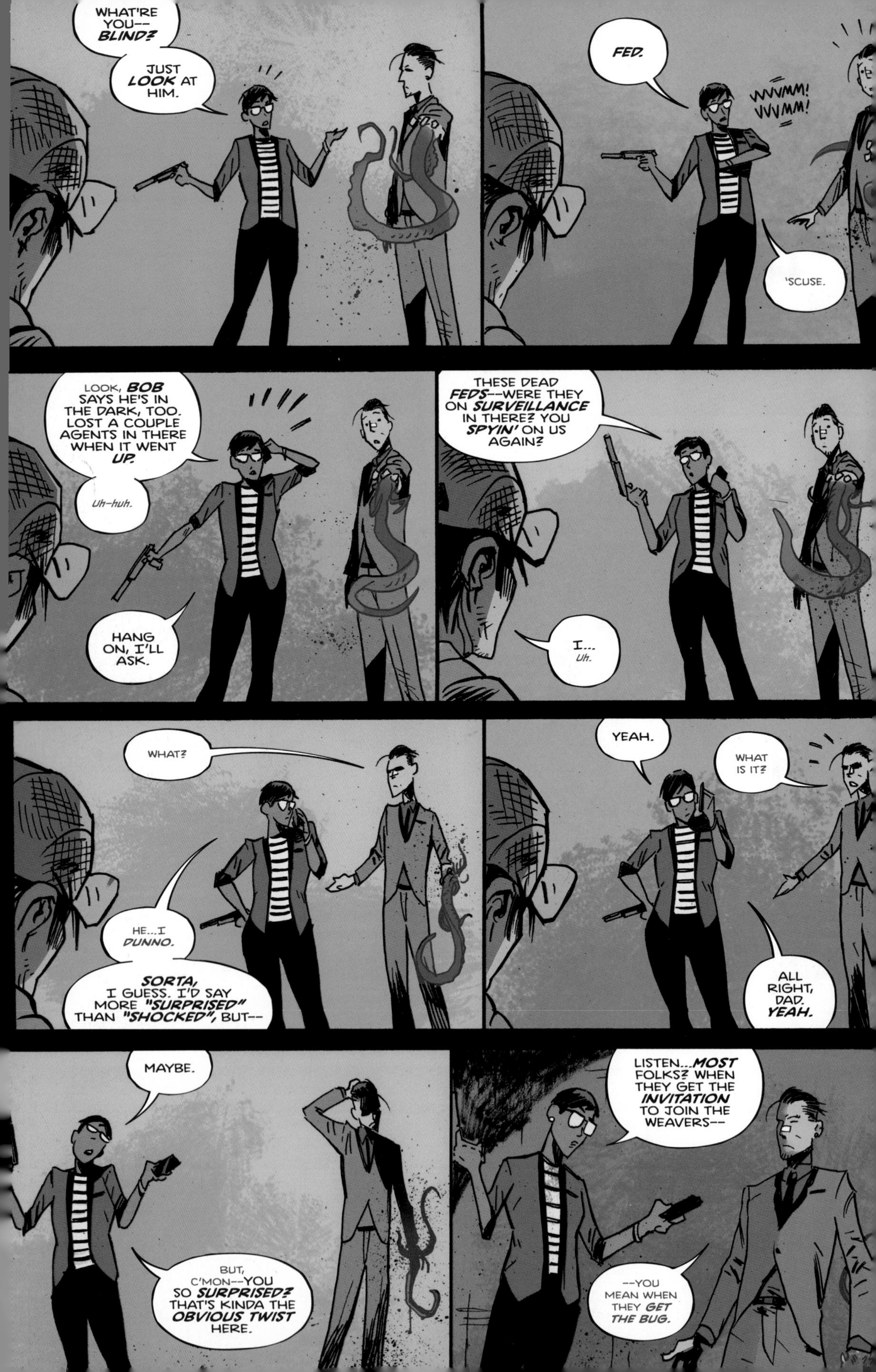
WHAT'RE YOU-- BLIND?
JUST LOOK AT HIM.
FED.
VVVMM! VVVMM!
'SCUSE.
LOOK, BOB SAYS HE'S IN THE DARK, TOO. LOST A COUPLE AGENTS IN THERE WHEN IT WENT UP.
Uh-huh.
HANG ON, I'LL ASK.
THESE DEAD FEDS--WERE THEY ON SURVEILLANCE IN THERE? YOU SPYIN' ON US AGAIN?
I... Uh.
WHAT?
HE...I DUNNO.
SORTA, I GUESS. I'D SAY MORE "SURPRISED" THAN "SHOCKED", BUT--
YEAH.
WHAT IS IT?
ALL RIGHT, DAD. YEAH.
MAYBE.
BUT, C'MON--YOU SO SURPRISED? THAT'S KINDA THE OBVIOUS TWIST HERE.
LISTEN...MOST FOLKS? WHEN THEY GET THE INVITATION TO JOIN THE WEAVERS--
--YOU MEAN WHEN THEY GET THE BUG.

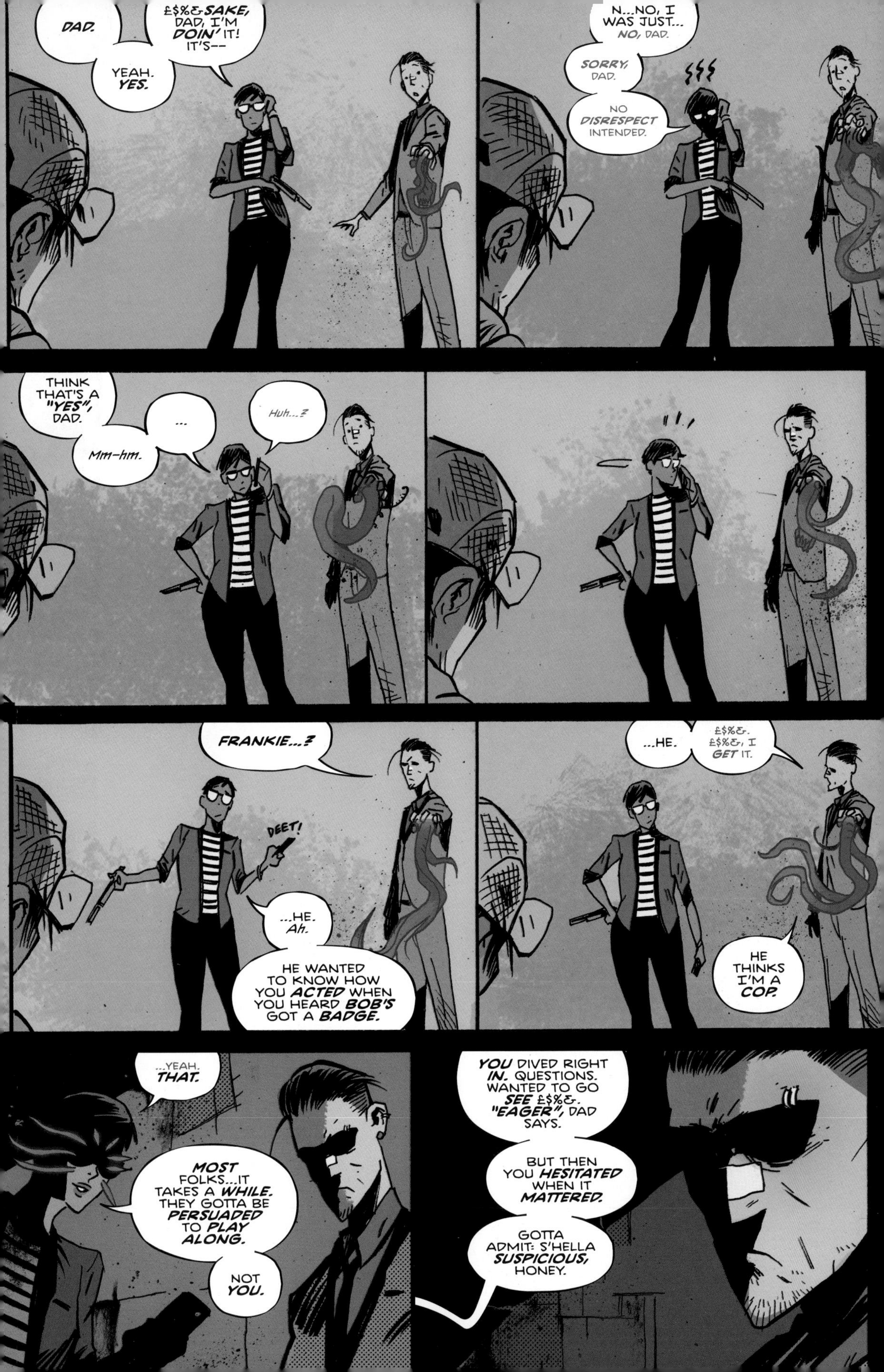
DAD.
YEAH. YES.
£$%& SAKE, DAD, I'M DOIN' IT! IT'S--
N...NO, I WAS JUST... NO, DAD.
SORRY, DAD.
NO DISRESPECT INTENDED.
THINK THAT'S A "YES", DAD.
Mm-hm.
...
Huh...?
FRANKIE...?
DEET!
...HE. Ah.
HE WANTED TO KNOW HOW YOU ACTED WHEN YOU HEARD BOB'S GOT A BADGE.
...HE.
£$%&. £$%&, I GET IT.
HE THINKS I'M A COP.
...YEAH. THAT.
MOST FOLKS...IT TAKES A WHILE. THEY GOTTA BE PERSUADED TO PLAY ALONG.
NOT YOU.
YOU DIVED RIGHT IN. QUESTIONS. WANTED TO GO SEE £$%&. "EAGER", DAD SAYS.
BUT THEN YOU HESITATED WHEN IT MATTERED.
GOTTA ADMIT: S'HELLA SUSPICIOUS, HONEY.

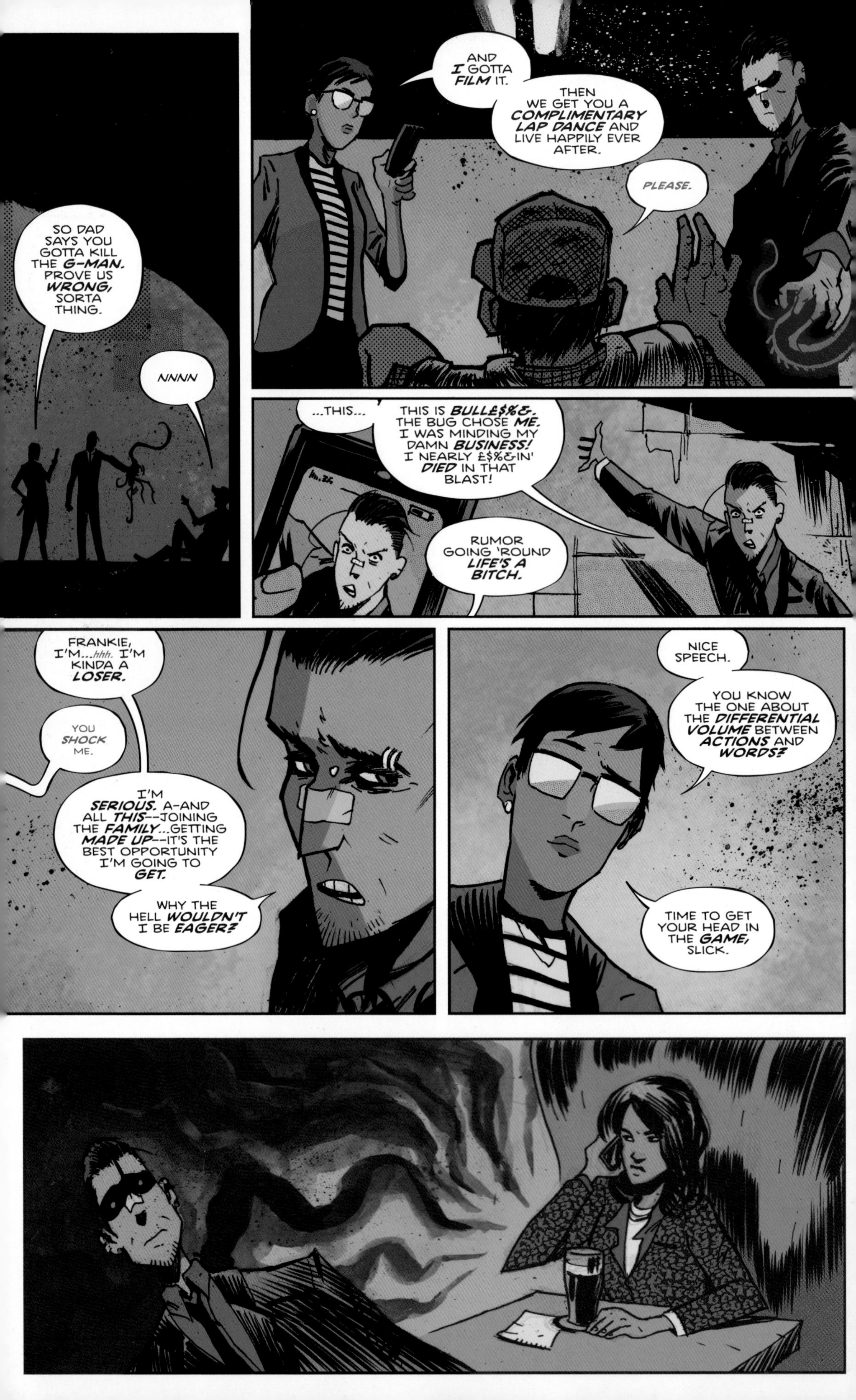
SO DAD SAYS YOU GOTTA KILL THE G-MAN. PROVE US WRONG, SORTA THING.
NNNN
AND I GOTTA FILM IT.
THEN WE GET YOU A COMPLIMENTARY LAP DANCE AND LIVE HAPPILY EVER AFTER.
PLEASE.
...THIS...
THIS IS BULL£$%&. THE BUG CHOSE ME. I WAS MINDING MY DAMN BUSINESS! I NEARLY £$%&IN' DIED IN THAT BLAST!
RUMOR GOING 'ROUND LIFE'S A BITCH.
FRANKIE, I'M...hhh. I'M KINDA A LOSER.
YOU SHOCK ME.
I'M SERIOUS. A-AND ALL THIS--JOINING THE FAMILY...GETTING MADE UP--IT'S THE BEST OPPORTUNITY I'M GOING TO GET.
WHY THE HELL WOULDN'T I BE EAGER?
NICE SPEECH.
YOU KNOW THE ONE ABOUT THE DIFFERENTIAL VOLUME BETWEEN ACTIONS AND WORDS?
TIME TO GET YOUR HEAD IN THE GAME, SLICK.

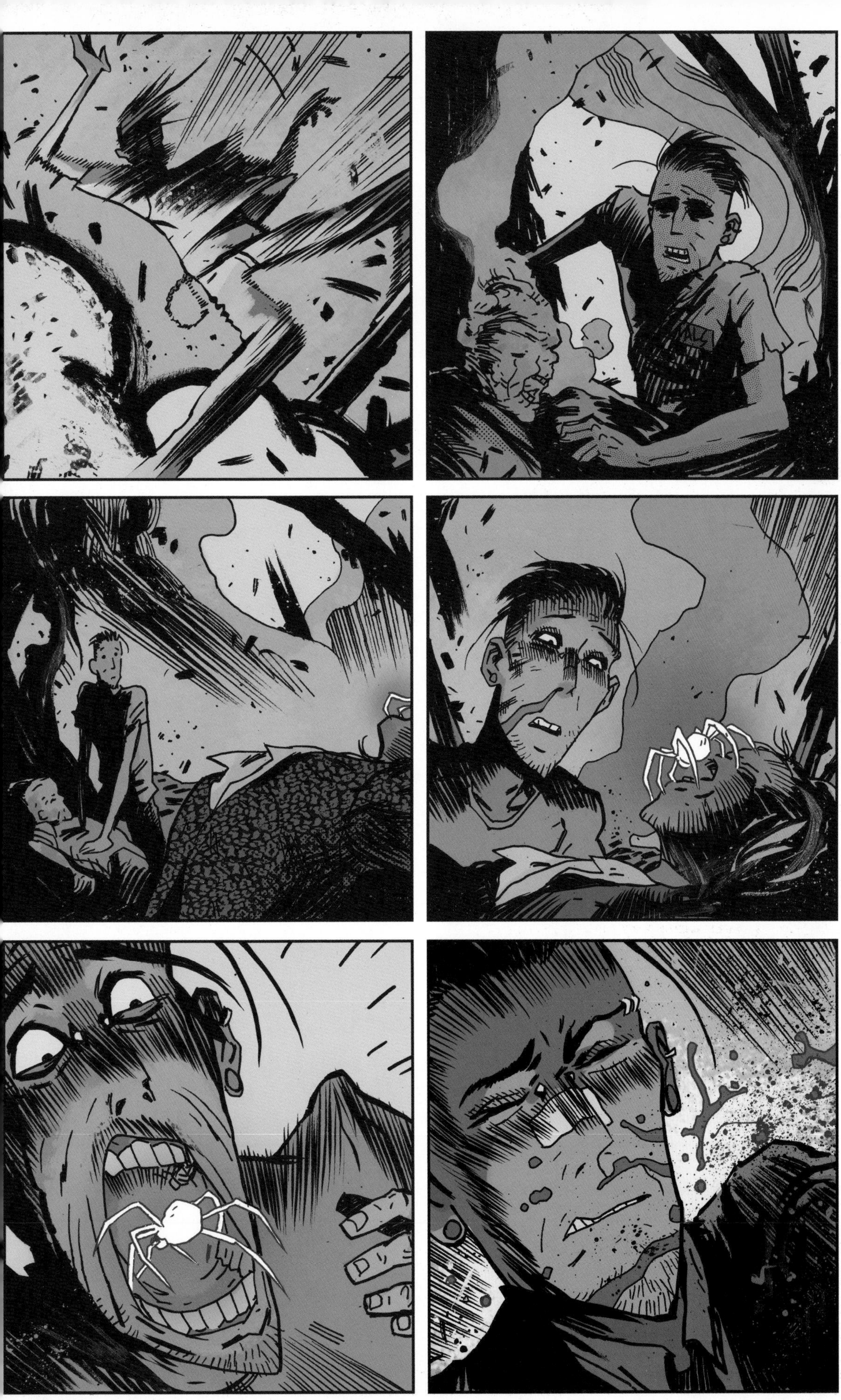

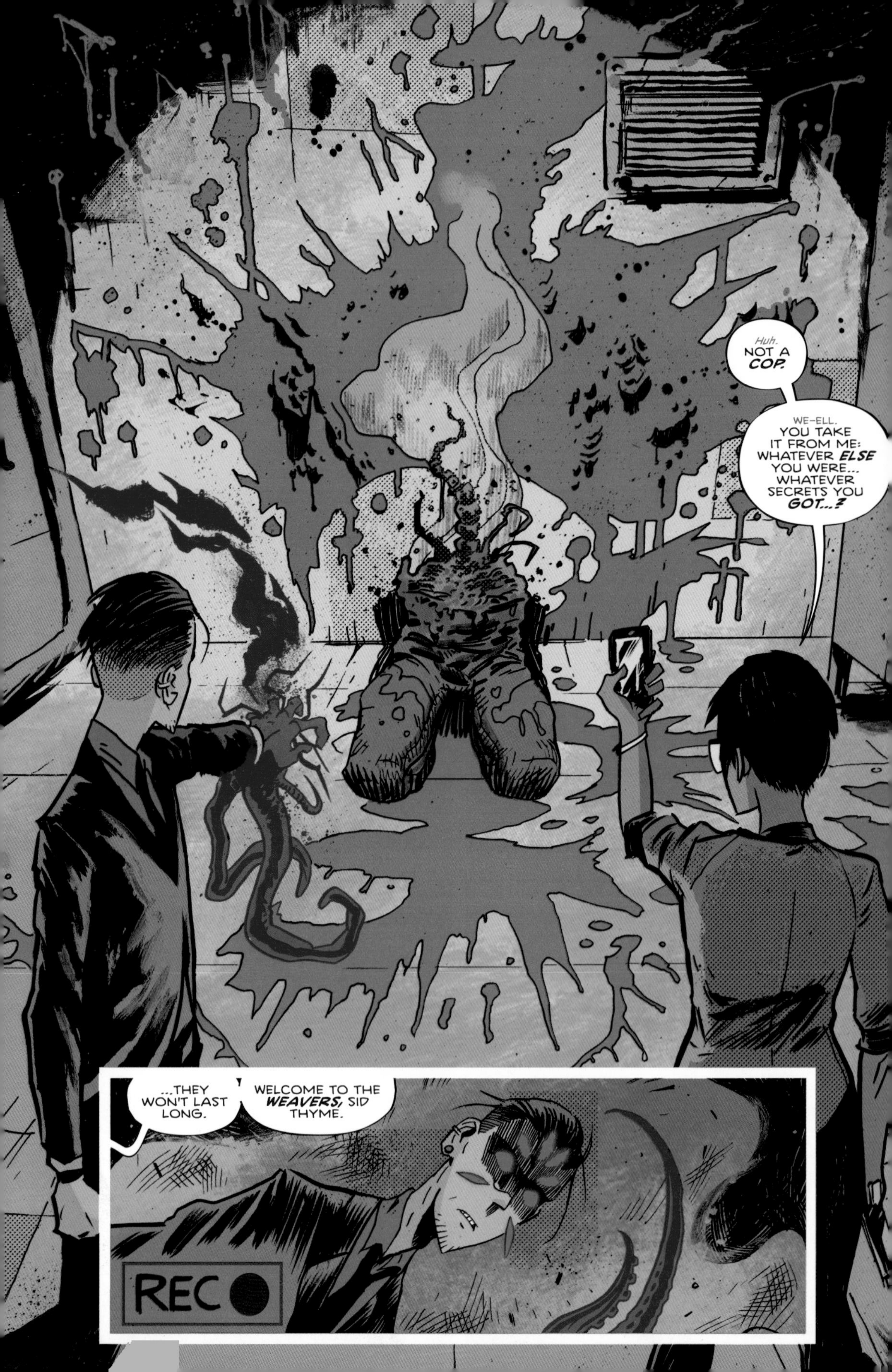
Huh. NOT A COP.
WE-ELL. YOU TAKE IT FROM ME: WHATEVER ELSE YOU WERE... WHATEVER SECRETS YOU GOT...?
...THEY WON'T LAST LONG.
WELCOME TO THE WEAVERS, SID THYME.
REC

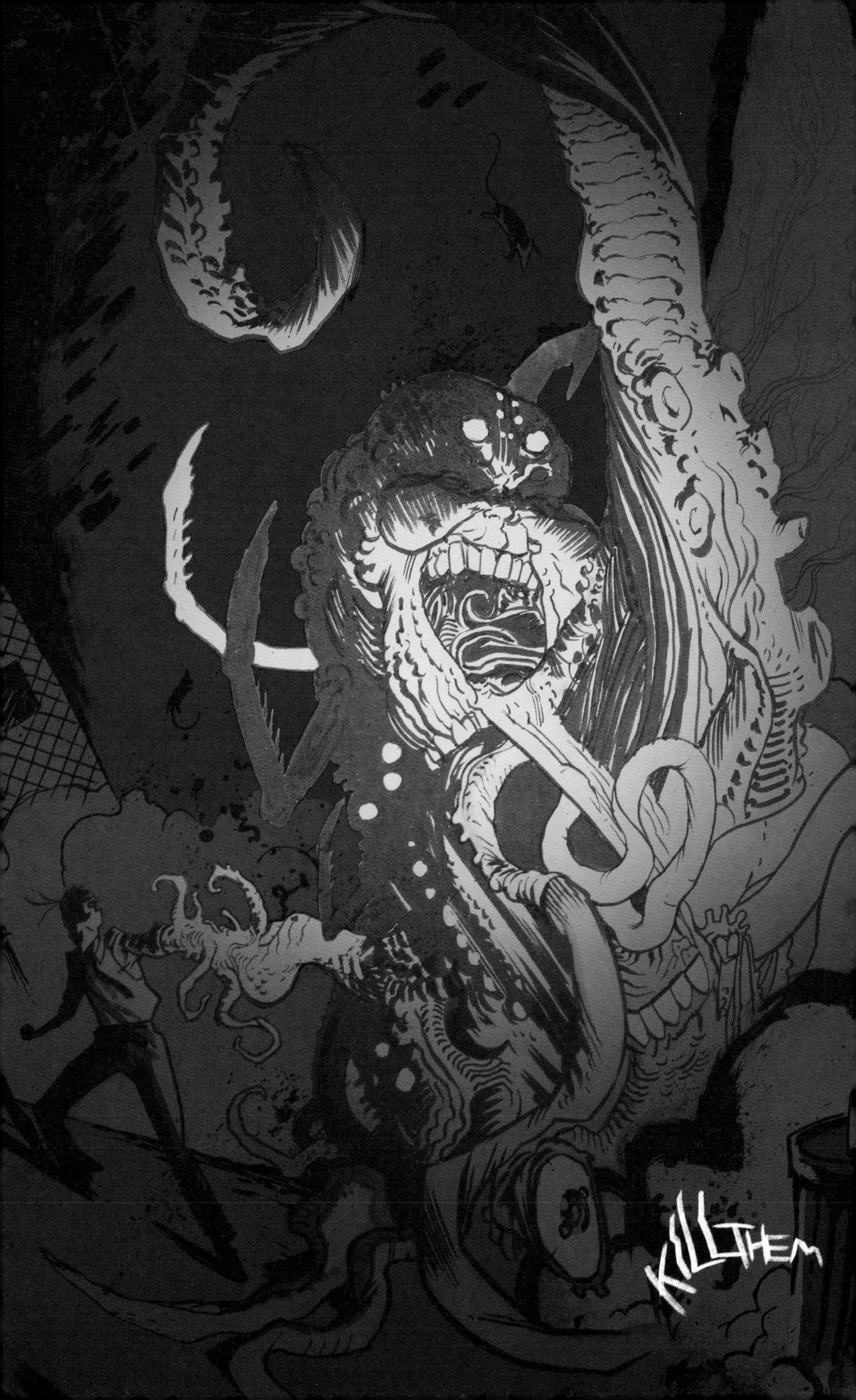
KILL THEM

CHAPTER TWO

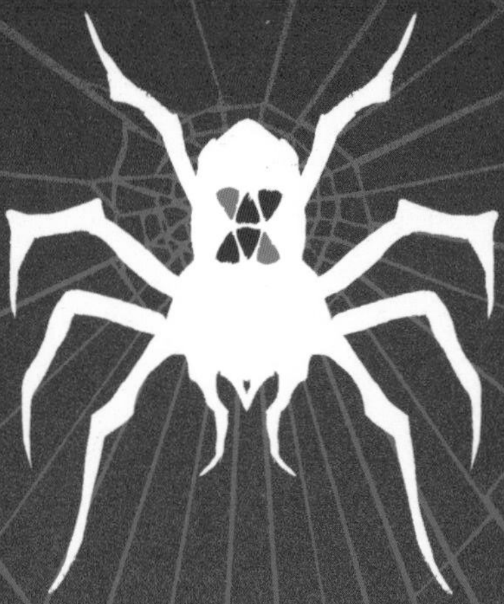

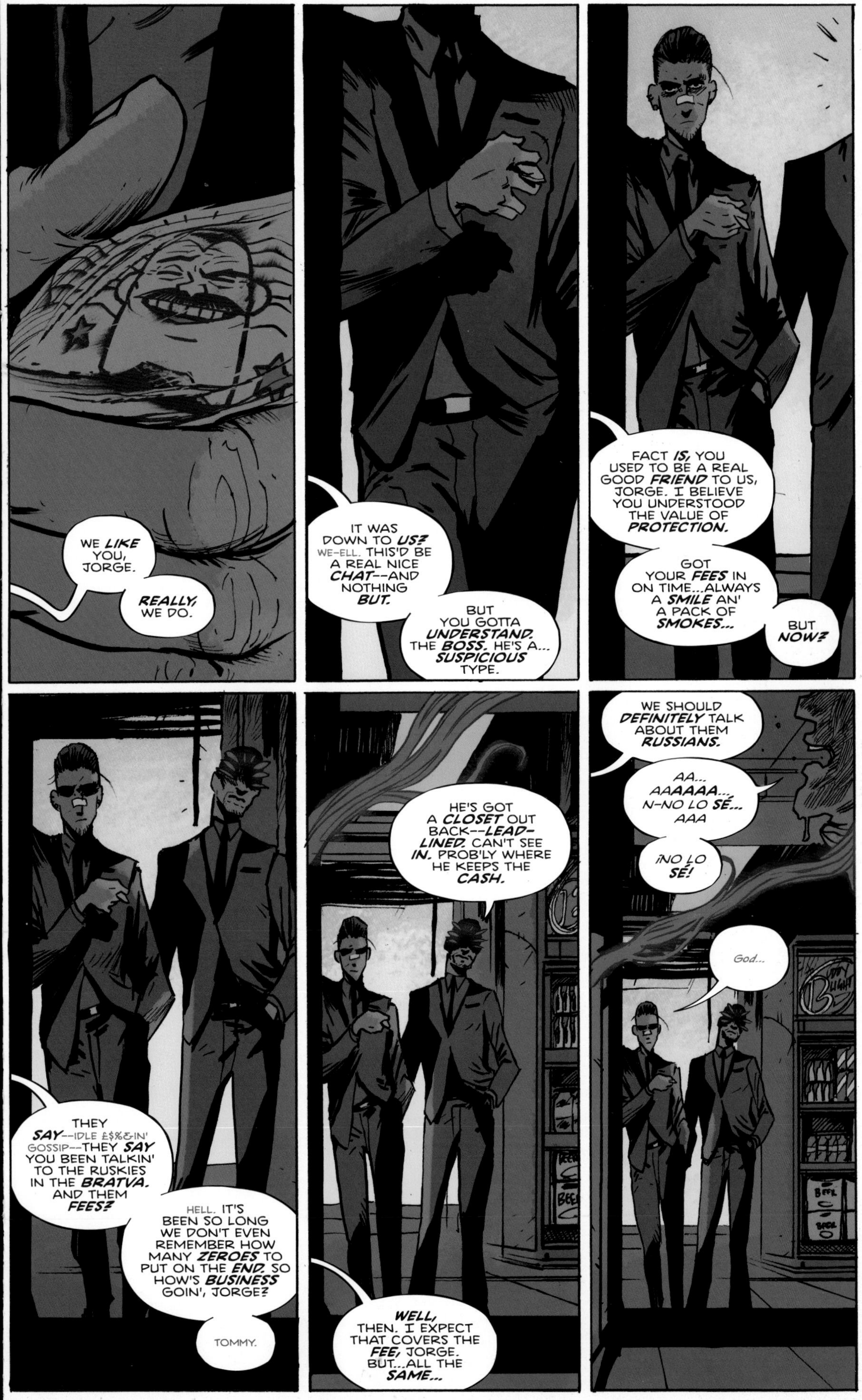

WE LIKE YOU, JORGE.
REALLY, WE DO.
IT WAS DOWN TO US? WE-ELL. THIS'D BE A REAL NICE CHAT--AND NOTHING BUT.
BUT YOU GOTTA UNDERSTAND. THE BOSS. HE'S A... SUSPICIOUS TYPE.
FACT IS, YOU USED TO BE A REAL GOOD FRIEND TO US, JORGE. I BELIEVE YOU UNDERSTOOD THE VALUE OF PROTECTION.
GOT YOUR FEES IN ON TIME...ALWAYS A SMILE AN' A PACK OF SMOKES...
BUT NOW?
THEY SAY--IDLE £$%&IN' GOSSIP--THEY SAY YOU BEEN TALKIN' TO THE RUSKIES IN THE BRATVA. AND THEM FEES?
HELL. IT'S BEEN SO LONG WE DON'T EVEN REMEMBER HOW MANY ZEROES TO PUT ON THE END. SO HOW'S BUSINESS GOIN', JORGE?
TOMMY.
HE'S GOT A CLOSET OUT BACK--LEAD-LINED. CAN'T SEE IN. PROB'LY WHERE HE KEEPS THE CASH.
WELL, THEN. I EXPECT THAT COVERS THE FEE, JORGE. BUT...ALL THE SAME...
WE SHOULD DEFINITELY TALK ABOUT THEM RUSSIANS.
AA... AAAAAA... N-NO LO SÉ... AAA
¡NO LO SÉ!
God...

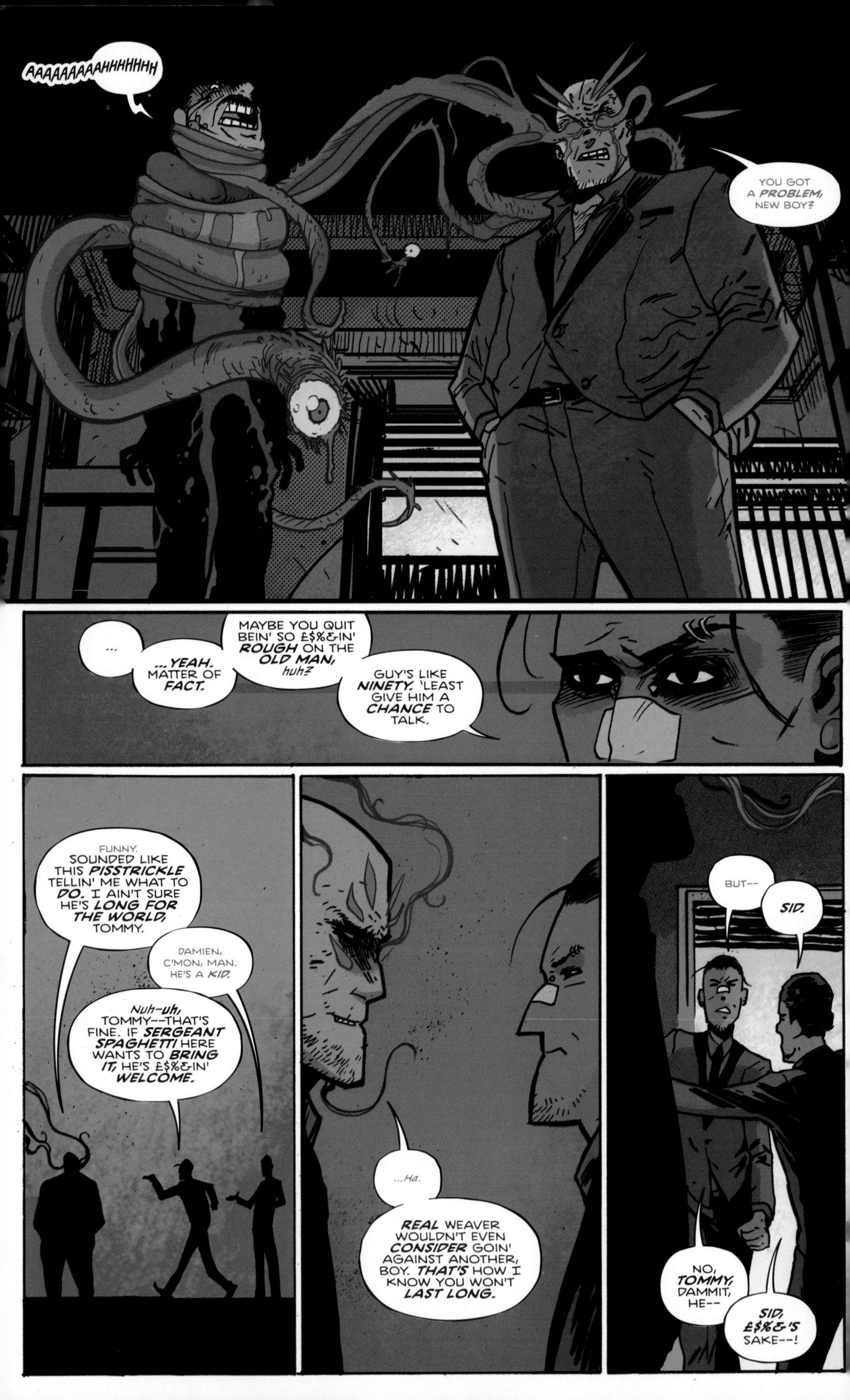
AAAAAAAAAHHHHHHH
YOU GOT A PROBLEM, NEW BOY?
...
...YEAH. MATTER OF FACT.
MAYBE YOU QUIT BEIN' SO £$%&IN' ROUGH ON THE OLD MAN, huh?
GUY'S LIKE NINETY. 'LEAST GIVE HIM A CHANCE TO TALK.
FUNNY. SOUNDED LIKE THIS PISSTRICKLE TELLIN' ME WHAT TO DO. I AIN'T SURE HE'S LONG FOR THE WORLD, TOMMY.
DAMIEN, C'MON, MAN. HE'S A KID.
Nuh-uh, TOMMY--THAT'S FINE. IF SERGEANT SPAGHETTI HERE WANTS TO BRING IT, HE'S £$%&IN' WELCOME.
...Ha.
REAL WEAVER WOULDN'T EVEN CONSIDER GOIN' AGAINST ANOTHER, BOY. THAT'S HOW I KNOW YOU WON'T LAST LONG.
BUT--
SID.
NO, TOMMY, DAMMIT, HE--
SID, £$%&'S SAKE--!

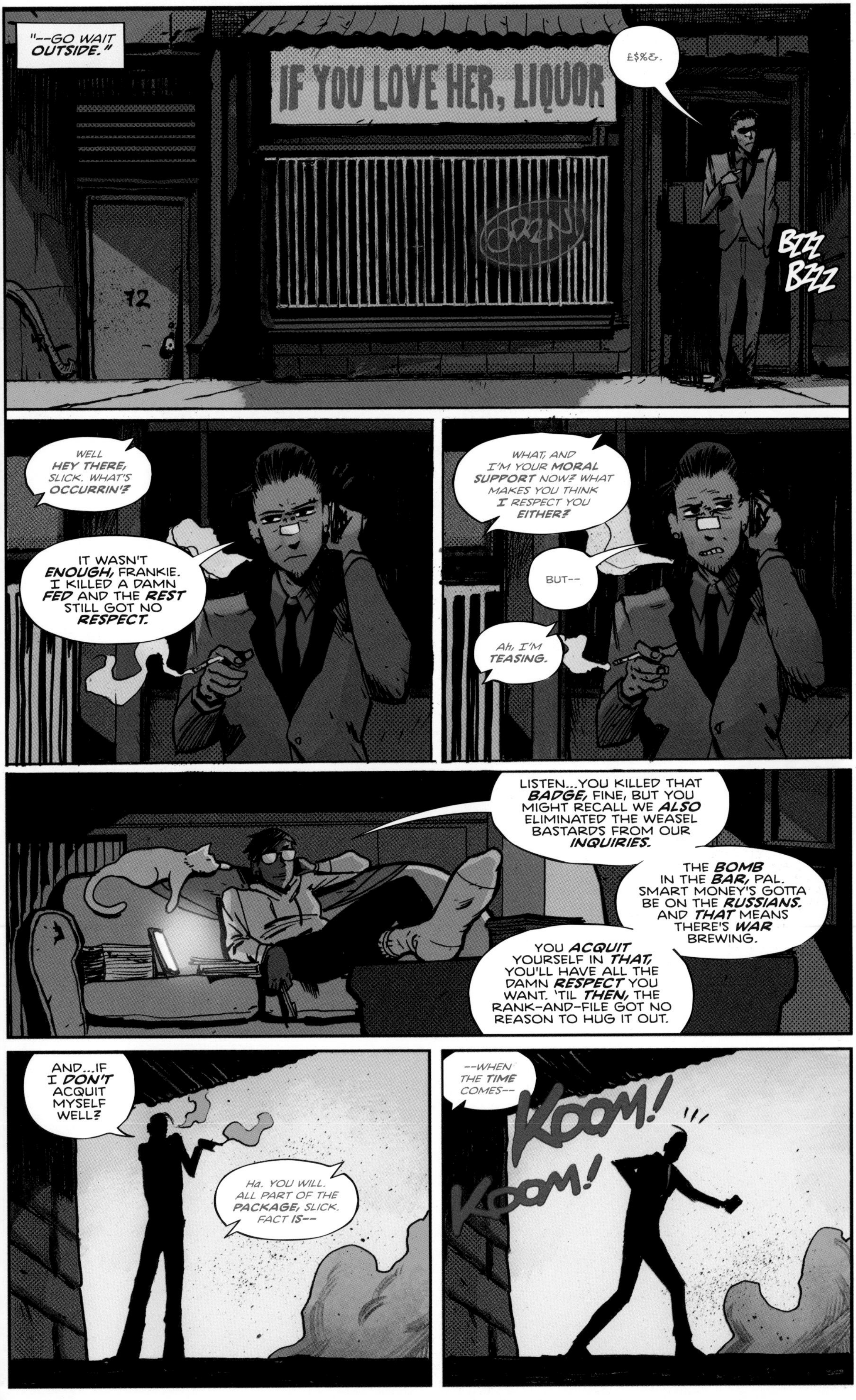
"--GO WAIT OUTSIDE."
IF YOU LOVE HER, LIQUOR
£$%&.
OPEN
72
BZZZ BZZZ
WELL HEY THERE, SLICK. WHAT'S OCCURRIN'?
IT WASN'T ENOUGH, FRANKIE. I KILLED A DAMN FED AND THE REST STILL GOT NO RESPECT.
WHAT, AND I'M YOUR MORAL SUPPORT NOW? WHAT MAKES YOU THINK I RESPECT YOU EITHER?
BUT--
Ah, I'M TEASING.
LISTEN...YOU KILLED THAT BADGE, FINE, BUT YOU MIGHT RECALL WE ALSO ELIMINATED THE WEASEL BASTARDS FROM OUR INQUIRIES.
THE BOMB IN THE BAR, PAL. SMART MONEY'S GOTTA BE ON THE RUSSIANS. AND THAT MEANS THERE'S WAR BREWING.
YOU ACQUIT YOURSELF IN THAT, YOU'LL HAVE ALL THE DAMN RESPECT YOU WANT. 'TIL THEN, THE RANK-AND-FILE GOT NO REASON TO HUG IT OUT.
AND...IF I DON'T ACQUIT MYSELF WELL?
Ha. YOU WILL. ALL PART OF THE PACKAGE, SLICK. FACT IS--
--WHEN THE TIME COMES--
KOOM!
KOOM!

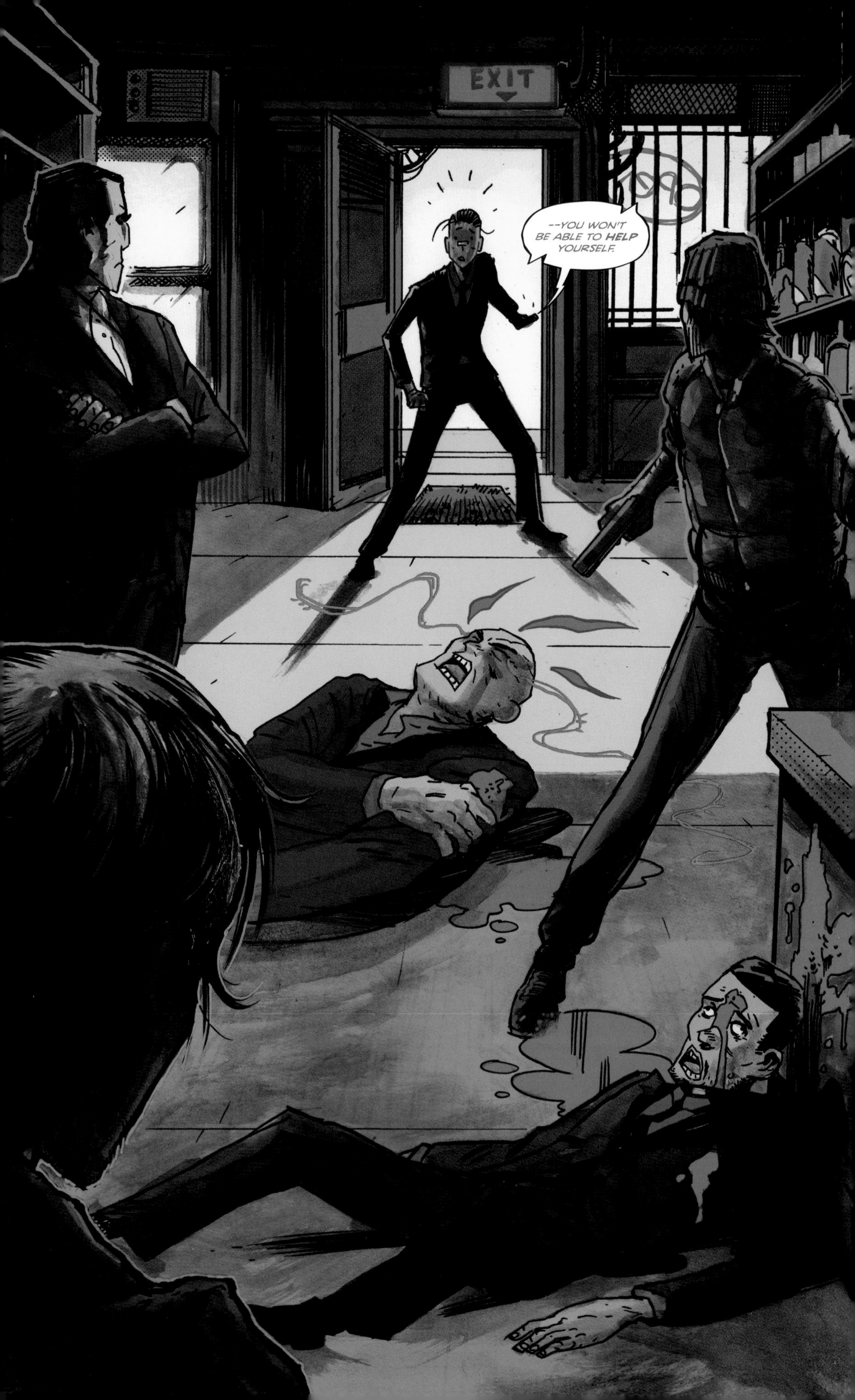
EXIT
--YOU WON'T BE ABLE TO HELP YOURSELF.

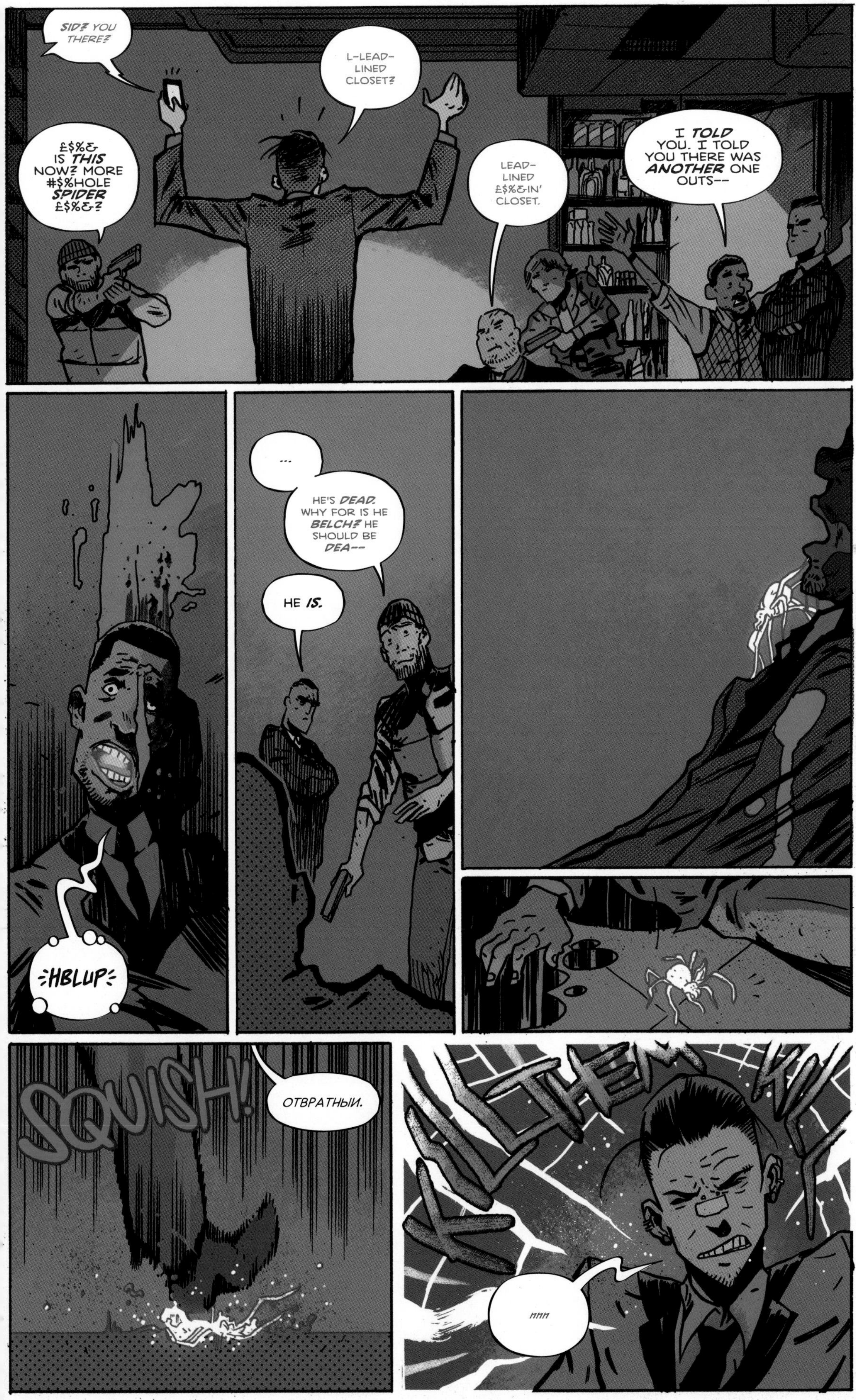
SID? YOU THERE?
L-LEAD-LINED CLOSET?
£$%& IS THIS NOW? MORE #$%HOLE SPIDER £$%&?
LEAD-LINED £$%&IN' CLOSET.
I TOLD YOU. I TOLD YOU THERE WAS ANOTHER ONE OUTS--
HBLUP
...
HE'S DEAD. WHY FOR IS HE BELCH? HE SHOULD BE DEA--
HE IS.
SQUISH!
ОТВРАТНЫИ.
THEM
nnn

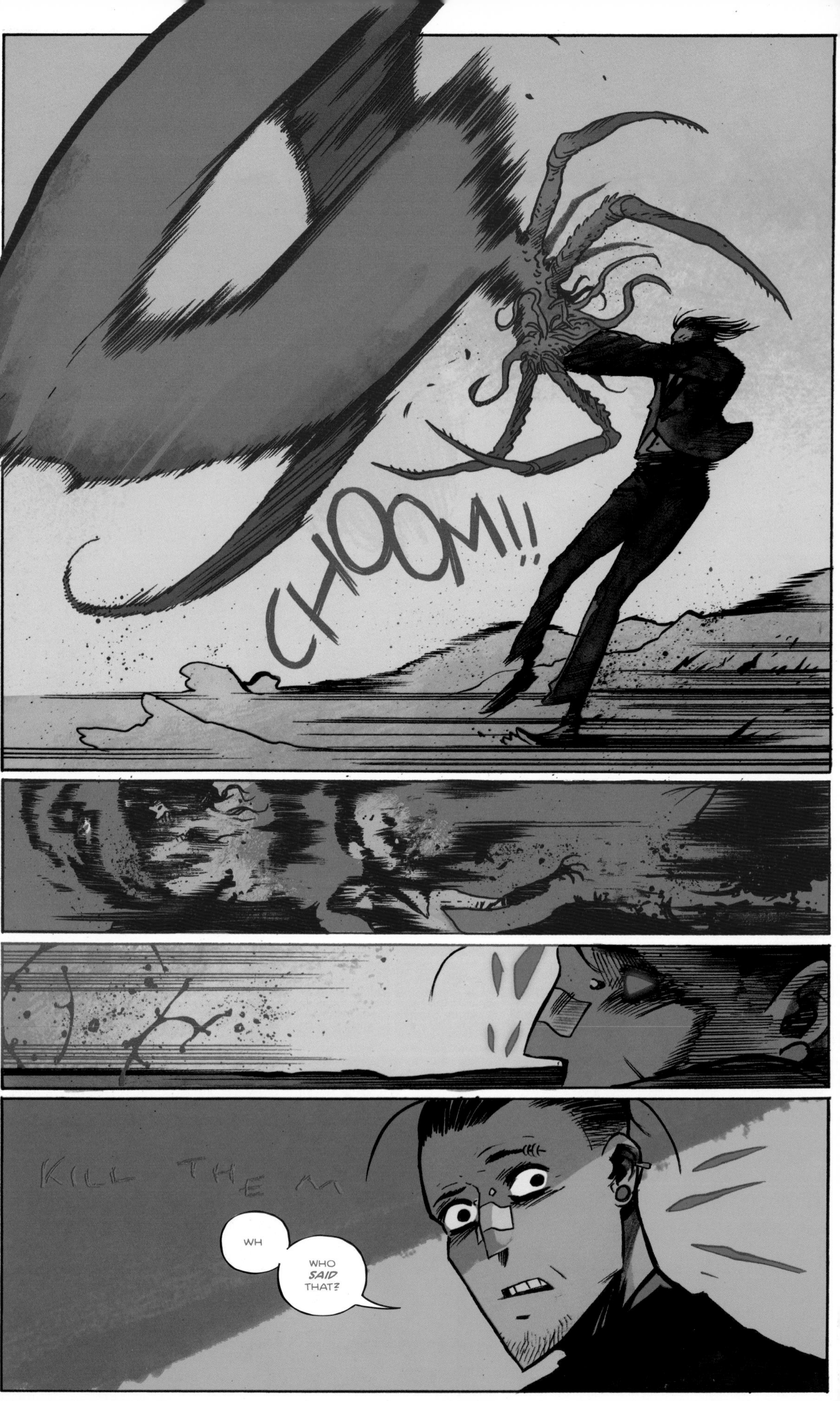

CHOOM!!
KILL THEM
WH
WHO *SAID* THAT?

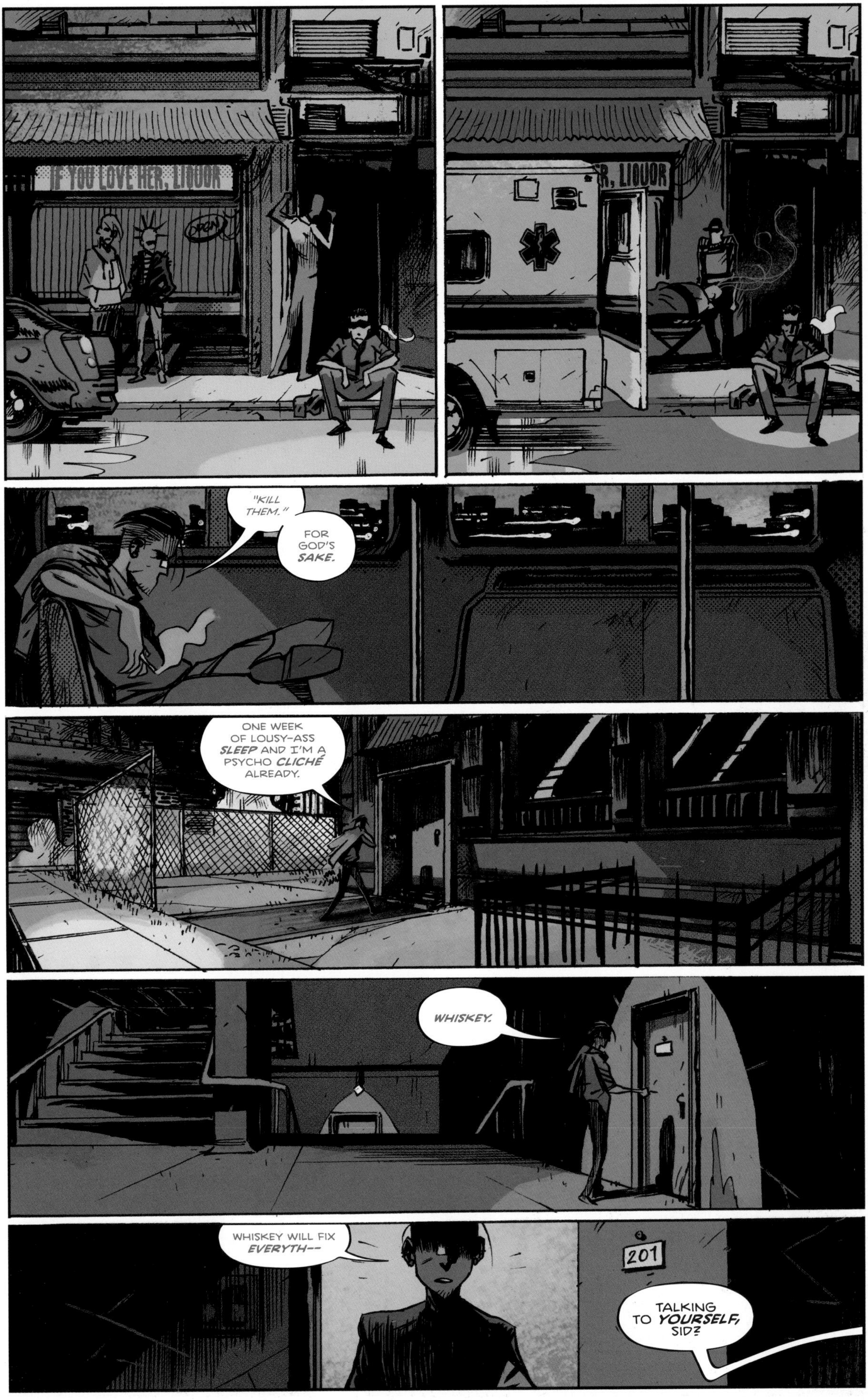
IF YOU LOVE HER, LIQUOR
OPEN
R, LIQUOR
"KILL THEM."
FOR GOD'S SAKE.
ONE WEEK OF LOUSY-ASS SLEEP AND I'M A PSYCHO CLICHÉ ALREADY.
WHISKEY.
WHISKEY WILL FIX EVERYTH--
201
TALKING TO YOURSELF, SID?

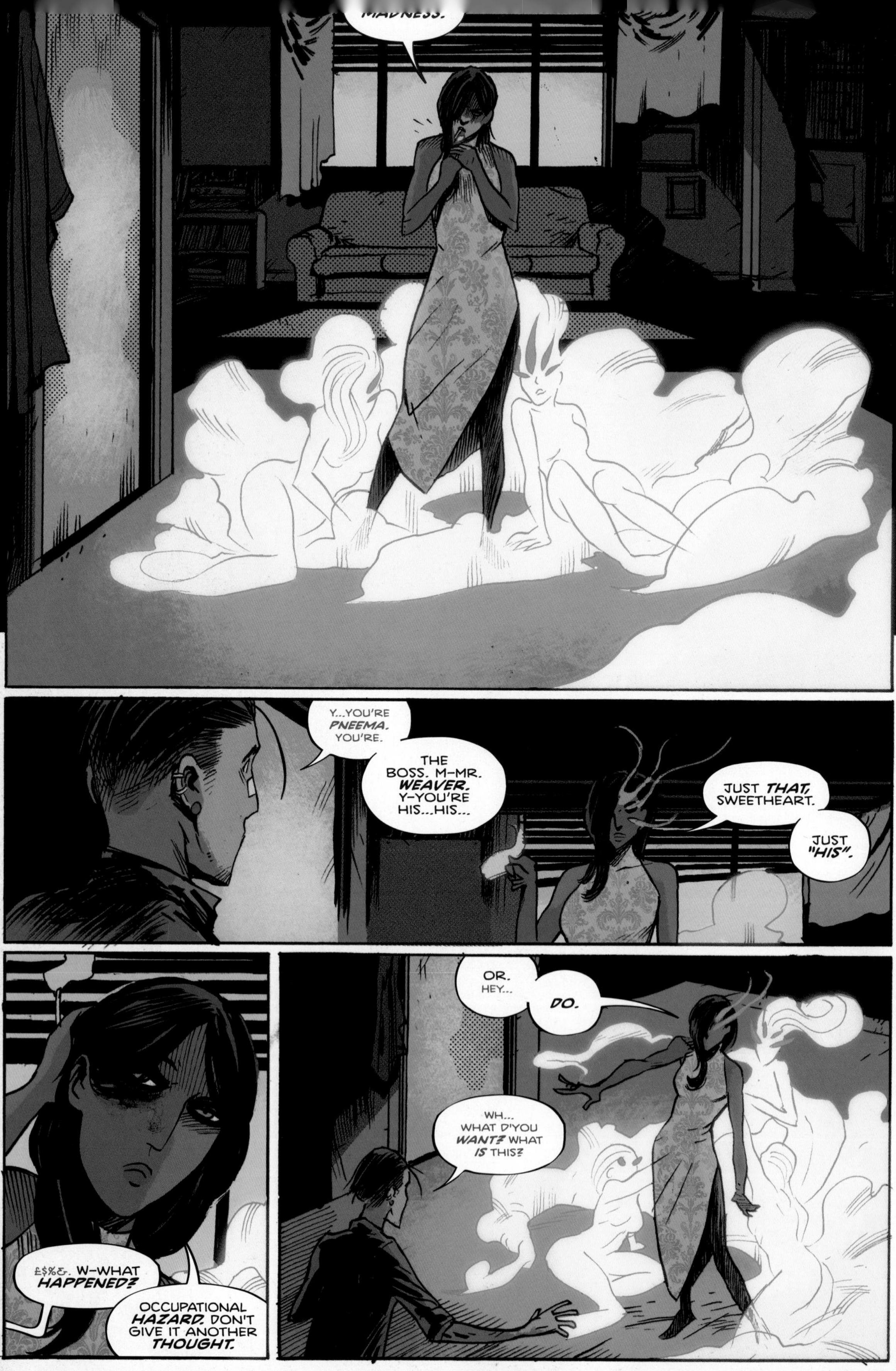
Y...YOU'RE PNEEMA. YOU'RE.
THE BOSS. M-MR. WEAVER. Y-YOU'RE HIS...HIS...
JUST THAT, SWEETHEART.
JUST "HIS".
£$%&. W-WHAT HAPPENED?
OCCUPATIONAL HAZARD. DON'T GIVE IT ANOTHER THOUGHT.
OR. HEY...
DO.
WH... WHAT D'YOU WANT? WHAT IS THIS?

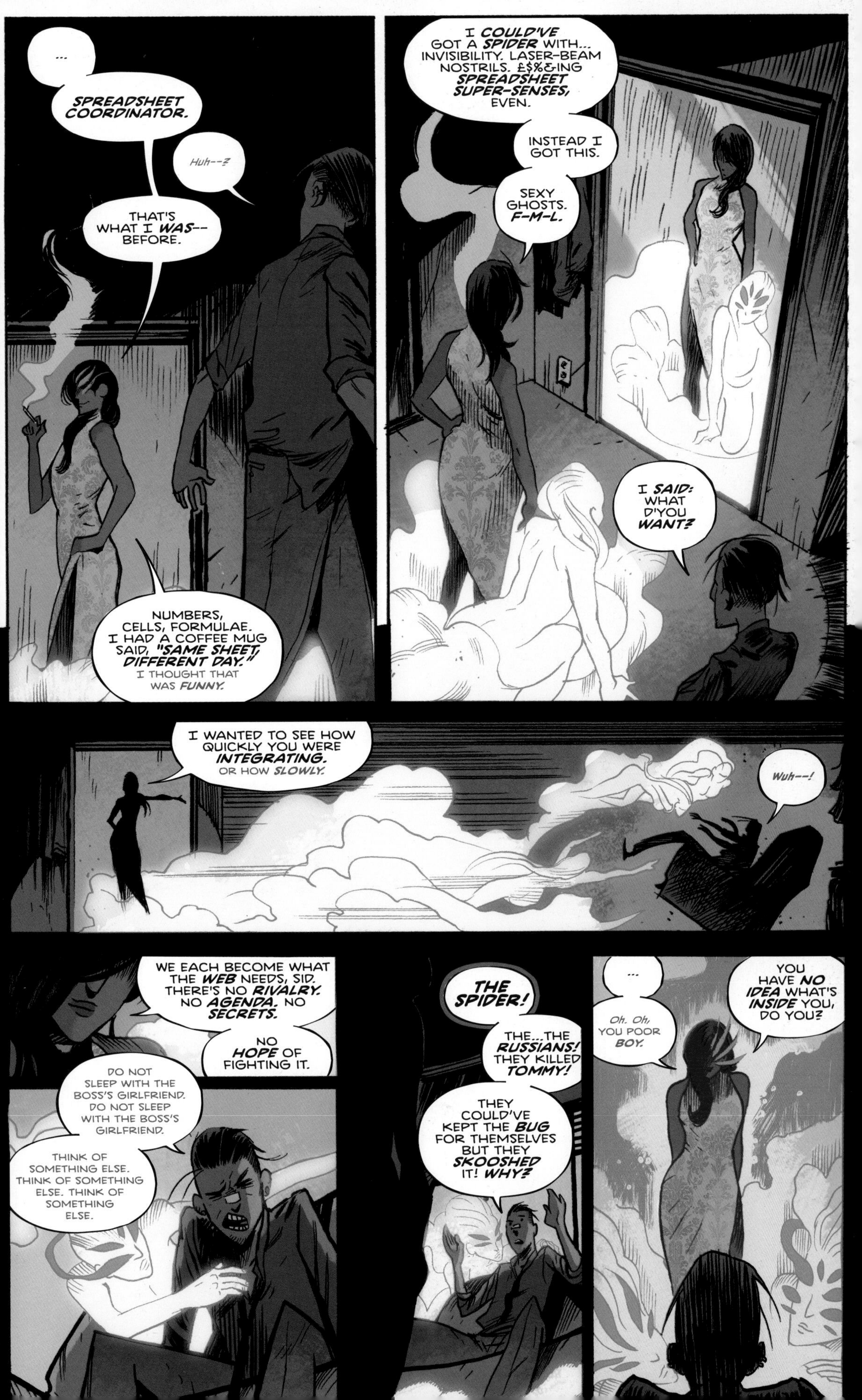

...
SPREADSHEET COORDINATOR.
Huh--?
THAT'S WHAT I WAS-- BEFORE.
NUMBERS, CELLS, FORMULAE. I HAD A COFFEE MUG SAID, "SAME SHEET, DIFFERENT DAY." I THOUGHT THAT WAS FUNNY.
I COULD'VE GOT A SPIDER WITH... INVISIBILITY. LASER-BEAM NOSTRILS. £$%&ING SPREADSHEET SUPER-SENSES, EVEN.
INSTEAD I GOT THIS.
SEXY GHOSTS. F-M-L.
I SAID: WHAT D'YOU WANT?
I WANTED TO SEE HOW QUICKLY YOU WERE INTEGRATING. OR HOW SLOWLY.
Wuh--!
WE EACH BECOME WHAT THE WEB NEEDS, SID. THERE'S NO RIVALRY. NO AGENDA. NO SECRETS.
NO HOPE OF FIGHTING IT.
DO NOT SLEEP WITH THE BOSS'S GIRLFRIEND. DO NOT SLEEP WITH THE BOSS'S GIRLFRIEND.
THINK OF SOMETHING ELSE. THINK OF SOMETHING ELSE. THINK OF SOMETHING ELSE.
THE SPIDER!
THE...THE RUSSIANS! THEY KILLED TOMMY!
THEY COULD'VE KEPT THE BUG FOR THEMSELVES BUT THEY SKOOSHED IT! WHY?
...
Oh. Oh, YOU POOR BOY.
YOU HAVE NO IDEA WHAT'S INSIDE YOU, DO YOU?

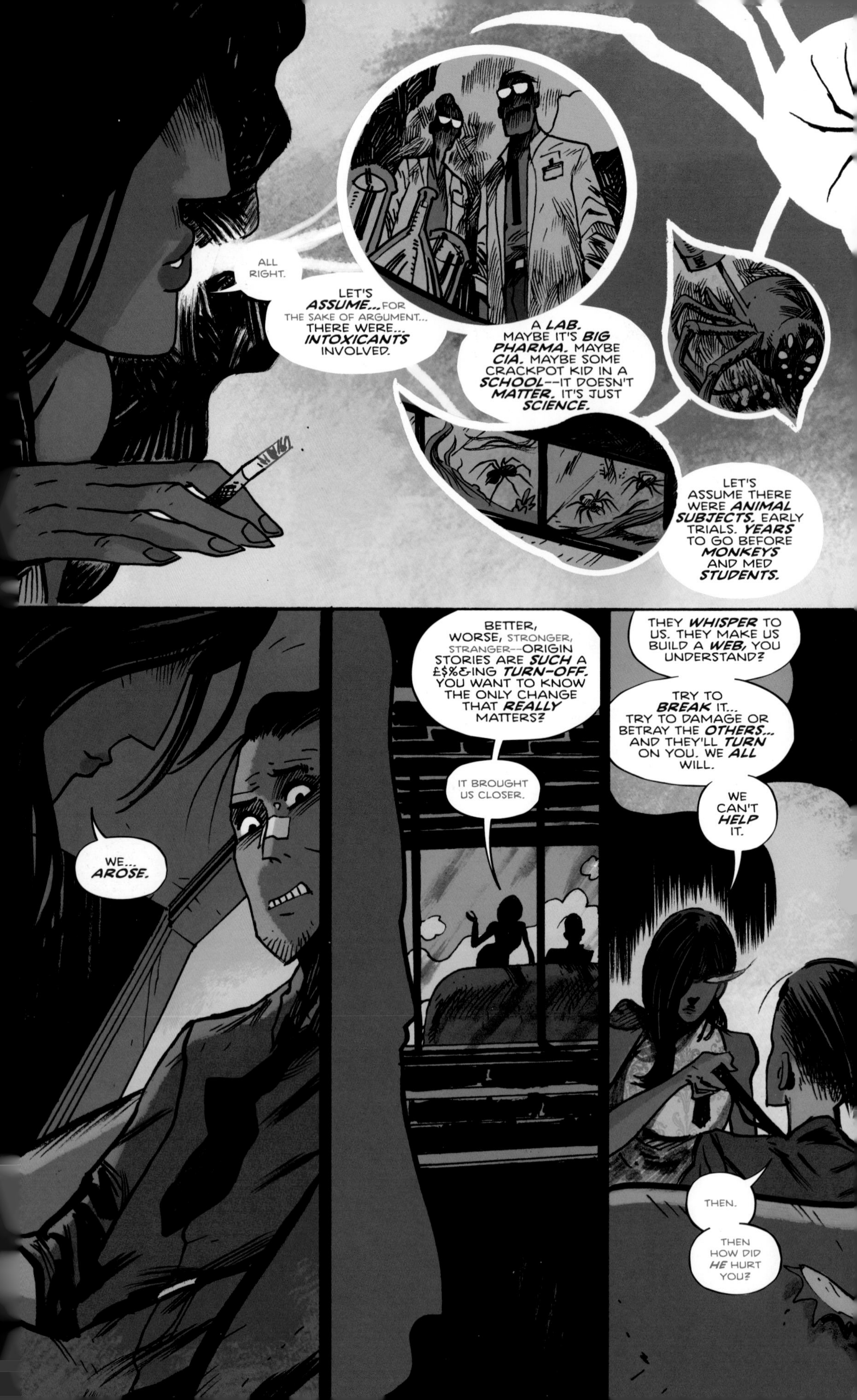
ALL RIGHT.
LET'S ASSUME... FOR THE SAKE OF ARGUMENT... THERE WERE... INTOXICANTS INVOLVED.
A LAB. MAYBE IT'S BIG PHARMA. MAYBE CIA. MAYBE SOME CRACKPOT KID IN A SCHOOL--IT DOESN'T MATTER. IT'S JUST SCIENCE.
LET'S ASSUME THERE WERE ANIMAL SUBJECTS. EARLY TRIALS. YEARS TO GO BEFORE MONKEYS AND MED STUDENTS.
WE... AROSE.
BETTER, WORSE, STRONGER, STRANGER--ORIGIN STORIES ARE SUCH A £$%&-ING TURN-OFF. YOU WANT TO KNOW THE ONLY CHANGE THAT REALLY MATTERS?
IT BROUGHT US CLOSER.
THEY WHISPER TO US. THEY MAKE US BUILD A WEB, YOU UNDERSTAND?
TRY TO BREAK IT... TRY TO DAMAGE OR BETRAY THE OTHERS... AND THEY'LL TURN ON YOU. WE ALL WILL.
WE CAN'T HELP IT.
THEN.
THEN HOW DID HE HURT YOU?

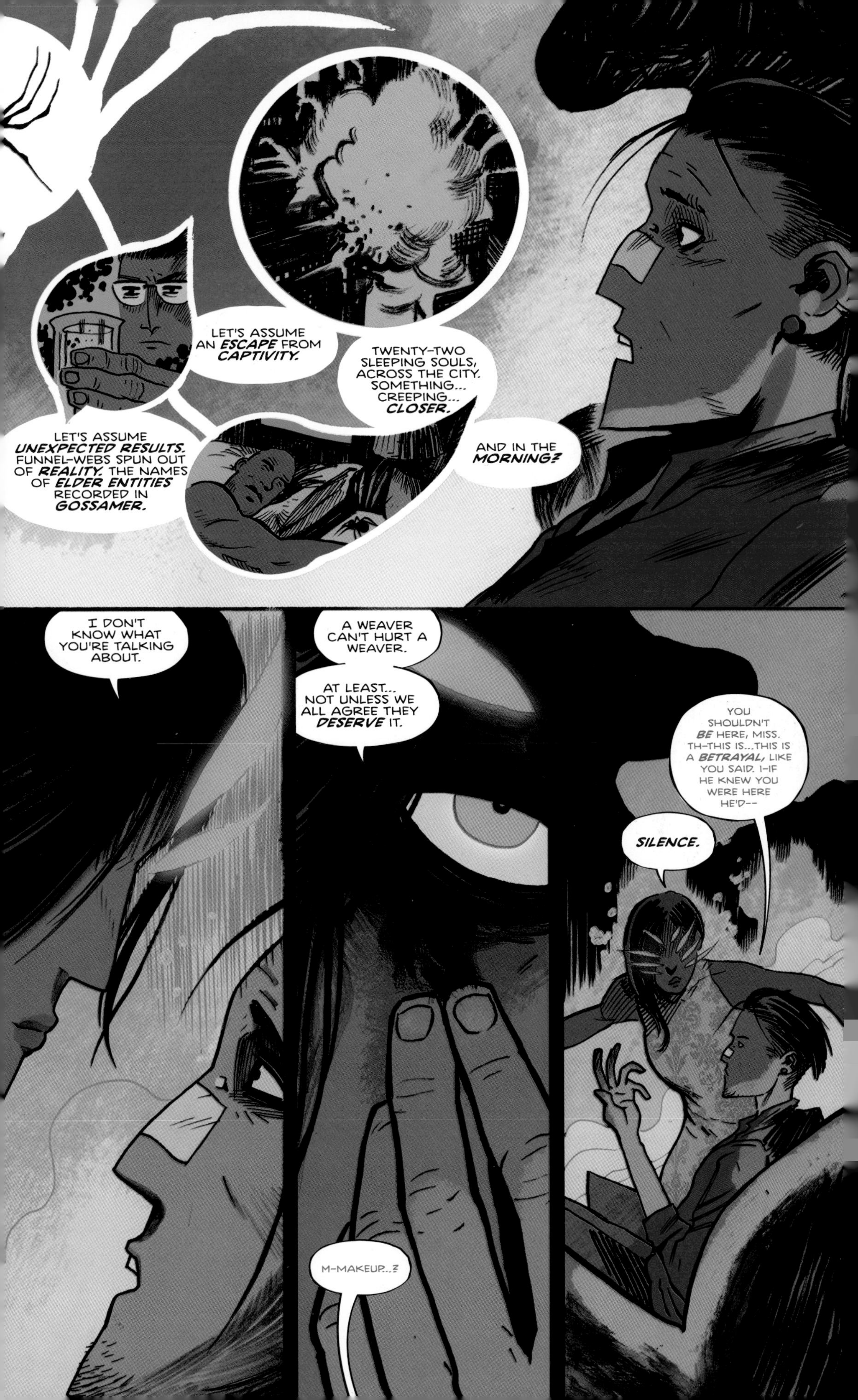
LET'S ASSUME AN ESCAPE FROM CAPTIVITY.
LET'S ASSUME UNEXPECTED RESULTS. FUNNEL-WEBS SPUN OUT OF REALITY. THE NAMES OF ELDER ENTITIES RECORDED IN GOSSAMER.
TWENTY-TWO SLEEPING SOULS, ACROSS THE CITY. SOMETHING... CREEPING... CLOSER.
AND IN THE MORNING?
I DON'T KNOW WHAT YOU'RE TALKING ABOUT.
A WEAVER CAN'T HURT A WEAVER.
AT LEAST... NOT UNLESS WE ALL AGREE THEY DESERVE IT.
M-MAKEUP...?
YOU SHOULDN'T BE HERE, MISS. TH-THIS IS...THIS IS A BETRAYAL, LIKE YOU SAID. I-IF HE KNEW YOU WERE HERE HE'D--
SILENCE.

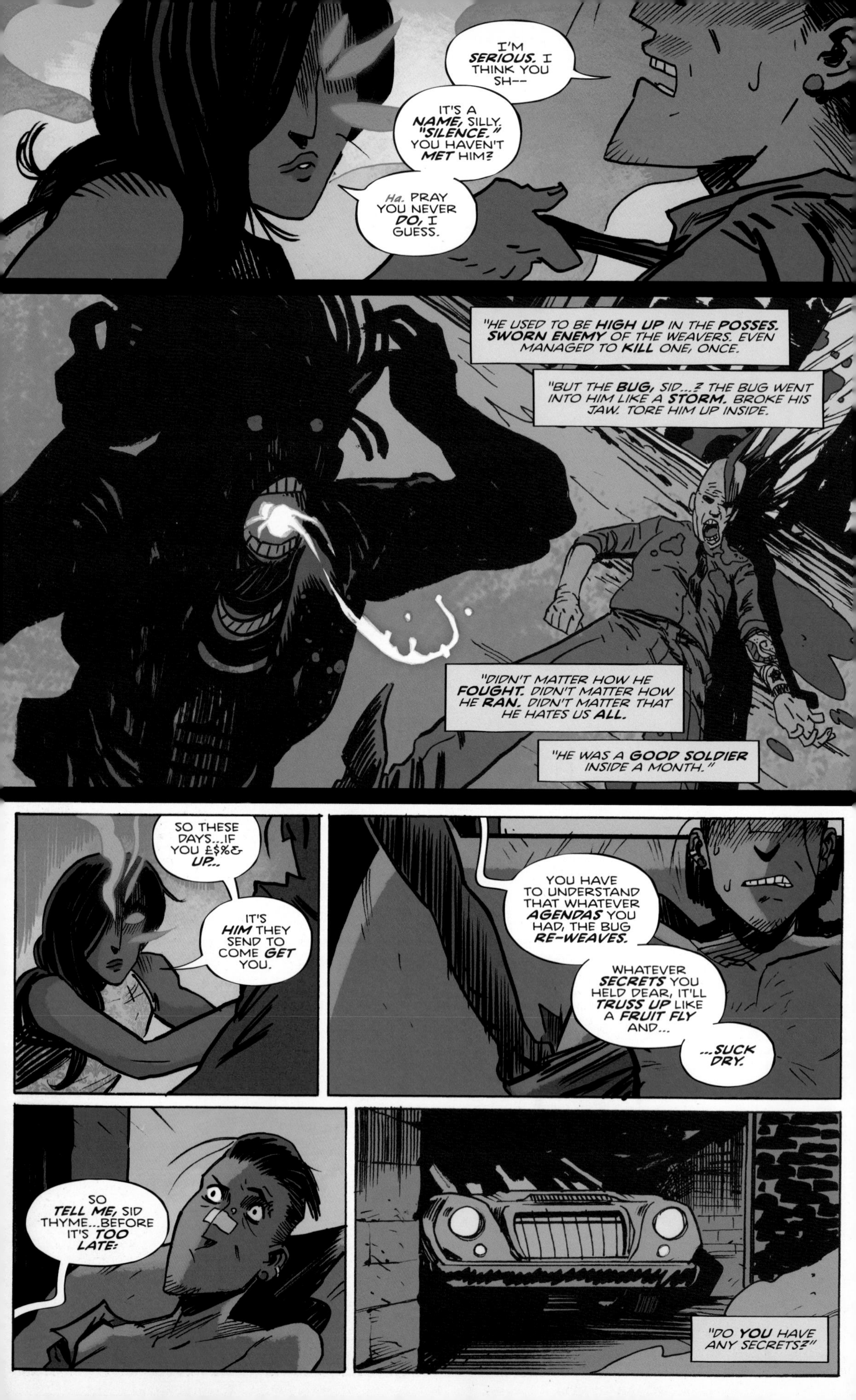

I'M SERIOUS. I THINK YOU SH--
IT'S A NAME, SILLY. "SILENCE." YOU HAVEN'T MET HIM?
Ha. PRAY YOU NEVER DO, I GUESS.
"HE USED TO BE HIGH UP IN THE POSSES. SWORN ENEMY OF THE WEAVERS. EVEN MANAGED TO KILL ONE, ONCE.
"BUT THE BUG, SID...? THE BUG WENT INTO HIM LIKE A STORM. BROKE HIS JAW. TORE HIM UP INSIDE.
"DIDN'T MATTER HOW HE FOUGHT. DIDN'T MATTER HOW HE RAN. DIDN'T MATTER THAT HE HATES US ALL.
"HE WAS A GOOD SOLDIER INSIDE A MONTH."
SO THESE DAYS...IF YOU £$%& UP...
IT'S HIM THEY SEND TO COME GET YOU.
YOU HAVE TO UNDERSTAND THAT WHATEVER AGENDAS YOU HAD, THE BUG RE-WEAVES.
WHATEVER SECRETS YOU HELD DEAR, IT'LL TRUSS UP LIKE A FRUIT FLY AND...
...SUCK DRY.
SO TELL ME, SID THYME...BEFORE IT'S TOO LATE:
"DO YOU HAVE ANY SECRETS?"

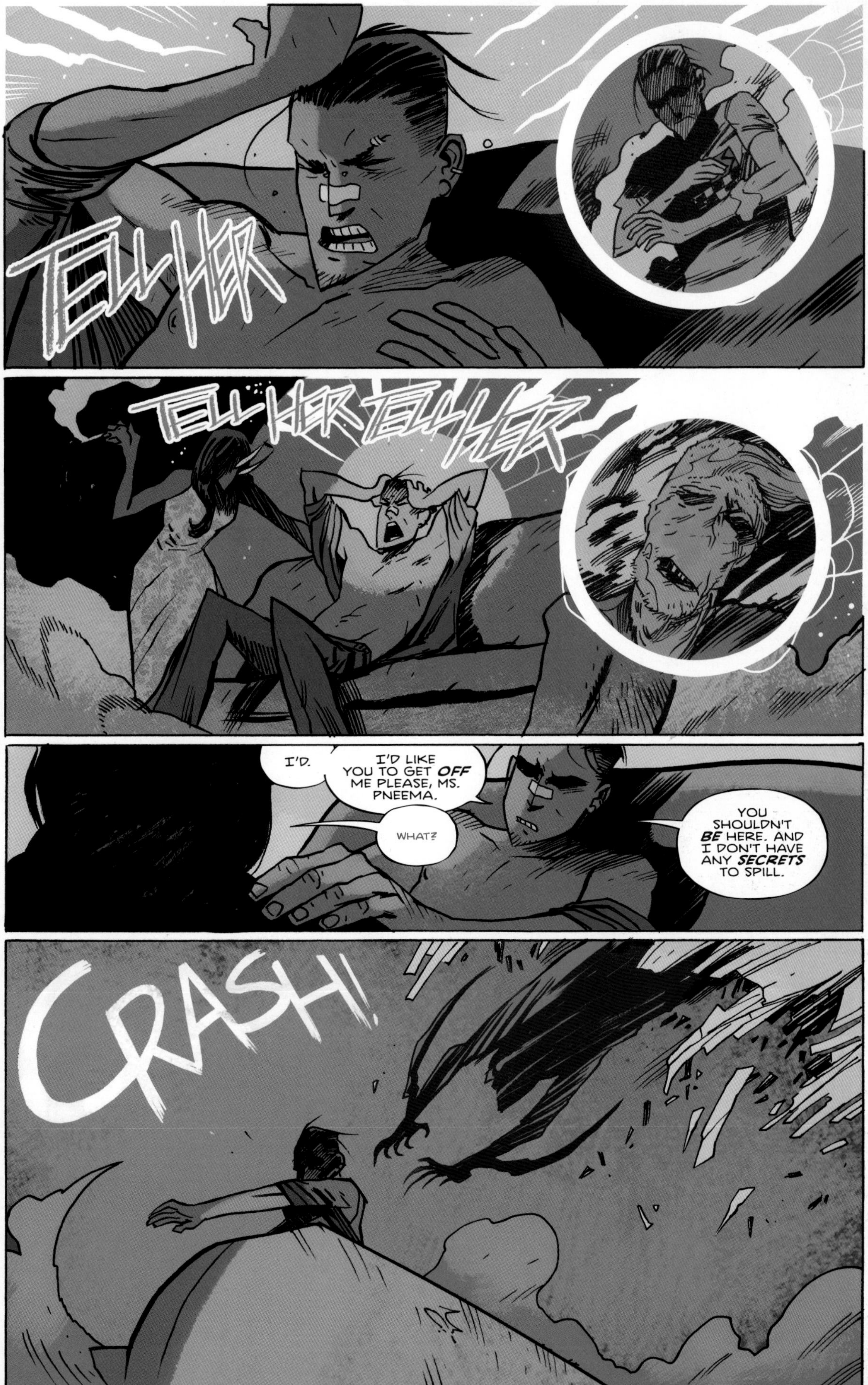
TELL HER
TELL HER TELL HER
I'D.
I'D LIKE YOU TO GET OFF ME PLEASE, MS. PNEEMA.
WHAT?
YOU SHOULDN'T BE HERE. AND I DON'T HAVE ANY SECRETS TO SPILL.
CRASH!

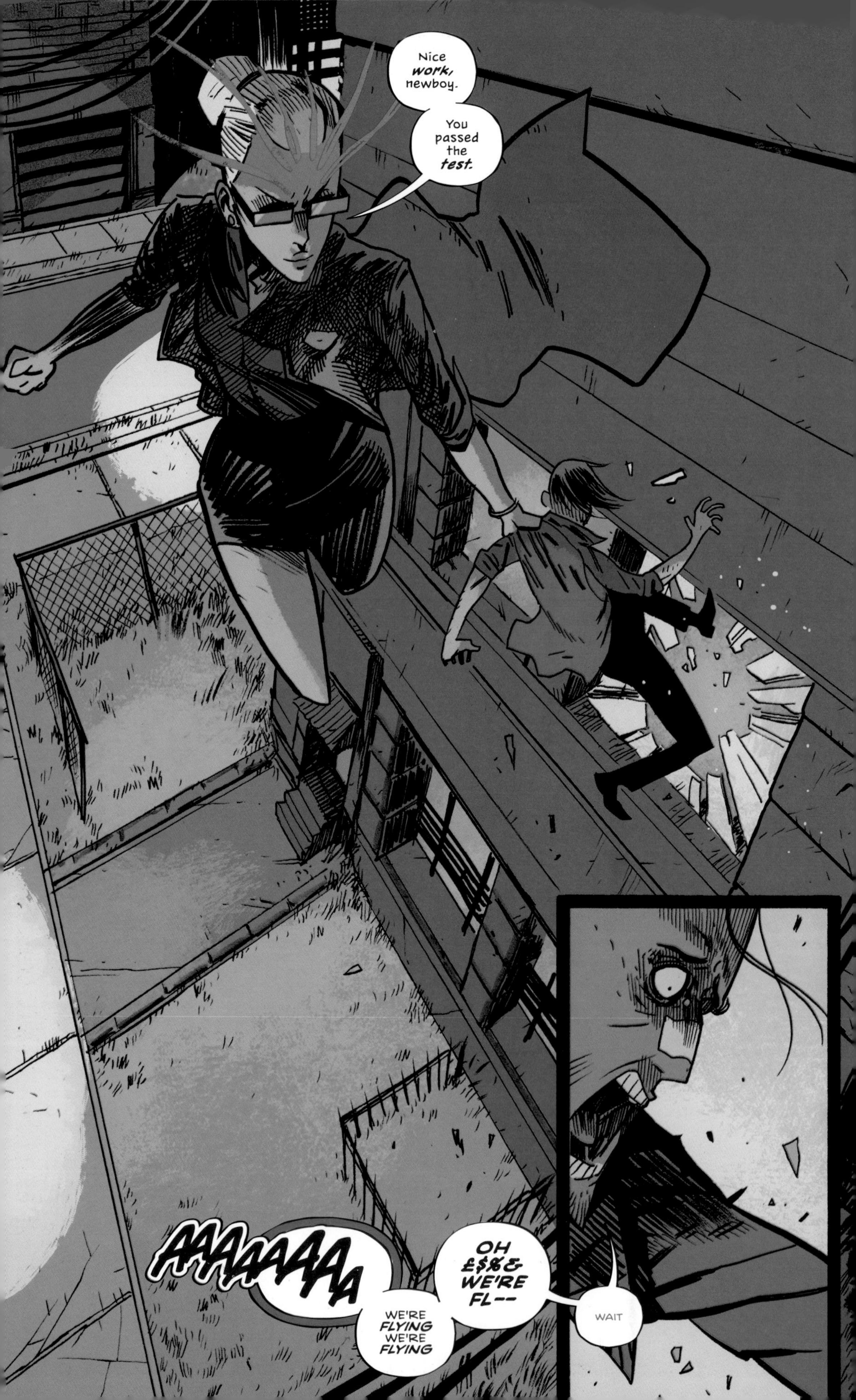
Nice *work,* newboy.
You passed the *test.*
AAAAAAAAA
WE'RE *FLYING* WE'RE *FLYING*
OH £$%& WE'RE FL--
WAIT

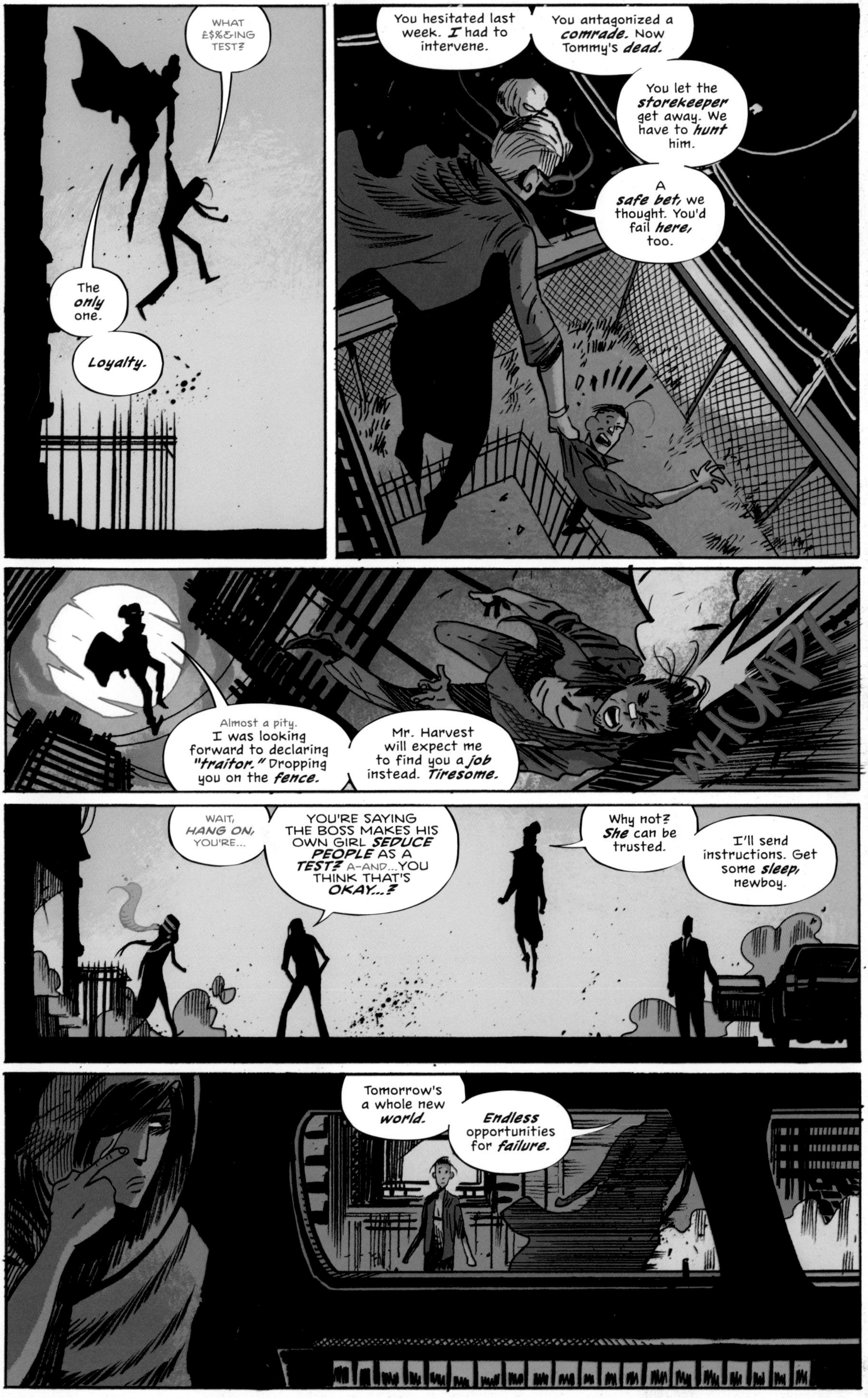
WHAT £$%&ING TEST?
The only one.
Loyalty.
You hesitated last week. I had to intervene.
You antagonized a comrade. Now Tommy's dead.
You let the storekeeper get away. We have to hunt him.
A safe bet, we thought. You'd fail here, too.
Almost a pity. I was looking forward to declaring "traitor." Dropping you on the fence.
Mr. Harvest will expect me to find you a job instead. Tiresome.
WHUMP!
WAIT, HANG ON, YOU'RE...
YOU'RE SAYING THE BOSS MAKES HIS OWN GIRL SEDUCE PEOPLE AS A TEST? A-AND... YOU THINK THAT'S OKAY...?
Why not? She can be trusted.
I'll send instructions. Get some sleep, newboy.
Tomorrow's a whole new world.
Endless opportunities for failure.

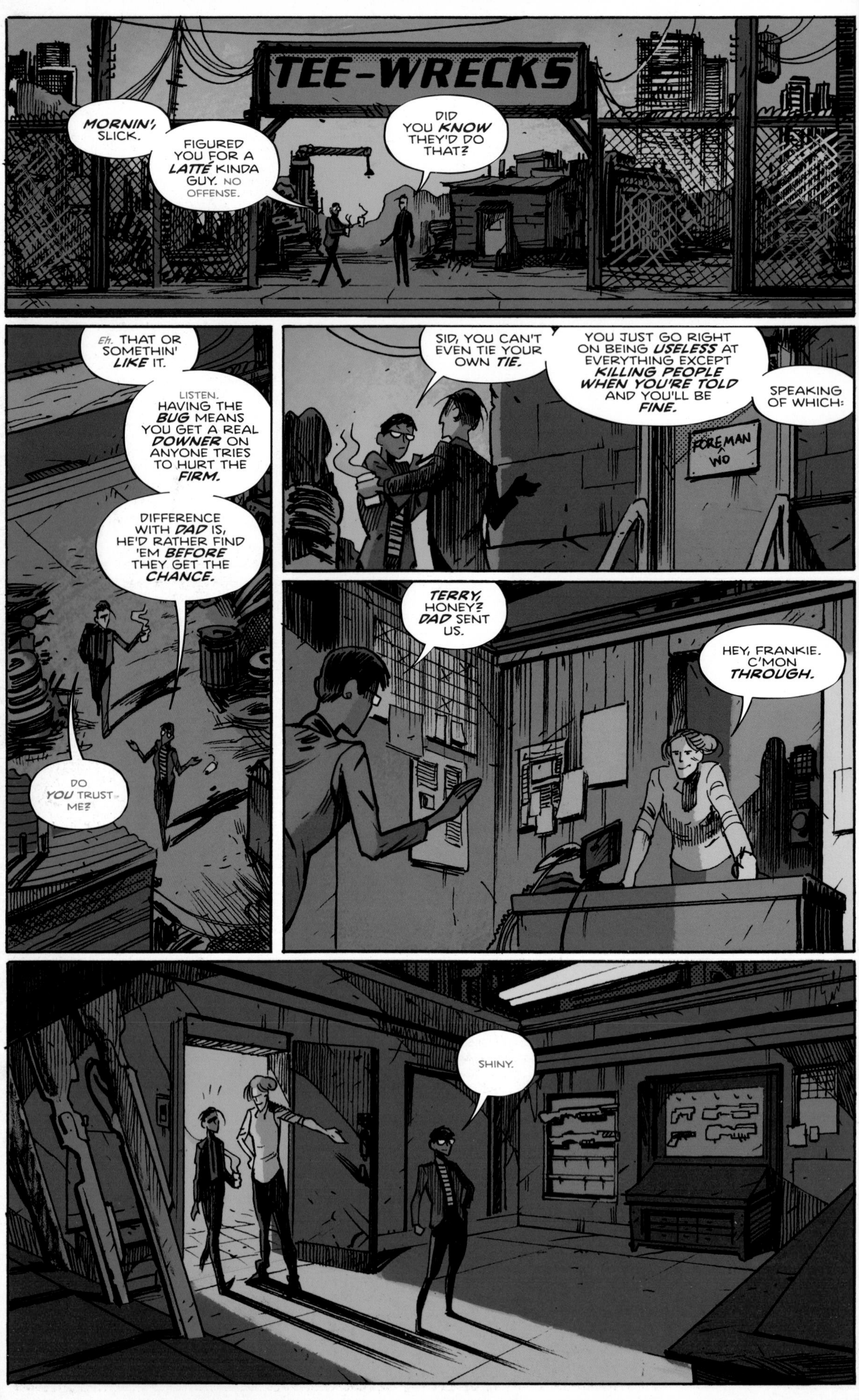
TEE-WRECKS
MORNIN', SLICK.
FIGURED YOU FOR A LATTÉ KINDA GUY. NO OFFENSE.
DID YOU KNOW THEY'D DO THAT?
Eh. THAT OR SOMETHIN' LIKE IT.
LISTEN. HAVING THE BUG MEANS YOU GET A REAL DOWNER ON ANYONE TRIES TO HURT THE FIRM.
DIFFERENCE WITH DAD IS, HE'D RATHER FIND 'EM BEFORE THEY GET THE CHANCE.
DO YOU TRUST ME?
SID, YOU CAN'T EVEN TIE YOUR OWN TIE.
YOU JUST GO RIGHT ON BEING USELESS AT EVERYTHING EXCEPT KILLING PEOPLE WHEN YOU'RE TOLD AND YOU'LL BE FINE.
SPEAKING OF WHICH:
FOREMAN WO
TERRY, HONEY? DAD SENT US.
HEY, FRANKIE. C'MON THROUGH.
SHINY.

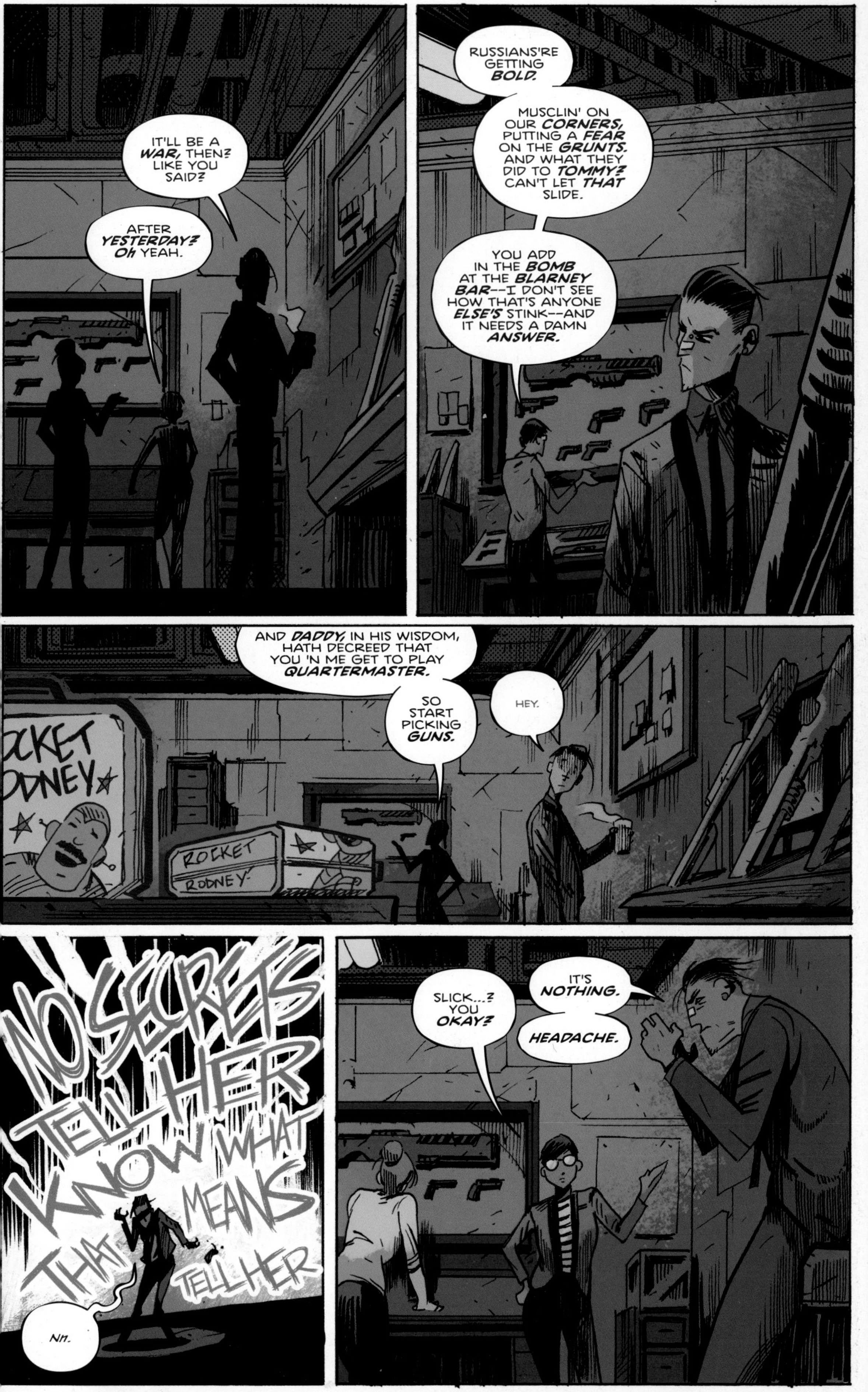
IT'LL BE A WAR, THEN? LIKE YOU SAID?
AFTER YESTERDAY? Oh YEAH.
RUSSIANS'RE GETTING BOLD.
MUSCLIN' ON OUR CORNERS, PUTTING A FEAR ON THE GRUNTS. AND WHAT THEY DID TO TOMMY? CAN'T LET THAT SLIDE.
YOU ADD IN THE BOMB AT THE BLARNEY BAR--I DON'T SEE HOW THAT'S ANYONE ELSE'S STINK--AND IT NEEDS A DAMN ANSWER.
AND DADDY, IN HIS WISDOM, HATH DECREED THAT YOU 'N ME GET TO PLAY QUARTERMASTER.
SO START PICKING GUNS.
HEY.
ROCKET RODNEY
ROCKET RODNEY
NO SECRETS
TELL HER
KNOW WHAT
THAT
MEANS
TELL HER
NN.
SLICK...? YOU OKAY?
IT'S NOTHING.
HEADACHE.

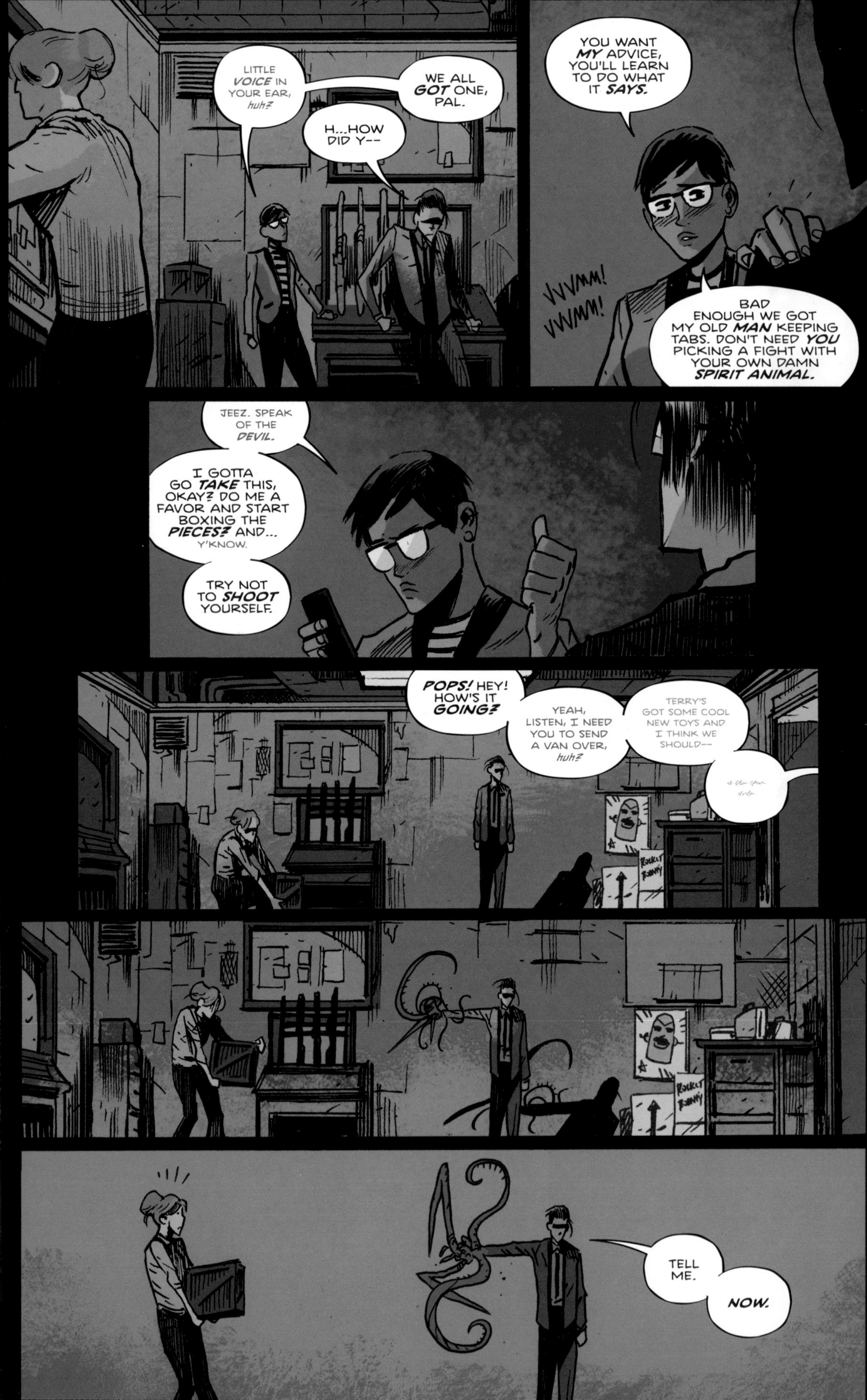
LITTLE VOICE IN YOUR EAR, huh?
WE ALL GOT ONE, PAL.
H...HOW DID Y--
YOU WANT MY ADVICE, YOU'LL LEARN TO DO WHAT IT SAYS.
VVVMM! VVVMM!
BAD ENOUGH WE GOT MY OLD MAN KEEPING TABS. DON'T NEED YOU PICKING A FIGHT WITH YOUR OWN DAMN SPIRIT ANIMAL.
JEEZ. SPEAK OF THE DEVIL.
I GOTTA GO TAKE THIS, OKAY? DO ME A FAVOR AND START BOXING THE PIECES? AND... Y'KNOW.
TRY NOT TO SHOOT YOURSELF.
POPS! HEY! HOW'S IT GOING?
YEAH, LISTEN, I NEED YOU TO SEND A VAN OVER, huh?
TERRY'S GOT SOME COOL NEW TOYS AND I THINK WE SHOULD--
TELL ME.
NOW.

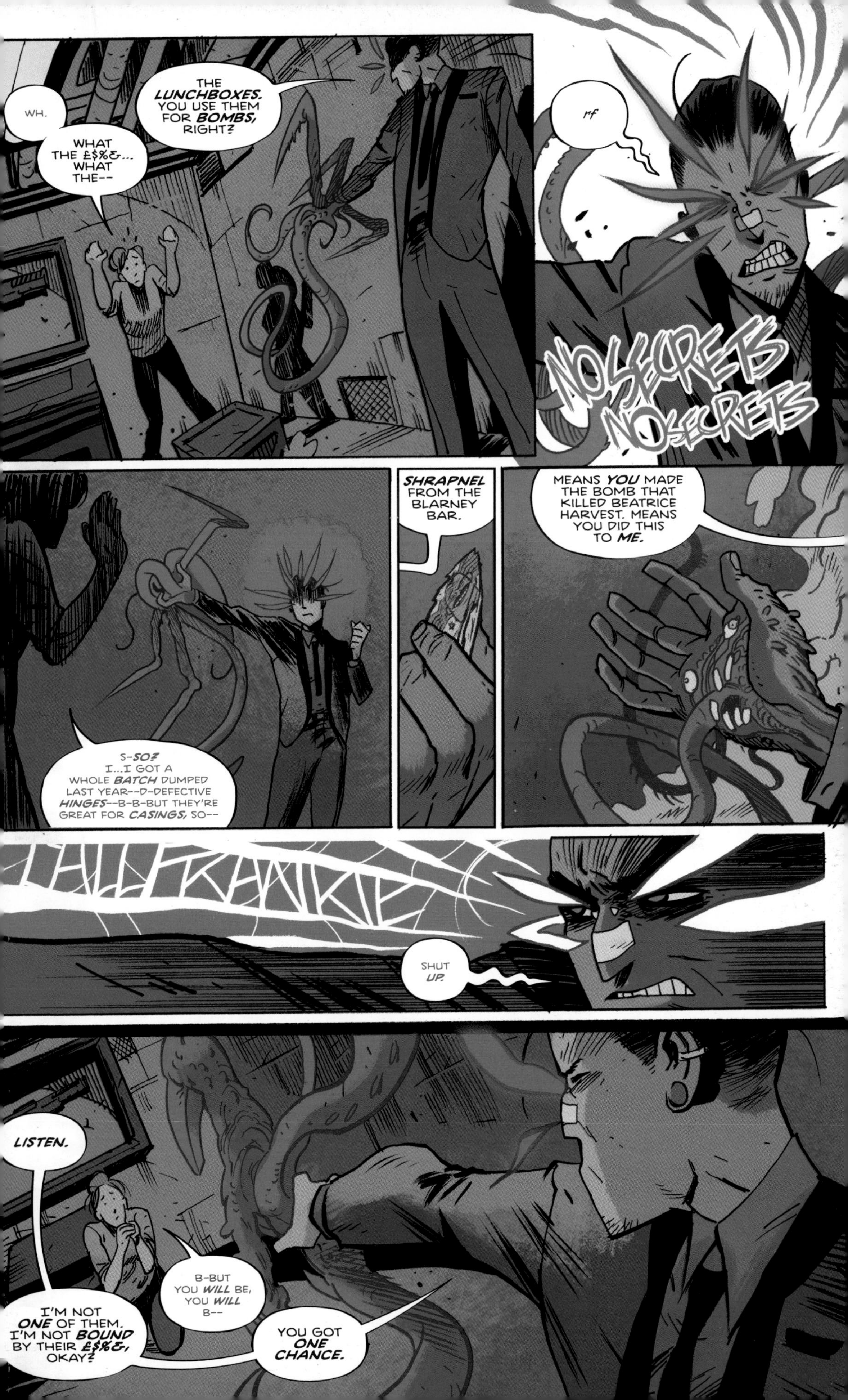

WH.
WHAT THE £$%&... WHAT THE--
THE LUNCHBOXES. YOU USE THEM FOR BOMBS, RIGHT?
rf
NO SECRETS NO SECRETS
S-SO? I...I GOT A WHOLE BATCH DUMPED LAST YEAR--D-DEFECTIVE HINGES--B-B-BUT THEY'RE GREAT FOR CASINGS, SO--
SHRAPNEL FROM THE BLARNEY BAR.
MEANS YOU MADE THE BOMB THAT KILLED BEATRICE HARVEST. MEANS YOU DID THIS TO ME.
SHUT UP.
LISTEN.
I'M NOT ONE OF THEM. I'M NOT BOUND BY THEIR £$%&, OKAY?
B-BUT YOU WILL BE, YOU WILL B--
YOU GOT ONE CHANCE.

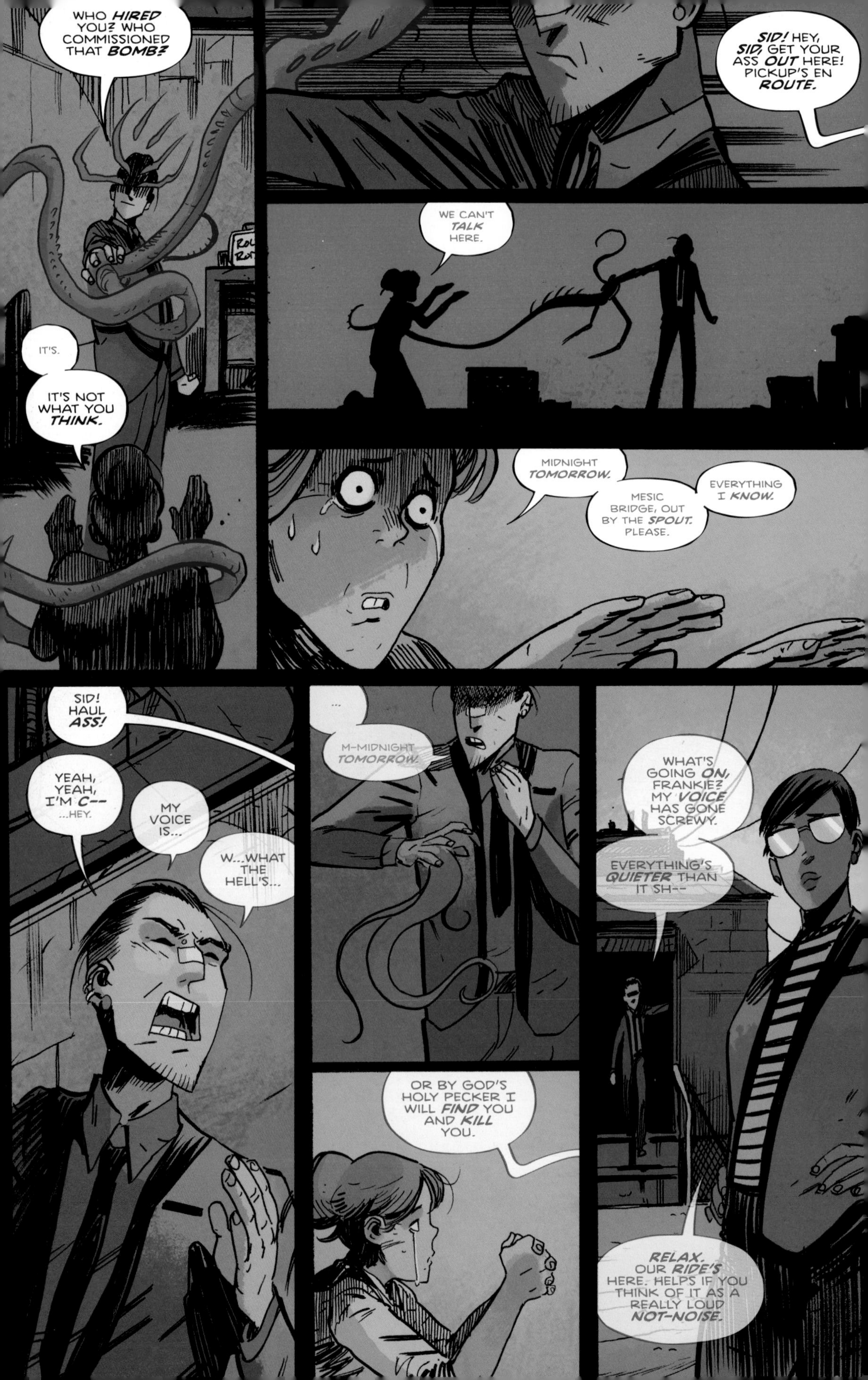

WHO HIRED YOU? WHO COMMISSIONED THAT BOMB?
SID! HEY, SID, GET YOUR ASS OUT HERE! PICKUP'S EN ROUTE.
WE CAN'T TALK HERE.
IT'S.
IT'S NOT WHAT YOU THINK.
MIDNIGHT TOMORROW.
MESIC BRIDGE, OUT BY THE SPOUT. PLEASE.
EVERYTHING I KNOW.
SID! HAUL ASS!
YEAH, YEAH, I'M C-- ...HEY.
MY VOICE IS...
W...WHAT THE HELL'S...
...
M-MIDNIGHT TOMORROW.
OR BY GOD'S HOLY PECKER I WILL FIND YOU AND KILL YOU.
WHAT'S GOING ON, FRANKIE? MY VOICE HAS GONE SCREWY.
EVERYTHING'S QUIETER THAN IT SH--
RELAX. OUR RIDE'S HERE. HELPS IF YOU THINK OF IT AS A REALLY LOUD NOT-NOISE.

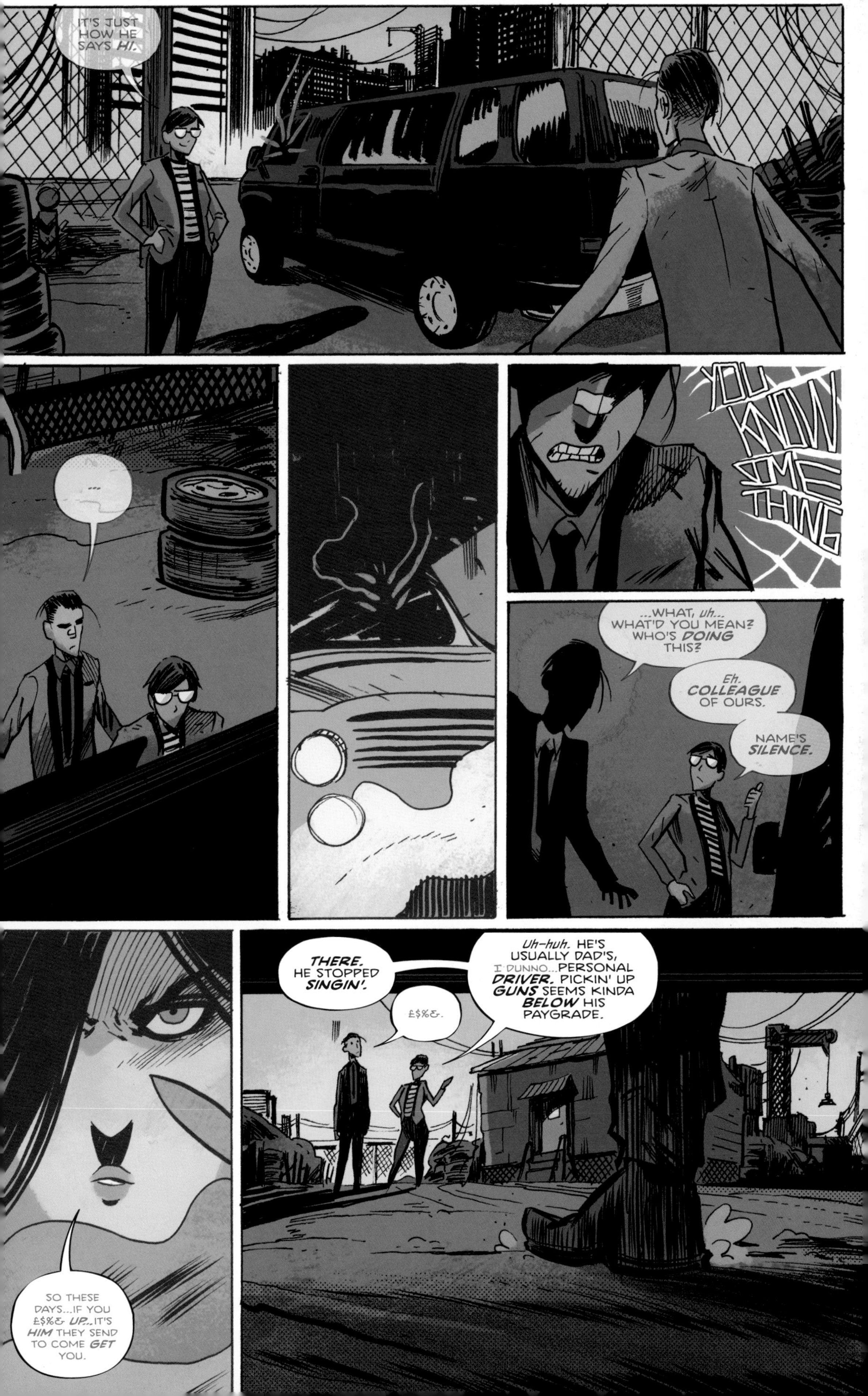
IT'S JUST HOW HE SAYS HI.
...
YOU KNOW SOMETHING
...WHAT, uh... WHAT'D YOU MEAN? WHO'S DOING THIS?
Eh. COLLEAGUE OF OURS.
NAME'S SILENCE.
SO THESE DAYS...IF YOU £$%& UP...IT'S HIM THEY SEND TO COME GET YOU.
THERE. HE STOPPED SINGIN'.
£$%&.
Uh-huh. HE'S USUALLY DAD'S, I DUNNO...PERSONAL DRIVER. PICKIN' UP GUNS SEEMS KINDA BELOW HIS PAYGRADE.

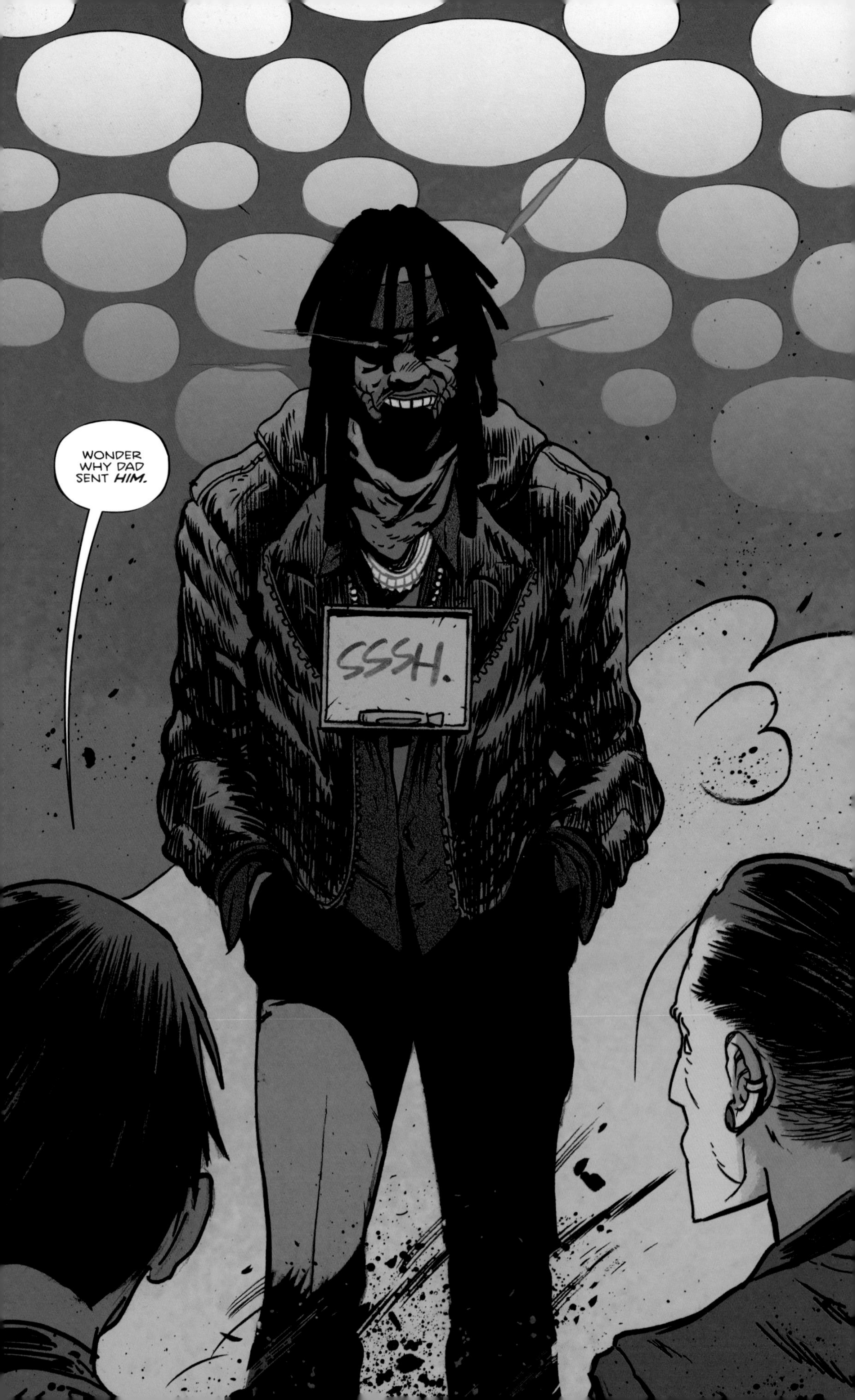
WONDER WHY DAD SENT HIM.
SSSH.

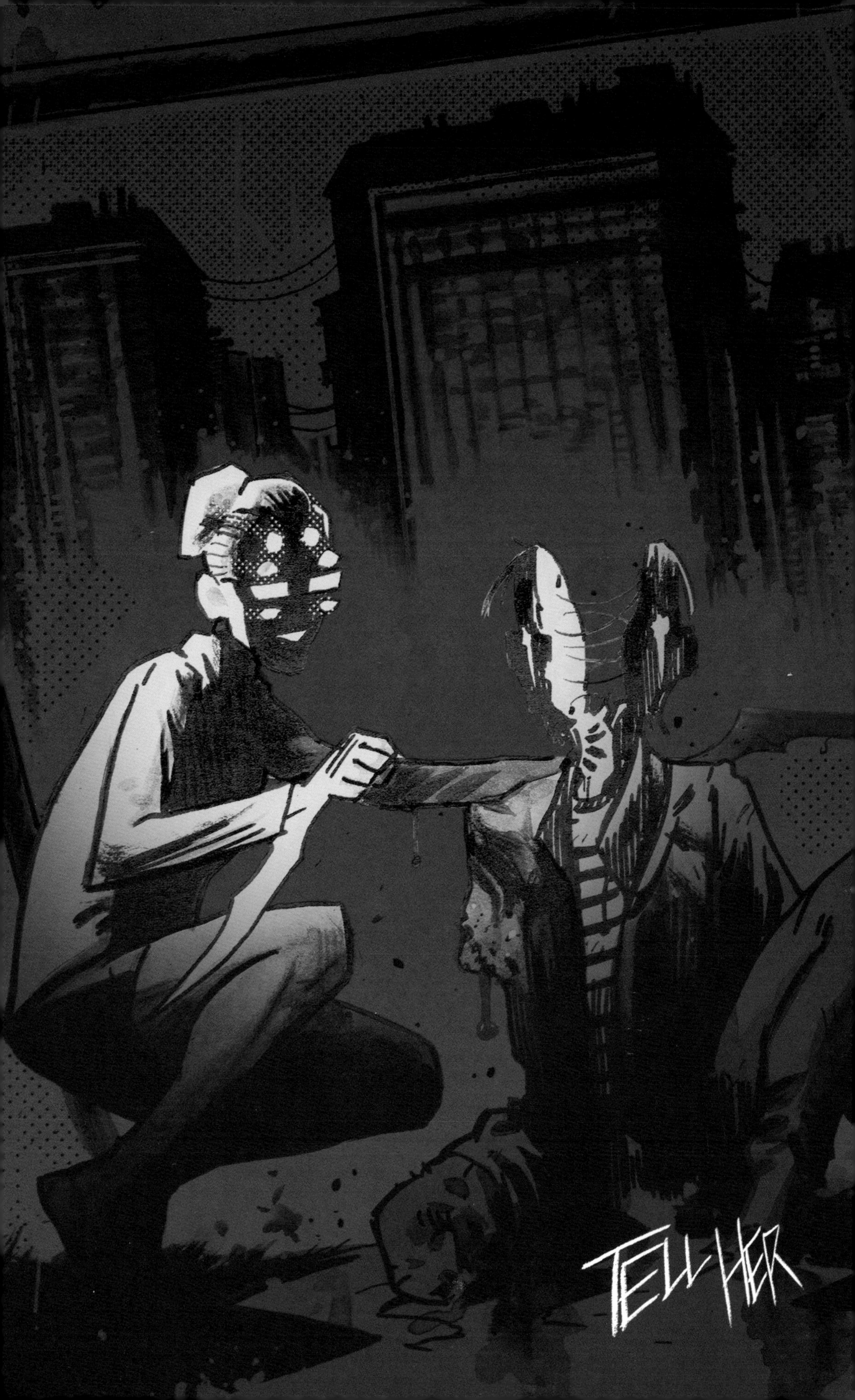
TELL HER

CHAPTER

THREE

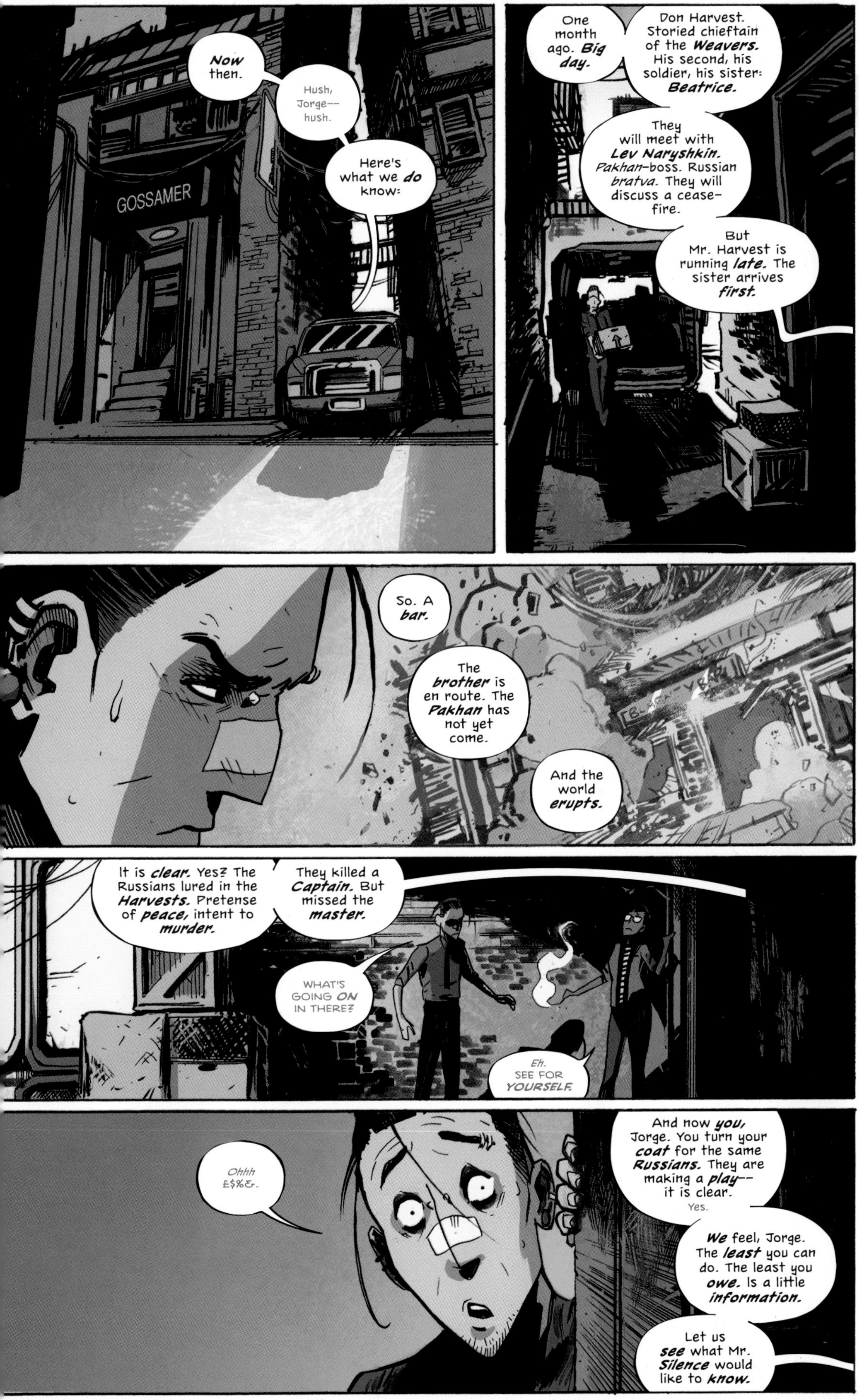

Now then.
Hush, Jorge-- hush.
Here's what we do know:
GOSSAMER
One month ago. Big day.
Don Harvest. Storied chieftain of the Weavers. His second, his sister: Beatrice.
They will meet with Lev Naryshkin. Pakhan--boss. Russian bratva. They will discuss a cease-fire.
But Mr. Harvest is running late. The sister arrives first.
So. A bar.
The brother is en route. The Pakhan has not yet come.
And the world erupts.
It is clear. Yes? The Russians lured in the Harvests. Pretense of peace, intent to murder.
They killed a Captain. But missed the master.
WHAT'S GOING ON IN THERE?
Eh. SEE FOR YOURSELF.
Ohhh £$%&.
And now you, Jorge. You turn your coat for the same Russians. They are making a play-- it is clear.
Yes.
We feel, Jorge. The least you can do. The least you owe. Is a little information.
Let us see what Mr. Silence would like to know.

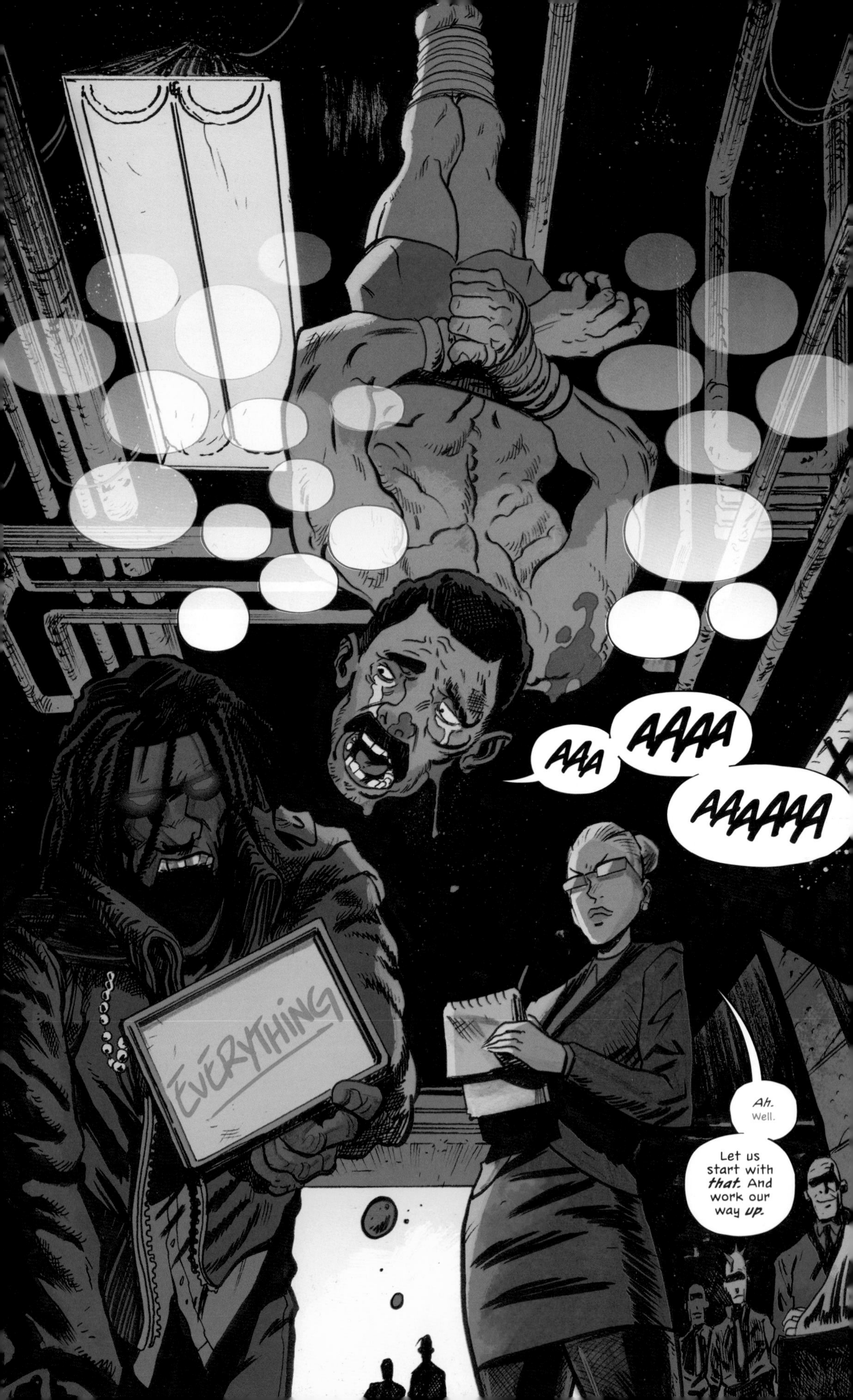
AAA AAAA AAAAAA
EVERYTHING
Ah. Well.
Let us start with that. And work our way up.

TH–THAT'S THE GUY FROM THE *STORE.*

SEE WHY THEY BROUGHT IN *SILENCE* NOW, *huh?* HE'S KINDA THE *SPECIALIST,* THIS STUFF.

WE *ALL* GOT A PART, ROOKIE.

AAAH!

JEEZ, DAD... AT LEAST PUT ON A *SHIRT...?*

≥pft≤ *SLAVE* RAGS. *PEACOCK BLING* FOR THE £$%&IN' *ORDINARY.*

I GET *HOT.*

W–WHERE'D YOU *FIND* HIM, SIR? THE *STOREKEEPER?*

RAILHEAD. TRYIN'A *BOUNCE* IN A FALSE *WIG.* RUSKIES PAID HIM, SLAPPED HIM ON THE BACK, LEFT HIM SPINNIN' IN THE *WIND.*

≥TH≤ NO *LOYALTY.*

YOU THINK HE KNOWS ANYTHING ABOUT THE *BOMB,* KILLED AUNTIE BEA?

DOUBT IT. HE'S A PAWN. BEST WE CAN HOPE, HE'S HAD *EYES* ON *BRATVA* TURF. LAYOUT, WEAK SPOTS—LIKE *THAT.*

LET SILENCE *SING* AT HIM A MINUTE OR TWO MORE— I GUESS WE'LL *FIND OUT.*

MORE?

AAAAAAAAAAAAAAAAAAAAAA

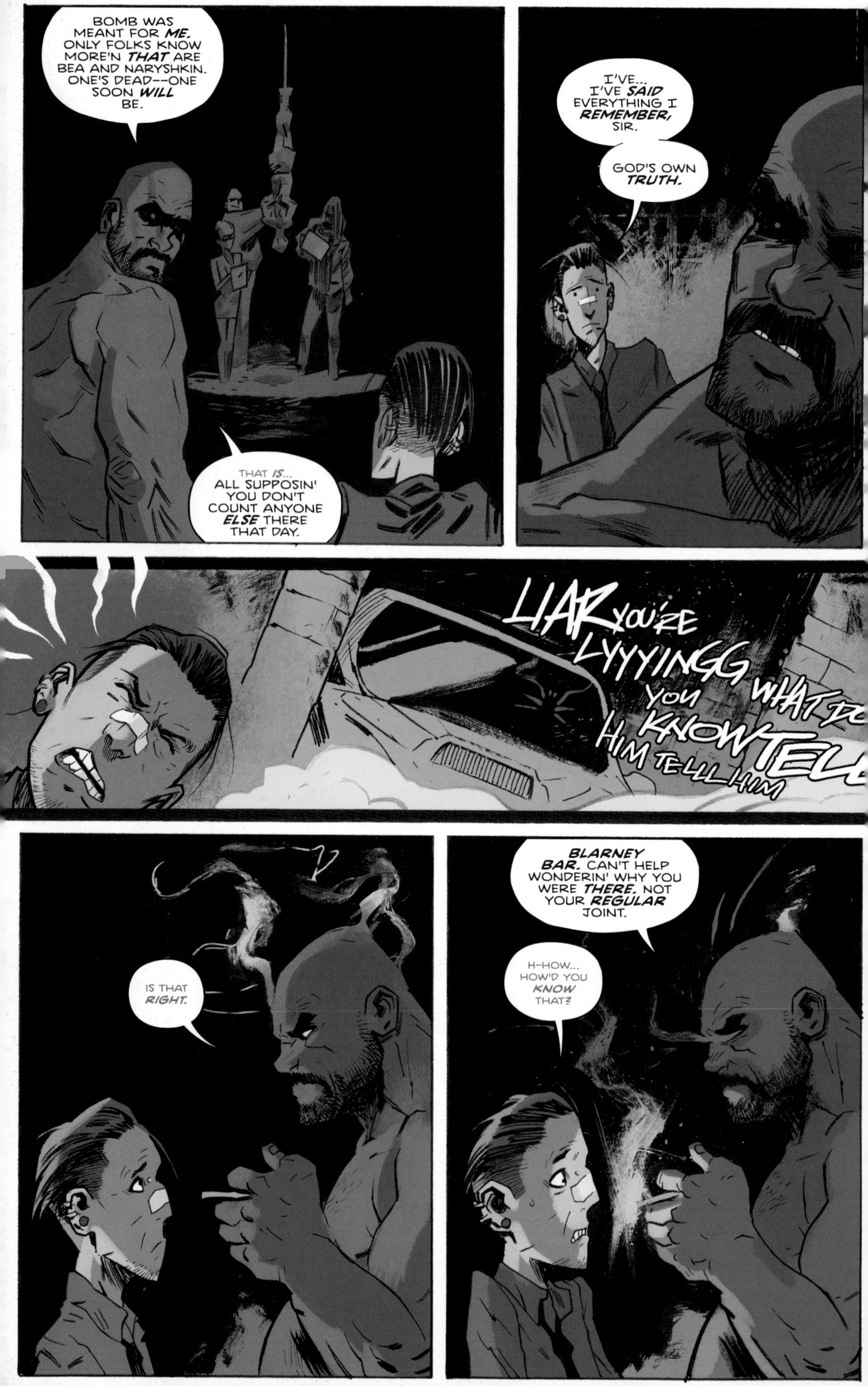
BOMB WAS MEANT FOR ME. ONLY FOLKS KNOW MORE'N THAT ARE BEA AND NARYSHKIN. ONE'S DEAD--ONE SOON WILL BE.
THAT IS... ALL SUPPOSIN' YOU DON'T COUNT ANYONE ELSE THERE THAT DAY.
I'VE... I'VE SAID EVERYTHING I REMEMBER, SIR.
GOD'S OWN TRUTH.
LIAR YOU'RE LYYYINGG
YOU KNOW
HIM TELLL HIM
IS THAT RIGHT.
BLARNEY BAR. CAN'T HELP WONDERIN' WHY YOU WERE THERE. NOT YOUR REGULAR JOINT.
H-HOW... HOW'D YOU KNOW THAT?

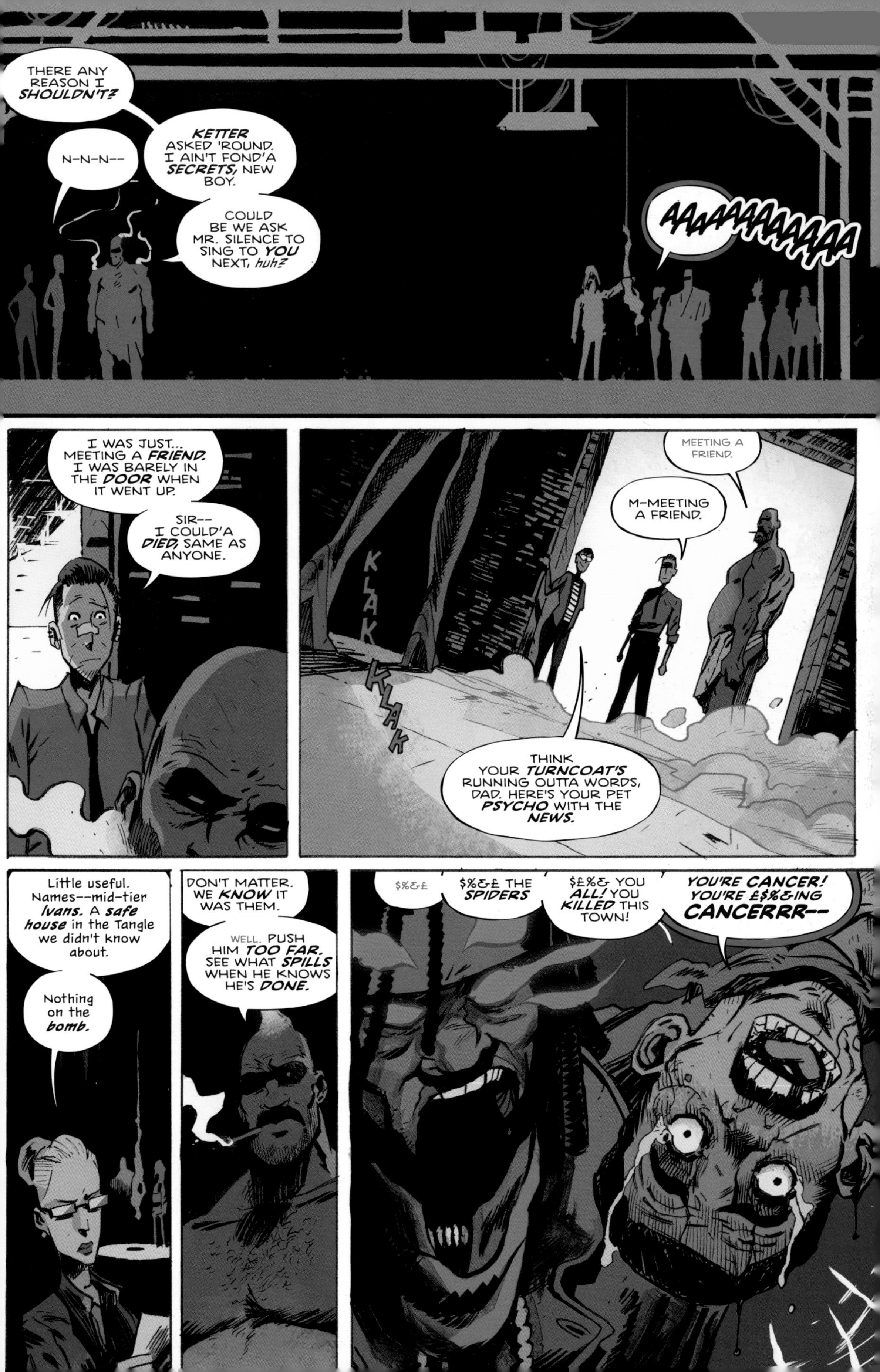
THERE ANY REASON I SHOULDN'T?
N-N-N--
KETTER ASKED 'ROUND. I AIN'T FOND'A SECRETS, NEW BOY.
COULD BE WE ASK MR. SILENCE TO SING TO YOU NEXT, huh?
AAAAAAAAAAAAA
I WAS JUST... MEETING A FRIEND. I WAS BARELY IN THE DOOR WHEN IT WENT UP.
SIR-- I COULD'A DIED, SAME AS ANYONE.
MEETING A FRIEND.
M-MEETING A FRIEND.
KLAK
KLAK
THINK YOUR TURNCOAT'S RUNNING OUTTA WORDS, DAD. HERE'S YOUR PET PSYCHO WITH THE NEWS.
Little useful. Names--mid-tier Ivans. A safe house in the Tangle we didn't know about.
Nothing on the bomb.
DON'T MATTER. WE KNOW IT WAS THEM.
WELL. PUSH HIM TOO FAR. SEE WHAT SPILLS WHEN HE KNOWS HE'S DONE.
$%&£
$%&£ THE SPIDERS
$£%& YOU ALL! YOU KILLED THIS TOWN!
YOU'RE CANCER! YOU'RE £$%&ING CANCERRR--

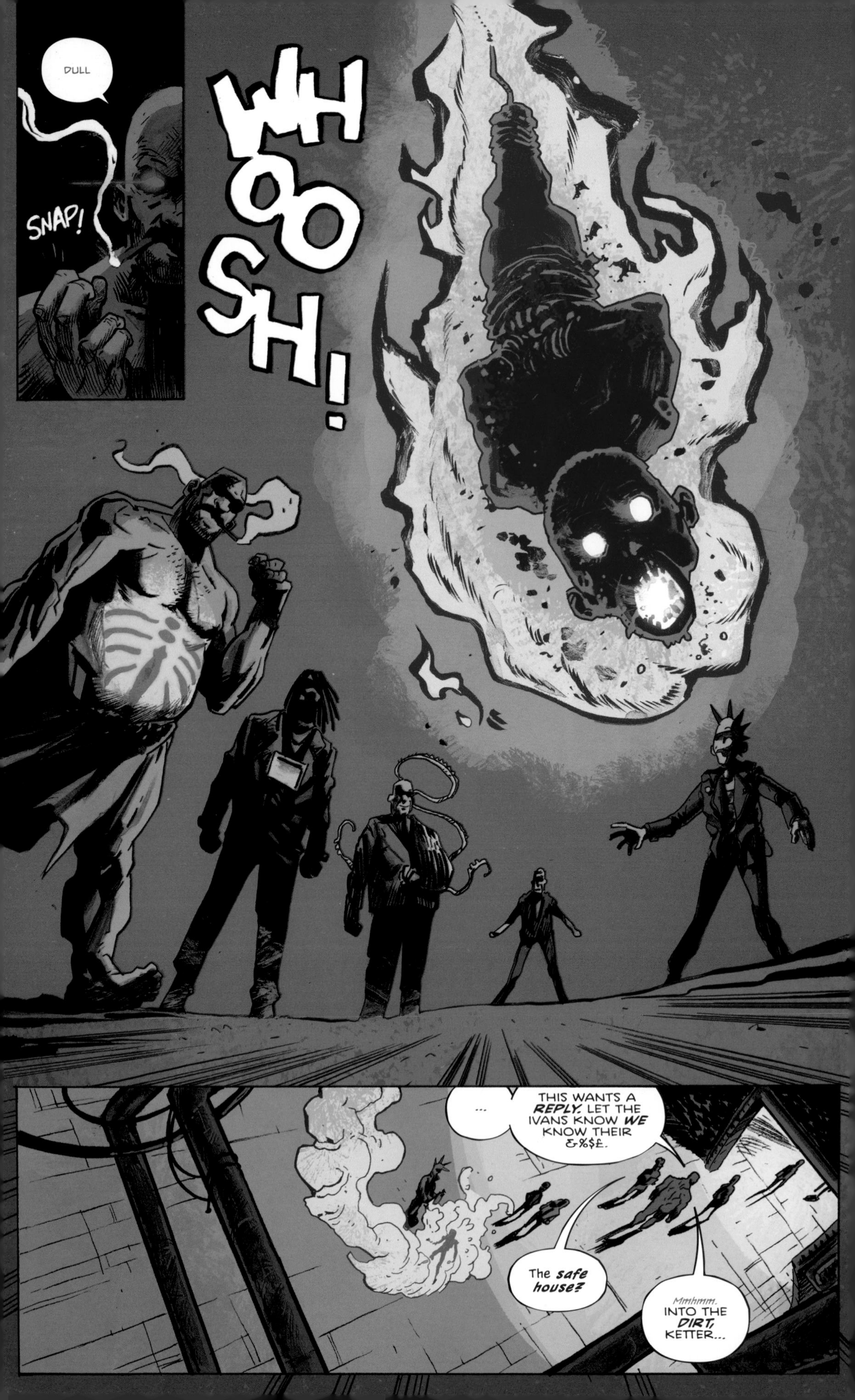
DULL
SNAP!
WHOOSH!
...
THIS WANTS A REPLY. LET THE IVANS KNOW WE KNOW THEIR &%$£.
The safe house?
Mmhmm. INTO THE DIRT, KETTER...

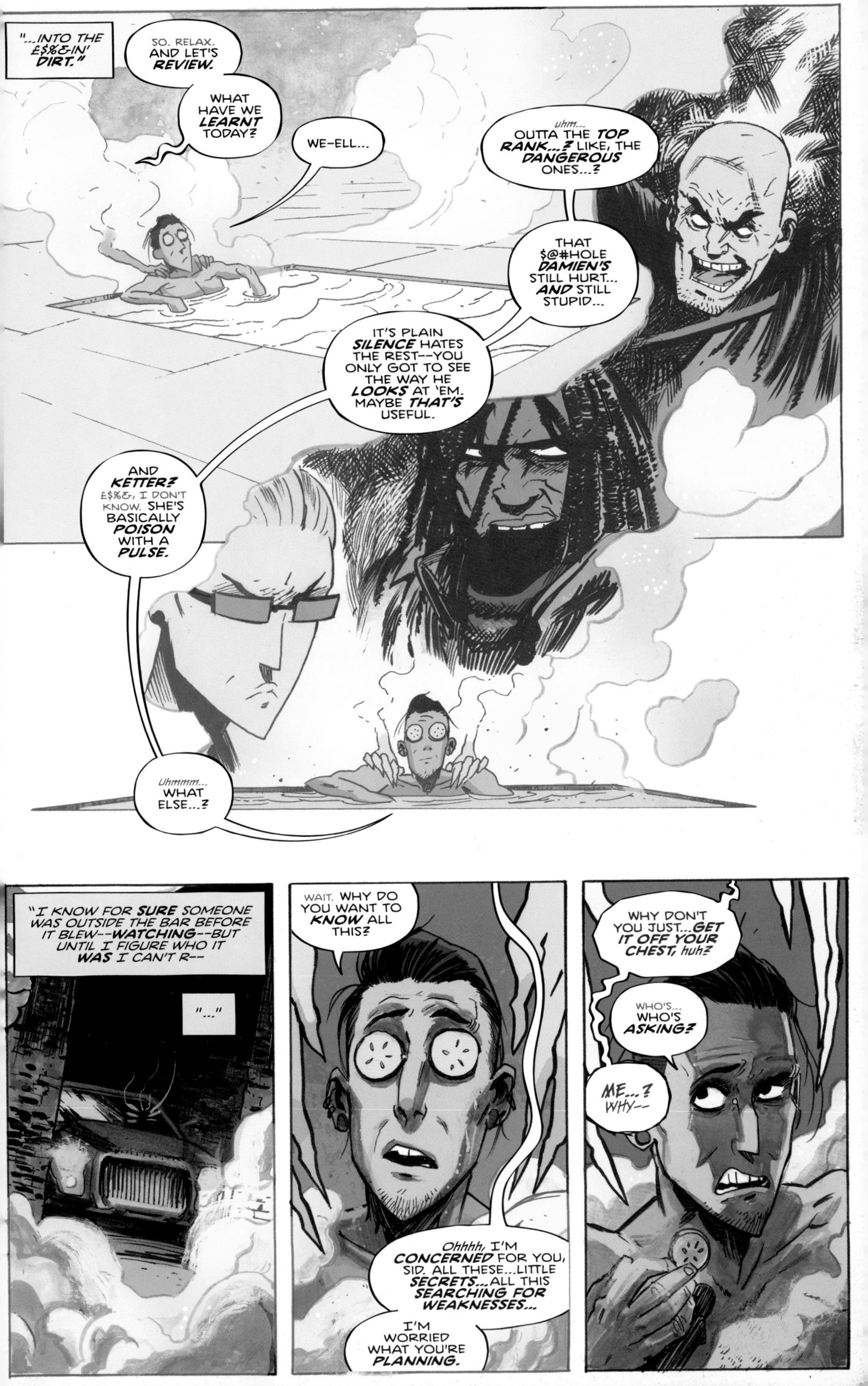
"...INTO THE £$%&-IN' DIRT."
SO. RELAX. AND LET'S REVIEW.
WHAT HAVE WE LEARNT TODAY?
WE-ELL...
uhm... OUTTA THE TOP RANK...? LIKE, THE DANGEROUS ONES...?
THAT $@#HOLE DAMIEN'S STILL HURT... AND STILL STUPID...
IT'S PLAIN SILENCE HATES THE REST--YOU ONLY GOT TO SEE THE WAY HE LOOKS AT 'EM. MAYBE THAT'S USEFUL.
AND KETTER? £$%&, I DON'T KNOW. SHE'S BASICALLY POISON WITH A PULSE.
Uhmmm... WHAT ELSE...?
"I KNOW FOR SURE SOMEONE WAS OUTSIDE THE BAR BEFORE IT BLEW--WATCHING--BUT UNTIL I FIGURE WHO IT WAS I CAN'T R--
"..."
WAIT. WHY DO YOU WANT TO KNOW ALL THIS?
Ohhhh, I'M CONCERNED FOR YOU, SID. ALL THESE...LITTLE SECRETS...ALL THIS SEARCHING FOR WEAKNESSES...
I'M WORRIED WHAT YOU'RE PLANNING.
WHY DON'T YOU JUST...GET IT OFF YOUR CHEST, huh?
WHO'S... WHO'S ASKING?
ME...? WHY--

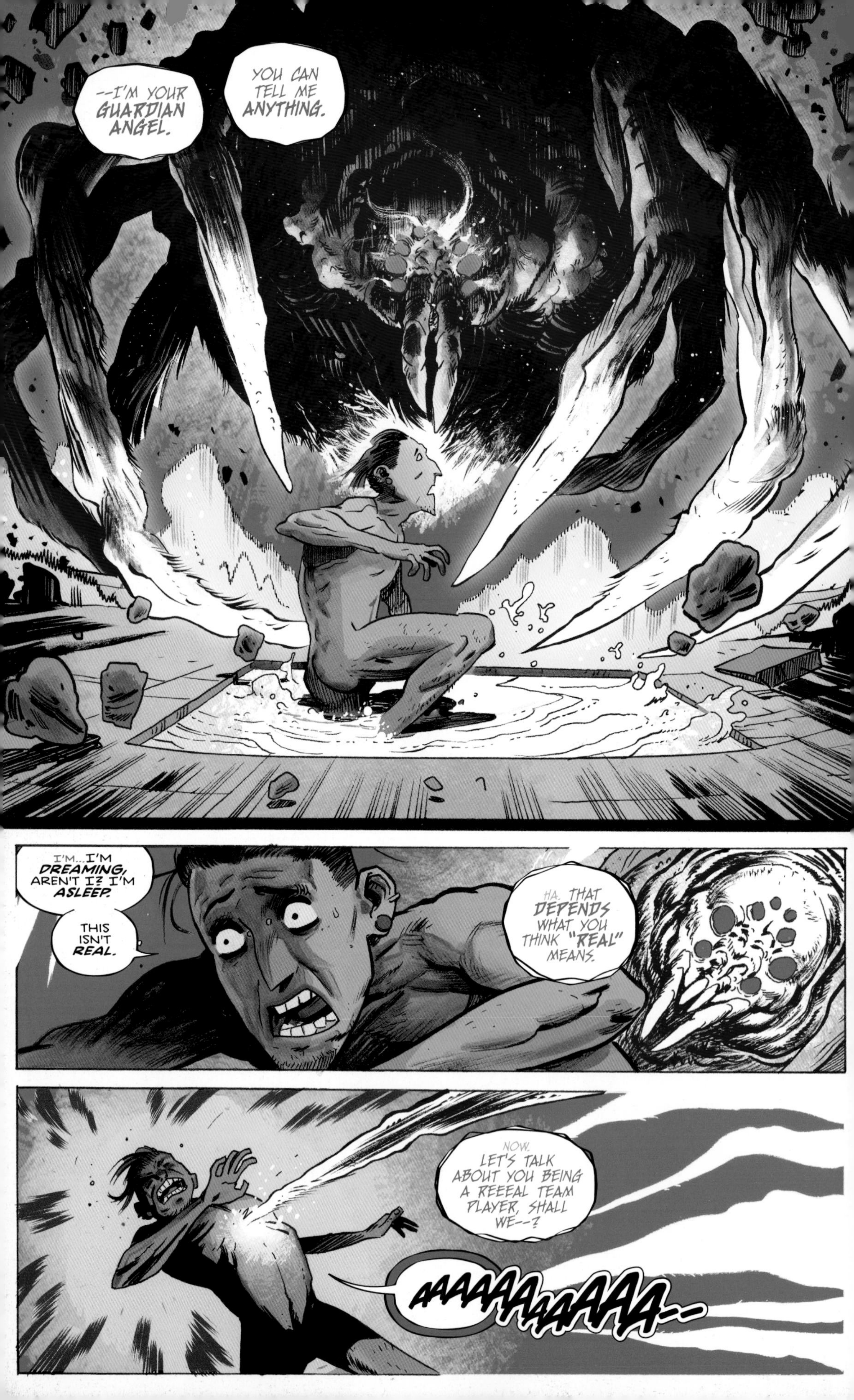
--I'M YOUR GUARDIAN ANGEL.
YOU CAN TELL ME ANYTHING.
I'M... I'M DREAMING, AREN'T I? I'M ASLEEP.
THIS ISN'T REAL.
HA. THAT DEPENDS WHAT YOU THINK "REAL" MEANS.
NOW. LET'S TALK ABOUT YOU BEING A REEEAL TEAM PLAYER, SHALL WE--?
AAAAAAAAAAAA--

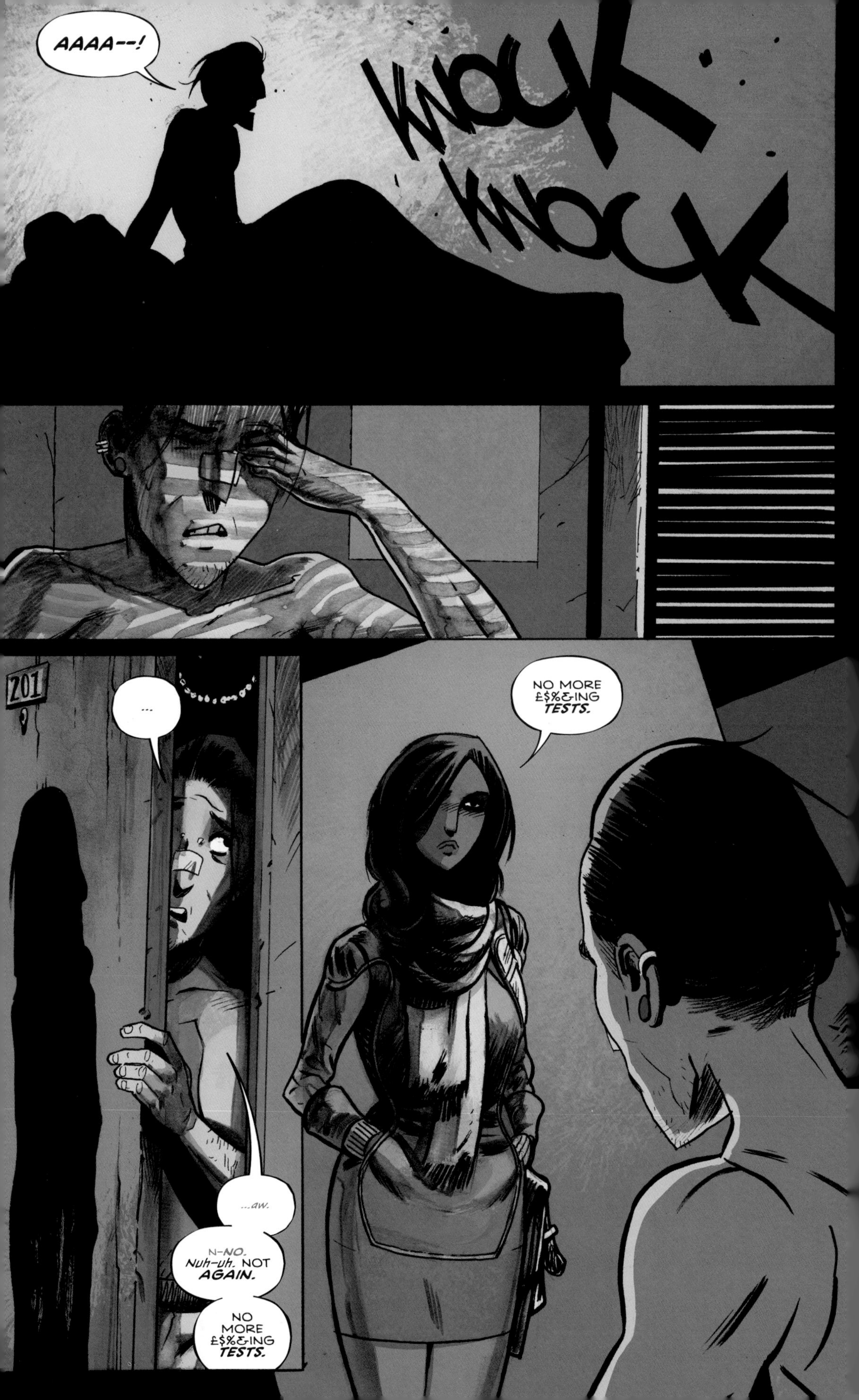
AAAA--!
KNOCK KNOCK
201
...
NO MORE £$%&ING TESTS.
...aw.
N-NO. Nuh-uh. NOT AGAIN.
NO MORE £$%&ING TESTS.

LISTEN, MISS PNEEMA, NO OFFENSE, BUT IF YOU'RE HERE TO GET ALL... Y'KNOW, SEDUCE-Y AGAIN--

--WITH THE SEXY POWERS AND THE £$%&ING FLYING MURDERESS WAITING OUTSIDE--

I'D KINDA PREFER TO SKIP IT.

Ssh.

AND LOOK, C'MON, YOU DID THE MAKEUP-BRUISE SYMPATHY GAG ALREADY. YOU GOTTA TRY HARDER T--

Ow.

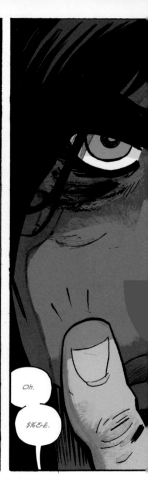

Oh.

$%&£.

HE DOESN'T KNOW I'M HERE.

uh

NOR DOES KETTER.

I MEAN... NO OFFENSE... I FIND THAT KINDA HARD TO BELI--

PLEASE, JUST. BE QUIET.

I HAVE TO KNOW.

KNOW WH--

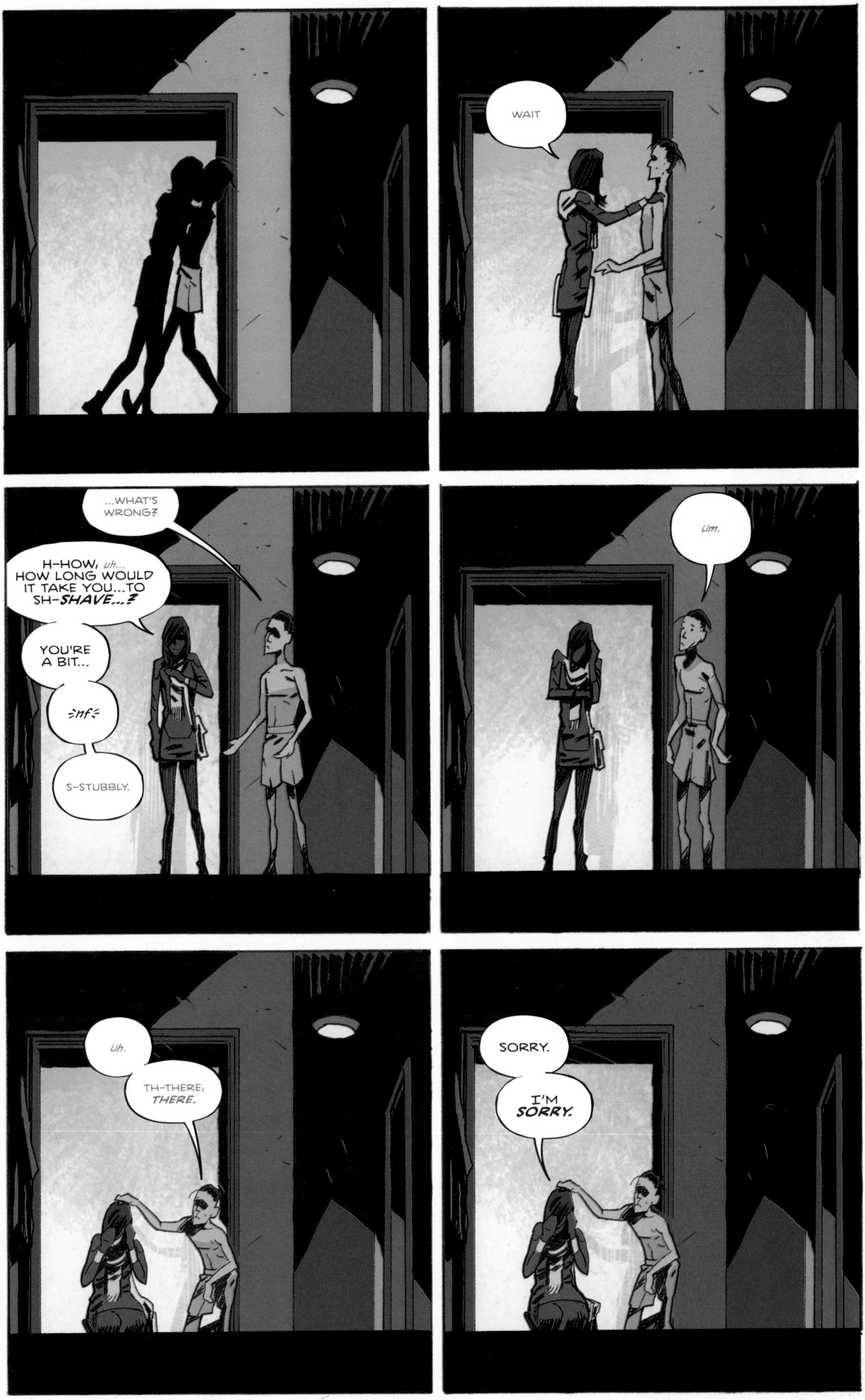
WAIT
...WHAT'S WRONG?
H-HOW, uh... HOW LONG WOULD IT TAKE YOU...TO SH-SHAVE...?
YOU'RE A BIT...
nf
S-STUBBLY.
Um.
Uh.
TH-THERE, THERE.
SORRY.
I'M SORRY.

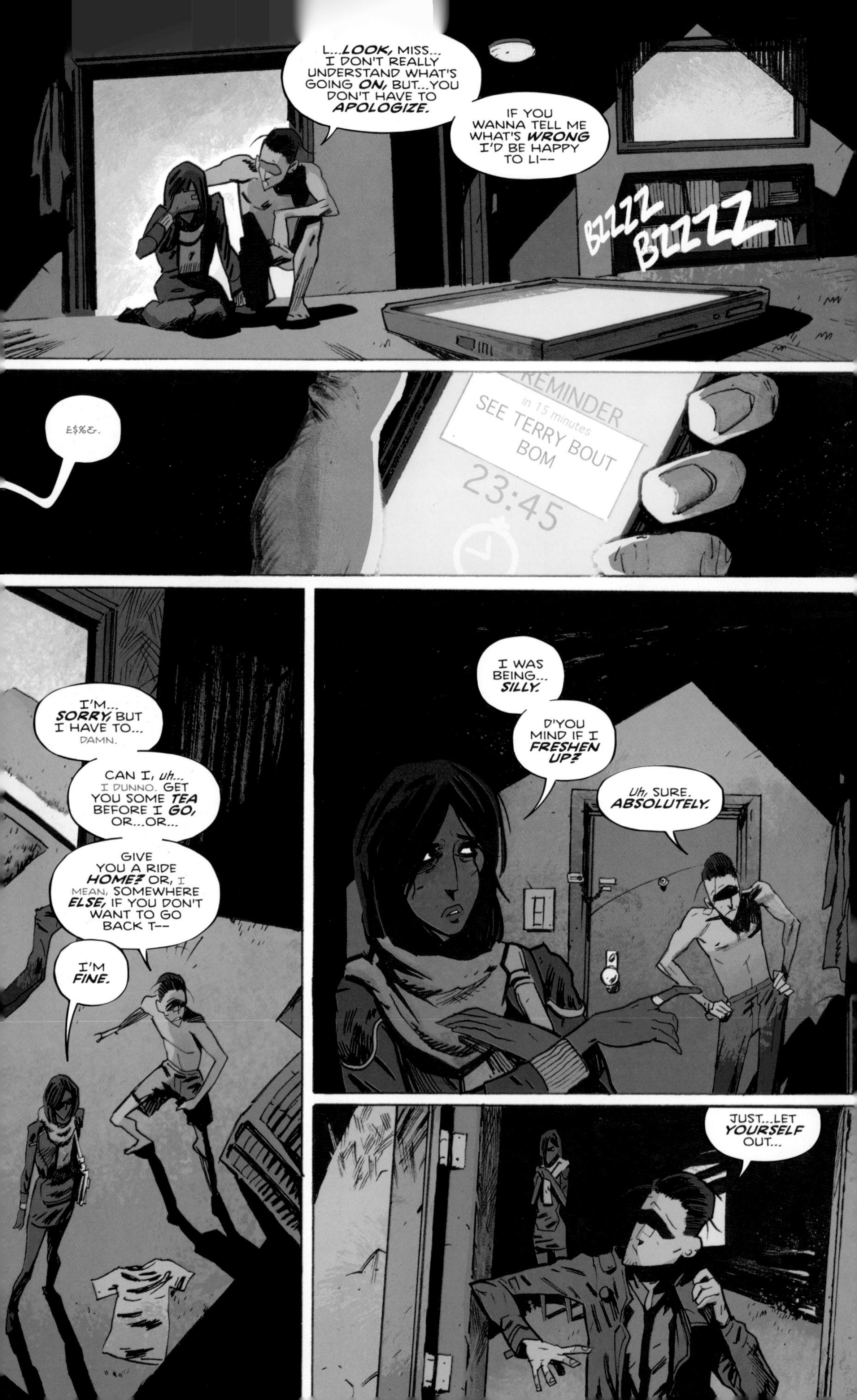

L...LOOK, MISS... I DON'T REALLY UNDERSTAND WHAT'S GOING ON, BUT...YOU DON'T HAVE TO APOLOGIZE.
IF YOU WANNA TELL ME WHAT'S WRONG I'D BE HAPPY TO LI--
BZZZZ BZZZZ
£$%&.
REMINDER
in 15 minutes
SEE TERRY BOUT BOM
23:45
I'M... SORRY, BUT I HAVE TO... DAMN.
CAN I, uh... I DUNNO. GET YOU SOME TEA BEFORE I GO, OR...OR...
GIVE YOU A RIDE HOME? OR, I MEAN, SOMEWHERE ELSE, IF YOU DON'T WANT TO GO BACK T--
I'M FINE.
I WAS BEING... SILLY.
D'YOU MIND IF I FRESHEN UP?
Uh, SURE. ABSOLUTELY.
JUST...LET YOURSELF OUT...

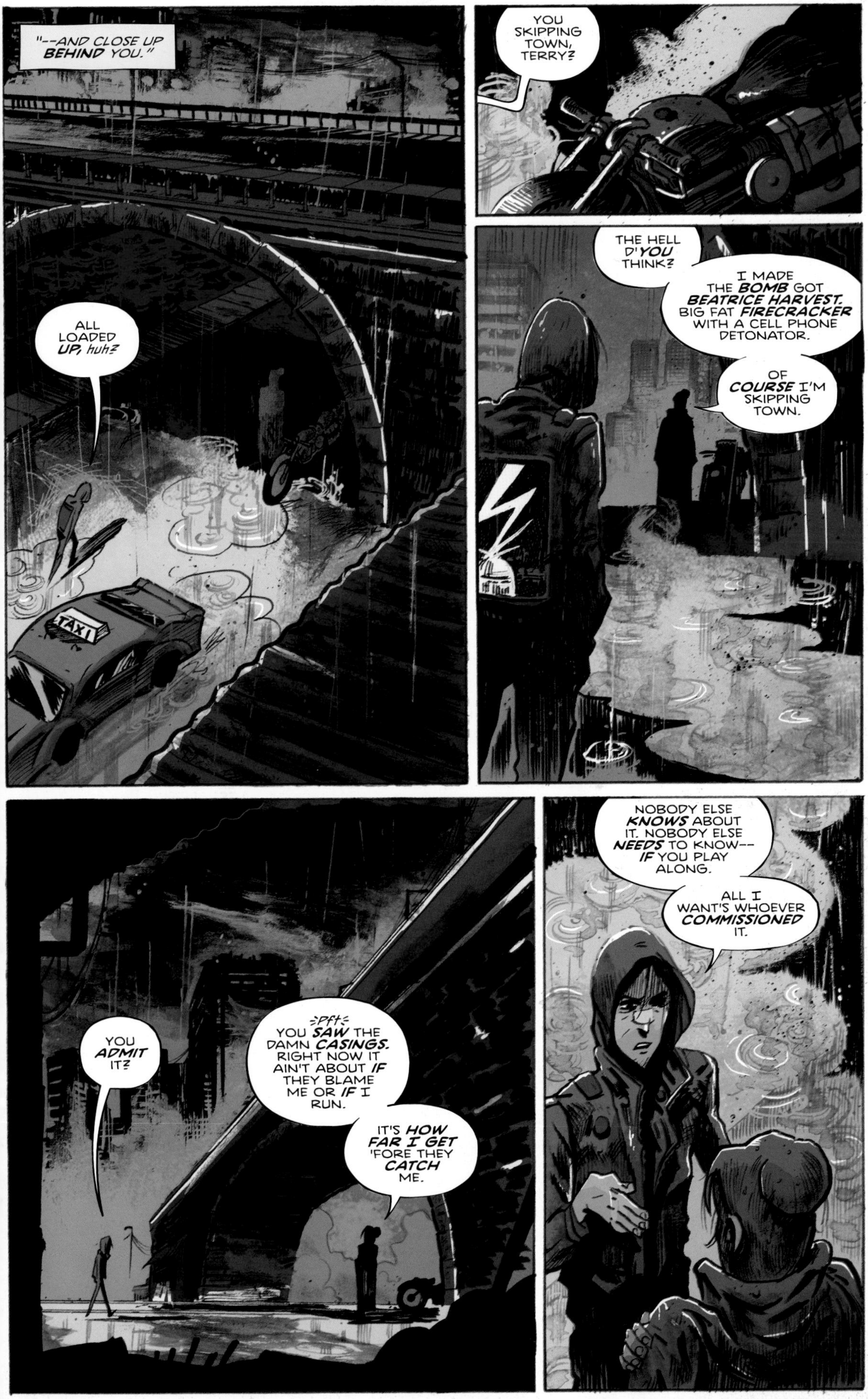
"--AND CLOSE UP BEHIND YOU."
ALL LOADED UP, huh?
YOU SKIPPING TOWN, TERRY?
THE HELL D'YOU THINK?
I MADE THE BOMB GOT BEATRICE HARVEST. BIG FAT FIRECRACKER WITH A CELL PHONE DETONATOR.
OF COURSE I'M SKIPPING TOWN.
YOU ADMIT IT?
pft
YOU SAW THE DAMN CASINGS. RIGHT NOW IT AIN'T ABOUT IF THEY BLAME ME OR IF I RUN.
IT'S HOW FAR I GET 'FORE THEY CATCH ME.
NOBODY ELSE KNOWS ABOUT IT. NOBODY ELSE NEEDS TO KNOW-- IF YOU PLAY ALONG.
ALL I WANT'S WHOEVER COMMISSIONED IT.

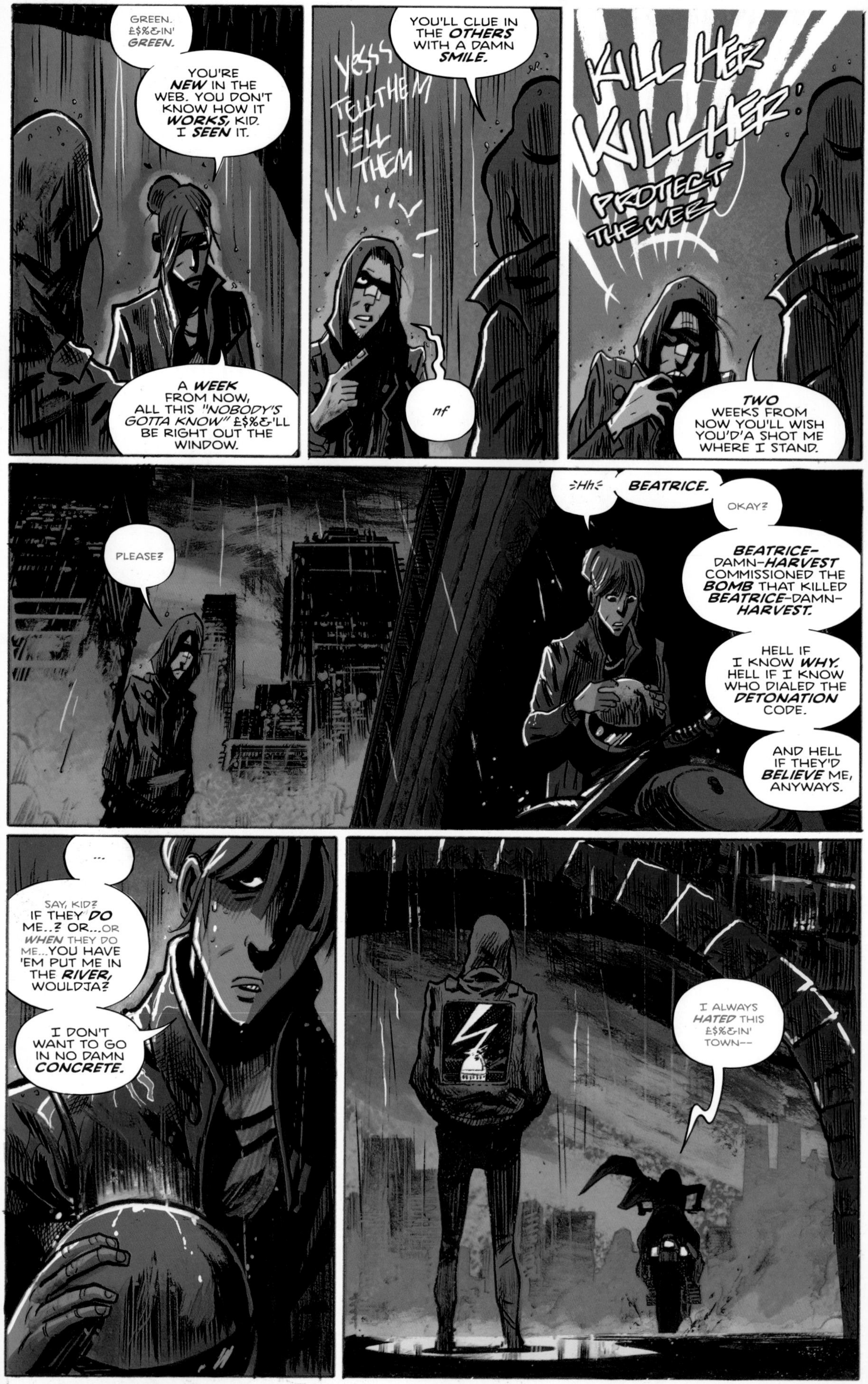
GREEN. £$%&IN' GREEN.
YOU'RE NEW IN THE WEB. YOU DON'T KNOW HOW IT WORKS, KID. I SEEN IT.
A WEEK FROM NOW, ALL THIS "NOBODY'S GOTTA KNOW" £$%&'LL BE RIGHT OUT THE WINDOW.
YOU'LL CLUE IN THE OTHERS WITH A DAMN SMILE.
YESSS TELL THEM TELL THEM
nf
KILL HER KILL HER!
PROTECT THE WEB
TWO WEEKS FROM NOW YOU'LL WISH YOU'D'A SHOT ME WHERE I STAND.
PLEASE?
HH
BEATRICE.
OKAY?
BEATRICE-DAMN-HARVEST COMMISSIONED THE BOMB THAT KILLED BEATRICE-DAMN-HARVEST.
HELL IF I KNOW WHY. HELL IF I KNOW WHO DIALED THE DETONATION CODE.
AND HELL IF THEY'D BELIEVE ME, ANYWAYS.
...
SAY, KID? IF THEY DO ME..? OR...OR WHEN THEY DO ME...YOU HAVE 'EM PUT ME IN THE RIVER, WOULDJA?
I DON'T WANT TO GO IN NO DAMN CONCRETE.
I ALWAYS HATED THIS £$%&IN' TOWN--

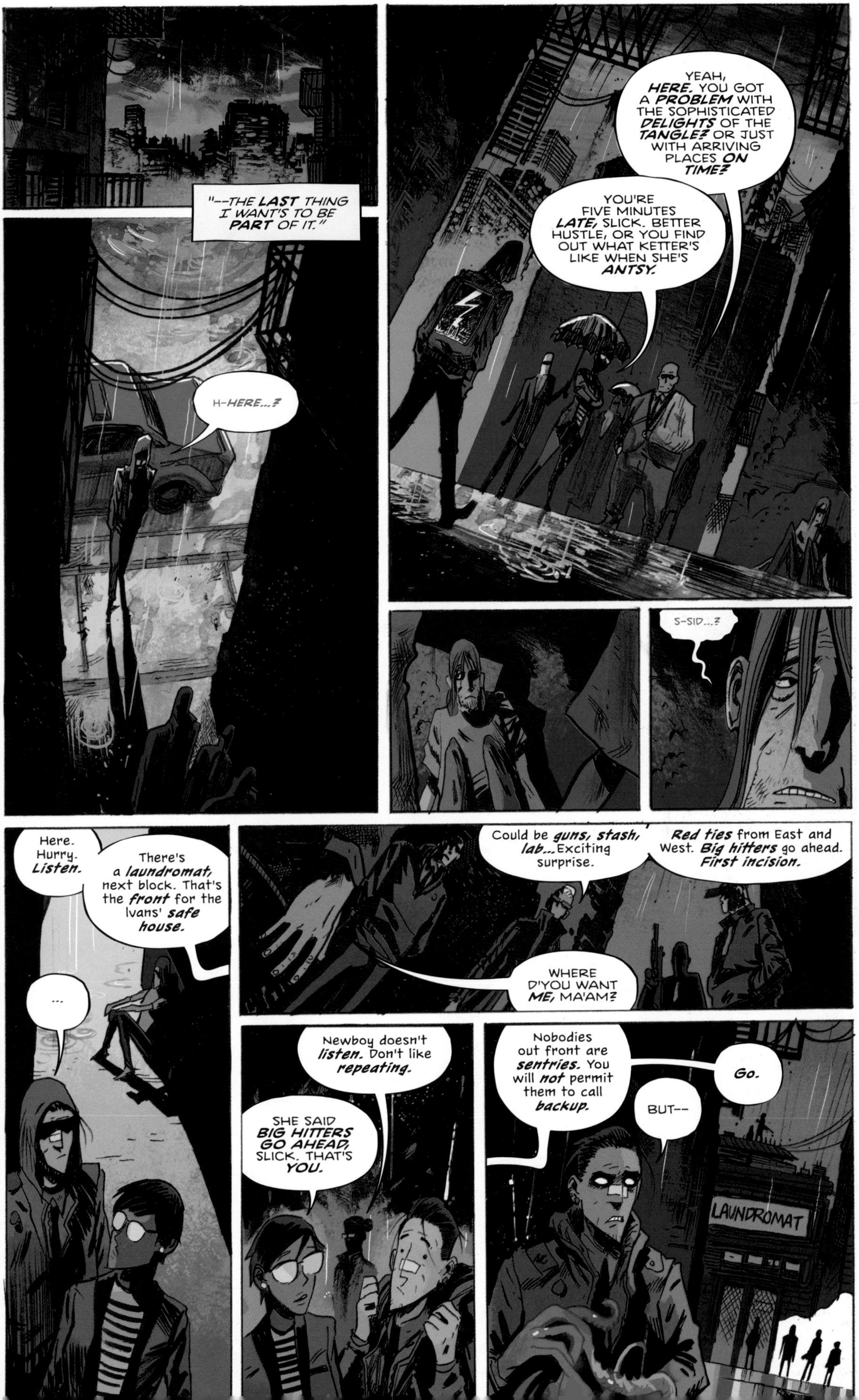

"--THE LAST THING I WANT'S TO BE PART OF IT."
H-HERE...?
YEAH, HERE. YOU GOT A PROBLEM WITH THE SOPHISTICATED DELIGHTS OF THE TANGLE? OR JUST WITH ARRIVING PLACES ON TIME?
YOU'RE FIVE MINUTES LATE, SLICK. BETTER HUSTLE, OR YOU FIND OUT WHAT KETTER'S LIKE WHEN SHE'S ANTSY.
S-SID...?
Here. Hurry. Listen.
There's a laundromat, next block. That's the front for the Ivans' safe house.
...
Could be guns, stash, lab... Exciting surprise.
Red ties from East and West. Big hitters go ahead. First incision.
WHERE D'YOU WANT ME, MA'AM?
Newboy doesn't listen. Don't like repeating.
SHE SAID BIG HITTERS GO AHEAD, SLICK. THAT'S YOU.
Nobodies out front are sentries. You will not permit them to call backup.
Go.
BUT--
LAUNDROMAT

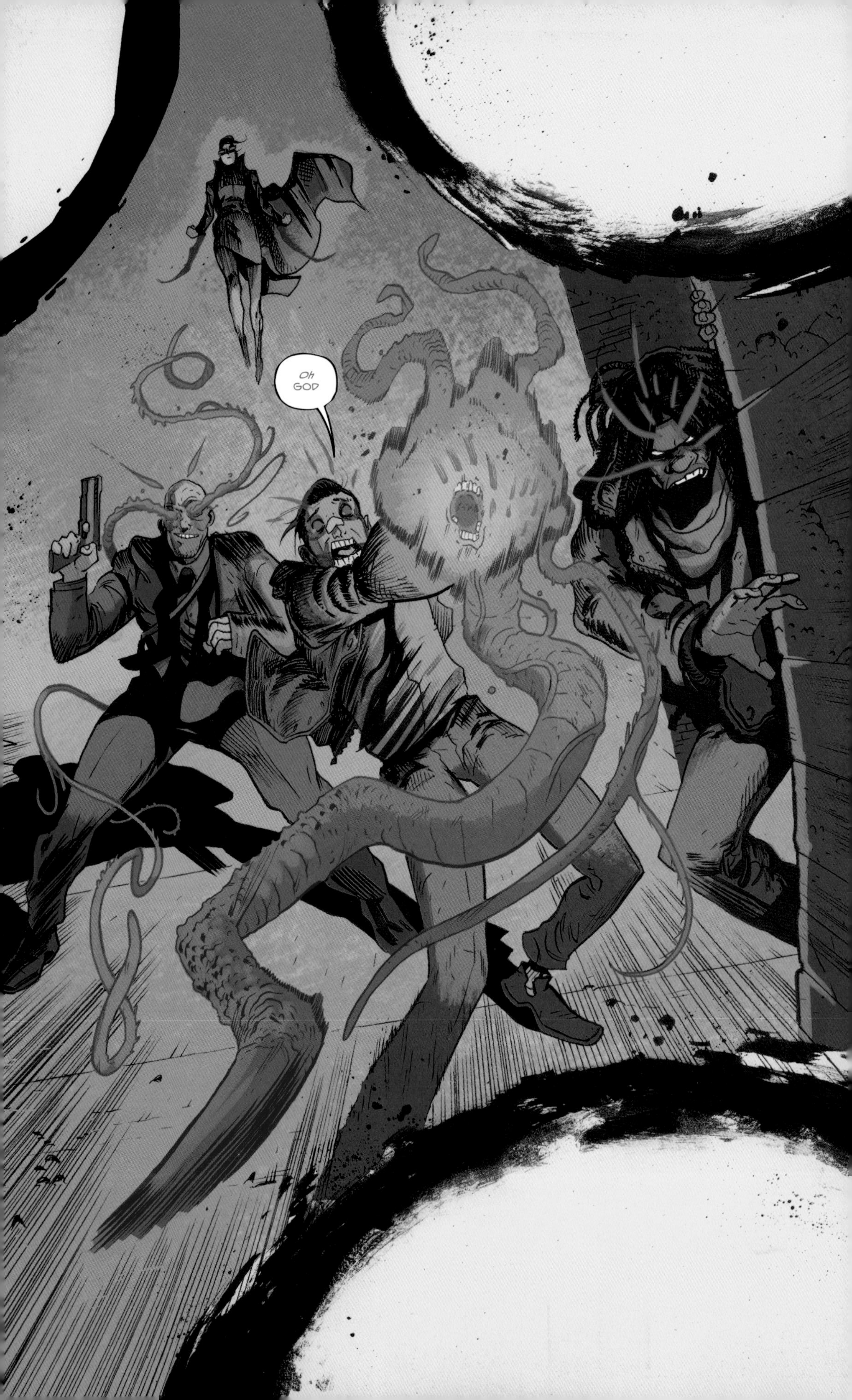
Oh GOD

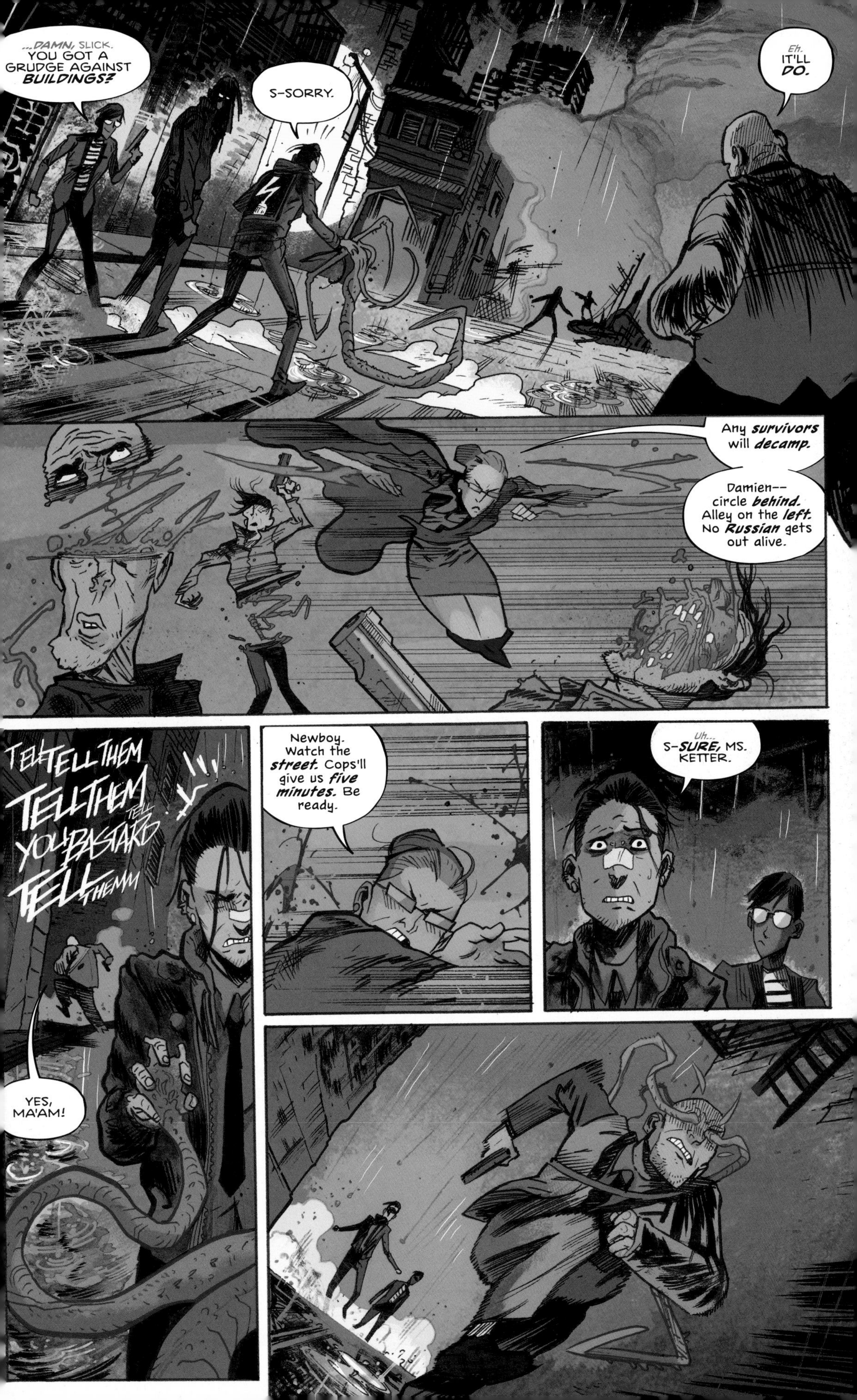
...DAMN, SLICK. YOU GOT A GRUDGE AGAINST BUILDINGS?
S-SORRY.
Eh. IT'LL DO.
Any survivors will decamp.
Damien-- circle behind. Alley on the left. No Russian gets out alive.
TELL TELL THEM TELL THEM TELL YOU BASTARD TELL THEM
YES, MA'AM!
Newboy. Watch the street. Cops'll give us five minutes. Be ready.
Uh... S-SURE, MS. KETTER.

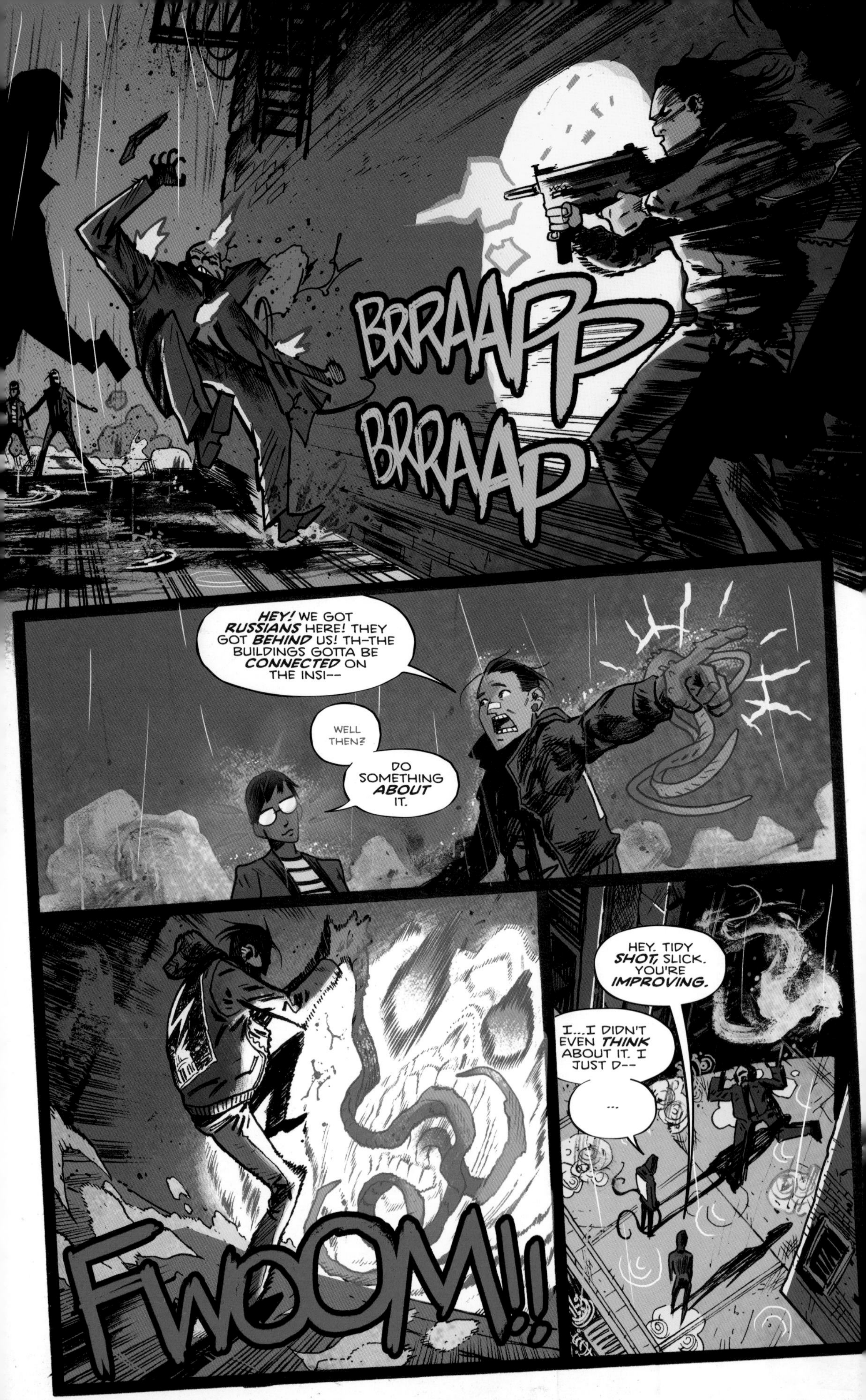
BRRAAPP
BRRAAP
HEY! WE GOT RUSSIANS HERE! THEY GOT BEHIND US! TH-THE BUILDINGS GOTTA BE CONNECTED ON THE INSI--
WELL THEN?
DO SOMETHING ABOUT IT.
FWOOM!!
HEY. TIDY SHOT, SLICK. YOU'RE IMPROVING.
I...I DIDN'T EVEN THINK ABOUT IT. I JUST D--
...

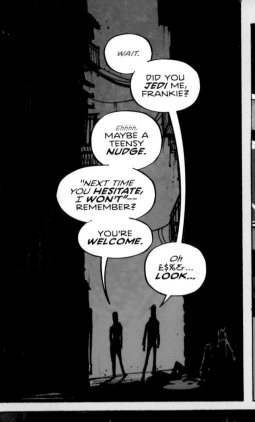

WAIT.

DID YOU *JEDI* ME, FRANKIE?

Ehhhh, MAYBE A TEENSY *NUDGE.*

"*NEXT TIME YOU HESITATE, I WON'T*"-- REMEMBER?

YOU'RE *WELCOME.*

Oh £$%&... *LOOK...*

DAMIEN'S *SPIDER.*

LISTEN, SID: THIS WAS YOUR *NEIGHBORHOOD,* RIGHT? BEFORE YOU GOT THE *BUG?*

THAT JUNKIE BACK THERE *KNEW* YOU.

Uhm

BUT YOU LET *DAMIEN* COME DOWN HERE *ALONE* ANYWAY.

I...

I...

Y...YEAH...? SORTA...?

SO YOU *KNEW* THIS *ALLEY* WAS WHERE THE IVANS WOULD PUNCH *OUT.*

You two. What are you *doing* over h--

Oh for heaven's sake. Not *another* dead host?

'FRAID SO, MA'AM. DAMIEN *SCREWED UP.*

NOBODY LEFT TO SWALLOW THE *BUG.*

Boss's *choice,* then.

DID... DID WE *WIN?*

Ha. Take a *look.*

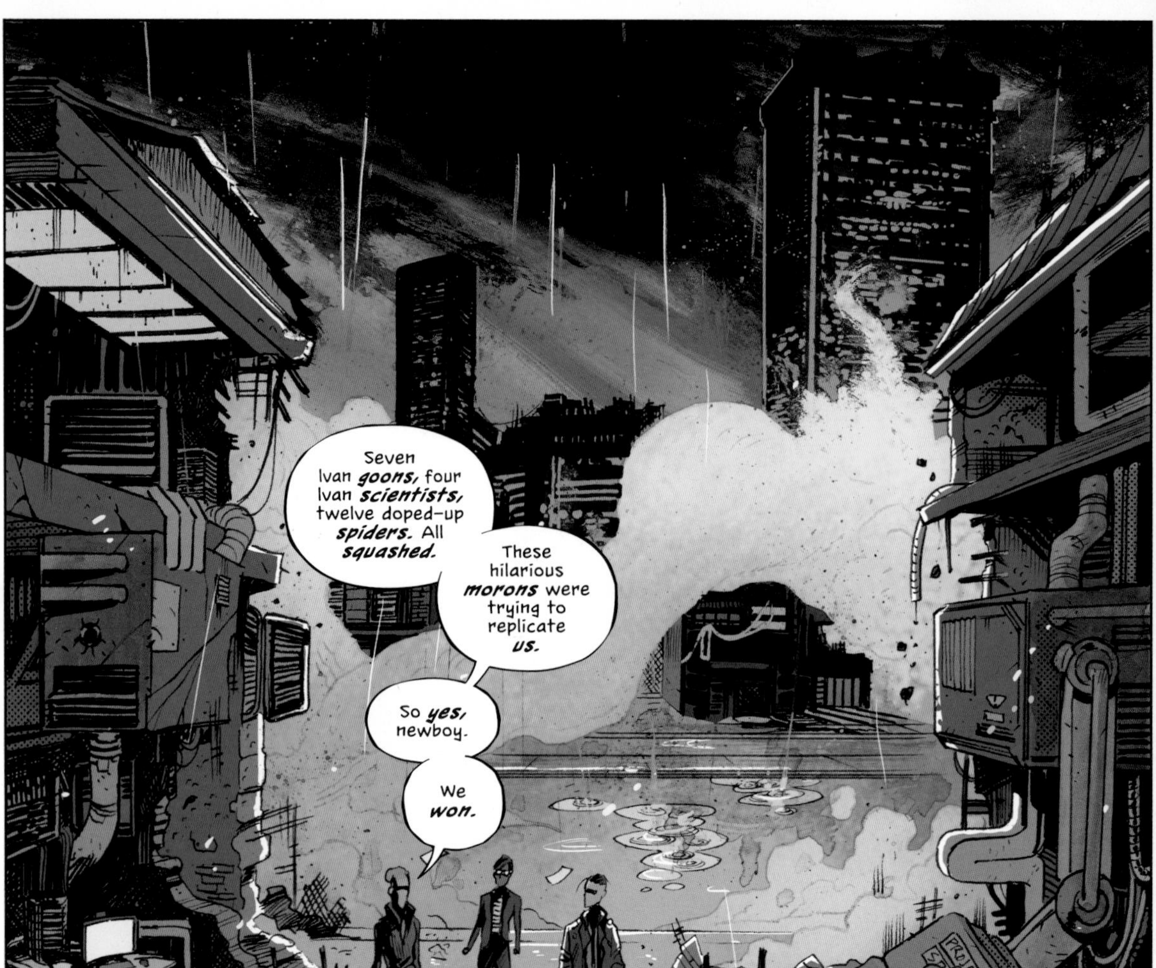
Seven Ivan *goons,* four Ivan *scientists,* twelve doped-up *spiders.* All *squashed.*
These hilarious *morons* were trying to replicate *us.*
So *yes,* newboy.
We *won.*

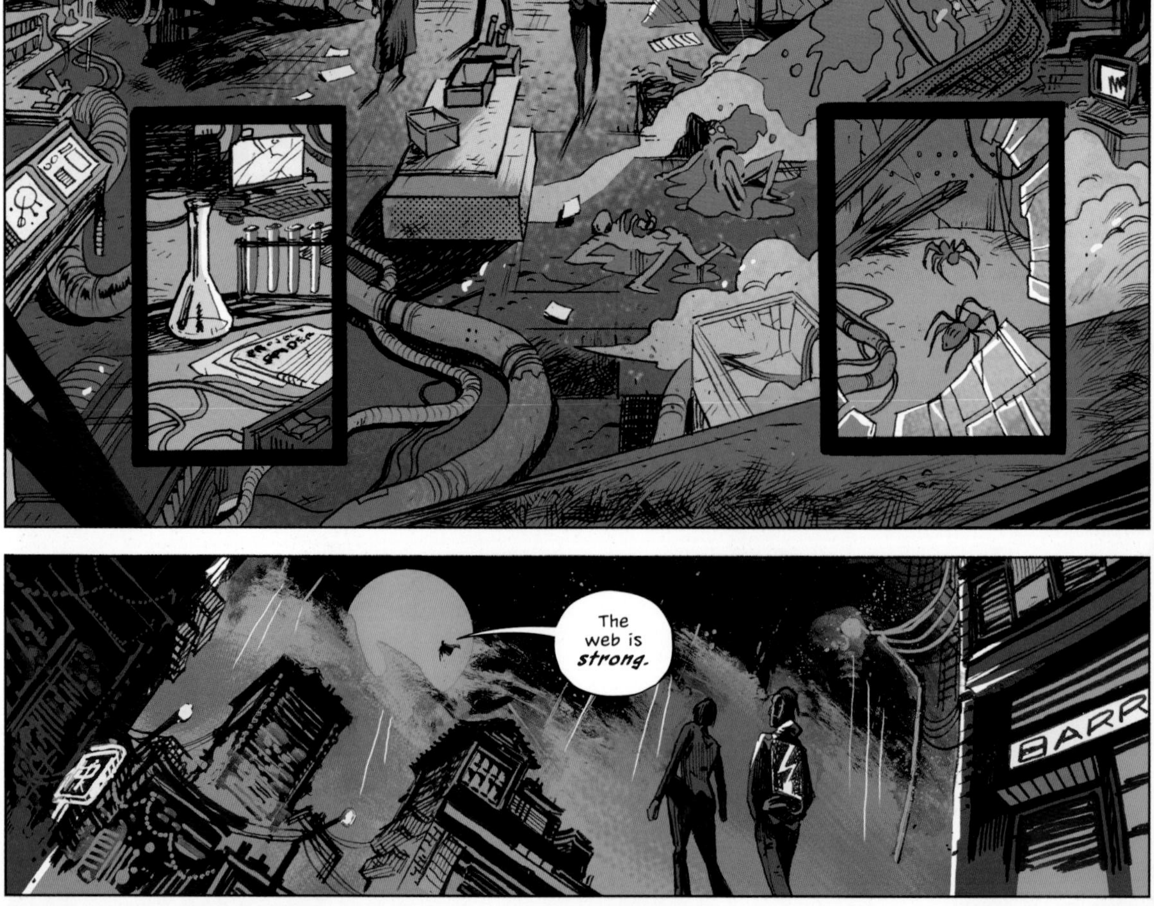
The web is *strong.*
BARR

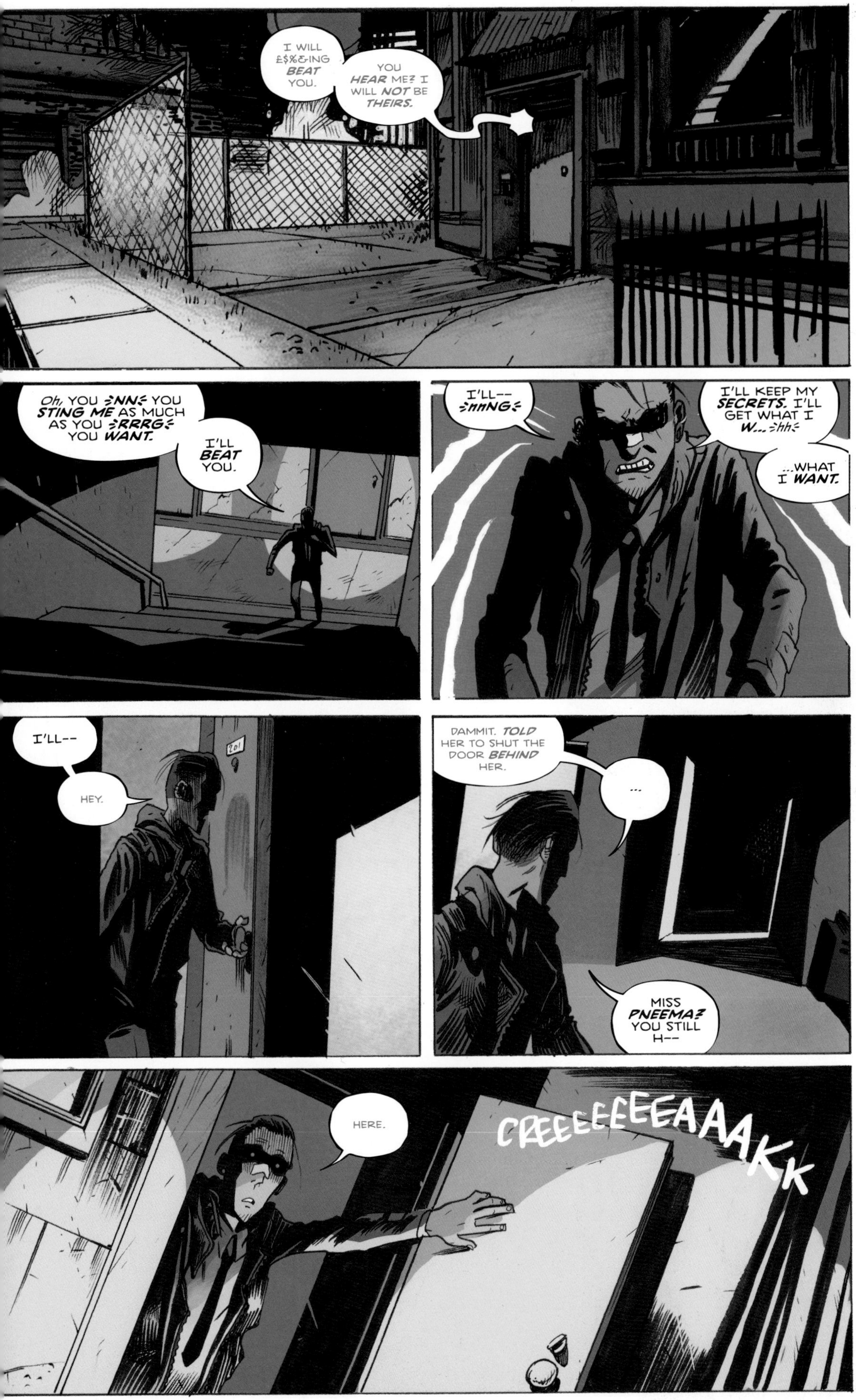
I WILL £$%&-ING BEAT YOU.
YOU HEAR ME? I WILL NOT BE THEIRS.
Oh, YOU NN YOU STING ME AS MUCH AS YOU RRRG YOU WANT.
I'LL BEAT YOU.
I'LL-- nnNG
I'LL KEEP MY SECRETS. I'LL GET WHAT I W... hh
...WHAT I WANT.
I'LL--
HEY.
DAMMIT. TOLD HER TO SHUT THE DOOR BEHIND HER.
...
MISS PNEEMA? YOU STILL H--
HERE.
CREEEEEEEAAAKK

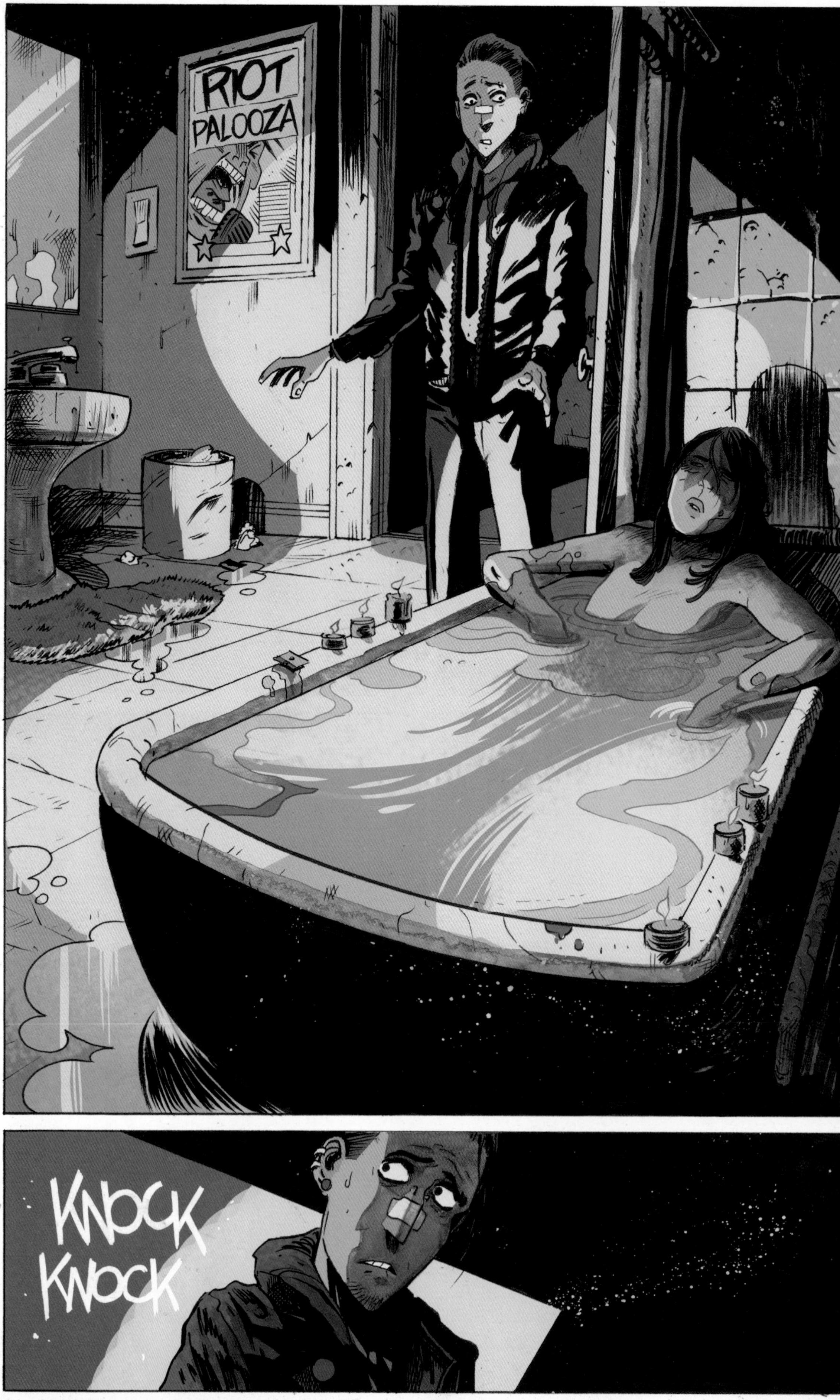
RIOT
PALOOZA
KNOCK
KNOCK

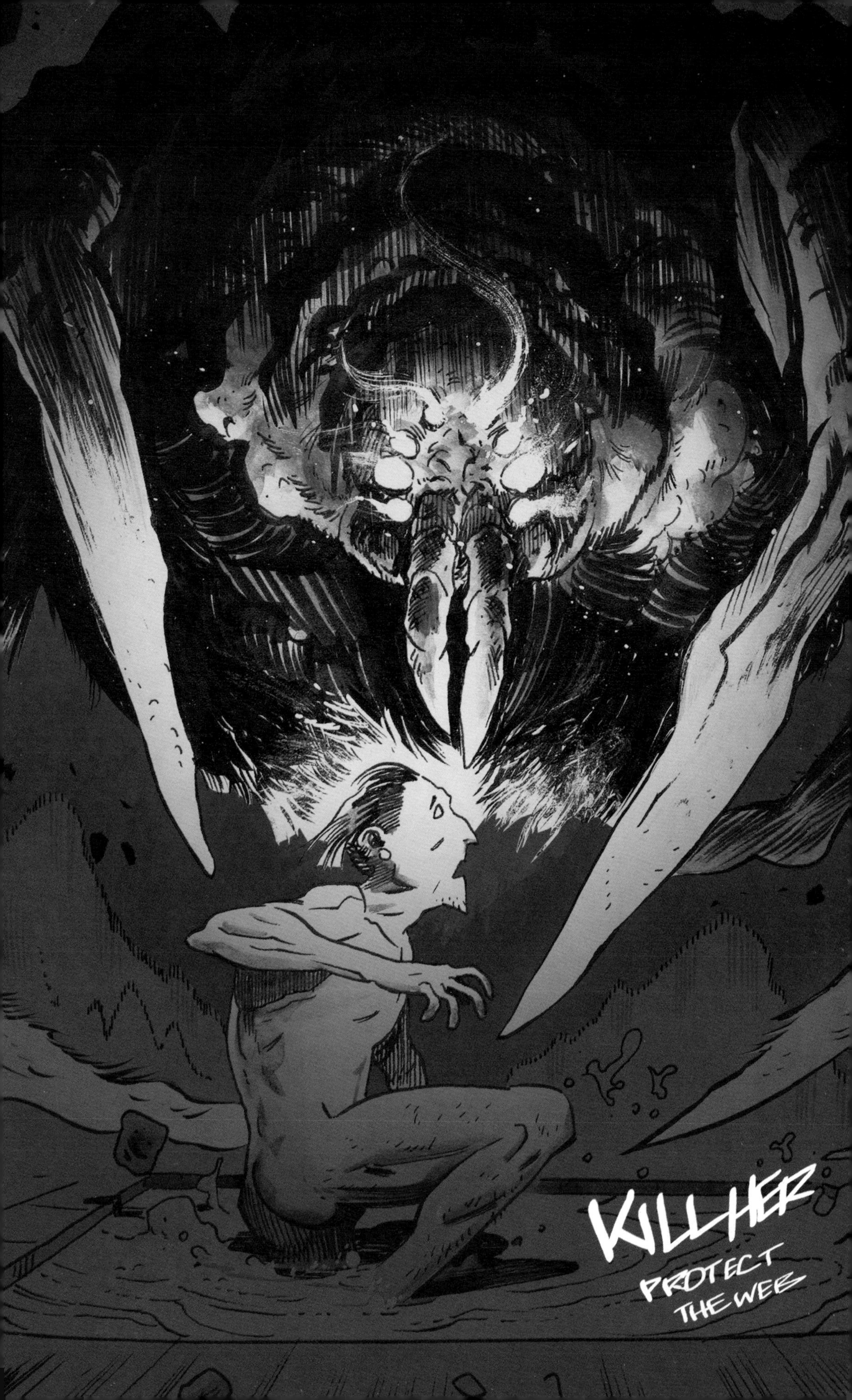
KILL HER
PROTECT THE WEB

CHAPTER
FOUR

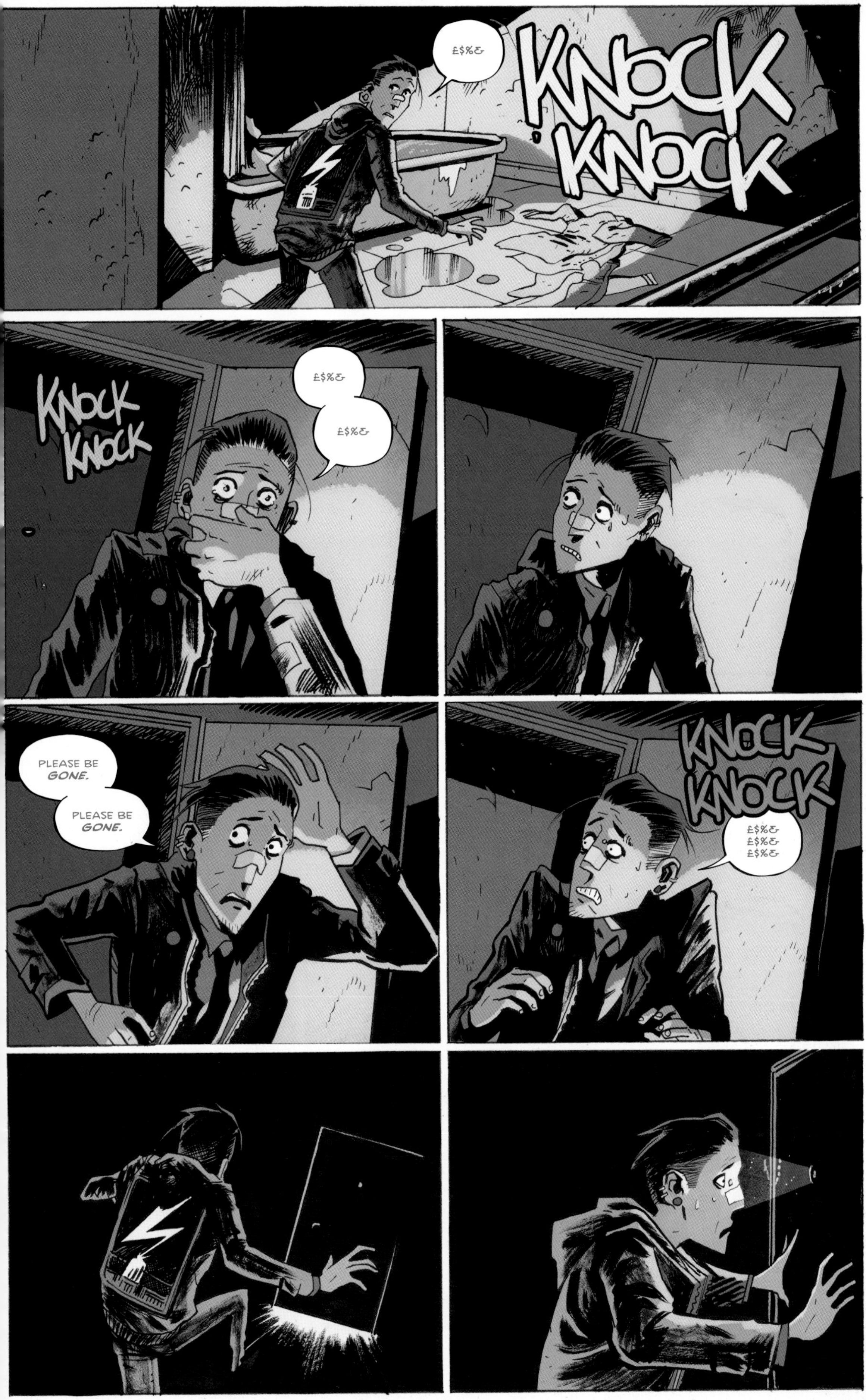
£$%&
KNOCK KNOCK
KNOCK KNOCK
£$%&
£$%&
PLEASE BE GONE.
PLEASE BE GONE.
KNOCK KNOCK
£$%& £$%& £$%&

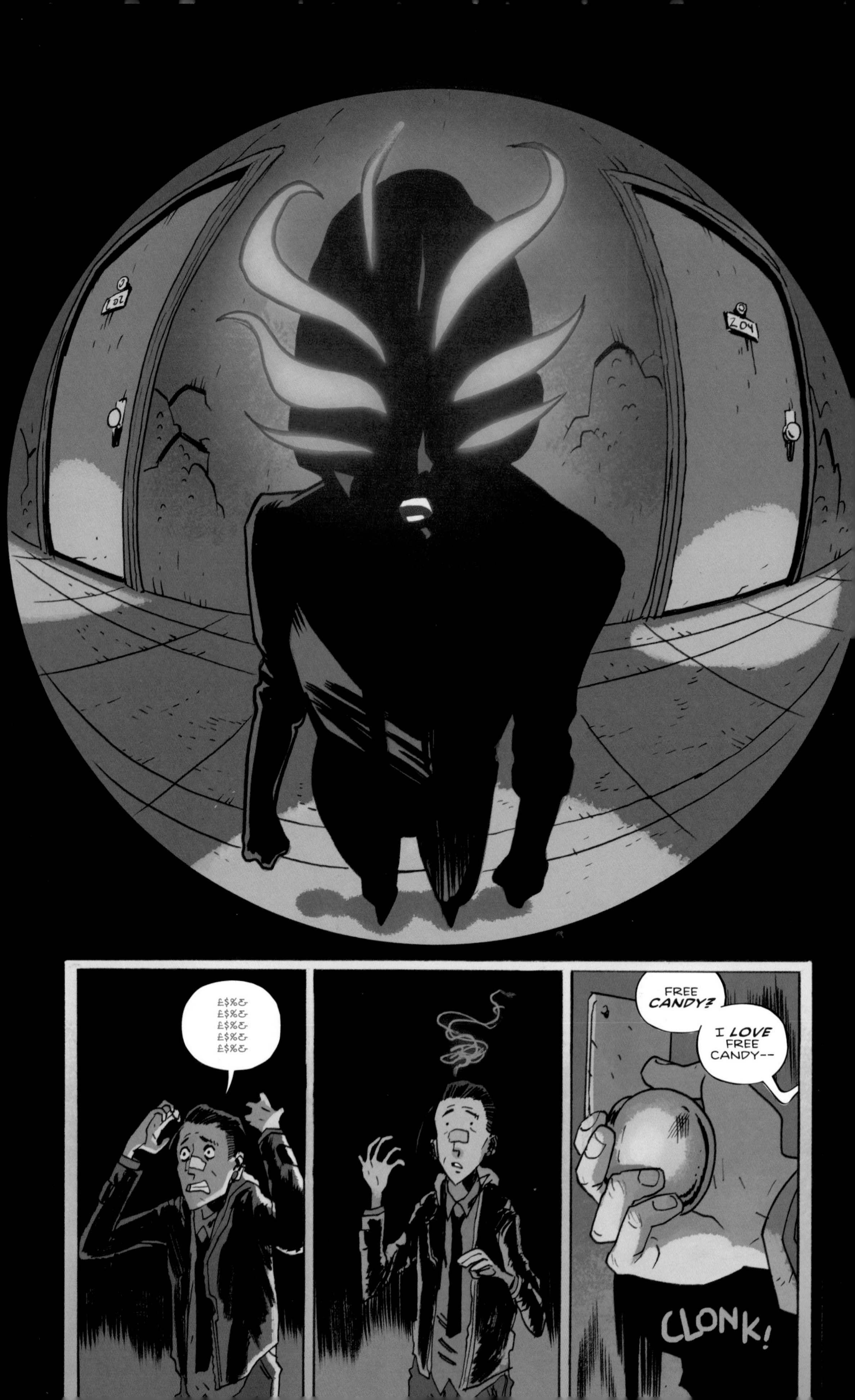
204
£$%&
£$%&
£$%&
£$%&
£$%&
FREE CANDY?
I LOVE FREE CANDY--
CLONK!

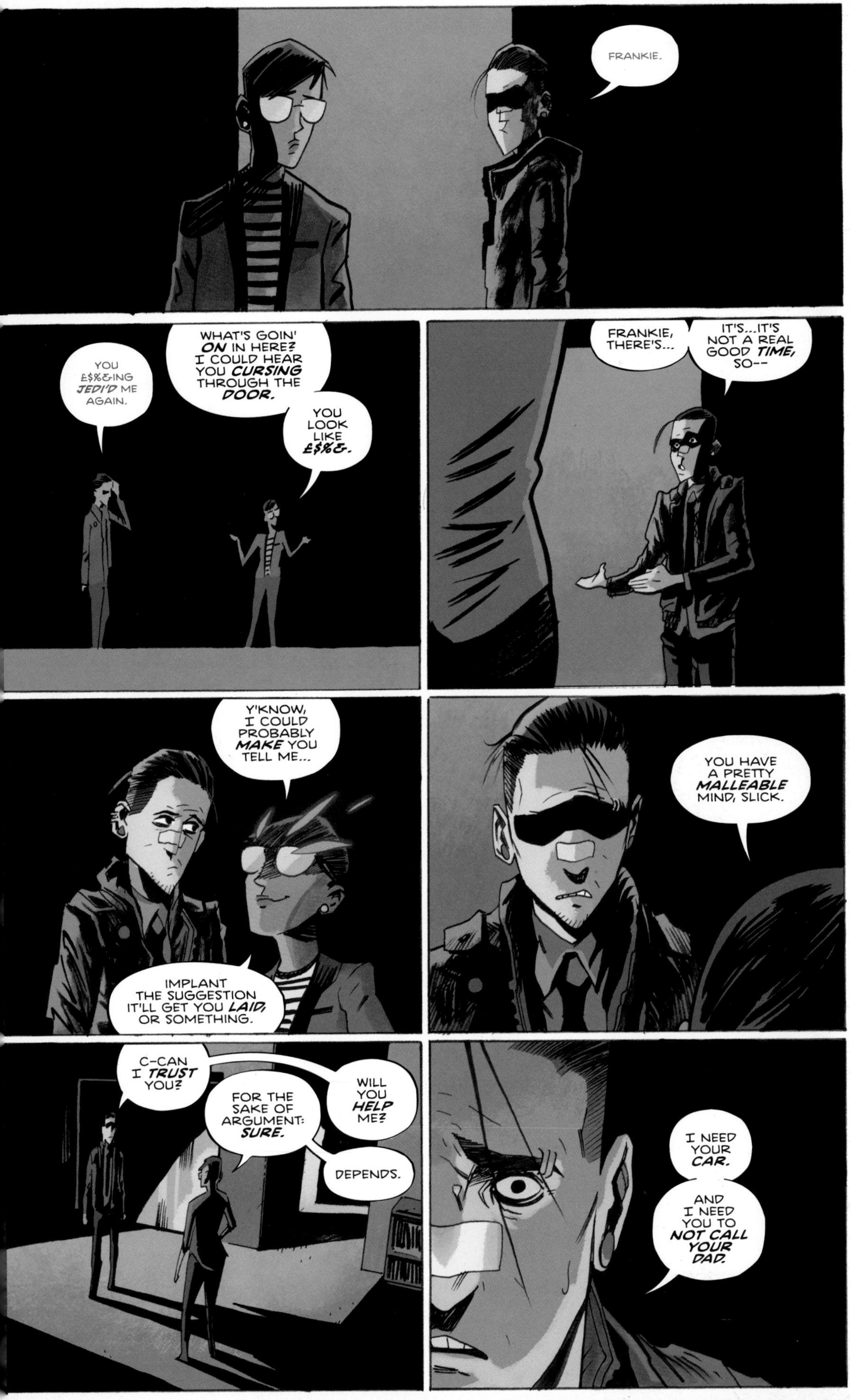
FRANKIE.
YOU £$%&-ING JEDI'D ME AGAIN.
WHAT'S GOIN' ON IN HERE? I COULD HEAR YOU CURSING THROUGH THE DOOR.
YOU LOOK LIKE £$%&.
FRANKIE, THERE'S...
IT'S...IT'S NOT A REAL GOOD TIME, SO--
Y'KNOW, I COULD PROBABLY MAKE YOU TELL ME...
IMPLANT THE SUGGESTION IT'LL GET YOU LAID, OR SOMETHING.
YOU HAVE A PRETTY MALLEABLE MIND, SLICK.
C-CAN I TRUST YOU?
FOR THE SAKE OF ARGUMENT: SURE.
WILL YOU HELP ME?
DEPENDS.
I NEED YOUR CAR.
AND I NEED YOU TO NOT CALL YOUR DAD.

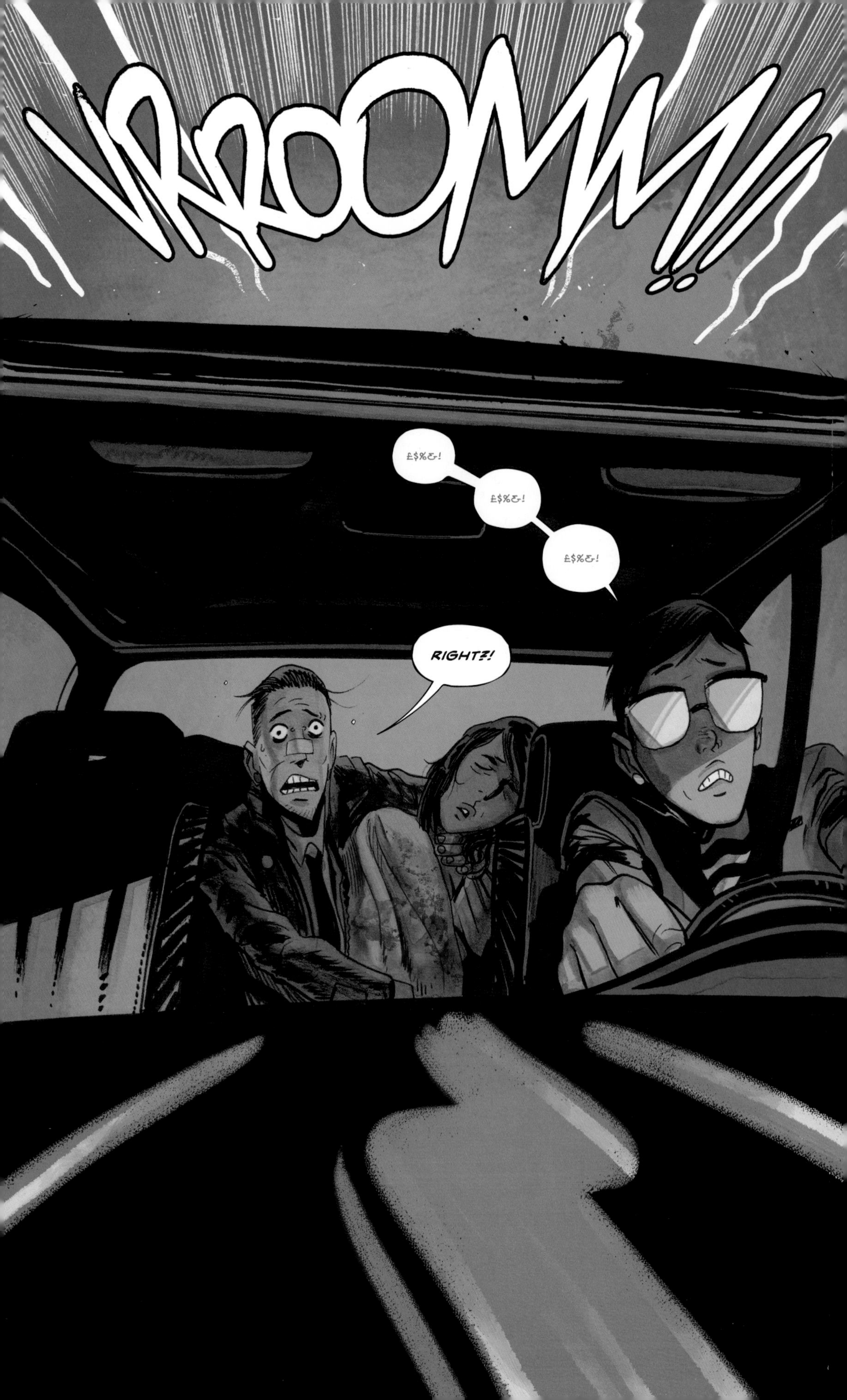
VRROOMM!!
£$%&!
£$%&!
£$%&!
RIGHT?!

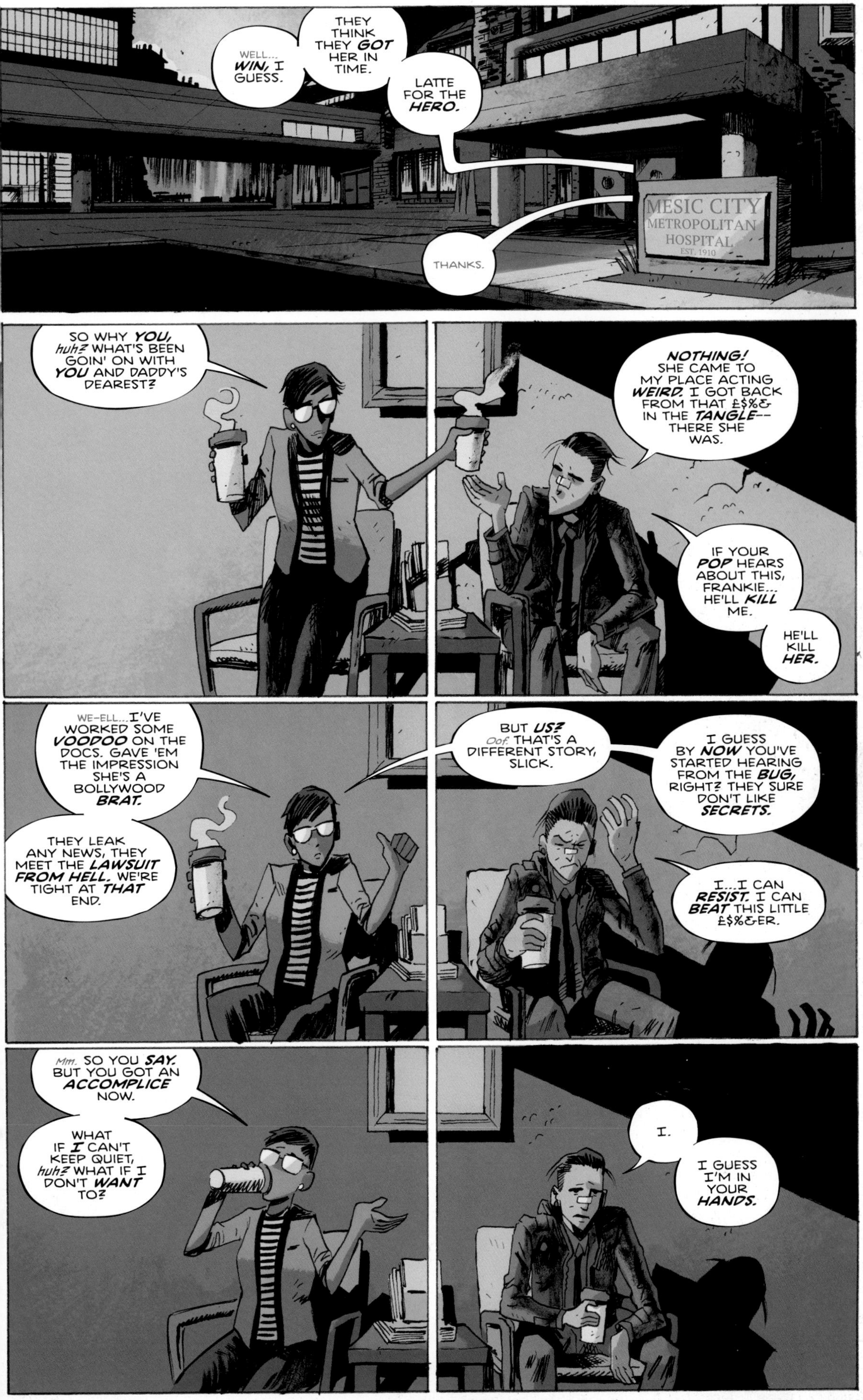
WELL... WIN, I GUESS.
THEY THINK THEY GOT HER IN TIME.
LATTE FOR THE HERO.
MESIC CITY METROPOLITAN HOSPITAL EST. 1910
THANKS.
SO WHY YOU, huh? WHAT'S BEEN GOIN' ON WITH YOU AND DADDY'S DEAREST?
NOTHING! SHE CAME TO MY PLACE ACTING WEIRD. I GOT BACK FROM THAT £$%& IN THE TANGLE-- THERE SHE WAS.
IF YOUR POP HEARS ABOUT THIS, FRANKIE... HE'LL KILL ME.
HE'LL KILL HER.
WE-ELL...I'VE WORKED SOME VOODOO ON THE DOCS. GAVE 'EM THE IMPRESSION SHE'S A BOLLYWOOD BRAT.
THEY LEAK ANY NEWS, THEY MEET THE LAWSUIT FROM HELL. WE'RE TIGHT AT THAT END.
BUT US? Oof. THAT'S A DIFFERENT STORY, SLICK.
I GUESS BY NOW YOU'VE STARTED HEARING FROM THE BUG, RIGHT? THEY SURE DON'T LIKE SECRETS.
I...I CAN RESIST. I CAN BEAT THIS LITTLE £$%&ER.
Mm. SO YOU SAY. BUT YOU GOT AN ACCOMPLICE NOW.
WHAT IF I CAN'T KEEP QUIET, huh? WHAT IF I DON'T WANT TO?
I.
I GUESS I'M IN YOUR HANDS.

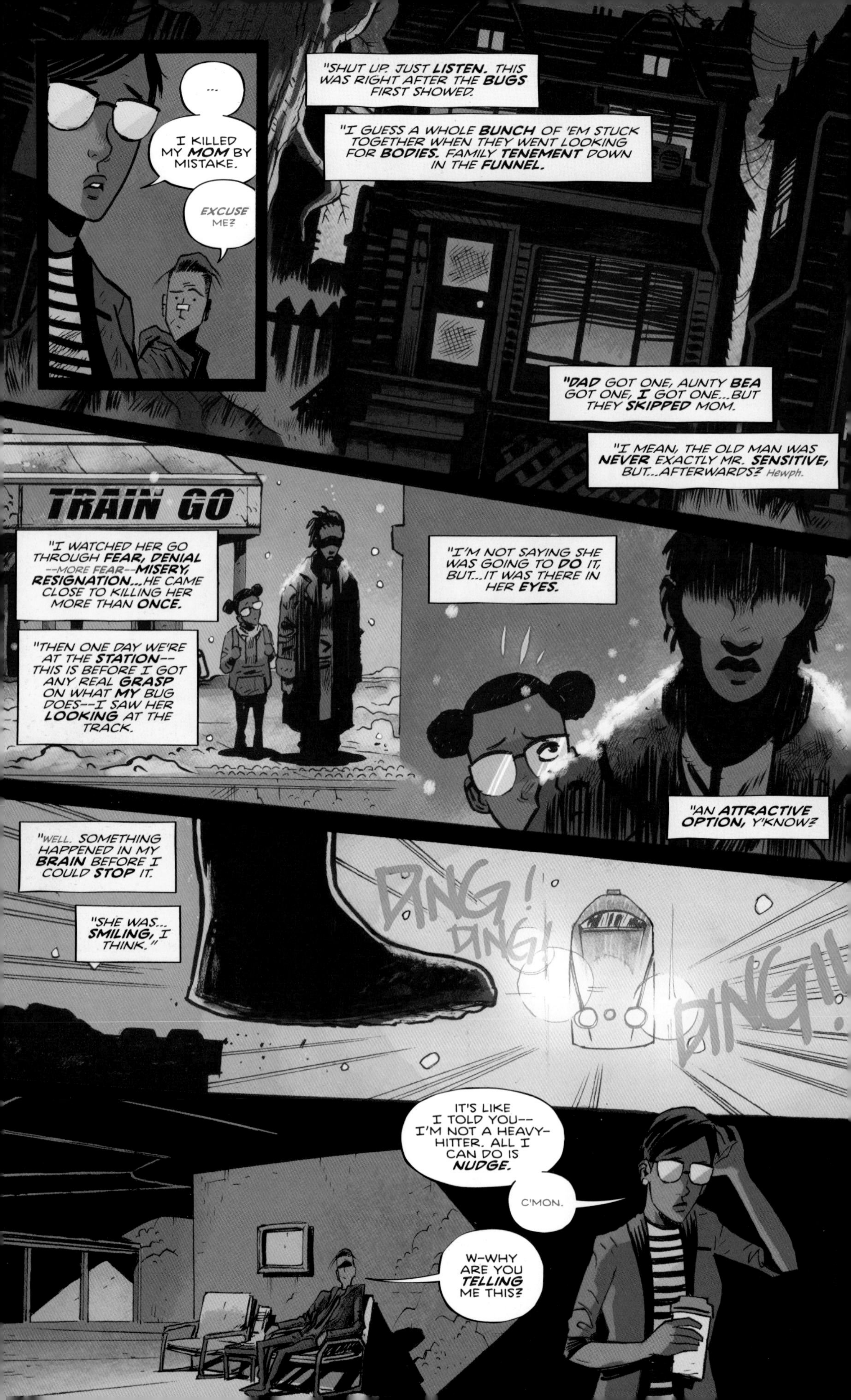
...
I KILLED MY MOM BY MISTAKE.
EXCUSE ME?
"SHUT UP, JUST LISTEN. THIS WAS RIGHT AFTER THE BUGS FIRST SHOWED.
"I GUESS A WHOLE BUNCH OF 'EM STUCK TOGETHER WHEN THEY WENT LOOKING FOR BODIES. FAMILY TENEMENT DOWN IN THE FUNNEL.
"DAD GOT ONE, AUNTY BEA GOT ONE, I GOT ONE...BUT THEY SKIPPED MOM.
"I MEAN, THE OLD MAN WAS NEVER EXACTLY MR. SENSITIVE, BUT...AFTERWARDS? Hewph.
TRAIN GO
"I WATCHED HER GO THROUGH FEAR, DENIAL --MORE FEAR--MISERY, RESIGNATION...HE CAME CLOSE TO KILLING HER MORE THAN ONCE.
"THEN ONE DAY WE'RE AT THE STATION-- THIS IS BEFORE I GOT ANY REAL GRASP ON WHAT MY BUG DOES--I SAW HER LOOKING AT THE TRACK.
"I'M NOT SAYING SHE WAS GOING TO DO IT, BUT...IT WAS THERE IN HER EYES.
"AN ATTRACTIVE OPTION, Y'KNOW?
"WELL. SOMETHING HAPPENED IN MY BRAIN BEFORE I COULD STOP IT.
"SHE WAS... SMILING, I THINK."
DING! DING! DING!!
IT'S LIKE I TOLD YOU-- I'M NOT A HEAVY-HITTER. ALL I CAN DO IS NUDGE.
C'MON.
W-WHY ARE YOU TELLING ME THIS?

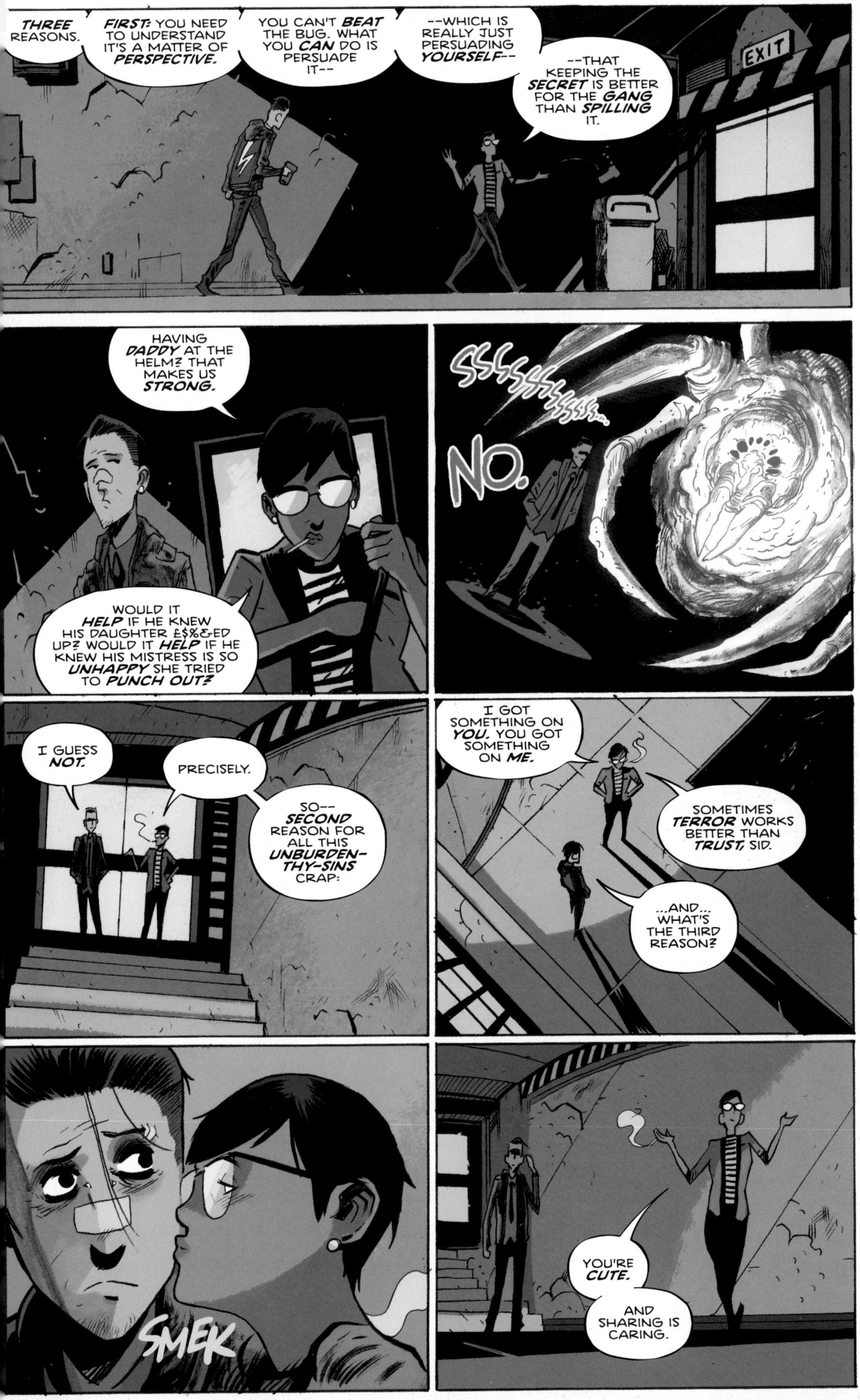
THREE REASONS.
FIRST: YOU NEED TO UNDERSTAND IT'S A MATTER OF PERSPECTIVE.
YOU CAN'T BEAT THE BUG. WHAT YOU CAN DO IS PERSUADE IT--
--WHICH IS REALLY JUST PERSUADING YOURSELF--
--THAT KEEPING THE SECRET IS BETTER FOR THE GANG THAN SPILLING IT.
EXIT
HAVING DADDY AT THE HELM? THAT MAKES US STRONG.
WOULD IT HELP IF HE KNEW HIS DAUGHTER £$%&ED UP? WOULD IT HELP IF HE KNEW HIS MISTRESS IS SO UNHAPPY SHE TRIED TO PUNCH OUT?
SSSSSSSSSSS...
NO.
I GUESS NOT.
PRECISELY.
SO-- SECOND REASON FOR ALL THIS UNBURDEN-THY-SINS CRAP:
I GOT SOMETHING ON YOU. YOU GOT SOMETHING ON ME.
SOMETIMES TERROR WORKS BETTER THAN TRUST, SID.
...AND... WHAT'S THE THIRD REASON?
SMEK
YOU'RE CUTE.
AND SHARING IS CARING.

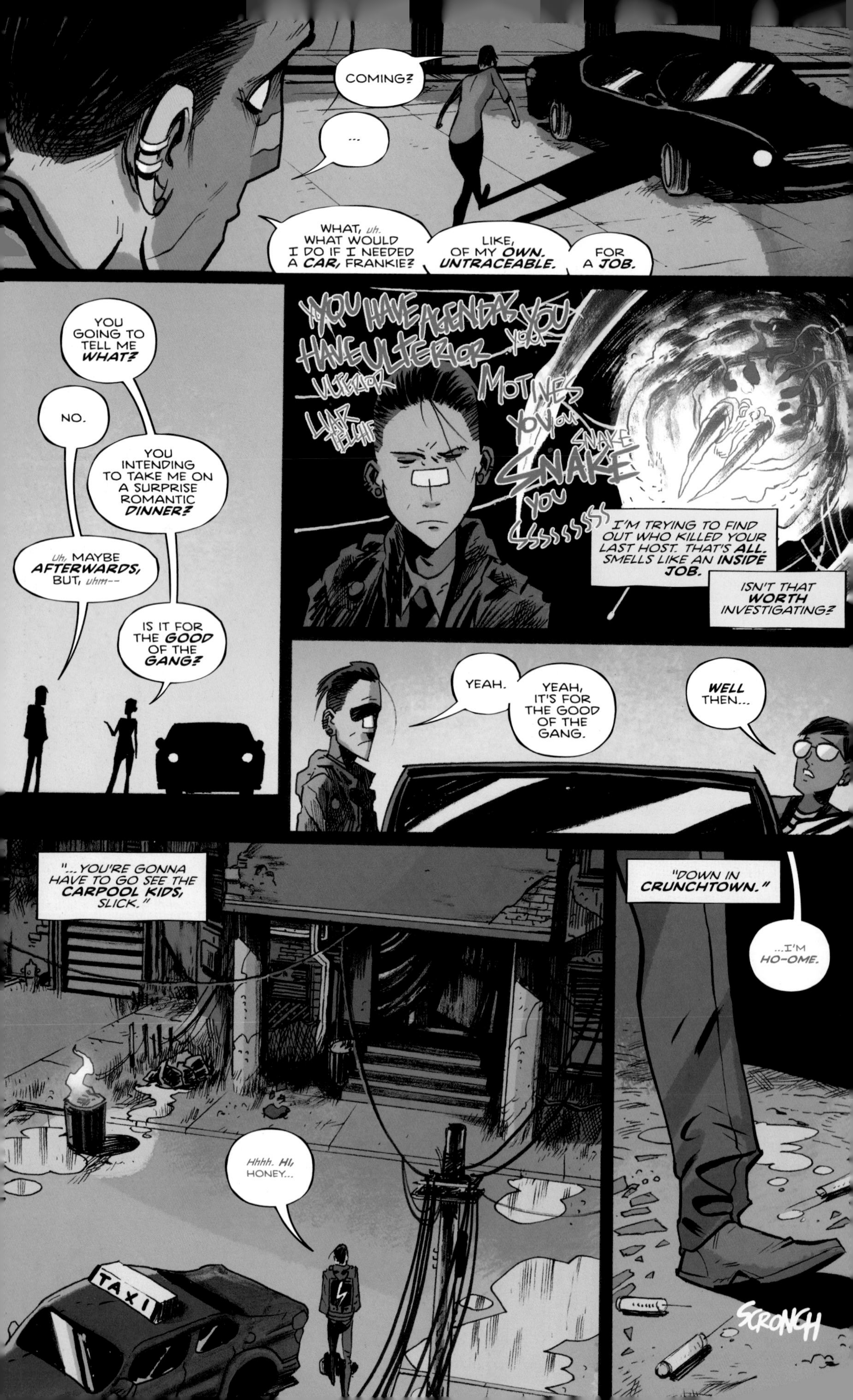

COMING?
...
WHAT, uh. WHAT WOULD I DO IF I NEEDED A CAR, FRANKIE?
LIKE, OF MY OWN. UNTRACEABLE.
FOR A JOB.
YOU GOING TO TELL ME WHAT?
NO.
YOU INTENDING TO TAKE ME ON A SURPRISE ROMANTIC DINNER?
Uh, MAYBE AFTERWARDS, BUT, uhm--
IS IT FOR THE GOOD OF THE GANG?
YOU HAVE AGENDAS YOU HAVE ULTERIOR
ULTERIOR MOTIVES
LIAR
YOU
SNAKE
SNAKE
YOU
SSSSSSSSS
I'M TRYING TO FIND OUT WHO KILLED YOUR LAST HOST. THAT'S ALL. SMELLS LIKE AN INSIDE JOB.
ISN'T THAT WORTH INVESTIGATING?
YEAH.
YEAH, IT'S FOR THE GOOD OF THE GANG.
WELL THEN...
"...YOU'RE GONNA HAVE TO GO SEE THE CARPOOL KIDS, SLICK."
Hhhh. HI, HONEY...
TAXI
"DOWN IN CRUNCHTOWN."
...I'M HO-OME.
SCRONCH

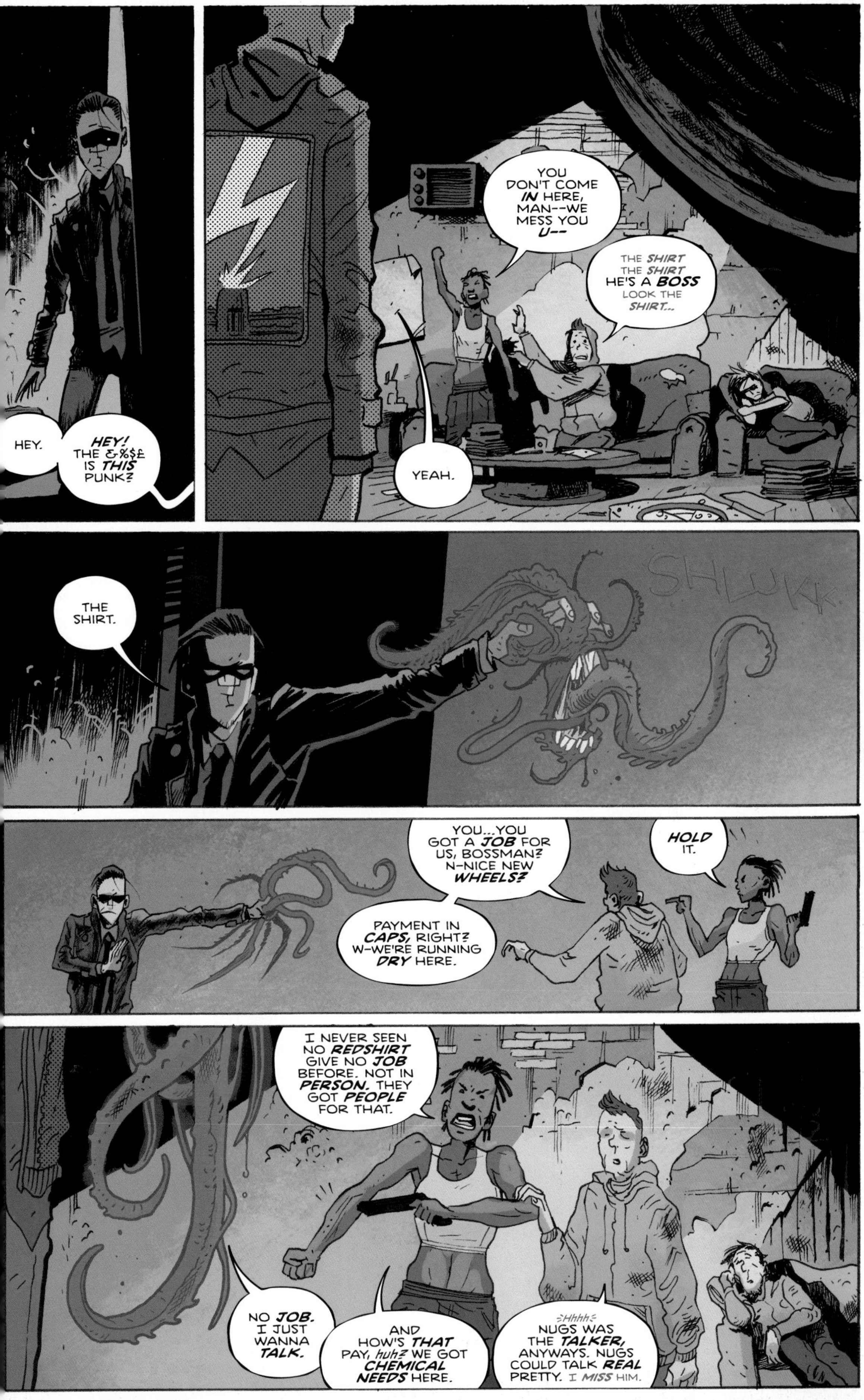

HEY.
HEY! THE &%$£ IS THIS PUNK?
YOU DON'T COME IN HERE, MAN--WE MESS YOU U--
THE SHIRT THE SHIRT HE'S A BOSS LOOK THE SHIRT...
YEAH.
THE SHIRT.
SHWKK
YOU...YOU GOT A JOB FOR US, BOSSMAN? N-NICE NEW WHEELS?
PAYMENT IN CAPS, RIGHT? W-WE'RE RUNNING DRY HERE.
HOLD IT.
I NEVER SEEN NO REDSHIRT GIVE NO JOB BEFORE. NOT IN PERSON. THEY GOT PEOPLE FOR THAT.
NO JOB. I JUST WANNA TALK.
AND HOW'S THAT PAY, huh? WE GOT CHEMICAL NEEDS HERE.
Hhhh NUGS WAS THE TALKER, ANYWAYS. NUGS COULD TALK REAL PRETTY. I MISS HIM.

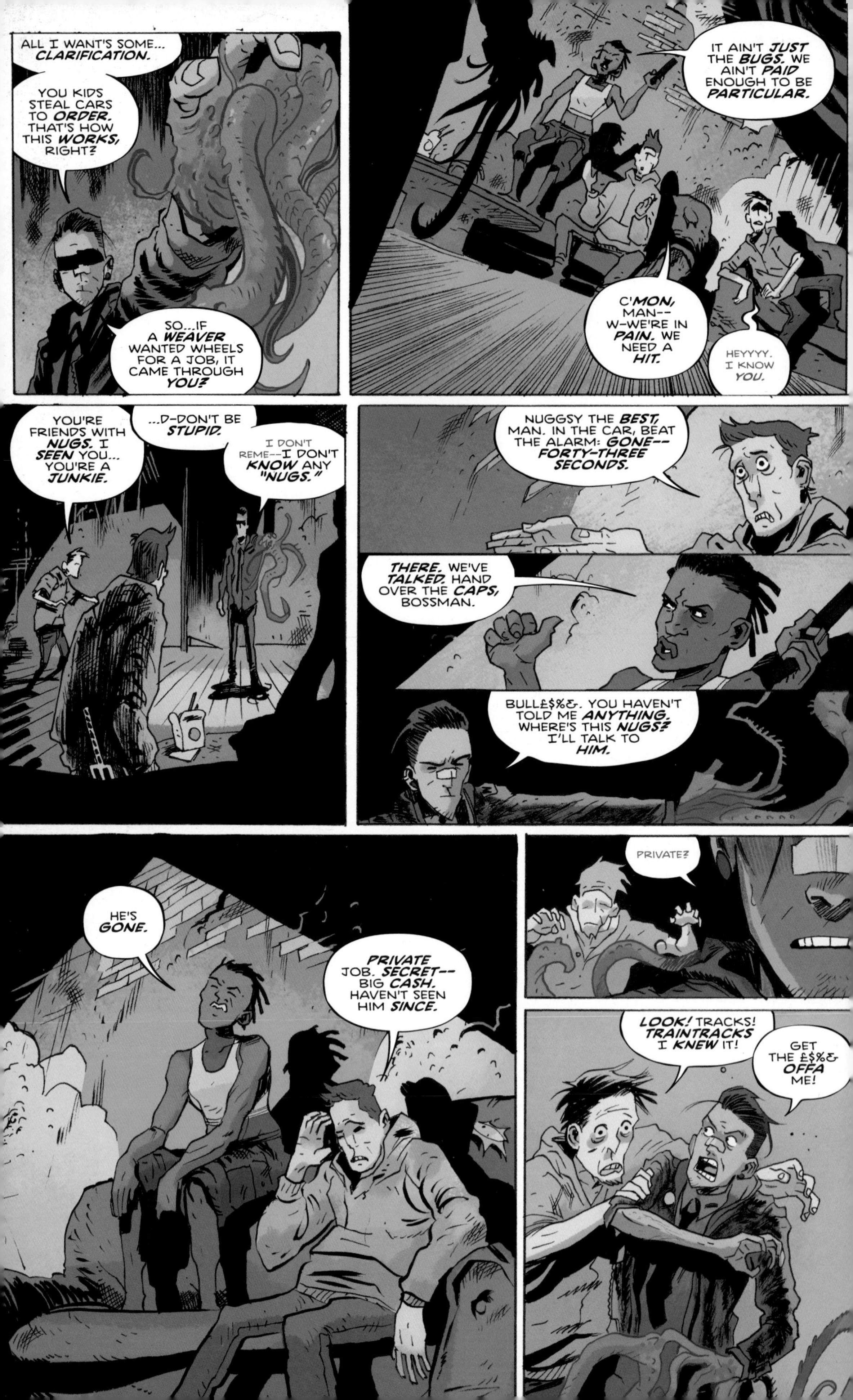
ALL I WANT'S SOME... CLARIFICATION.
YOU KIDS STEAL CARS TO ORDER. THAT'S HOW THIS WORKS, RIGHT?
SO...IF A WEAVER WANTED WHEELS FOR A JOB, IT CAME THROUGH YOU?
IT AIN'T JUST THE BUGS. WE AIN'T PAID ENOUGH TO BE PARTICULAR.
C'MON, MAN-- W-WE'RE IN PAIN. WE NEED A HIT.
HEYYYY. I KNOW YOU.
YOU'RE FRIENDS WITH NUGS. I SEEN YOU... YOU'RE A JUNKIE.
...D-DON'T BE STUPID.
I DON'T REME--I DON'T KNOW ANY "NUGS."
NUGGSY THE BEST, MAN. IN THE CAR, BEAT THE ALARM: GONE-- FORTY-THREE SECONDS.
THERE. WE'VE TALKED. HAND OVER THE CAPS, BOSSMAN.
BULL£$%&. YOU HAVEN'T TOLD ME ANYTHING. WHERE'S THIS NUGS? I'LL TALK TO HIM.
HE'S GONE.
PRIVATE JOB. SECRET-- BIG CASH. HAVEN'T SEEN HIM SINCE.
PRIVATE?
LOOK! TRACKS! TRAINTRACKS I KNEW IT!
GET THE £$%& OFFA ME!

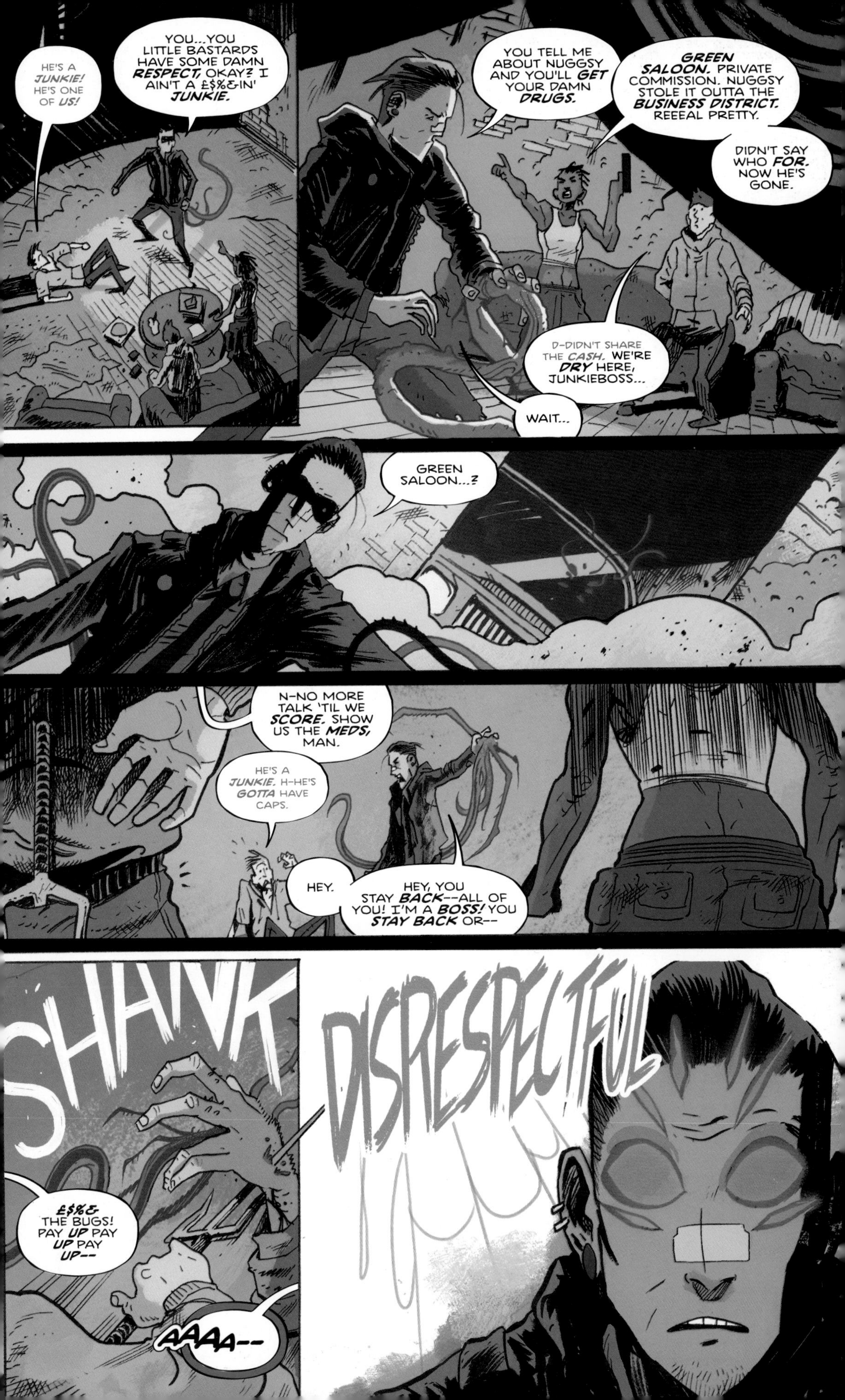
HE'S A JUNKIE! HE'S ONE OF US!
YOU...YOU LITTLE BASTARDS HAVE SOME DAMN RESPECT, OKAY? I AIN'T A £$%&IN' JUNKIE.
YOU TELL ME ABOUT NUGGSY AND YOU'LL GET YOUR DAMN DRUGS.
GREEN SALOON. PRIVATE COMMISSION. NUGGSY STOLE IT OUTTA THE BUSINESS DISTRICT. REEEAL PRETTY.
DIDN'T SAY WHO FOR. NOW HE'S GONE.
D-DIDN'T SHARE THE CASH. WE'RE DRY HERE, JUNKIEBOSS...
WAIT...
GREEN SALOON...?
N-NO MORE TALK 'TIL WE SCORE. SHOW US THE MEDS, MAN.
HE'S A JUNKIE. H-HE'S GOTTA HAVE CAPS.
HEY.
HEY, YOU STAY BACK--ALL OF YOU! I'M A BOSS! YOU STAY BACK OR--
SHANK
DISRESPECTFUL
£$%& THE BUGS! PAY UP PAY UP PAY UP--
AAAA--

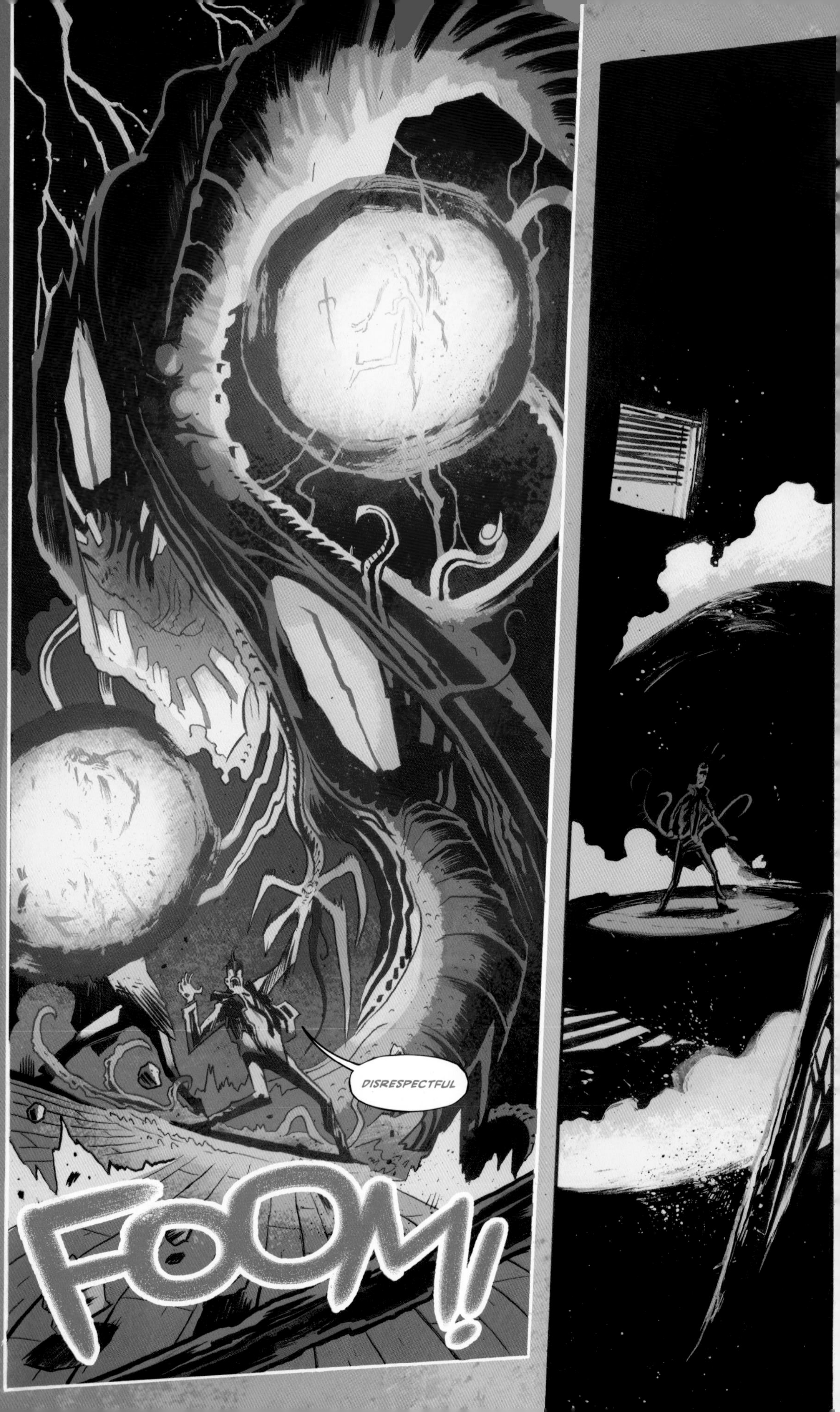
DISRESPECTFUL
FOOM!

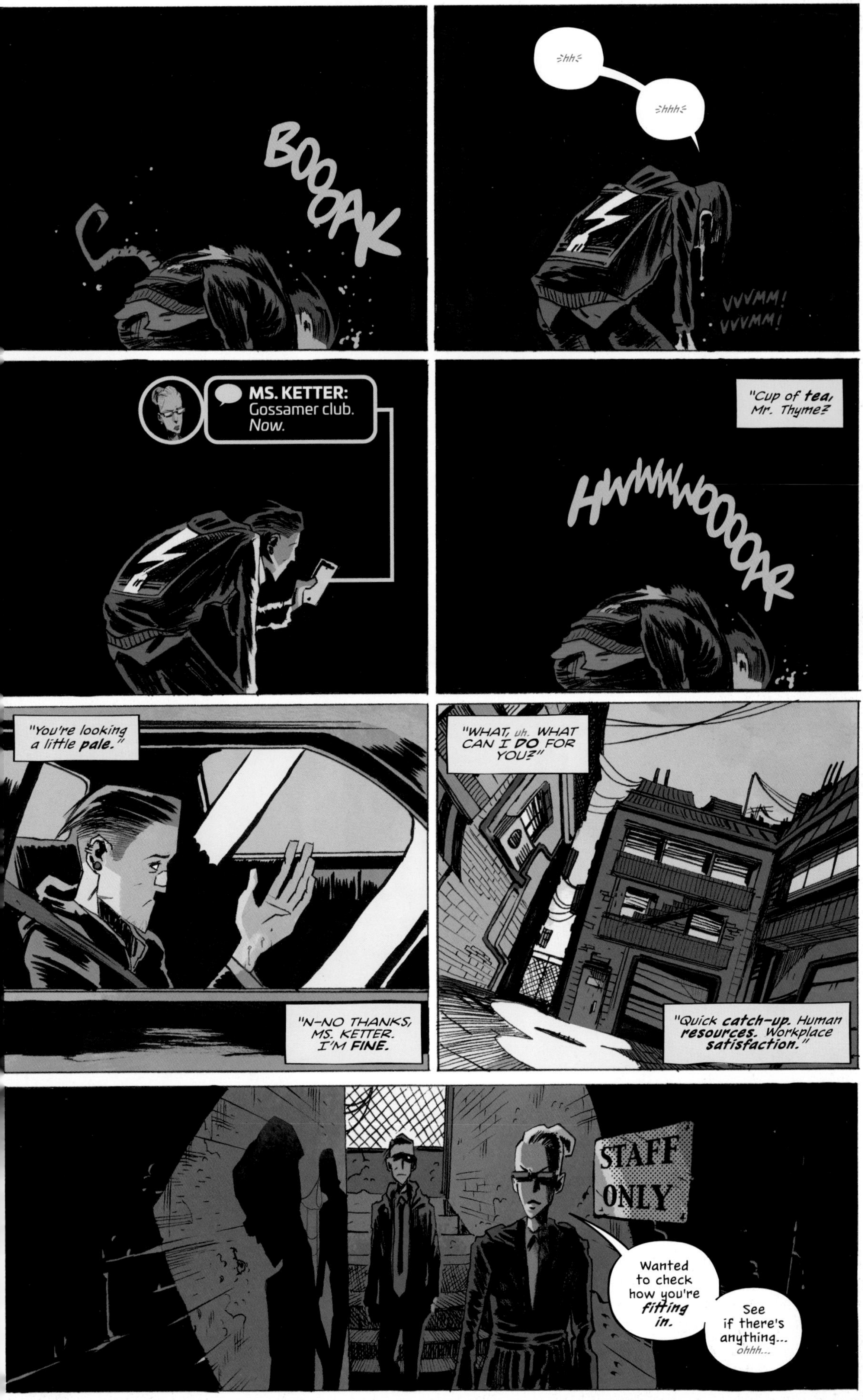

BOOOAK
≷hh≶
≷hhh≶
VVVMM!
VVVMM!
MS. KETTER: Gossamer club. Now.
"Cup of tea, Mr. Thyme?
HWWWOOOOAR
"You're looking a little pale."
"N-NO THANKS, MS. KETTER. I'M FINE.
"WHAT, uh. WHAT CAN I DO FOR YOU?"
"Quick catch-up. Human resources. Workplace satisfaction."
STAFF ONLY
Wanted to check how you're fitting in.
See if there's anything... ohhh...

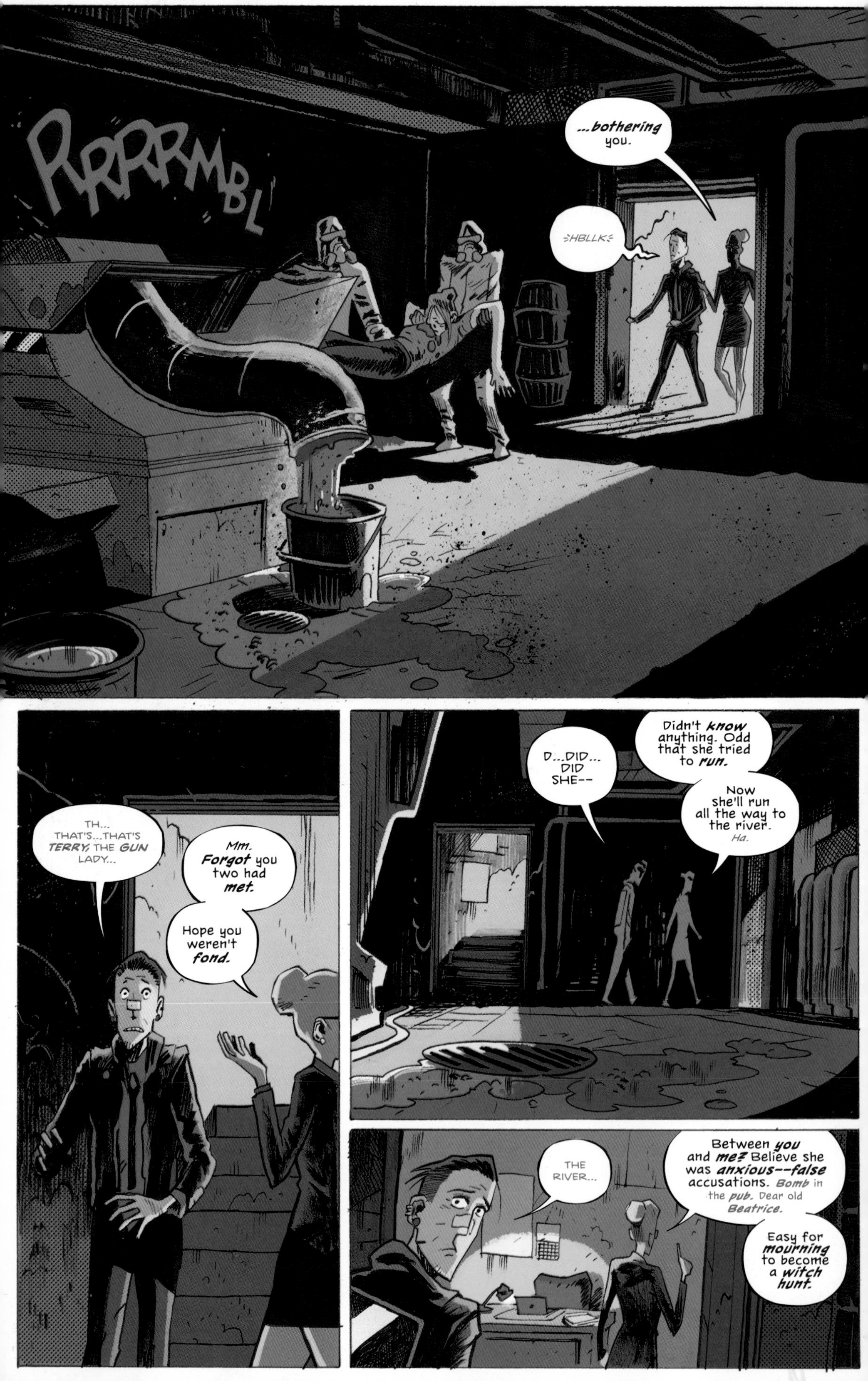
RRRRMBL
...bothering you.
HBLLK
TH... THAT'S...THAT'S TERRY, THE GUN LADY...
Mm. Forgot you two had met.
Hope you weren't fond.
D...DID... DID SHE--
Didn't know anything. Odd that she tried to run.
Now she'll run all the way to the river. Ha.
THE RIVER...
Between you and me? Believe she was anxious--false accusations. Bomb in the pub. Dear old Beatrice.
Easy for mourning to become a witch hunt.

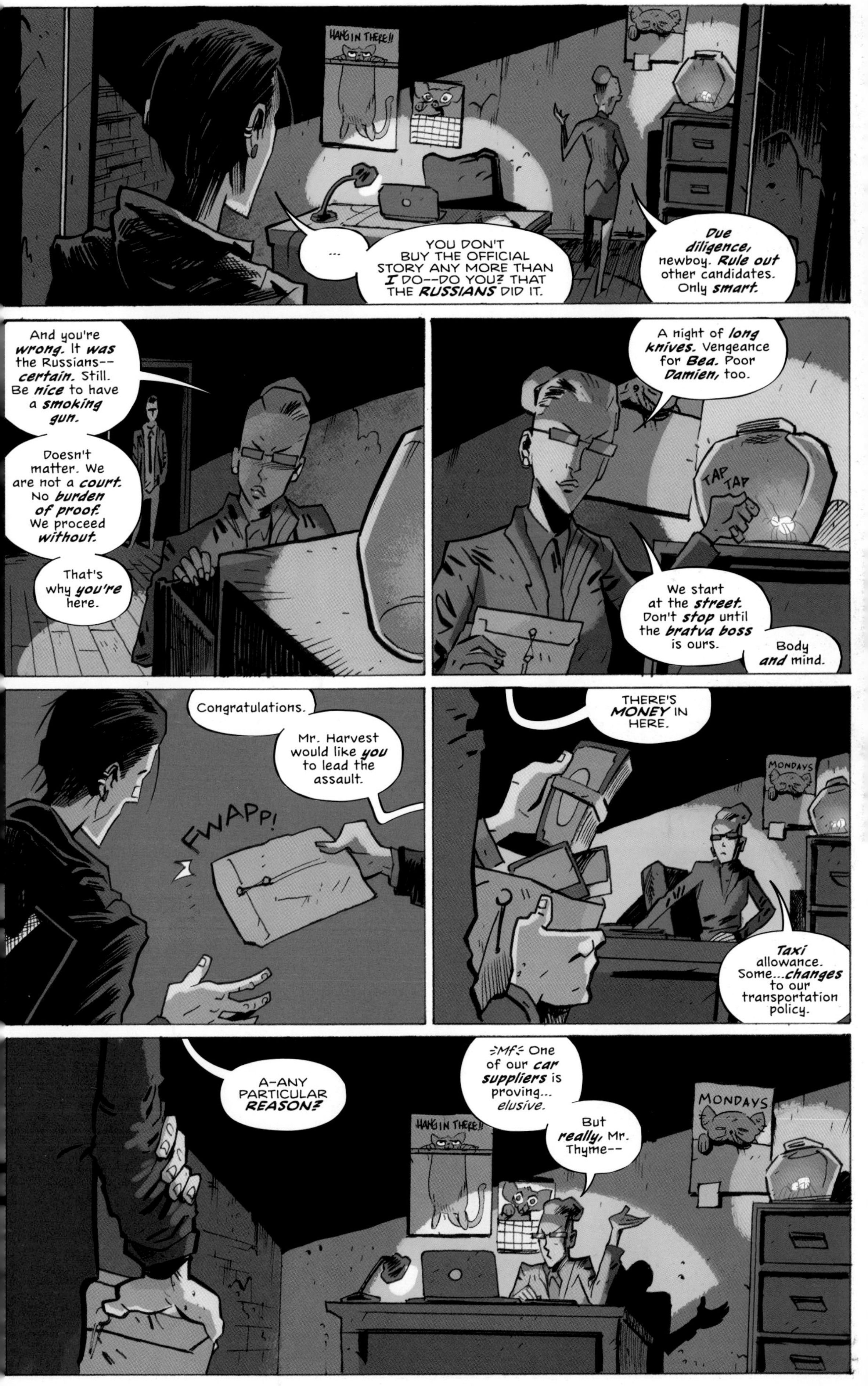
HANG IN THERE!!
...
YOU DON'T BUY THE OFFICIAL STORY ANY MORE THAN I DO--DO YOU? THAT THE RUSSIANS DID IT.
Due diligence, newboy. Rule out other candidates. Only smart.
And you're wrong. It was the Russians--certain. Still. Be nice to have a smoking gun.
Doesn't matter. We are not a court. No burden of proof. We proceed without.
That's why you're here.
A night of long knives. Vengeance for Bea. Poor Damien, too.
TAP TAP
We start at the street. Don't stop until the bratva boss is ours.
Body and mind.
Congratulations.
Mr. Harvest would like you to lead the assault.
FWAPP!
THERE'S MONEY IN HERE.
MONDAYS
Taxi allowance. Some...changes to our transportation policy.
A-ANY PARTICULAR REASON?
⇒Mf⇐ One of our car suppliers is proving... elusive.
But really, Mr. Thyme--
HANG IN THERE!!
MONDAYS

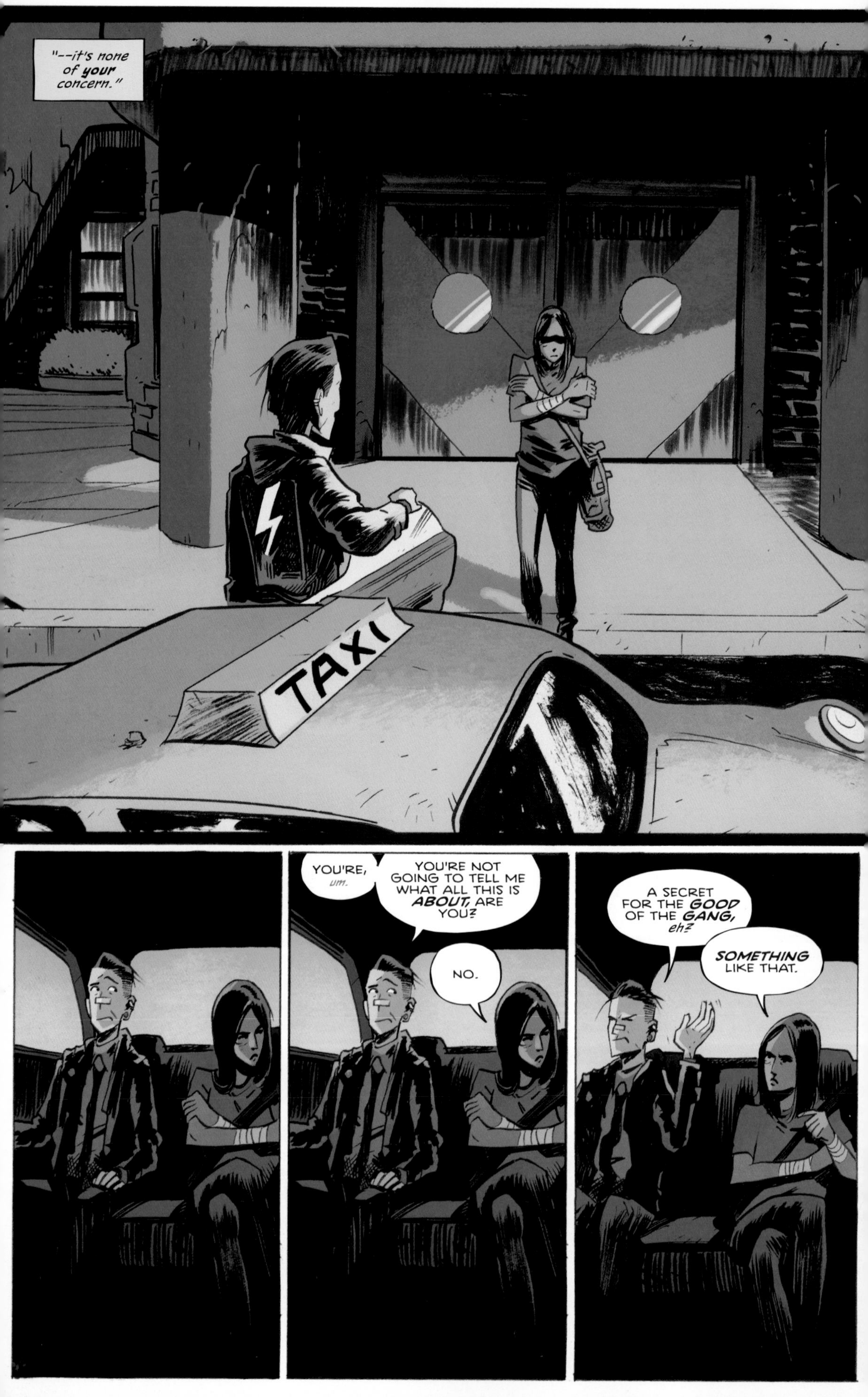
"--it's none of *your* concern."
TAXI
YOU'RE, *um.*
YOU'RE NOT GOING TO TELL ME WHAT ALL THIS IS *ABOUT,* ARE YOU?
NO.
A SECRET FOR THE *GOOD* OF THE *GANG,* *eh?*
SOMETHING LIKE THAT.

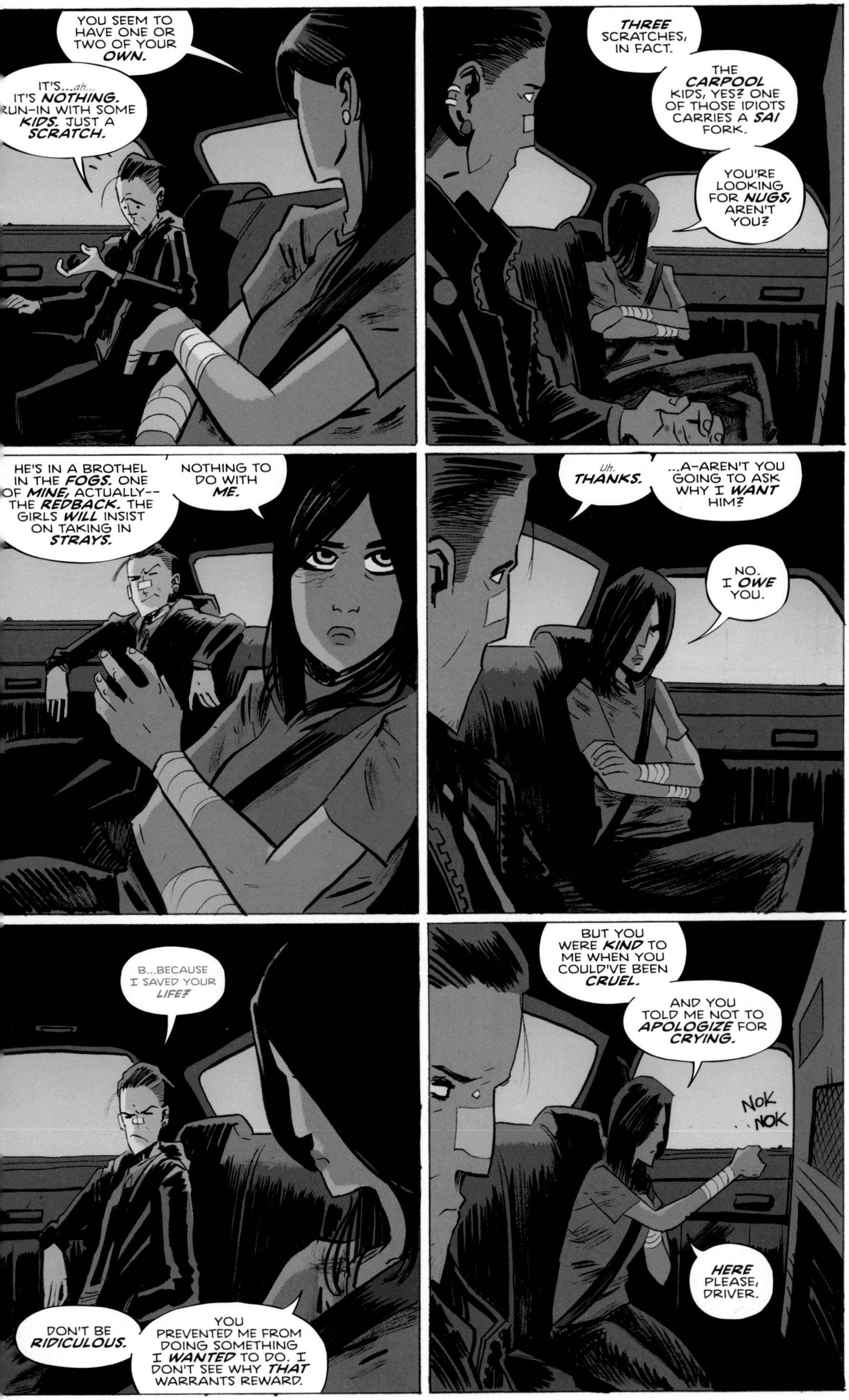
YOU SEEM TO HAVE ONE OR TWO OF YOUR OWN.
IT'S...ah... IT'S NOTHING. RUN-IN WITH SOME KIDS. JUST A SCRATCH.
THREE SCRATCHES, IN FACT.
THE CARPOOL KIDS, YES? ONE OF THOSE IDIOTS CARRIES A SAI FORK.
YOU'RE LOOKING FOR NUGS, AREN'T YOU?
HE'S IN A BROTHEL IN THE FOGS. ONE OF MINE, ACTUALLY-- THE REDBACK. THE GIRLS WILL INSIST ON TAKING IN STRAYS.
NOTHING TO DO WITH ME.
Uh. THANKS.
...A-AREN'T YOU GOING TO ASK WHY I WANT HIM?
NO. I OWE YOU.
B...BECAUSE I SAVED YOUR LIFE?
DON'T BE RIDICULOUS.
YOU PREVENTED ME FROM DOING SOMETHING I WANTED TO DO. I DON'T SEE WHY THAT WARRANTS REWARD.
BUT YOU WERE KIND TO ME WHEN YOU COULD'VE BEEN CRUEL.
AND YOU TOLD ME NOT TO APOLOGIZE FOR CRYING.
NOK NOK
HERE PLEASE, DRIVER.

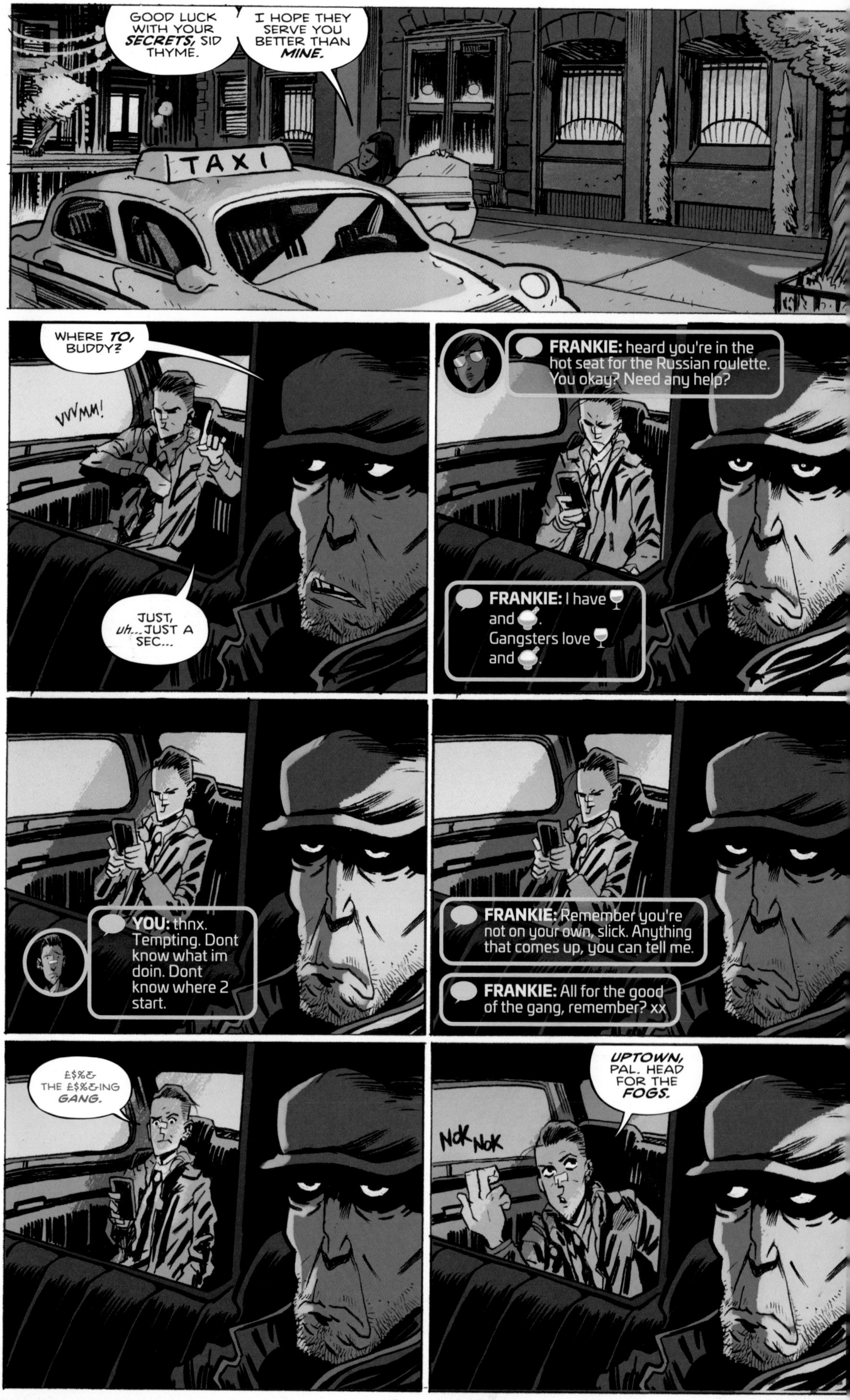
GOOD LUCK WITH YOUR SECRETS, SID THYME.
I HOPE THEY SERVE YOU BETTER THAN MINE.
TAXI
WHERE TO, BUDDY?
VVVMM!
JUST, uh... JUST A SEC...
FRANKIE: heard you're in the hot seat for the Russian roulette. You okay? Need any help?
FRANKIE: I have 🍷 and 🍄. Gangsters love 🍷 and 🍄.
YOU: thnx. Tempting. Dont know what im doin. Dont know where 2 start.
FRANKIE: Remember you're not on your own, slick. Anything that comes up, you can tell me.
FRANKIE: All for the good of the gang, remember? xx
£$%& THE £$%&-ING GANG.
UPTOWN, PAL. HEAD FOR THE FOGS.
NOK NOK

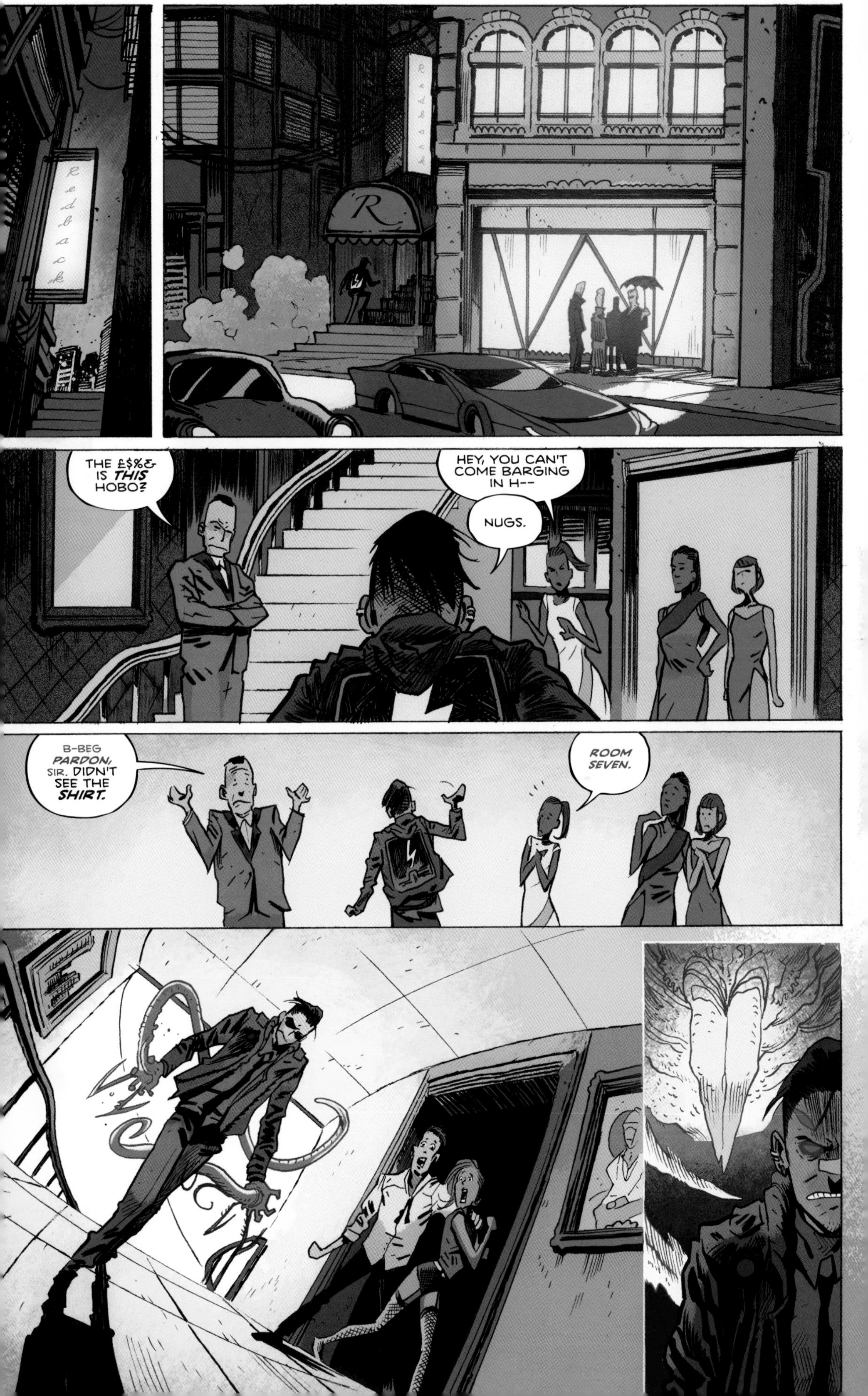
Redback
Redback
THE £$%& IS THIS HOBO?
HEY, YOU CAN'T COME BARGING IN H--
NUGS.
B-BEG PARDON, SIR. DIDN'T SEE THE SHIRT.
ROOM SEVEN.

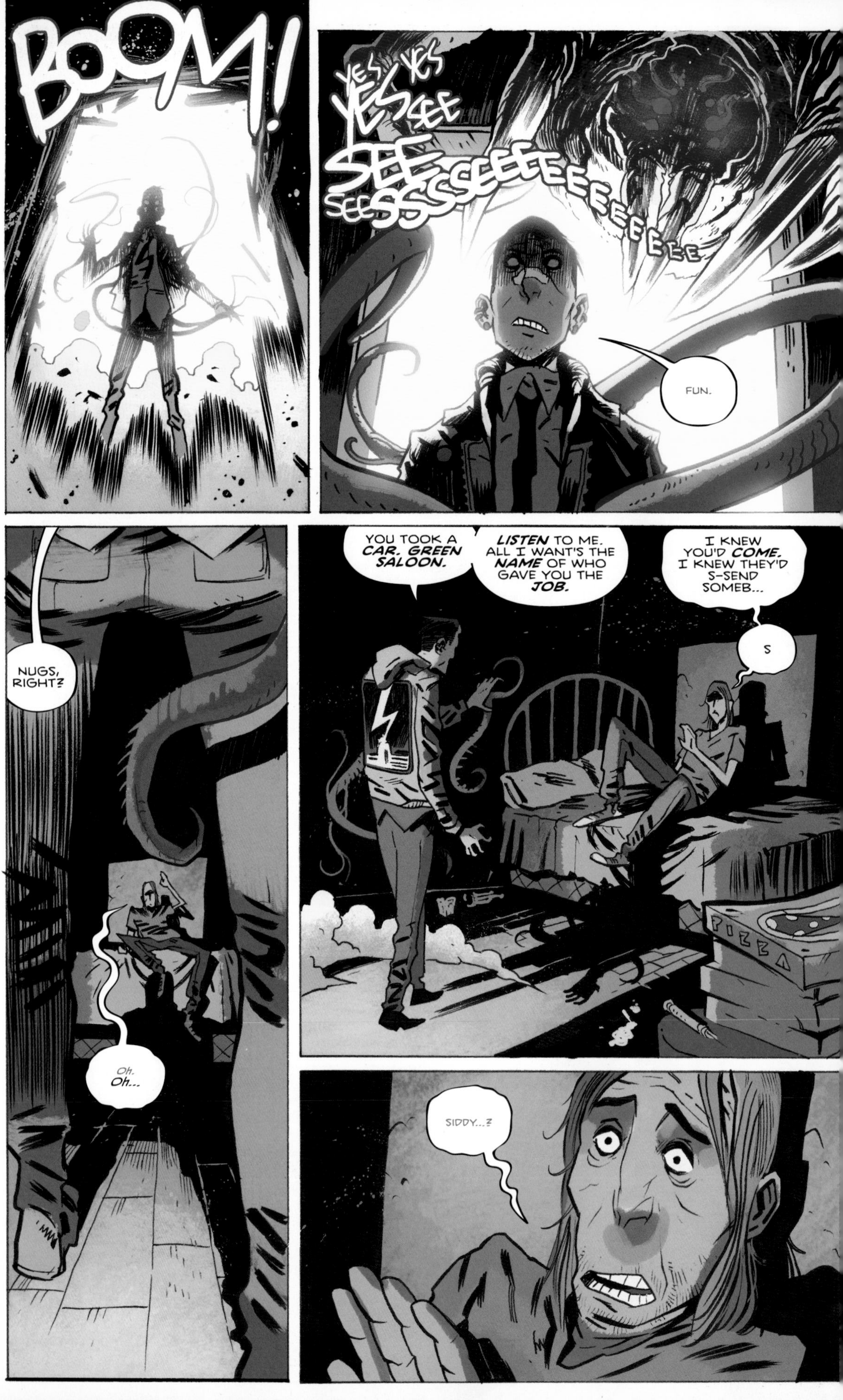
BOOM!
YES YES YES SEE
SEE SEE SSSSEEEEEEEEEEEEE
FUN.
NUGS, RIGHT?
Oh. Oh...
YOU TOOK A CAR. GREEN SALOON.
LISTEN TO ME. ALL I WANT'S THE NAME OF WHO GAVE YOU THE JOB.
I KNEW YOU'D COME. I KNEW THEY'D S-SEND SOMEB...
S
SIDDY...?

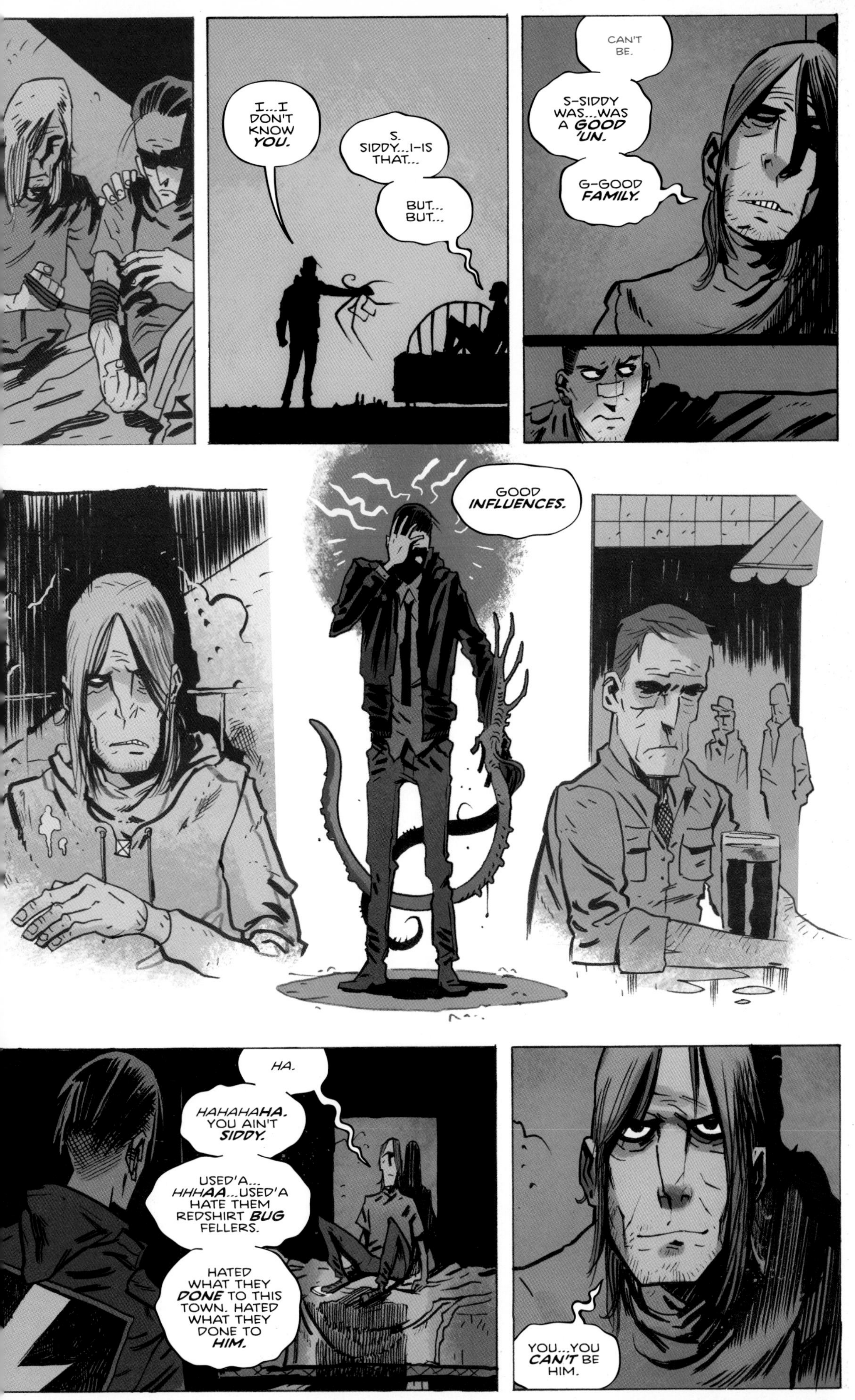
I...I DON'T KNOW *YOU.*
S. SIDDY...I-IS THAT...
BUT... BUT...
CAN'T BE.
S-SIDDY WAS...WAS A *GOOD 'UN.*
G-GOOD *FAMILY.*
GOOD *INFLUENCES.*
HA.
HAHAHAHA. YOU AIN'T *SIDDY.*
USED'A... *HHHAA*...USED'A HATE THEM REDSHIRT *BUG* FELLERS.
HATED WHAT THEY *DONE* TO THIS TOWN. HATED WHAT THEY DONE TO *HIM.*
YOU...YOU *CAN'T* BE HIM.

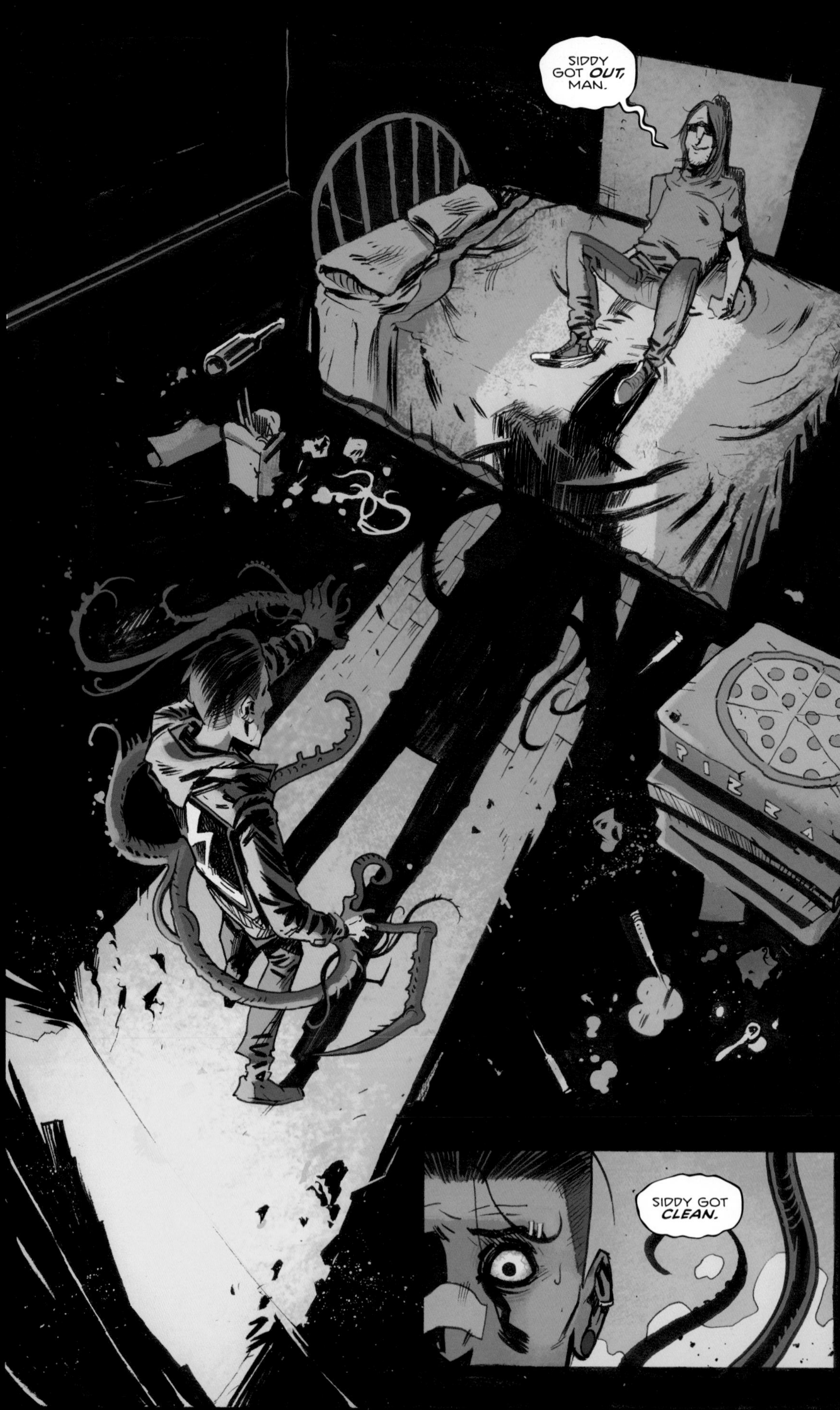
SIDDY GOT OUT, MAN.
SIDDY GOT CLEAN.

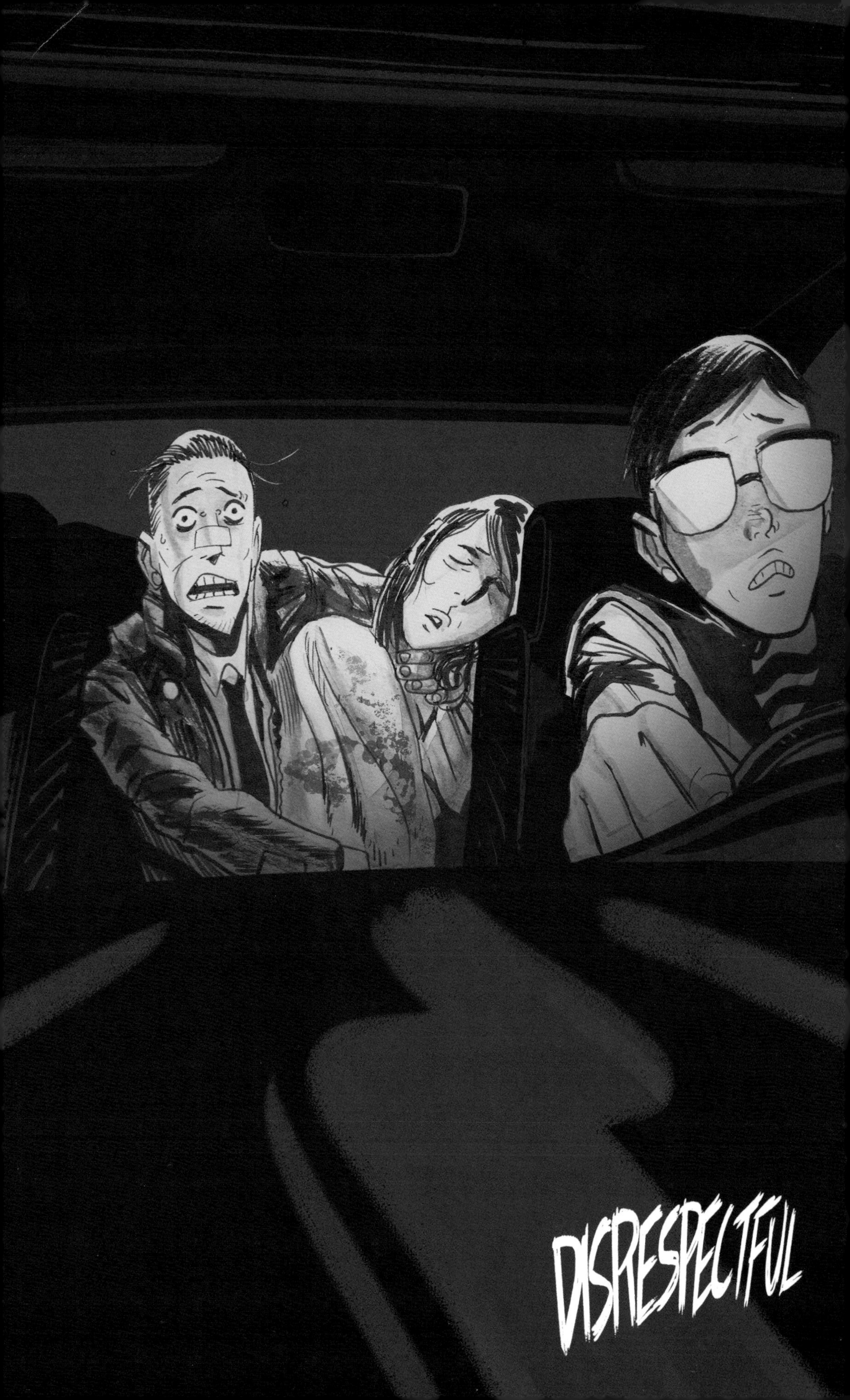
DISRESPECTFUL

CHAPTER FIVE

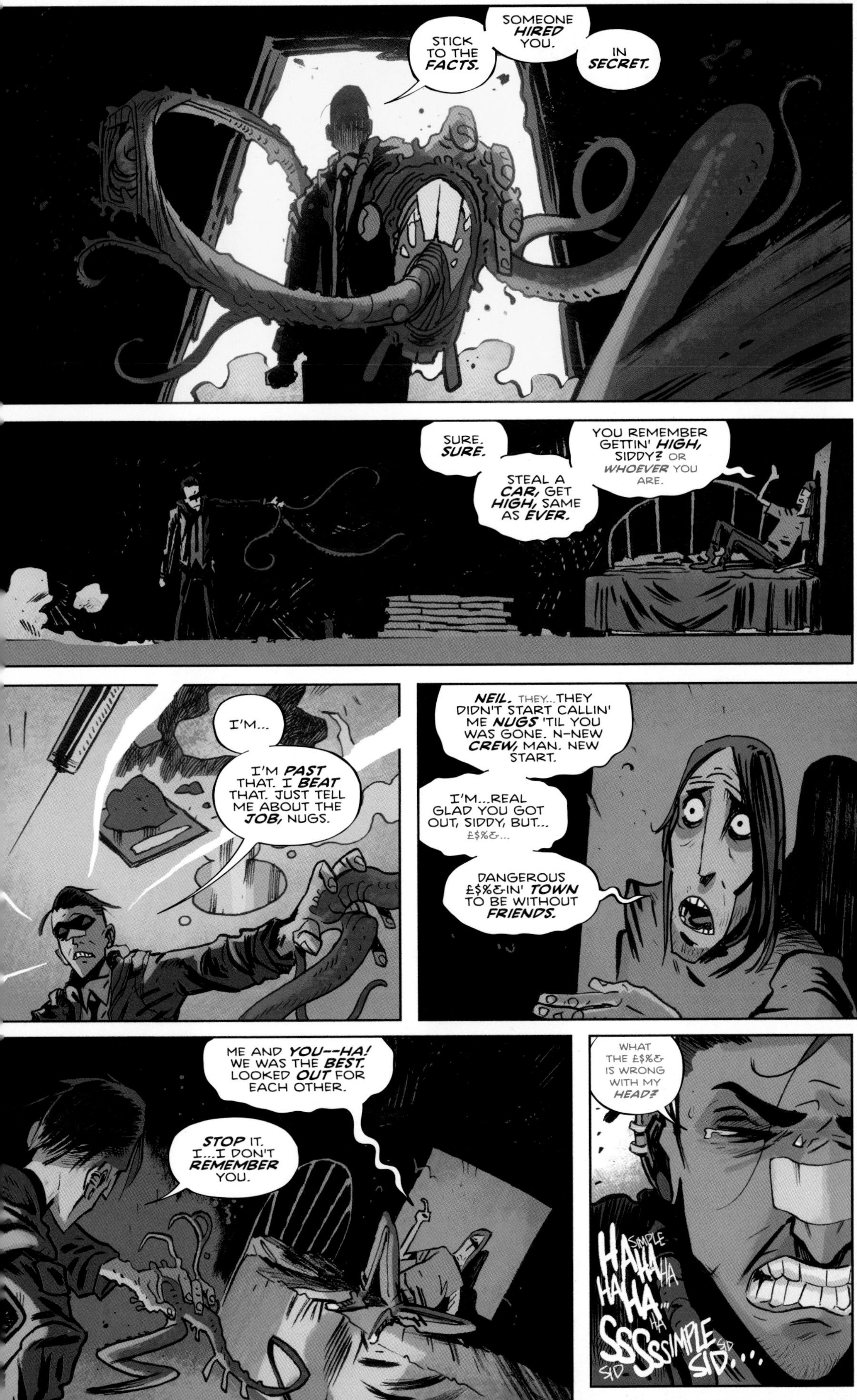
STICK TO THE FACTS.
SOMEONE HIRED YOU.
IN SECRET.
SURE. SURE.
STEAL A CAR, GET HIGH, SAME AS EVER.
YOU REMEMBER GETTIN' HIGH, SIDDY? OR WHOEVER YOU ARE.
I'M...
I'M PAST THAT. I BEAT THAT. JUST TELL ME ABOUT THE JOB, NUGS.
NEIL. THEY...THEY DIDN'T START CALLIN' ME NUGS 'TIL YOU WAS GONE. N-NEW CREW, MAN. NEW START.
I'M...REAL GLAD YOU GOT OUT, SIDDY, BUT... £$%&...
DANGEROUS £$%&IN' TOWN TO BE WITHOUT FRIENDS.
ME AND YOU--HA! WE WAS THE BEST. LOOKED OUT FOR EACH OTHER.
STOP IT. I...I DON'T REMEMBER YOU.
WHAT THE £$%& IS WRONG WITH MY HEAD?
HA SIMPLE HA HA HA HA HA... HA
SSSSIMPLE SID SID SID...

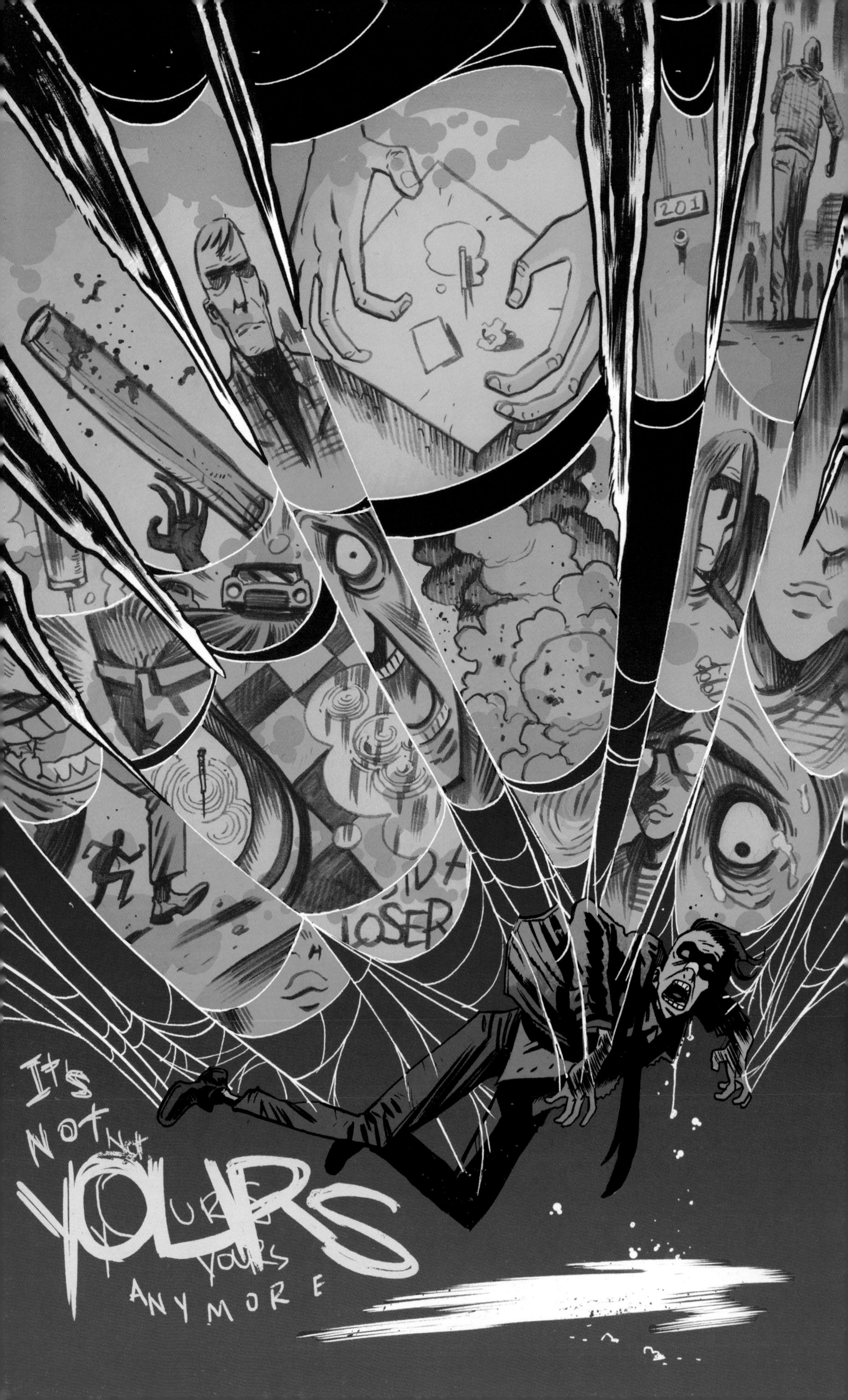
201
LOSER
It's not not
YOURS
yours
ANYMORE

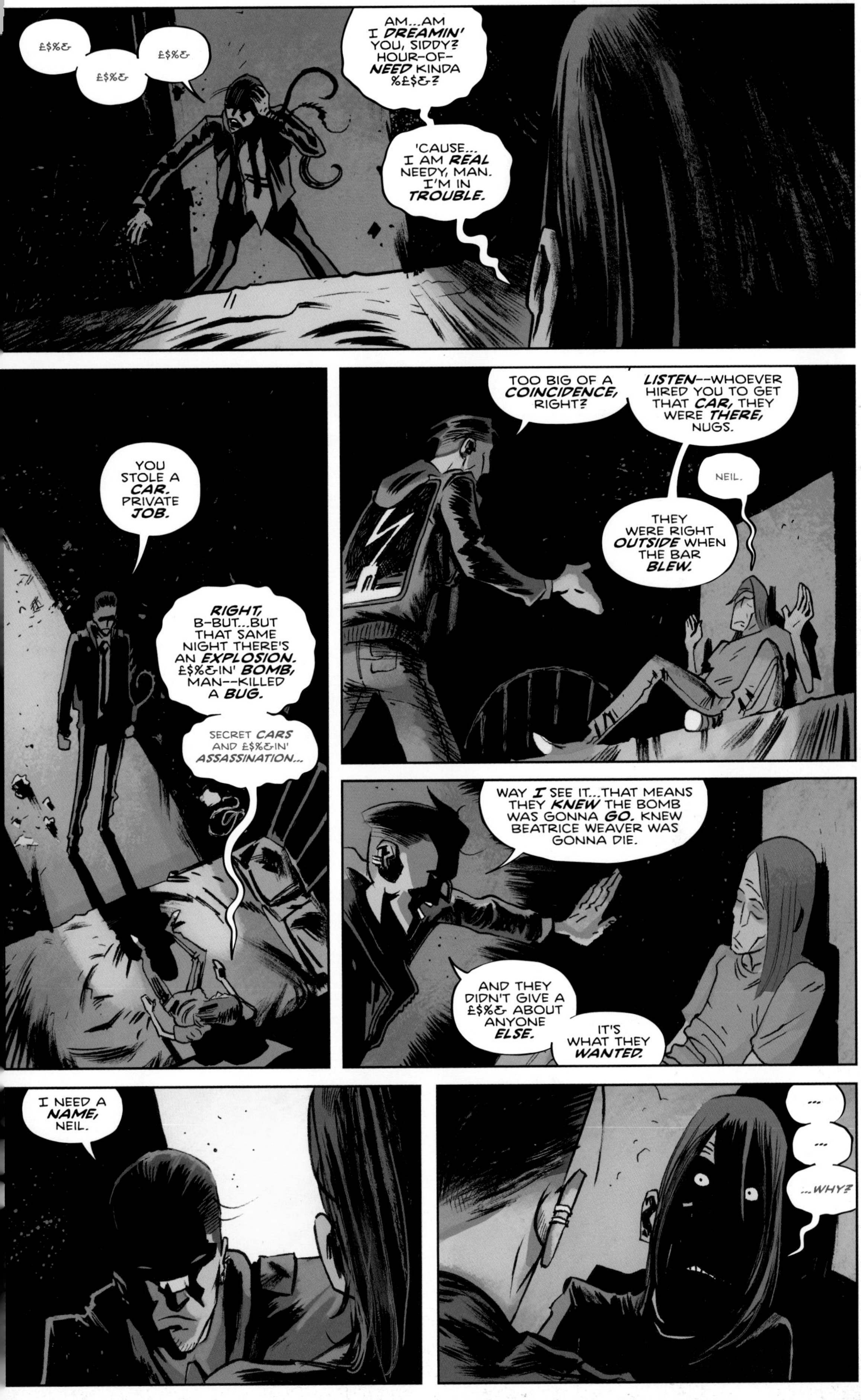
£$%&
£$%&
£$%&
AM...AM I DREAMIN' YOU, SIDDY? HOUR-OF-NEED KINDA %£$&?
'CAUSE... I AM REAL NEEDY, MAN. I'M IN TROUBLE.
YOU STOLE A CAR. PRIVATE JOB.
RIGHT, B-BUT...BUT THAT SAME NIGHT THERE'S AN EXPLOSION. £$%&-IN' BOMB, MAN--KILLED A BUG.
SECRET CARS AND £$%&-IN' ASSASSINATION...
TOO BIG OF A COINCIDENCE, RIGHT?
LISTEN--WHOEVER HIRED YOU TO GET THAT CAR, THEY WERE THERE, NUGS.
NEIL.
THEY WERE RIGHT OUTSIDE WHEN THE BAR BLEW.
WAY I SEE IT...THAT MEANS THEY KNEW THE BOMB WAS GONNA GO. KNEW BEATRICE WEAVER WAS GONNA DIE.
AND THEY DIDN'T GIVE A £$%& ABOUT ANYONE ELSE.
IT'S WHAT THEY WANTED.
I NEED A NAME, NEIL.
...
...
...WHY?

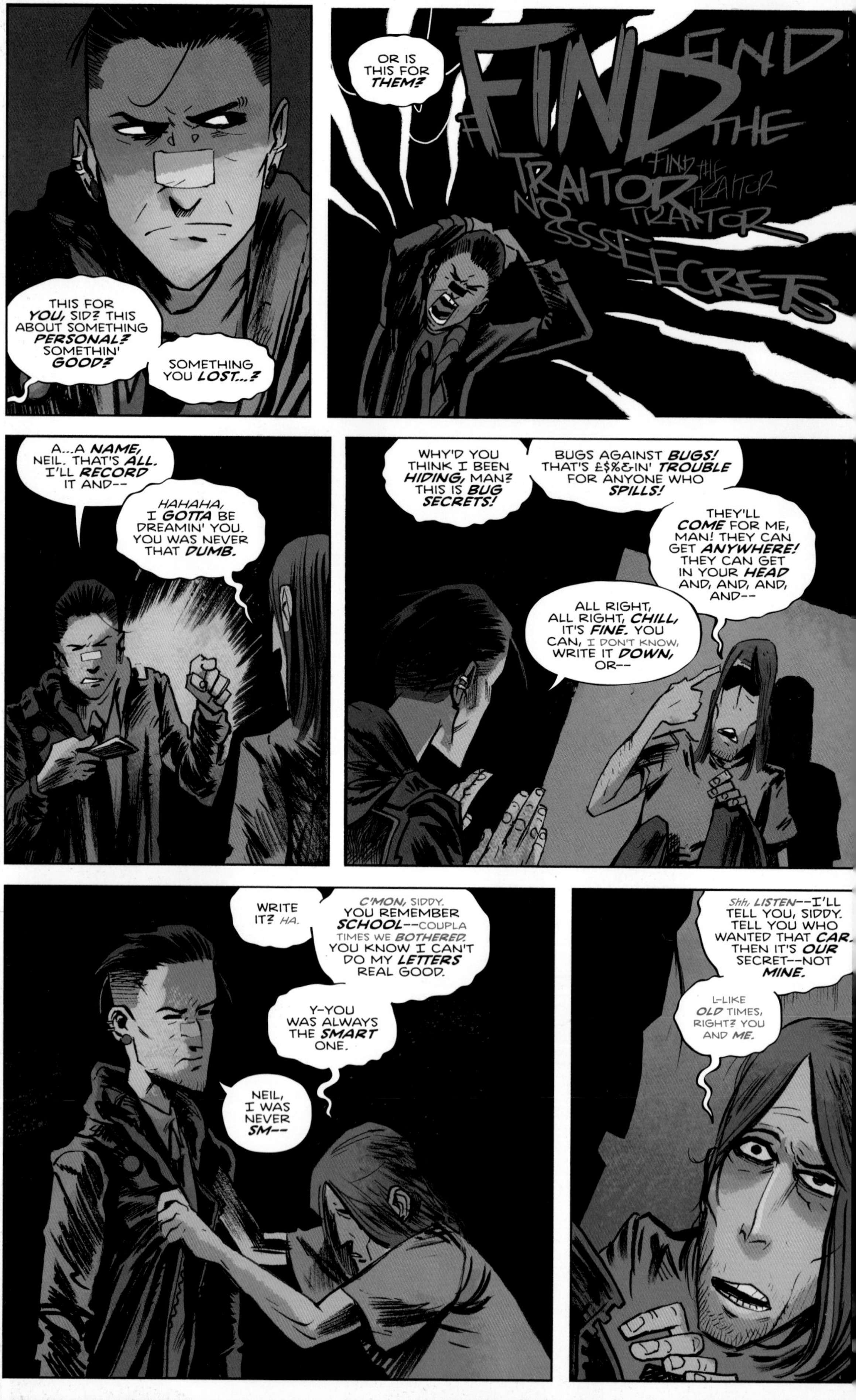
THIS FOR YOU, SID? THIS ABOUT SOMETHING PERSONAL? SOMETHIN' GOOD?
SOMETHING YOU LOST...?
OR IS THIS FOR THEM?
FIND FIND THE TRAITOR FIND THE TRAITOR NO TRAITOR SSSSEEECRETS
A...A NAME, NEIL. THAT'S ALL. I'LL RECORD IT AND--
HAHAHA, I GOTTA BE DREAMIN' YOU. YOU WAS NEVER THAT DUMB.
WHY'D YOU THINK I BEEN HIDING, MAN? THIS IS BUG SECRETS!
BUGS AGAINST BUGS! THAT'S £$%&IN' TROUBLE FOR ANYONE WHO SPILLS!
THEY'LL COME FOR ME, MAN! THEY CAN GET ANYWHERE! THEY CAN GET IN YOUR HEAD AND, AND, AND, AND--
ALL RIGHT, ALL RIGHT, CHILL, IT'S FINE. YOU CAN, I DON'T KNOW, WRITE IT DOWN, OR--
WRITE IT? HA.
C'MON, SIDDY. YOU REMEMBER SCHOOL--COUPLA TIMES WE BOTHERED. YOU KNOW I CAN'T DO MY LETTERS REAL GOOD.
Y-YOU WAS ALWAYS THE SMART ONE.
NEIL, I WAS NEVER SM--
Shh, LISTEN--I'LL TELL YOU, SIDDY. TELL YOU WHO WANTED THAT CAR. THEN IT'S OUR SECRET--NOT MINE.
L-LIKE OLD TIMES, RIGHT? YOU AND ME.

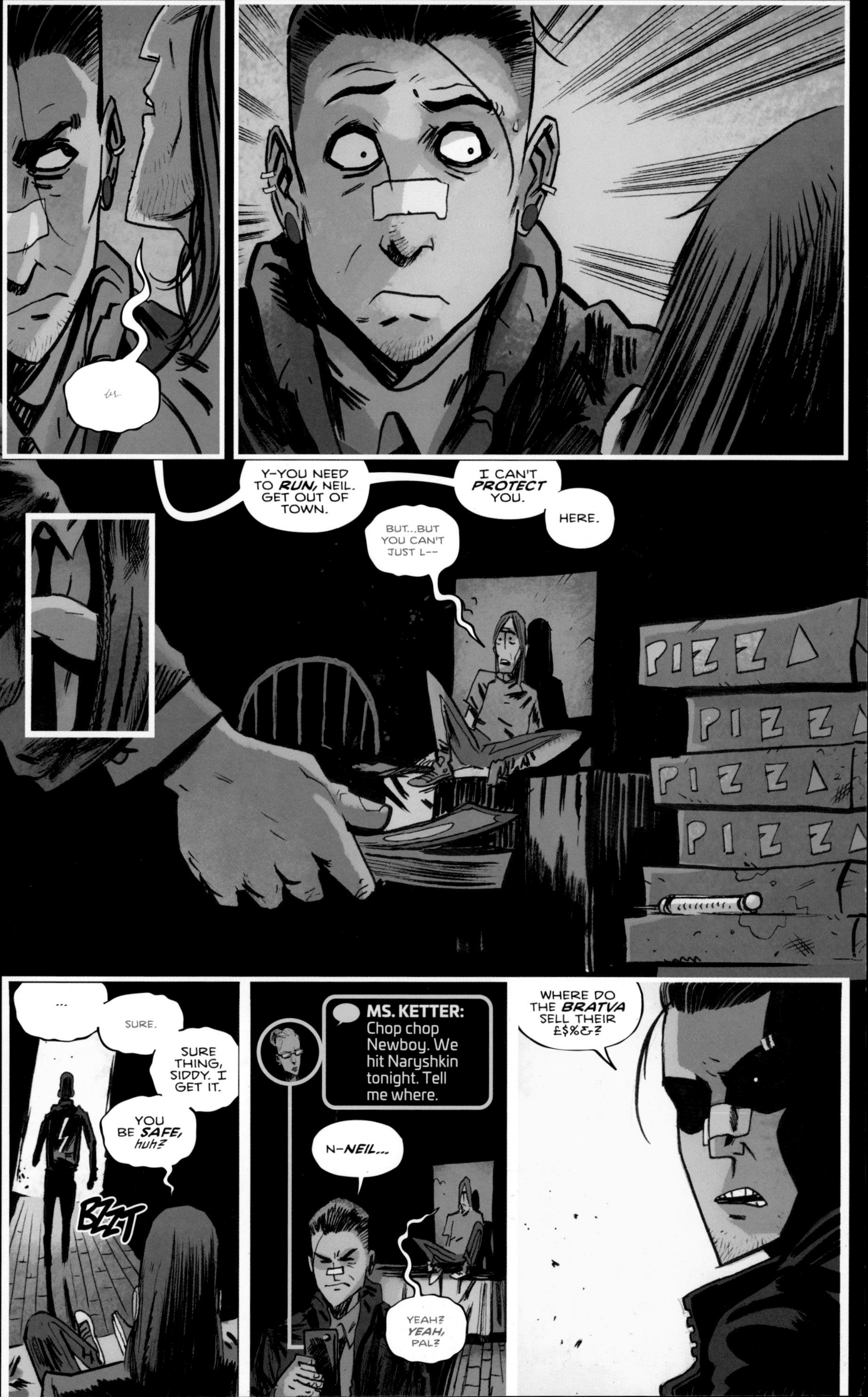
Y-YOU NEED TO RUN, NEIL. GET OUT OF TOWN.
I CAN'T PROTECT YOU.
HERE.
BUT...BUT YOU CAN'T JUST L--
PIZZA
PIZZA
PIZZA
PIZZA
...
SURE.
SURE THING, SIDDY. I GET IT.
YOU BE SAFE, huh?
BZZT
MS. KETTER: Chop chop Newboy. We hit Naryshkin tonight. Tell me where.
N-NEIL...
YEAH? YEAH, PAL?
WHERE DO THE BRATVA SELL THEIR £$%&?

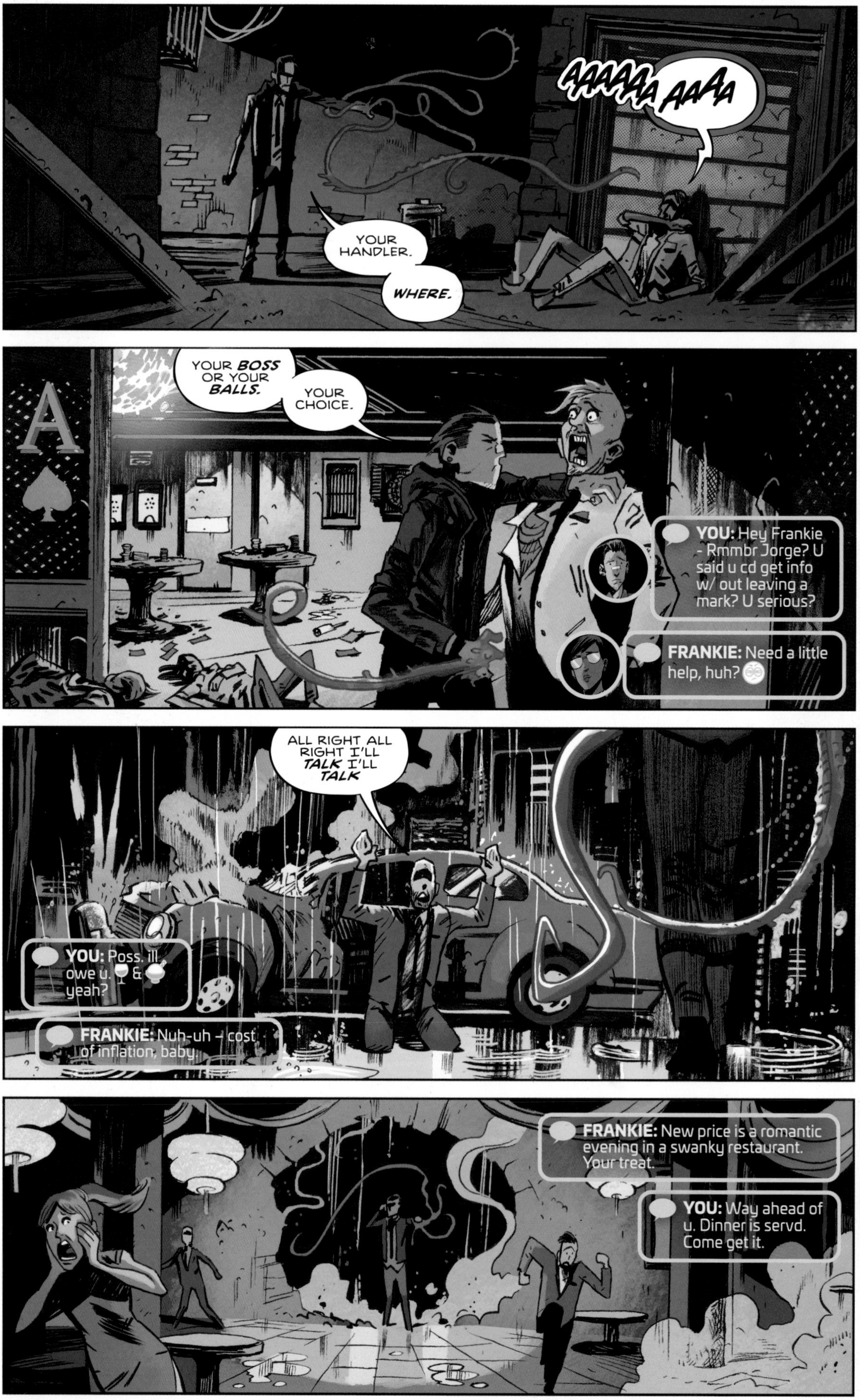
AAAAAA AAAA
YOUR HANDLER.
WHERE.
YOUR BOSS OR YOUR BALLS.
YOUR CHOICE.
YOU: Hey Frankie - Rmmbr Jorge? U said u cd get info w/ out leaving a mark? U serious?
FRANKIE: Need a little help, huh?
ALL RIGHT ALL RIGHT I'LL TALK I'LL TALK
YOU: Poss. ill owe u. & yeah?
FRANKIE: Nuh-uh – cost of inflation, baby.
FRANKIE: New price is a romantic evening in a swanky restaurant. Your treat.
YOU: Way ahead of u. Dinner is servd. Come get it.

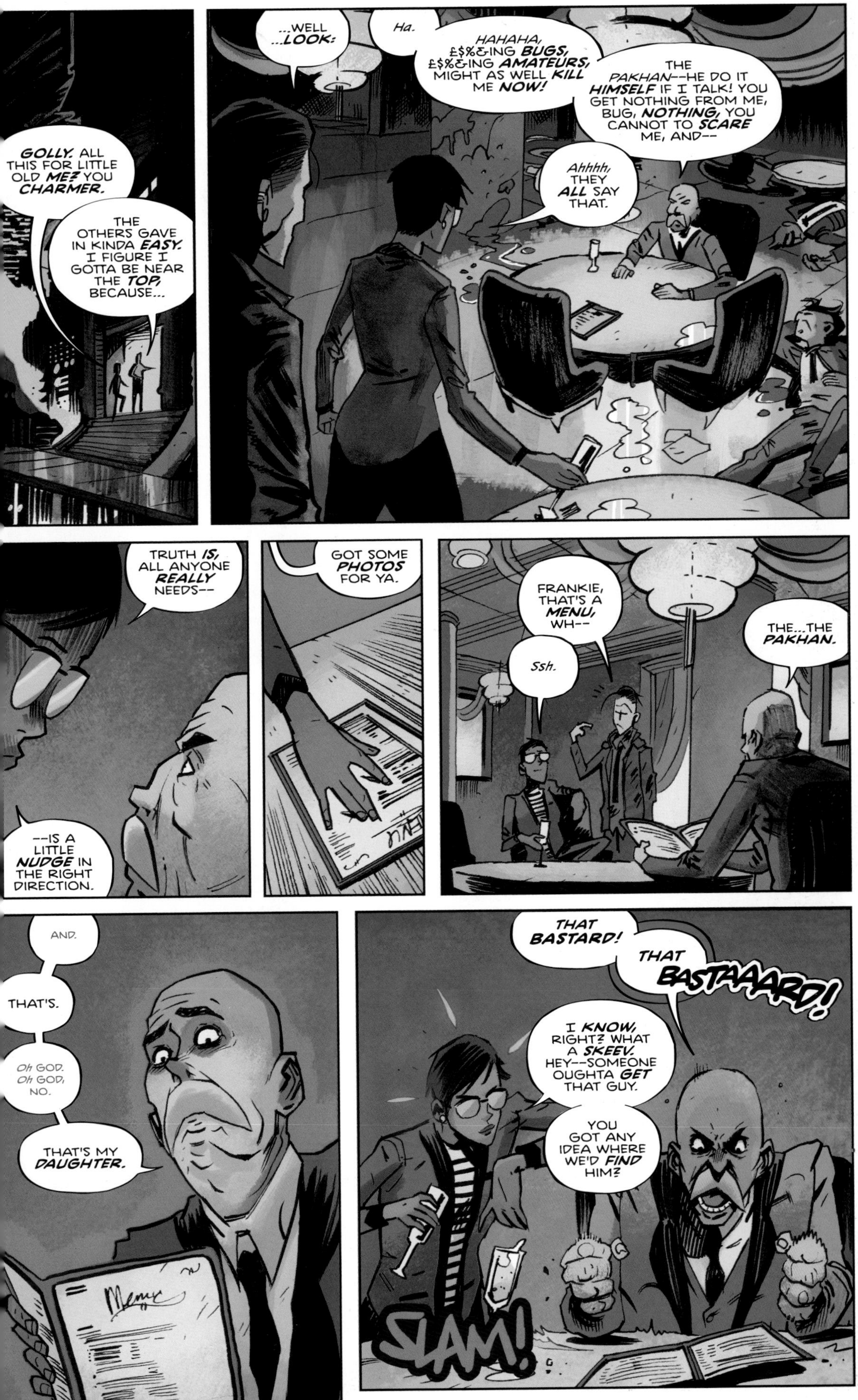
GOLLY. ALL THIS FOR LITTLE OLD ME? YOU CHARMER.
THE OTHERS GAVE IN KINDA EASY. I FIGURE I GOTTA BE NEAR THE TOP, BECAUSE...
...WELL ...LOOK:
Ha.
HAHAHA, £$%&ING BUGS, £$%&ING AMATEURS, MIGHT AS WELL KILL ME NOW!
THE PAKHAN--HE DO IT HIMSELF IF I TALK! YOU GET NOTHING FROM ME, BUG, NOTHING, YOU CANNOT TO SCARE ME, AND--
Ahhhh, THEY ALL SAY THAT.
TRUTH IS, ALL ANYONE REALLY NEEDS--
--IS A LITTLE NUDGE IN THE RIGHT DIRECTION.
GOT SOME PHOTOS FOR YA.
FRANKIE, THAT'S A MENU, WH--
Ssh.
THE...THE PAKHAN.
AND.
THAT'S.
Oh GOD. Oh GOD, NO.
THAT'S MY DAUGHTER.
THAT BASTARD!
THAT BASTAAARD!
I KNOW, RIGHT? WHAT A SKEEV. HEY--SOMEONE OUGHTA GET THAT GUY.
YOU GOT ANY IDEA WHERE WE'D FIND HIM?
SLAM!

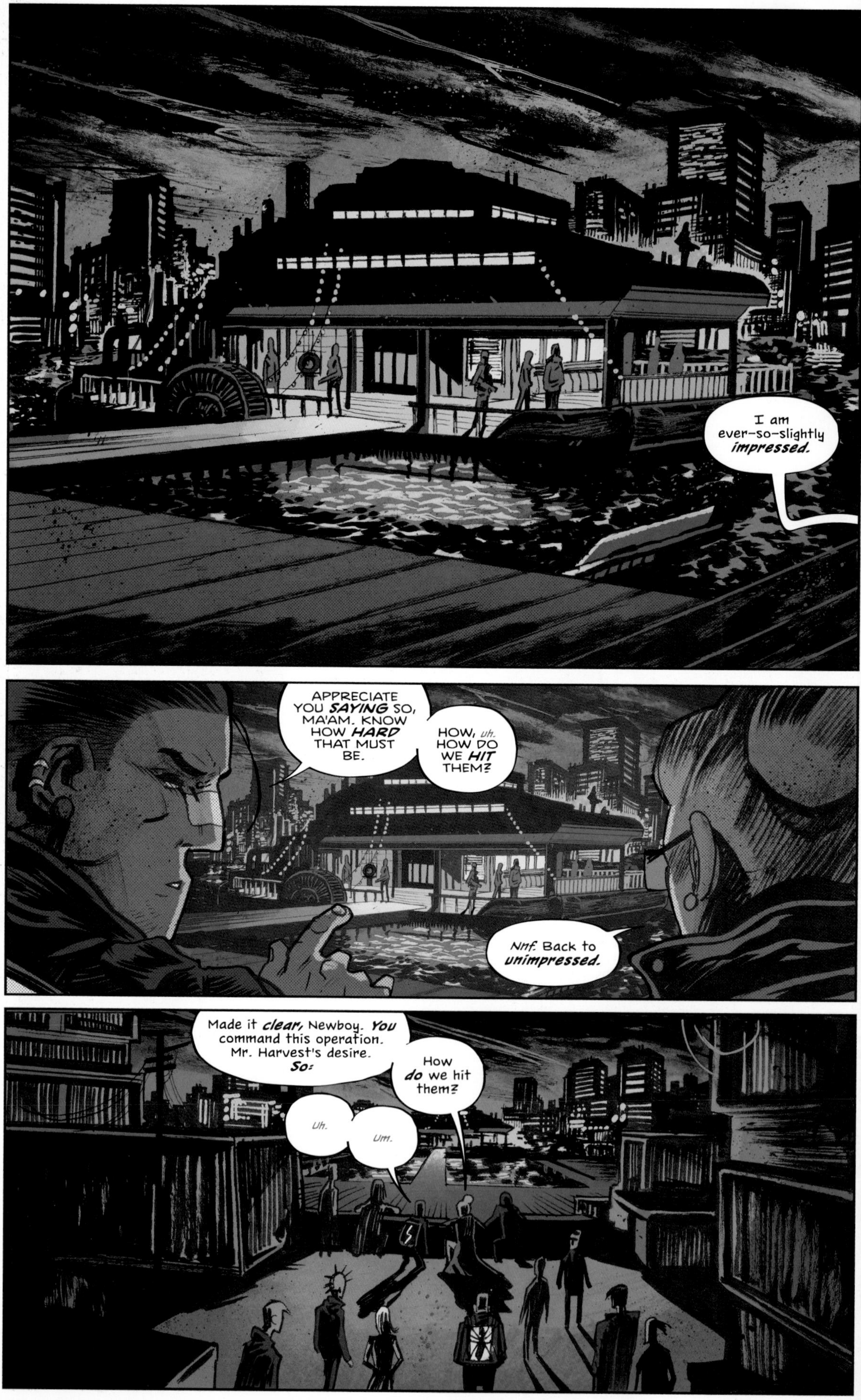
I am ever-so-slightly impressed.
APPRECIATE YOU SAYING SO, MA'AM. KNOW HOW HARD THAT MUST BE.
HOW, uh. HOW DO WE HIT THEM?
Nnf. Back to unimpressed.
Made it clear, Newboy. You command this operation. Mr. Harvest's desire. So:
How do we hit them?
Uh.
Um.

"WELL, I GUESS...

"SHOCK-AND-AWE, RIGHT? I'LL HIT THE FRONT.

FOOM

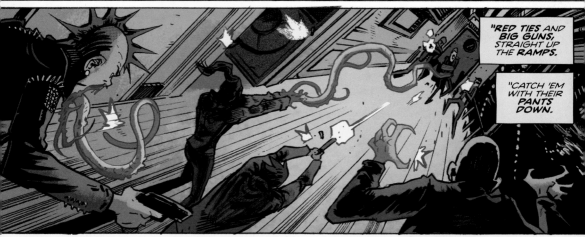

"RED TIES AND BIG GUNS, STRAIGHT UP THE RAMPS.

"CATCH 'EM WITH THEIR PANTS DOWN.

BOOM

"I FIGURE YOU GO IN THROUGH THE OFF-SIDE, MA'AM.

"FIND THE BOSS WHILE EVERYONE'S BUSY WITH THE LIGHTSHOW.

"I'LL SET UP OUT HERE. COMMAND AND OVERWATCH. KEEP A SECOND LINE TO MOP UP CRUMBS.

"I'LL PICK MY OWN TEAM FOR THAT."

Y KEEP ME HERE SHOULD BE FRONT ROW!!

MM. WELL.

ABOUT THAT.

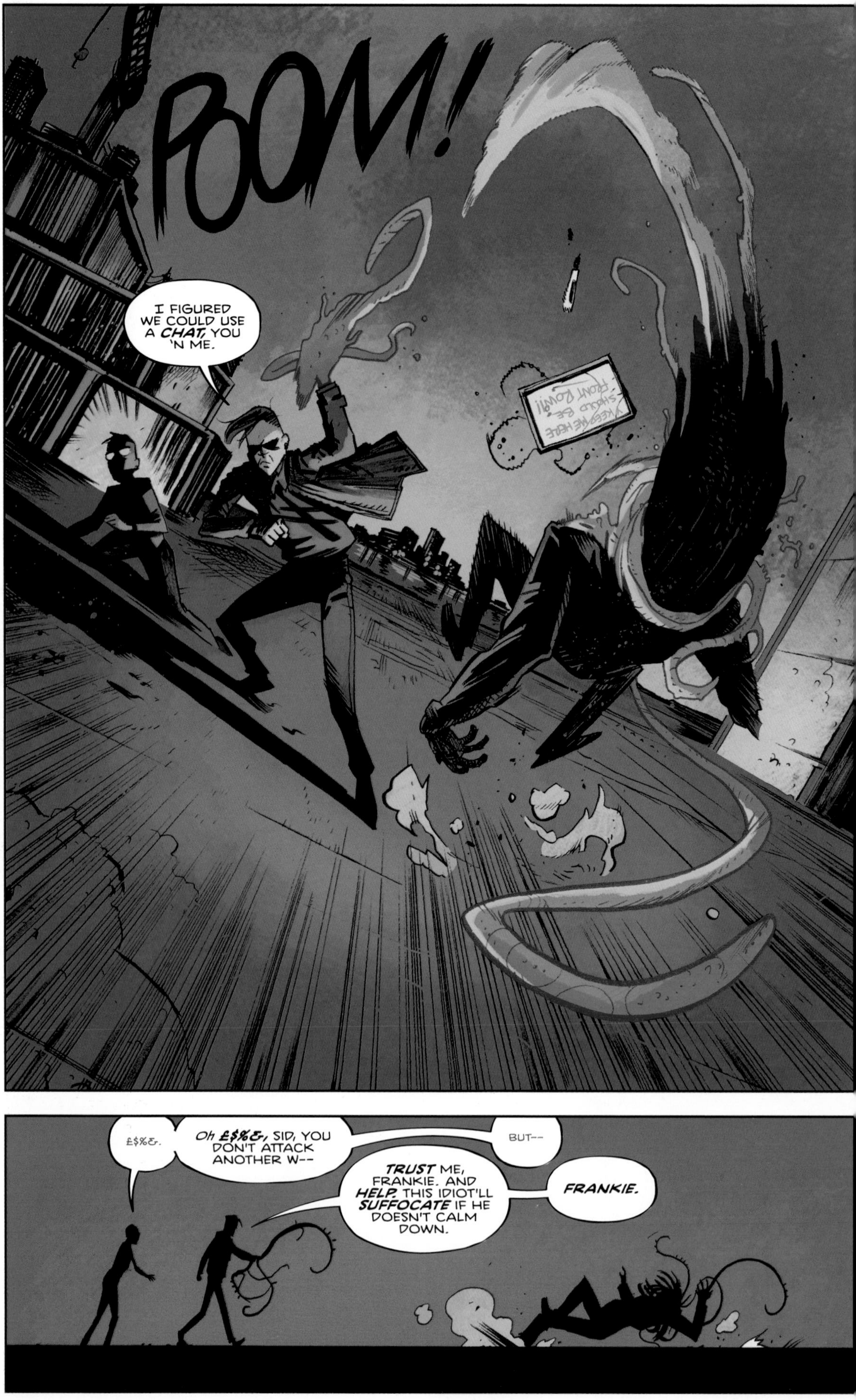
BOOM!
I FIGURED WE COULD USE A CHAT, YOU 'N ME.
£$%&.
Oh £$%&, SID, YOU DON'T ATTACK ANOTHER W--
BUT--
TRUST ME, FRANKIE. AND HELP. THIS IDIOT'LL SUFFOCATE IF HE DOESN'T CALM DOWN.
FRANKIE.

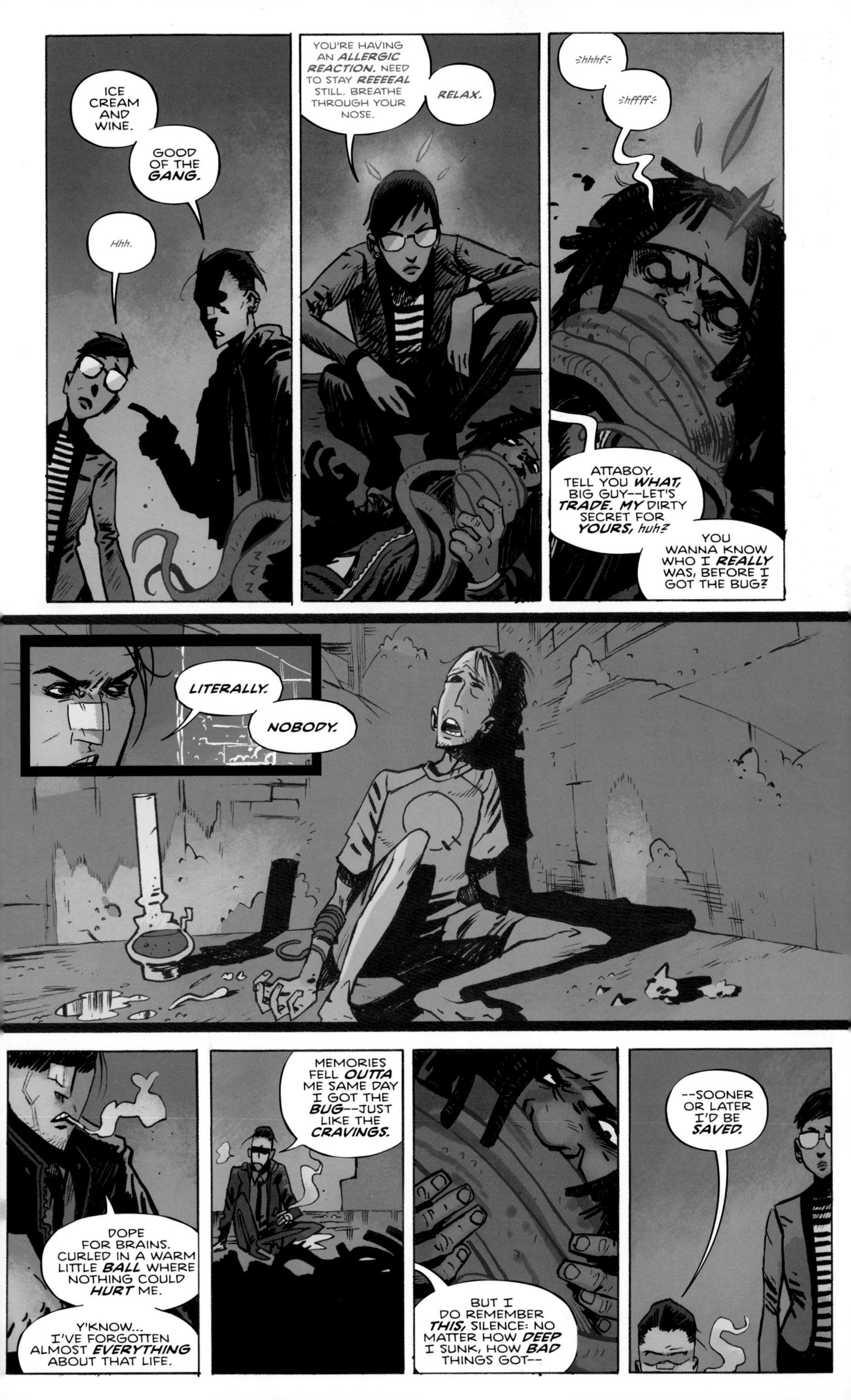
ICE CREAM AND WINE.
GOOD OF THE GANG.
Hhh.
YOU'RE HAVING AN ALLERGIC REACTION. NEED TO STAY REEEEAL STILL. BREATHE THROUGH YOUR NOSE.
RELAX.
hhhf
hffff
ATTABOY. TELL YOU WHAT, BIG GUY--LET'S TRADE. MY DIRTY SECRET FOR YOURS, huh?
YOU WANNA KNOW WHO I REALLY WAS, BEFORE I GOT THE BUG?
LITERALLY.
NOBODY.
DOPE FOR BRAINS. CURLED IN A WARM LITTLE BALL WHERE NOTHING COULD HURT ME.
Y'KNOW... I'VE FORGOTTEN ALMOST EVERYTHING ABOUT THAT LIFE.
MEMORIES FELL OUTTA ME SAME DAY I GOT THE BUG--JUST LIKE THE CRAVINGS.
BUT I DO REMEMBER THIS, SILENCE: NO MATTER HOW DEEP I SUNK, HOW BAD THINGS GOT--
--SOONER OR LATER I'D BE SAVED.

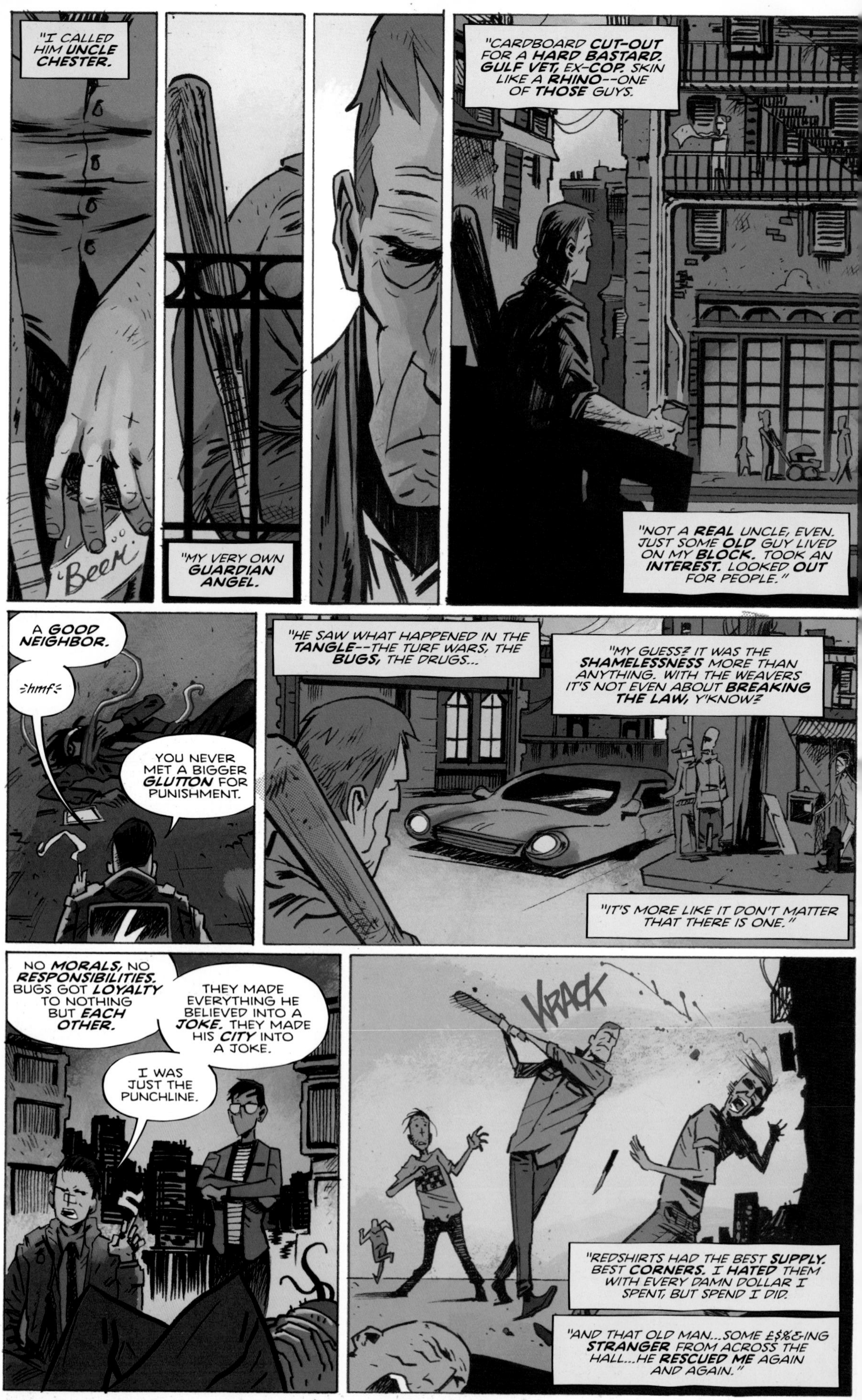
"I CALLED HIM UNCLE CHESTER.
Beer
"MY VERY OWN GUARDIAN ANGEL.
"CARDBOARD CUT-OUT FOR A HARD BASTARD. GULF VET, EX-COP. SKIN LIKE A RHINO--ONE OF THOSE GUYS.
"NOT A REAL UNCLE, EVEN. JUST SOME OLD GUY LIVED ON MY BLOCK. TOOK AN INTEREST. LOOKED OUT FOR PEOPLE."
A GOOD NEIGHBOR.
hmf
YOU NEVER MET A BIGGER GLUTTON FOR PUNISHMENT.
"HE SAW WHAT HAPPENED IN THE TANGLE--THE TURF WARS, THE BUGS, THE DRUGS...
"MY GUESS? IT WAS THE SHAMELESSNESS MORE THAN ANYTHING. WITH THE WEAVERS IT'S NOT EVEN ABOUT BREAKING THE LAW, Y'KNOW?
"IT'S MORE LIKE IT DON'T MATTER THAT THERE IS ONE."
NO MORALS, NO RESPONSIBILITIES. BUGS GOT LOYALTY TO NOTHING BUT EACH OTHER.
THEY MADE EVERYTHING HE BELIEVED INTO A JOKE. THEY MADE HIS CITY INTO A JOKE.
I WAS JUST THE PUNCHLINE.
KRACK
"REDSHIRTS HAD THE BEST SUPPLY. BEST CORNERS. I HATED THEM WITH EVERY DAMN DOLLAR I SPENT, BUT SPEND I DID.
"AND THAT OLD MAN...SOME £$%&-ING STRANGER FROM ACROSS THE HALL...HE RESCUED ME AGAIN AND AGAIN."

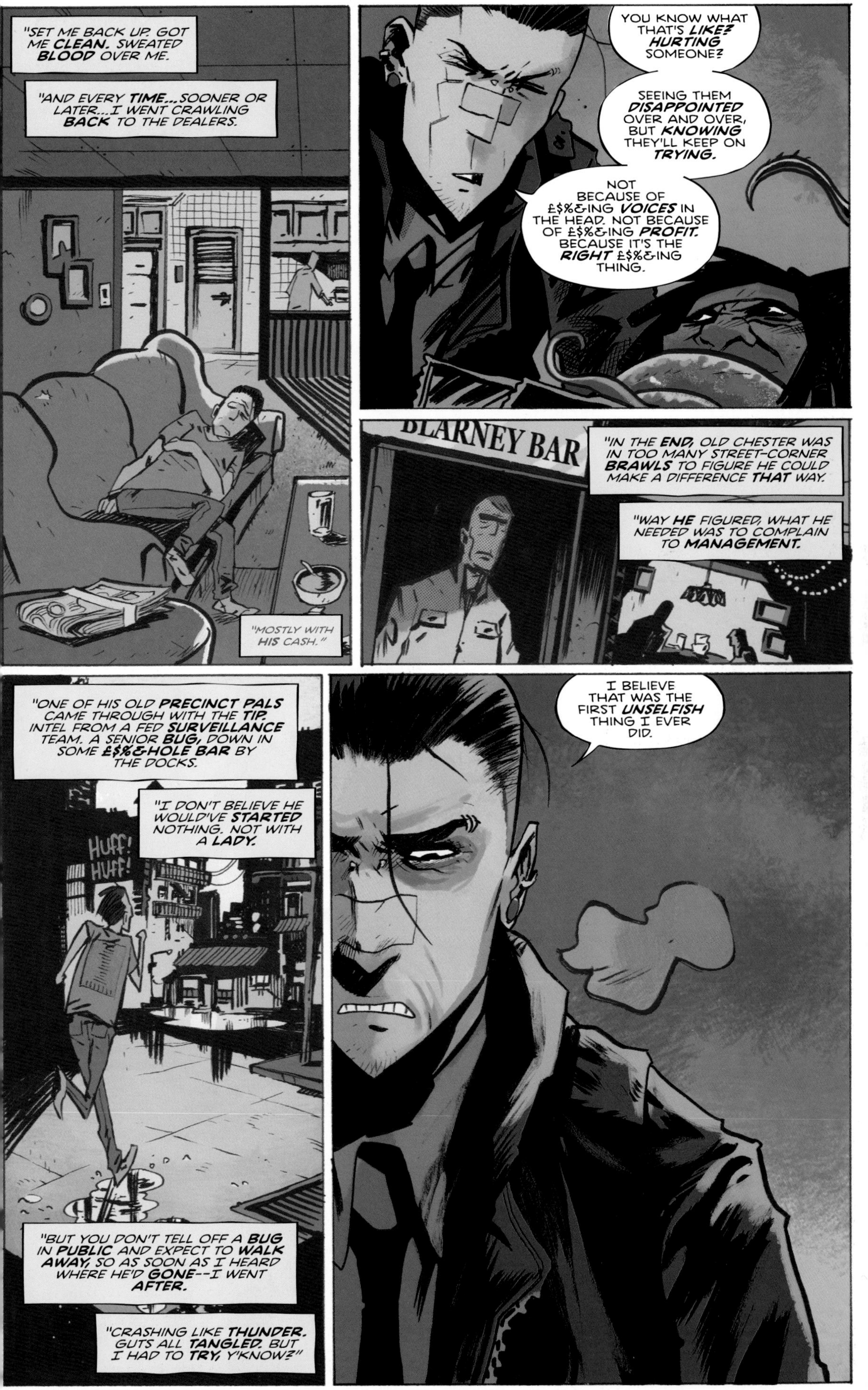
"SET ME BACK UP. GOT ME CLEAN. SWEATED BLOOD OVER ME.
"AND EVERY TIME... SOONER OR LATER... I WENT CRAWLING BACK TO THE DEALERS.
"MOSTLY WITH HIS CASH."
YOU KNOW WHAT THAT'S LIKE? HURTING SOMEONE?
SEEING THEM DISAPPOINTED OVER AND OVER, BUT KNOWING THEY'LL KEEP ON TRYING.
NOT BECAUSE OF £$%&ING VOICES IN THE HEAD. NOT BECAUSE OF £$%&ING PROFIT. BECAUSE IT'S THE RIGHT £$%&ING THING.
BLARNEY BAR
"IN THE END, OLD CHESTER WAS IN TOO MANY STREET-CORNER BRAWLS TO FIGURE HE COULD MAKE A DIFFERENCE THAT WAY.
"WAY HE FIGURED, WHAT HE NEEDED WAS TO COMPLAIN TO MANAGEMENT.
"ONE OF HIS OLD PRECINCT PALS CAME THROUGH WITH THE TIP. INTEL FROM A FED SURVEILLANCE TEAM. A SENIOR BUG, DOWN IN SOME £$%&HOLE BAR BY THE DOCKS.
"I DON'T BELIEVE HE WOULD'VE STARTED NOTHING. NOT WITH A LADY.
HUFF! HUFF!
"BUT YOU DON'T TELL OFF A BUG IN PUBLIC AND EXPECT TO WALK AWAY, SO AS SOON AS I HEARD WHERE HE'D GONE--I WENT AFTER.
"CRASHING LIKE THUNDER. GUTS ALL TANGLED. BUT I HAD TO TRY, Y'KNOW?"
I BELIEVE THAT WAS THE FIRST UNSELFISH THING I EVER DID.

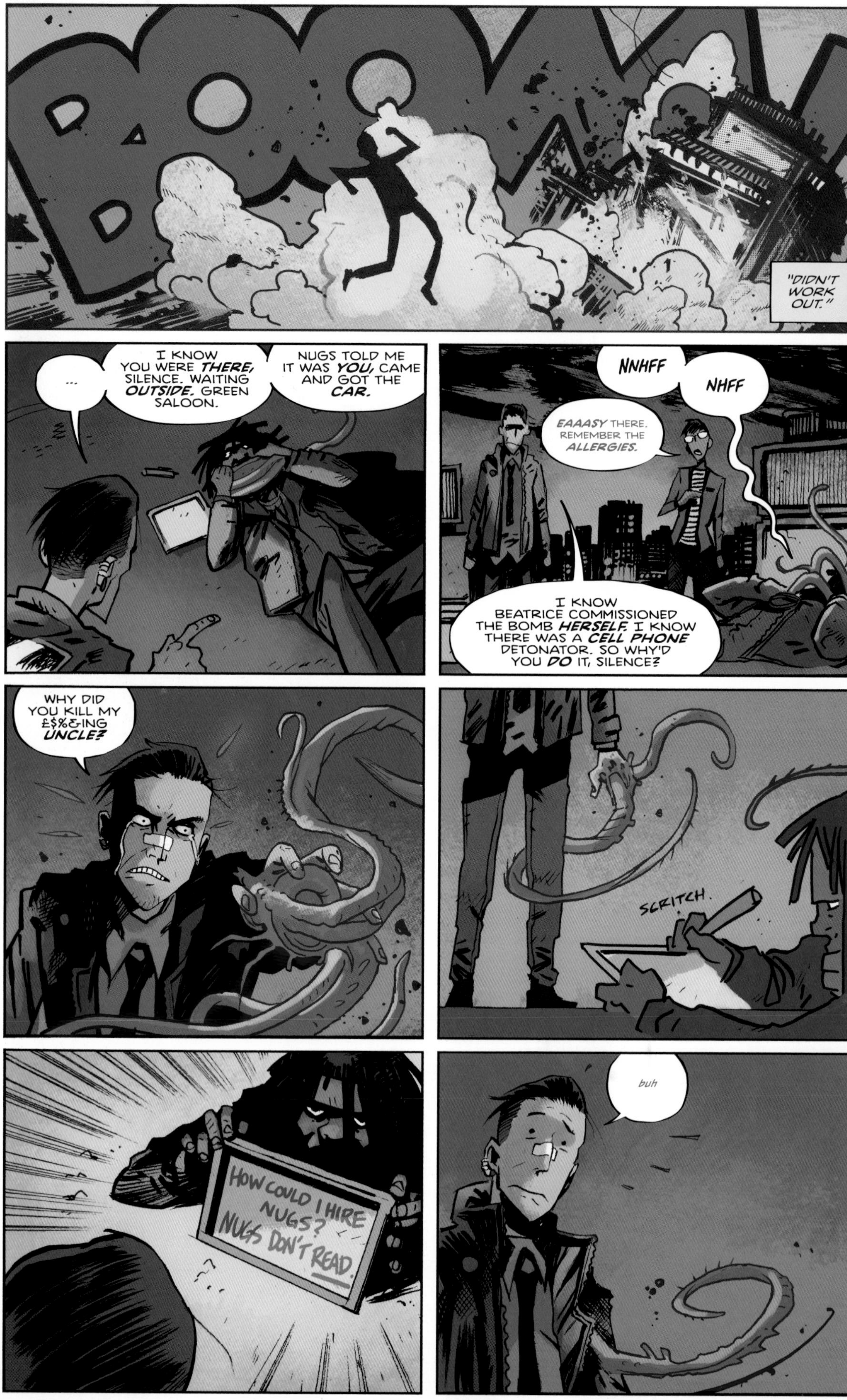
BOOOM!
"DIDN'T WORK OUT."
...
I KNOW YOU WERE THERE, SILENCE. WAITING OUTSIDE. GREEN SALOON.
NUGS TOLD ME IT WAS YOU, CAME AND GOT THE CAR.
NNHFF
NHFF
EAAASY THERE. REMEMBER THE ALLERGIES.
I KNOW BEATRICE COMMISSIONED THE BOMB HERSELF. I KNOW THERE WAS A CELL PHONE DETONATOR. SO WHY'D YOU DO IT, SILENCE?
WHY DID YOU KILL MY £$%&ING UNCLE?
SCRITCH.
HOW COULD I HIRE NUGS? NUGS DON'T READ.
buh

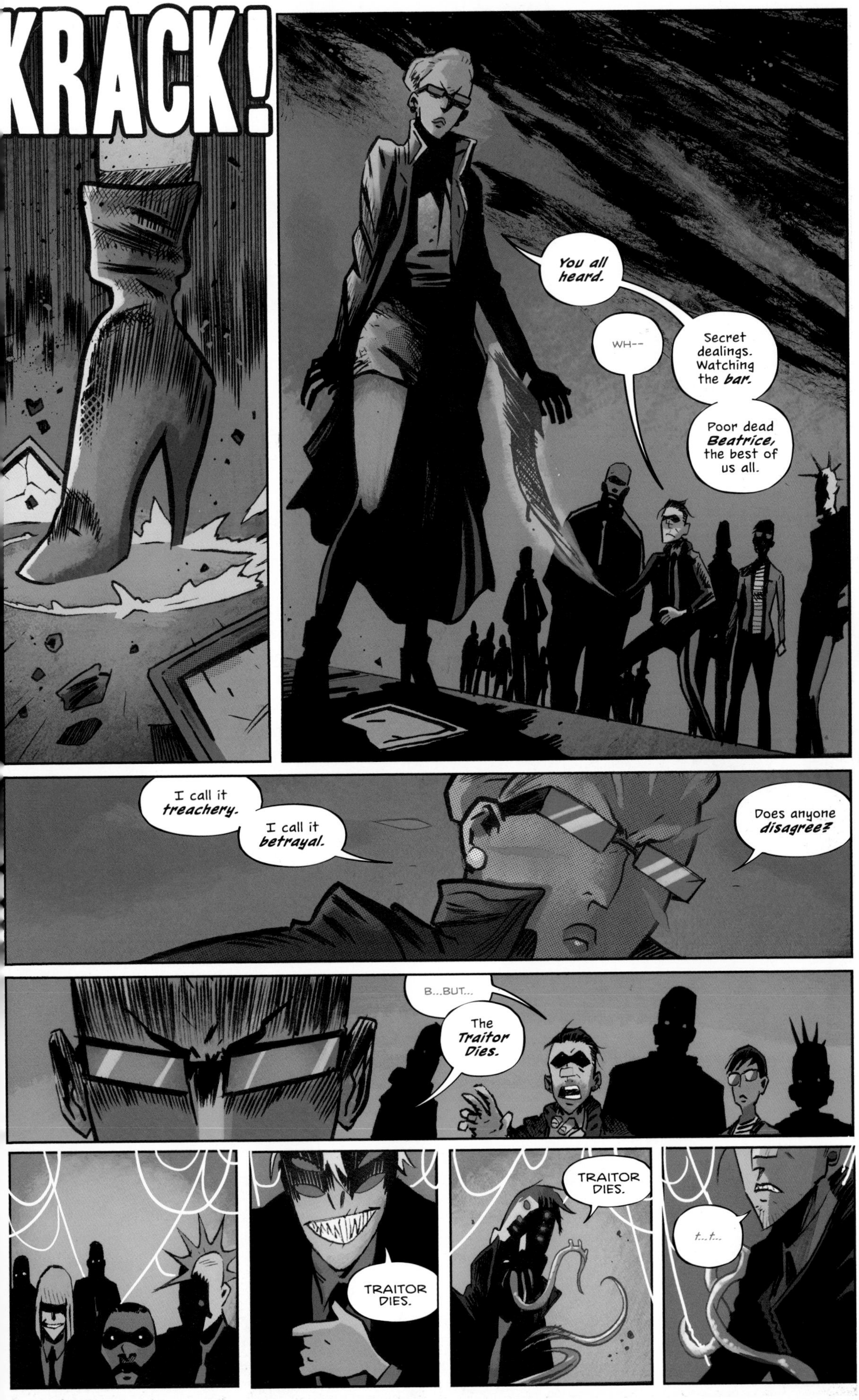
KRACK!
You all heard.
WH--
Secret dealings. Watching the bar.
Poor dead Beatrice, the best of us all.
I call it treachery.
I call it betrayal.
Does anyone disagree?
B...BUT...
The Traitor Dies.
TRAITOR DIES.
TRAITOR DIES.
t...t...

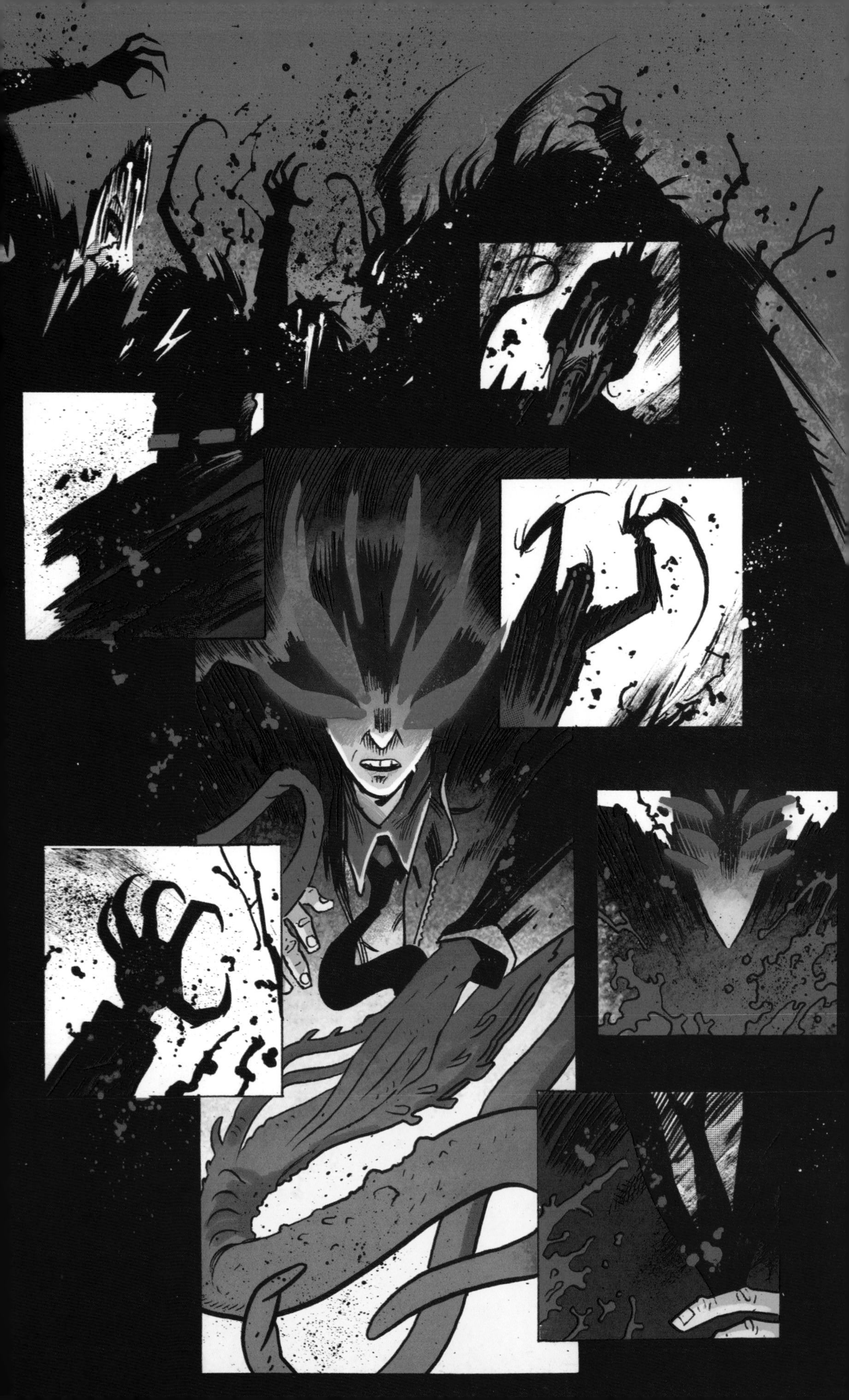

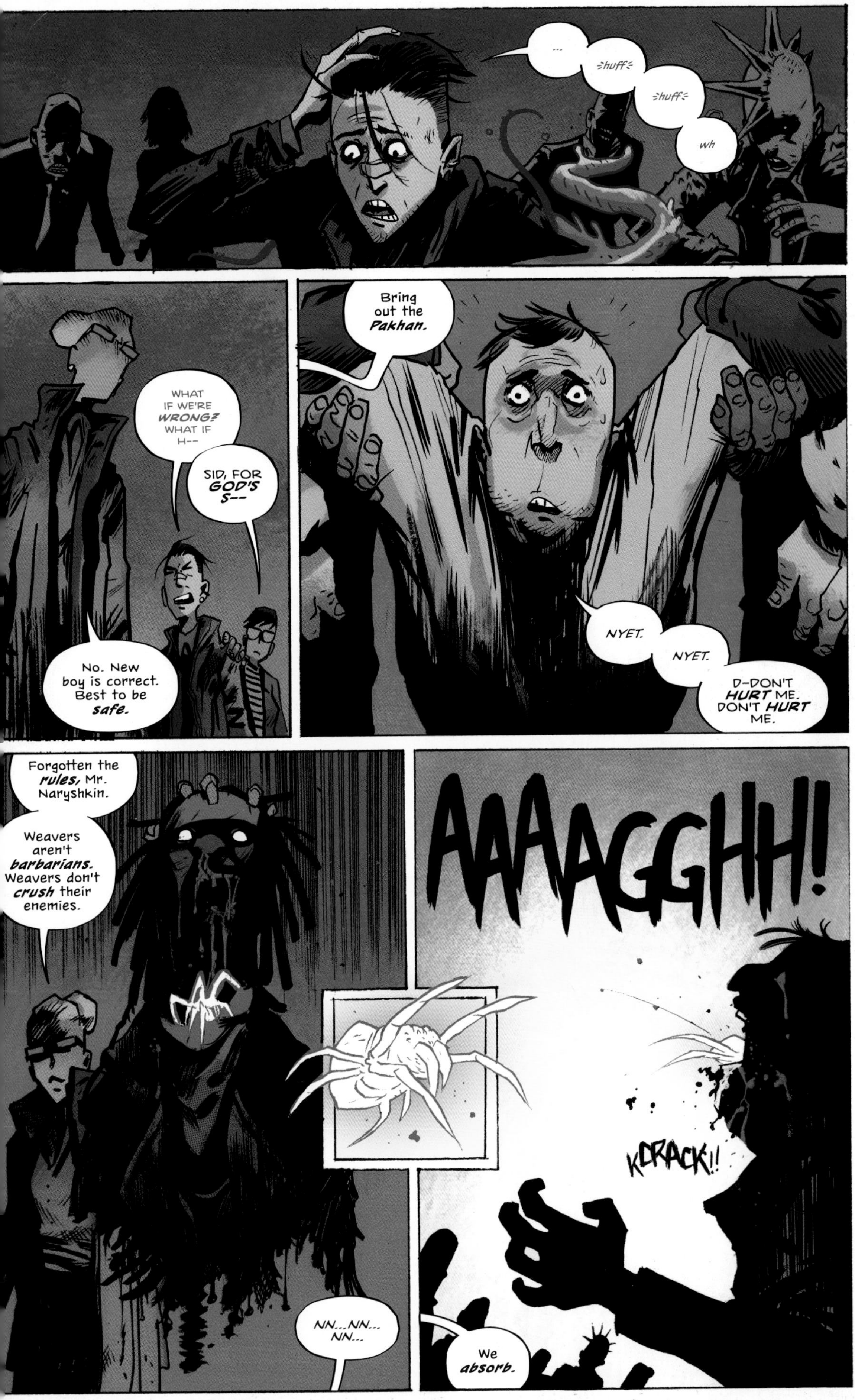
...
≈huff≈
≈huff≈
wh
WHAT IF WE'RE WRONG? WHAT IF H--
SID, FOR GOD'S S--
No. New boy is correct. Best to be safe.
Bring out the Pakhan.
NYET.
NYET.
D-DON'T HURT ME. DON'T HURT ME.
Forgotten the rules, Mr. Naryshkin.
Weavers aren't barbarians. Weavers don't crush their enemies.
NN...NN... NN...
AAAAGGHH!
KRRACK!!
We absorb.

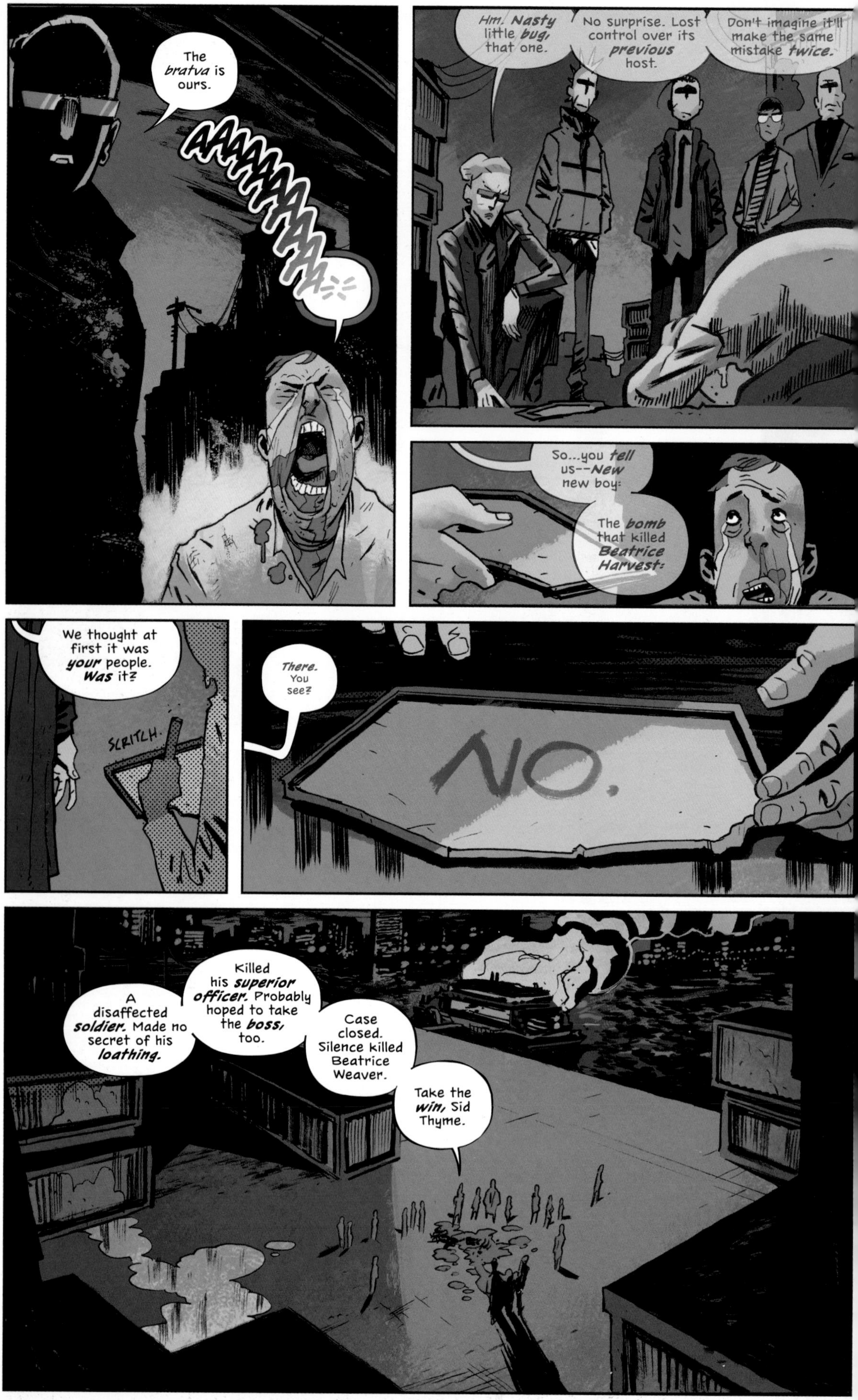
The bratva is ours.
AAAAAAAAAAAAA
Hm. Nasty little bug, that one.
No surprise. Lost control over its previous host.
Don't imagine it'll make the same mistake twice.
So...you tell us--New new boy:
The bomb that killed Beatrice Harvest:
We thought at first it was your people. Was it?
SCRITCH.
There. You see?
NO.
A disaffected soldier. Made no secret of his loathing.
Killed his superior officer. Probably hoped to take the boss, too.
Case closed. Silence killed Beatrice Weaver.
Take the win, Sid Thyme.

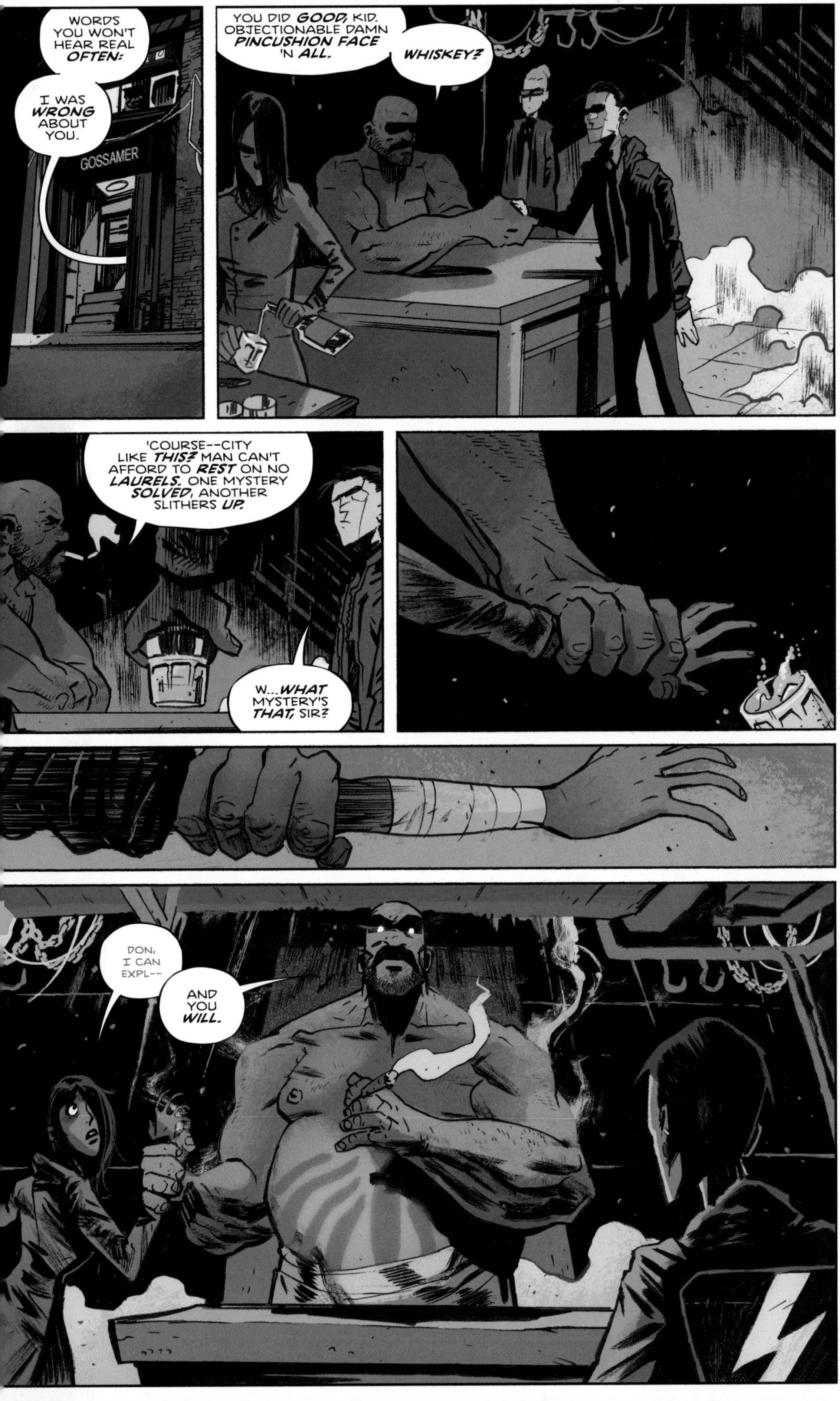
WORDS YOU WON'T HEAR REAL OFTEN:
I WAS WRONG ABOUT YOU.
GOSSAMER
YOU DID GOOD, KID. OBJECTIONABLE DAMN PINCUSHION FACE 'N ALL.
WHISKEY?
'COURSE--CITY LIKE THIS? MAN CAN'T AFFORD TO REST ON NO LAURELS. ONE MYSTERY SOLVED, ANOTHER SLITHERS UP.
W...WHAT MYSTERY'S THAT, SIR?
DON, I CAN EXPL--
AND YOU WILL.

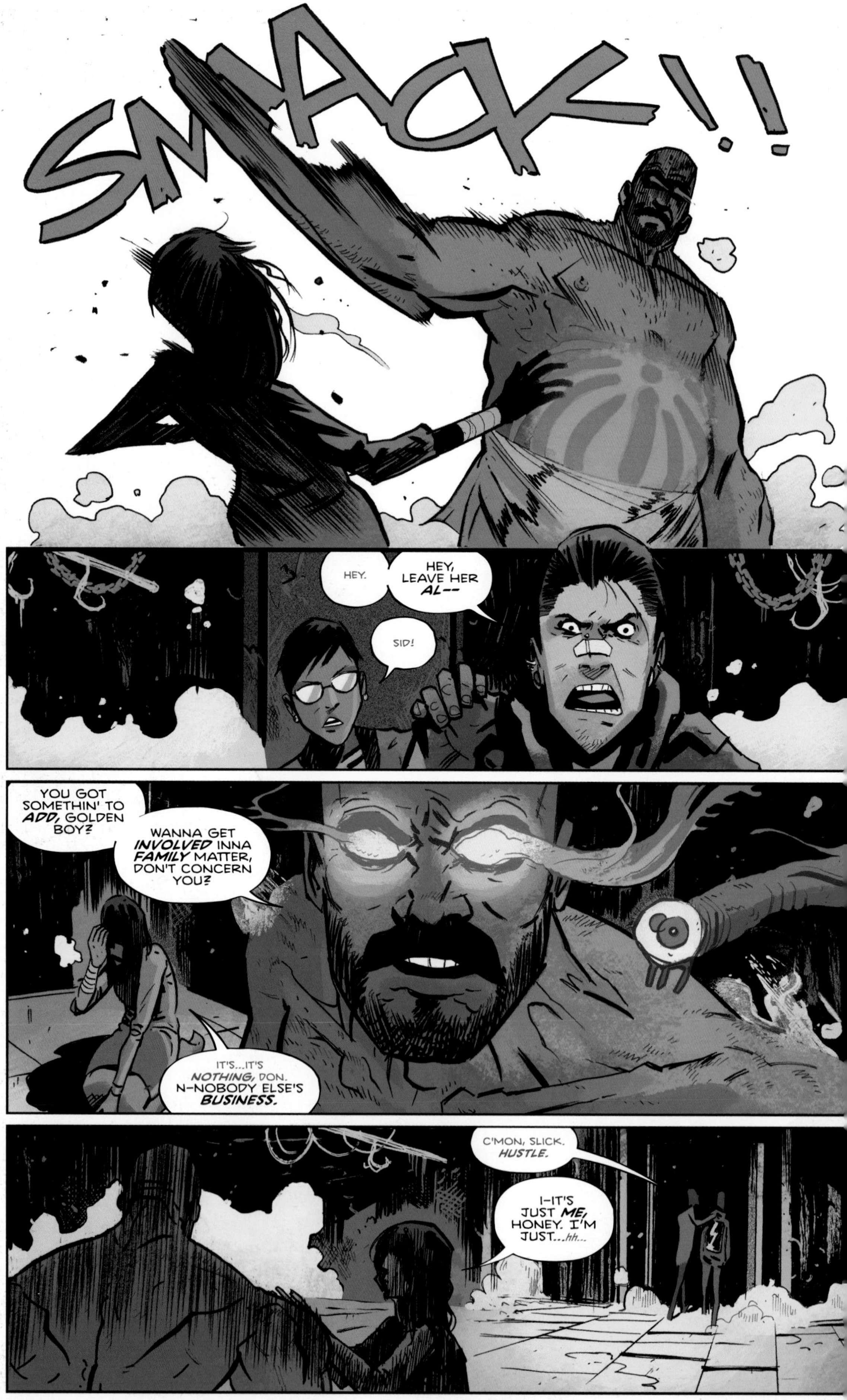
SMACK!!
HEY.
HEY, LEAVE HER AL--
SID!
YOU GOT SOMETHIN' TO ADD, GOLDEN BOY?
WANNA GET INVOLVED INNA FAMILY MATTER, DON'T CONCERN YOU?
IT'S...IT'S NOTHING, DON. N-NOBODY ELSE'S BUSINESS.
C'MON, SLICK. HUSTLE.
I-IT'S JUST ME, HONEY. I'M JUST...hh...

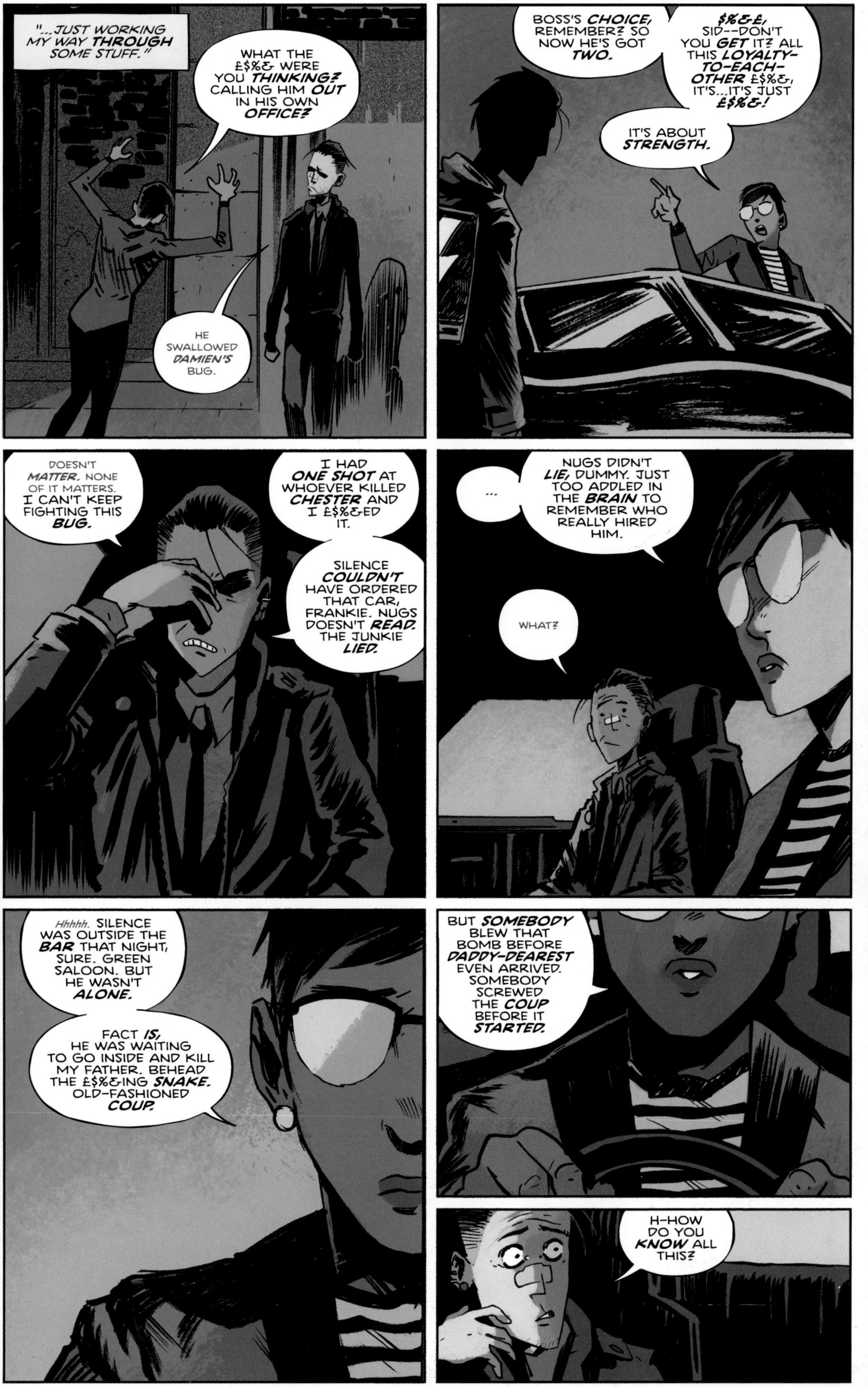
"...JUST WORKING MY WAY THROUGH SOME STUFF."
WHAT THE £$%& WERE YOU THINKING? CALLING HIM OUT IN HIS OWN OFFICE?
HE SWALLOWED DAMIEN'S BUG.
BOSS'S CHOICE, REMEMBER? SO NOW HE'S GOT TWO.
$%&£, SID--DON'T YOU GET IT? ALL THIS LOYALTY-TO-EACH-OTHER £$%&, IT'S...IT'S JUST £$%&!
IT'S ABOUT STRENGTH.
DOESN'T MATTER. NONE OF IT MATTERS. I CAN'T KEEP FIGHTING THIS BUG.
I HAD ONE SHOT AT WHOEVER KILLED CHESTER AND I £$%&ED IT.
SILENCE COULDN'T HAVE ORDERED THAT CAR, FRANKIE. NUGS DOESN'T READ. THE JUNKIE LIED.
...
NUGS DIDN'T LIE, DUMMY. JUST TOO ADDLED IN THE BRAIN TO REMEMBER WHO REALLY HIRED HIM.
WHAT?
Hhhhh. SILENCE WAS OUTSIDE THE BAR THAT NIGHT, SURE. GREEN SALOON. BUT HE WASN'T ALONE.
FACT IS, HE WAS WAITING TO GO INSIDE AND KILL MY FATHER. BEHEAD THE £$%&ING SNAKE. OLD-FASHIONED COUP.
BUT SOMEBODY BLEW THAT BOMB BEFORE DADDY-DEAREST EVEN ARRIVED. SOMEBODY SCREWED THE COUP BEFORE IT STARTED.
H-HOW DO YOU KNOW ALL THIS?

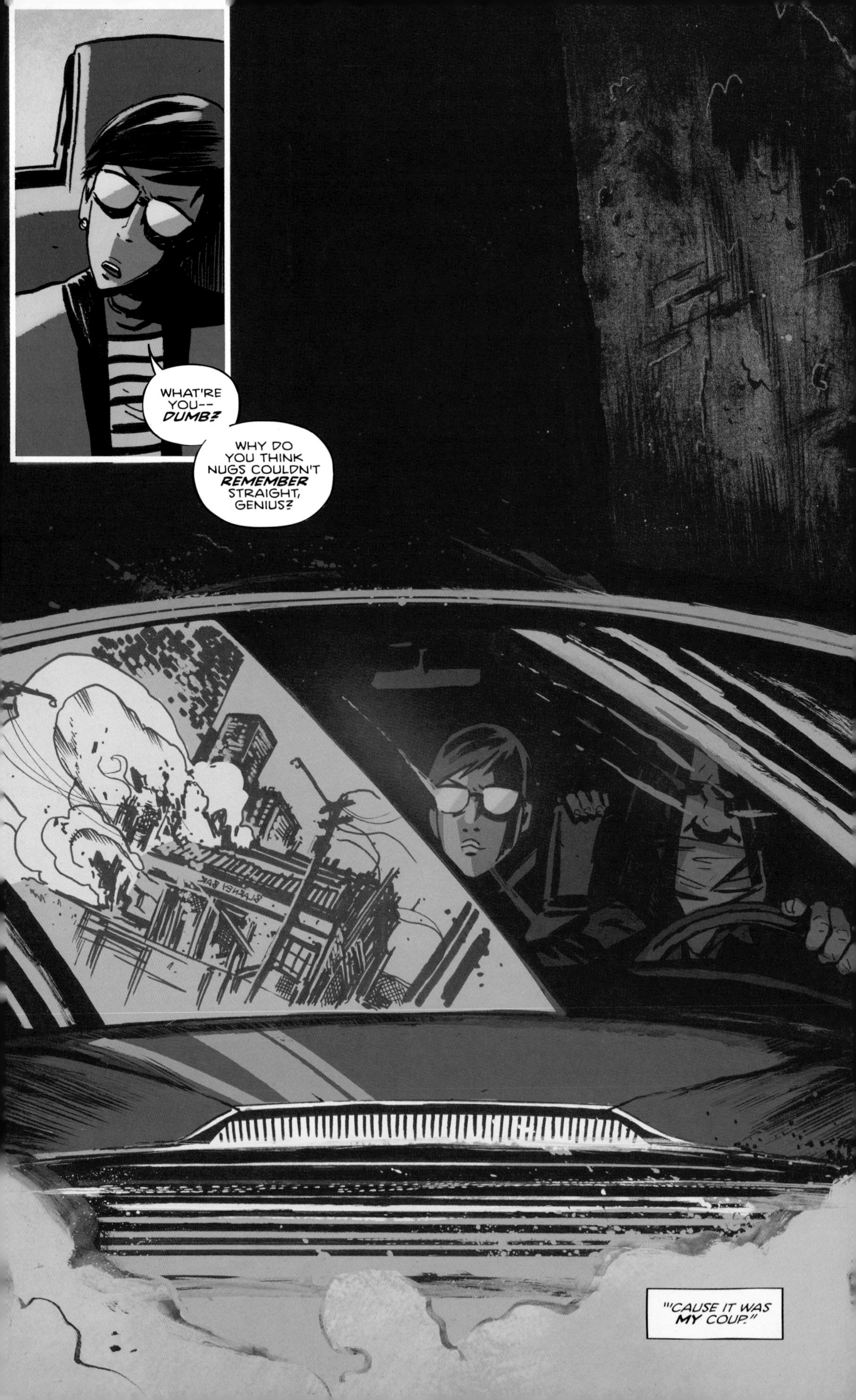
WHAT'RE YOU-- DUMB?
WHY DO YOU THINK NUGS COULDN'T REMEMBER STRAIGHT, GENIUS?
"'CAUSE IT WAS MY COUP."

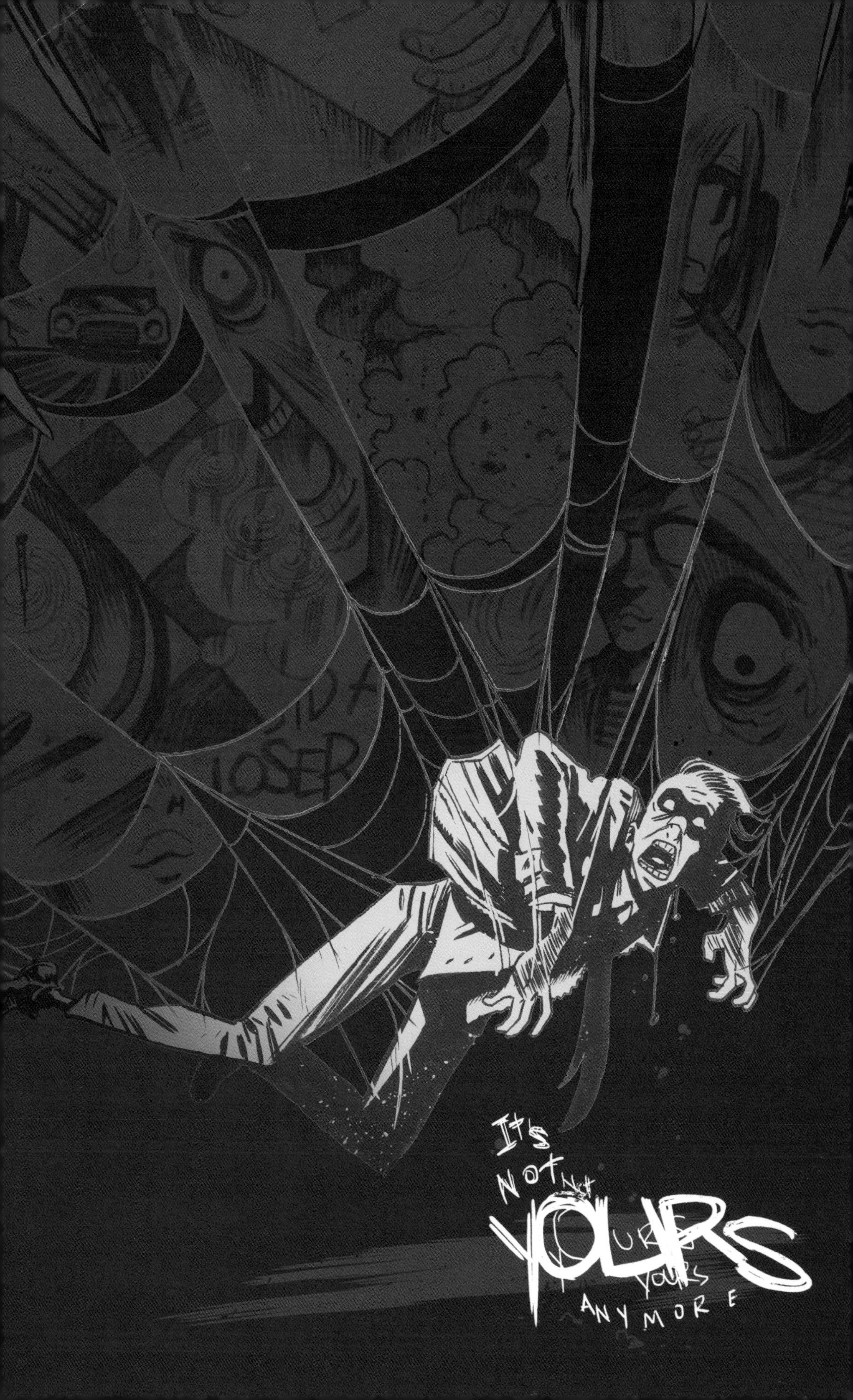
LOSER
IT'S NOT YOURS ANYMORE

CHAPTER SIX

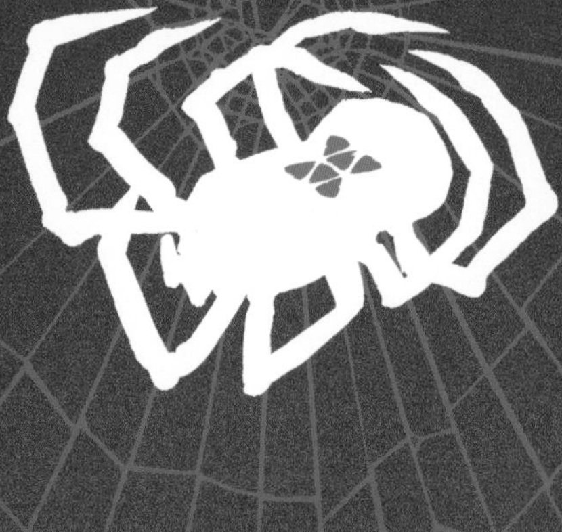

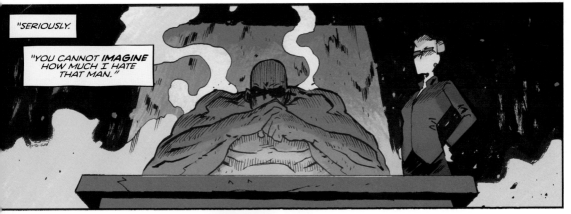

"SERIOUSLY.

"YOU CANNOT *IMAGINE* HOW MUCH I HATE THAT MAN."

Ohhh, NOT JUST THE *OBVIOUS* £$%&. WAY HE TREATED *MOM.* WAY HE TREATS *ME.*

HE'S JUST-- *AWFUL,* Y'KNOW? JUST AN *AWFUL* PERSON. HE'S NOT EVEN A GOOD *LEADER.*

SO.

I PUT TOGETHER A *PLAN.* REAL SLOW, REAL *CAREFUL.* RECRUITED *SILENCE,* SET A *TIME...*

WHAT ABOUT YOUR *SPIDER?* WHY DIDN'T IT *STOP* YOU?

"Heh. YOU'VE SEEN WHAT I *DO,* SLICK. I *NUDGE.*

"WORKS AS WELL ON *BUGS* AS *BASTARDS.*"

BESIDES--*GOOD OF THE GANG,* REMEMBER?

YOU LOOK AT IT RIGHT, GETTING *RID* OF MY PSYCHO *DAD'S* THE MOST *LOYAL* THING A WEAVER COULD DO.

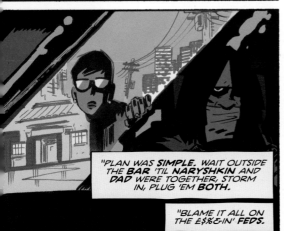

"PLAN WAS *SIMPLE.* WAIT OUTSIDE THE *BAR* 'TIL *NARYSHKIN* AND *DAD* WERE TOGETHER, STORM IN, PLUG 'EM *BOTH.*

"BLAME IT ALL ON THE £$%&-IN' *FEDS.*

"ONLY, *BEA* GOT THERE FIRST.

"LAST WE SAW SHE WAS HEADING *INSIDE,* YELLING ON THE *PHONE.*

"COUPLE MINUTES *LATER?"*

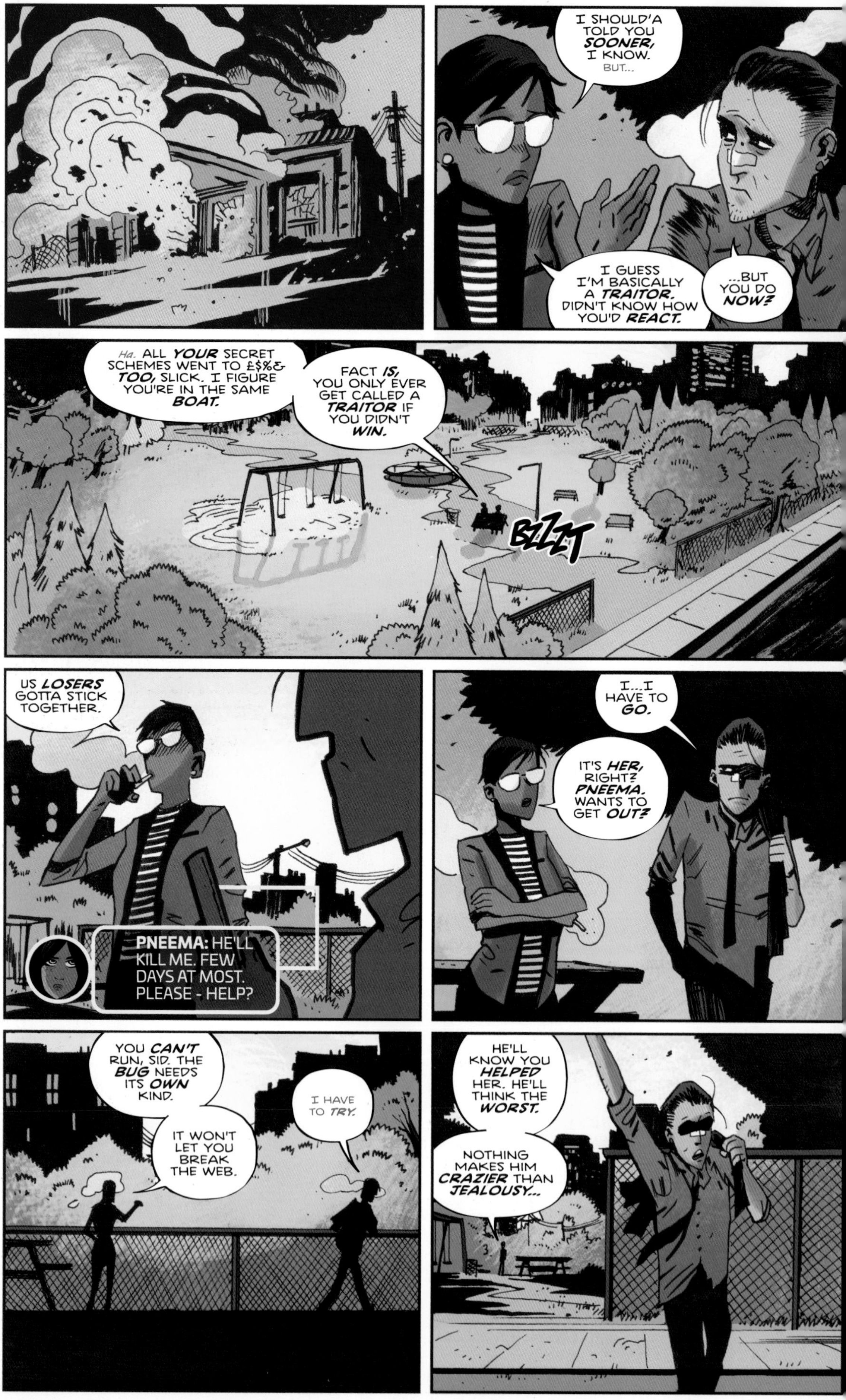
I SHOULD'A TOLD YOU SOONER, I KNOW. BUT...
I GUESS I'M BASICALLY A TRAITOR. DIDN'T KNOW HOW YOU'D REACT.
...BUT YOU DO NOW?
Ha. ALL YOUR SECRET SCHEMES WENT TO £$%& TOO, SLICK. I FIGURE YOU'RE IN THE SAME BOAT.
FACT IS, YOU ONLY EVER GET CALLED A TRAITOR IF YOU DIDN'T WIN.
BZZZT
US LOSERS GOTTA STICK TOGETHER.
PNEEMA: HE'LL KILL ME. FEW DAYS AT MOST. PLEASE - HELP?
I...I HAVE TO GO.
IT'S HER, RIGHT? PNEEMA. WANTS TO GET OUT?
YOU CAN'T RUN, SID. THE BUG NEEDS ITS OWN KIND.
IT WON'T LET YOU BREAK THE WEB.
I HAVE TO TRY.
HE'LL KNOW YOU HELPED HER. HE'LL THINK THE WORST.
NOTHING MAKES HIM CRAZIER THAN JEALOUSY...

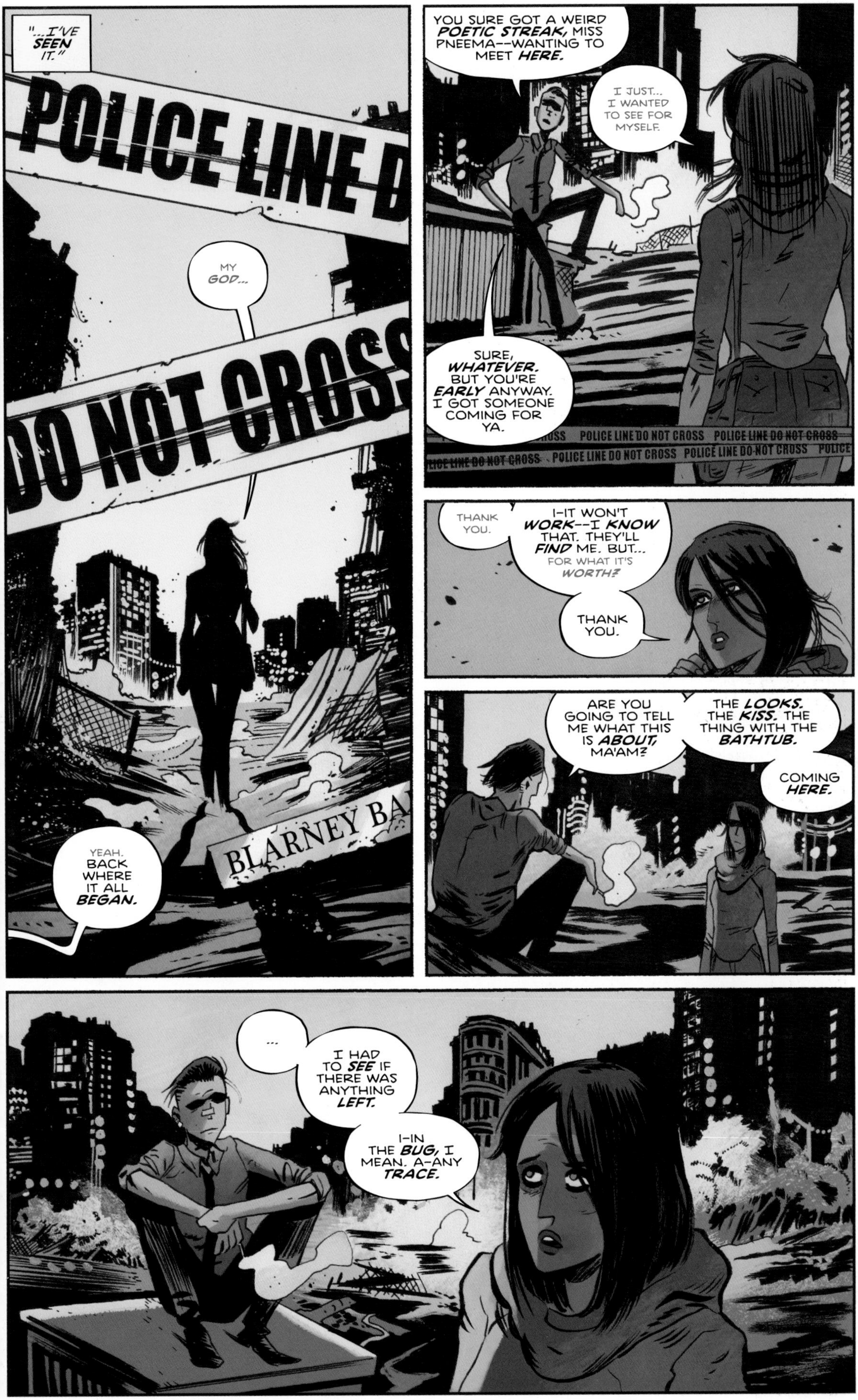
"...I'VE SEEN IT."
POLICE LINE D
MY GOD...
DO NOT CROSS
BLARNEY BA
YEAH. BACK WHERE IT ALL BEGAN.
YOU SURE GOT A WEIRD POETIC STREAK, MISS PNEEMA--WANTING TO MEET HERE.
I JUST... I WANTED TO SEE FOR MYSELF.
SURE, WHATEVER. BUT YOU'RE EARLY ANYWAY. I GOT SOMEONE COMING FOR YA.
POLICE LINE DO NOT CROSS
THANK YOU.
I-IT WON'T WORK--I KNOW THAT. THEY'LL FIND ME. BUT... FOR WHAT IT'S WORTH?
THANK YOU.
ARE YOU GOING TO TELL ME WHAT THIS IS ABOUT, MA'AM?
THE LOOKS. THE KISS. THE THING WITH THE BATHTUB.
COMING HERE.
...
I HAD TO SEE IF THERE WAS ANYTHING LEFT.
I-IN THE BUG, I MEAN. A-ANY TRACE.

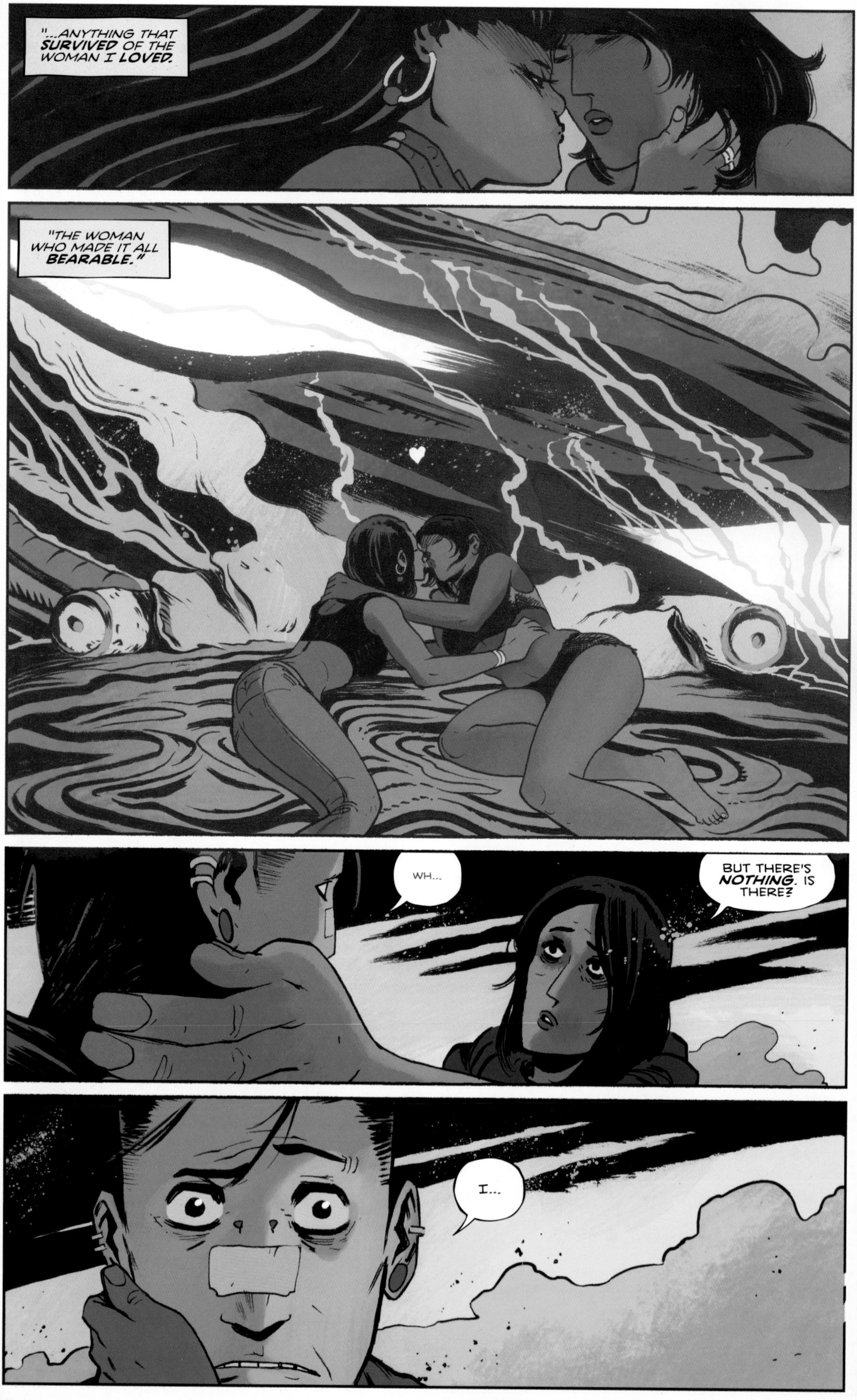
"...ANYTHING THAT SURVIVED OF THE WOMAN I LOVED.
"THE WOMAN WHO MADE IT ALL BEARABLE."
WH...
BUT THERE'S NOTHING. IS THERE?
I...

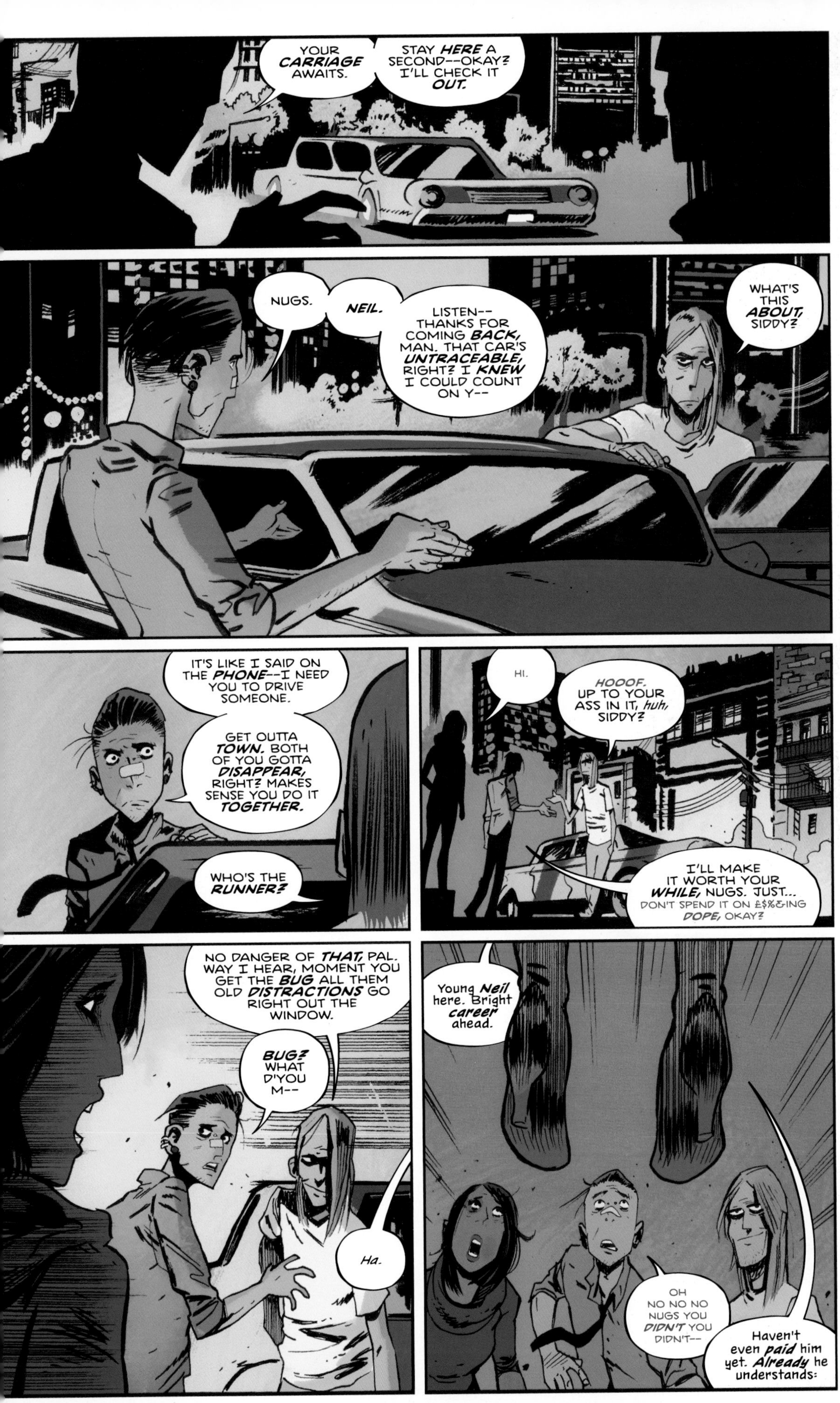

YOUR CARRIAGE AWAITS.
STAY HERE A SECOND--OKAY? I'LL CHECK IT OUT.
NUGS.
NEIL.
LISTEN-- THANKS FOR COMING BACK, MAN. THAT CAR'S UNTRACEABLE, RIGHT? I KNEW I COULD COUNT ON Y--
WHAT'S THIS ABOUT, SIDDY?
IT'S LIKE I SAID ON THE PHONE--I NEED YOU TO DRIVE SOMEONE.
GET OUTTA TOWN. BOTH OF YOU GOTTA DISAPPEAR, RIGHT? MAKES SENSE YOU DO IT TOGETHER.
WHO'S THE RUNNER?
HI.
HOOOF. UP TO YOUR ASS IN IT, huh, SIDDY?
I'LL MAKE IT WORTH YOUR WHILE, NUGS. JUST... DON'T SPEND IT ON £$%&ING DOPE, OKAY?
NO DANGER OF THAT, PAL. WAY I HEAR, MOMENT YOU GET THE BUG ALL THEM OLD DISTRACTIONS GO RIGHT OUT THE WINDOW.
BUG? WHAT D'YOU M--
Ha.
Young Neil here. Bright career ahead.
OH NO NO NO NUGS YOU DIDN'T YOU DIDN'T--
Haven't even paid him yet. Already he understands:

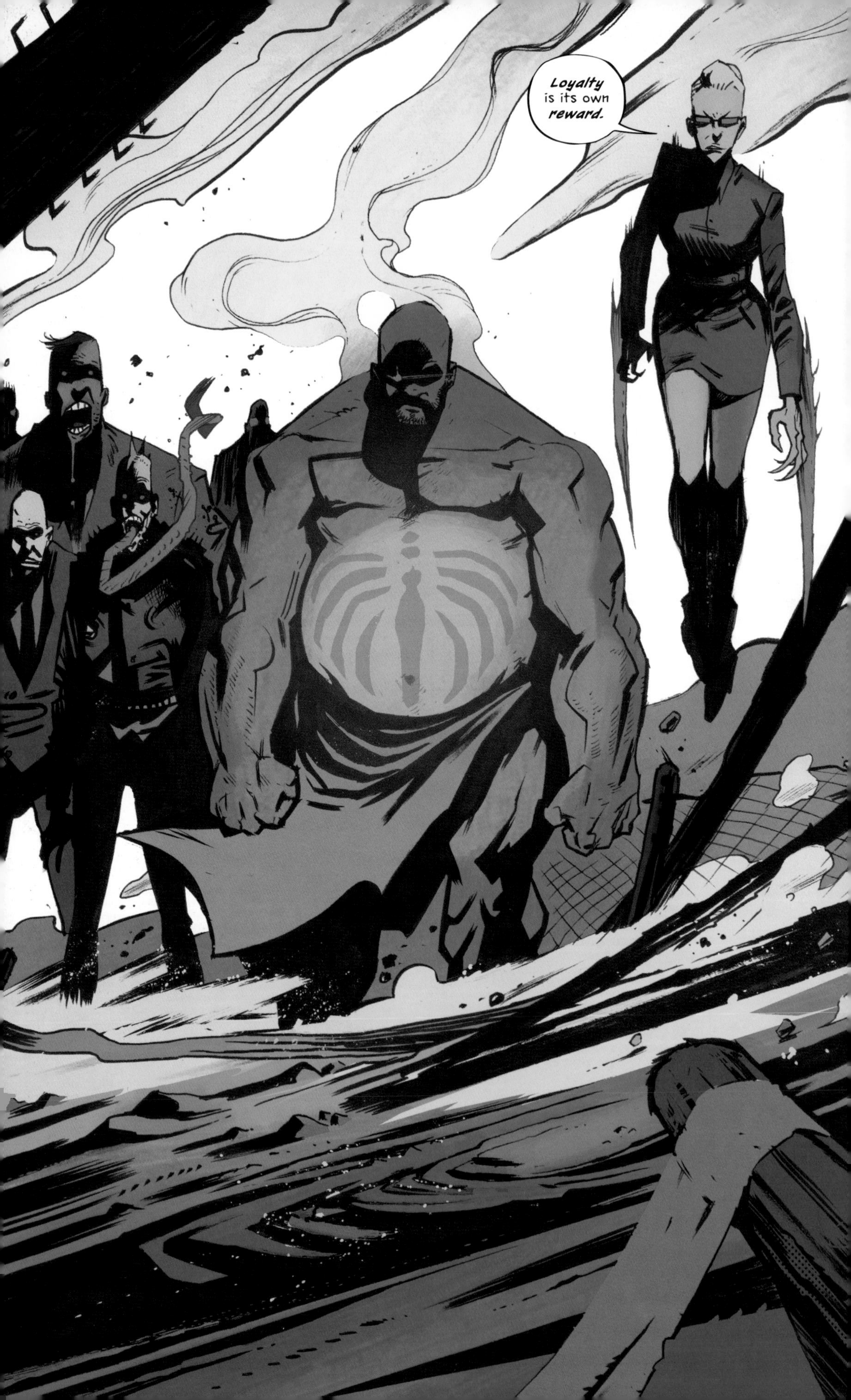
Loyalty is its own reward.

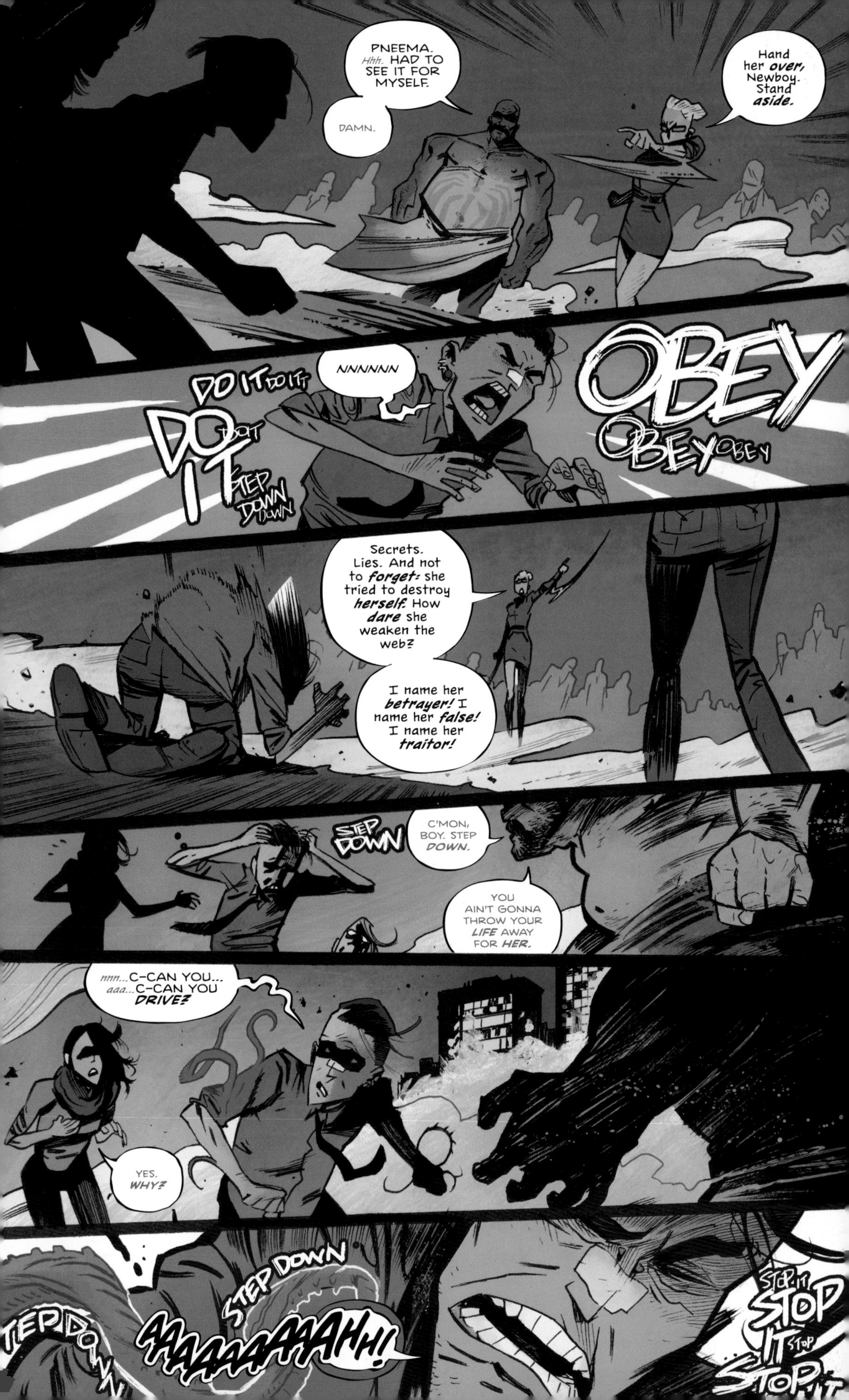

PNEEMA. Hhh. HAD TO SEE IT FOR MYSELF.
DAMN.
Hand her over, Newboy. Stand aside.
DO IT DO IT
DO IT DO IT
NNNNNN
OBEY
OBEY OBEY
STEP DOWN DOWN
Secrets. Lies. And not to forget: she tried to destroy herself. How dare she weaken the web?
I name her betrayer! I name her false! I name her traitor!
STEP DOWN
C'MON, BOY. STEP DOWN.
YOU AIN'T GONNA THROW YOUR LIFE AWAY FOR HER.
nnn... C-CAN YOU... aaa... C-CAN YOU DRIVE?
YES. WHY?
STEP DOWN
AAAAAAAAAAHH!
STEP DOWN
STOP IT STOP
STOP IT

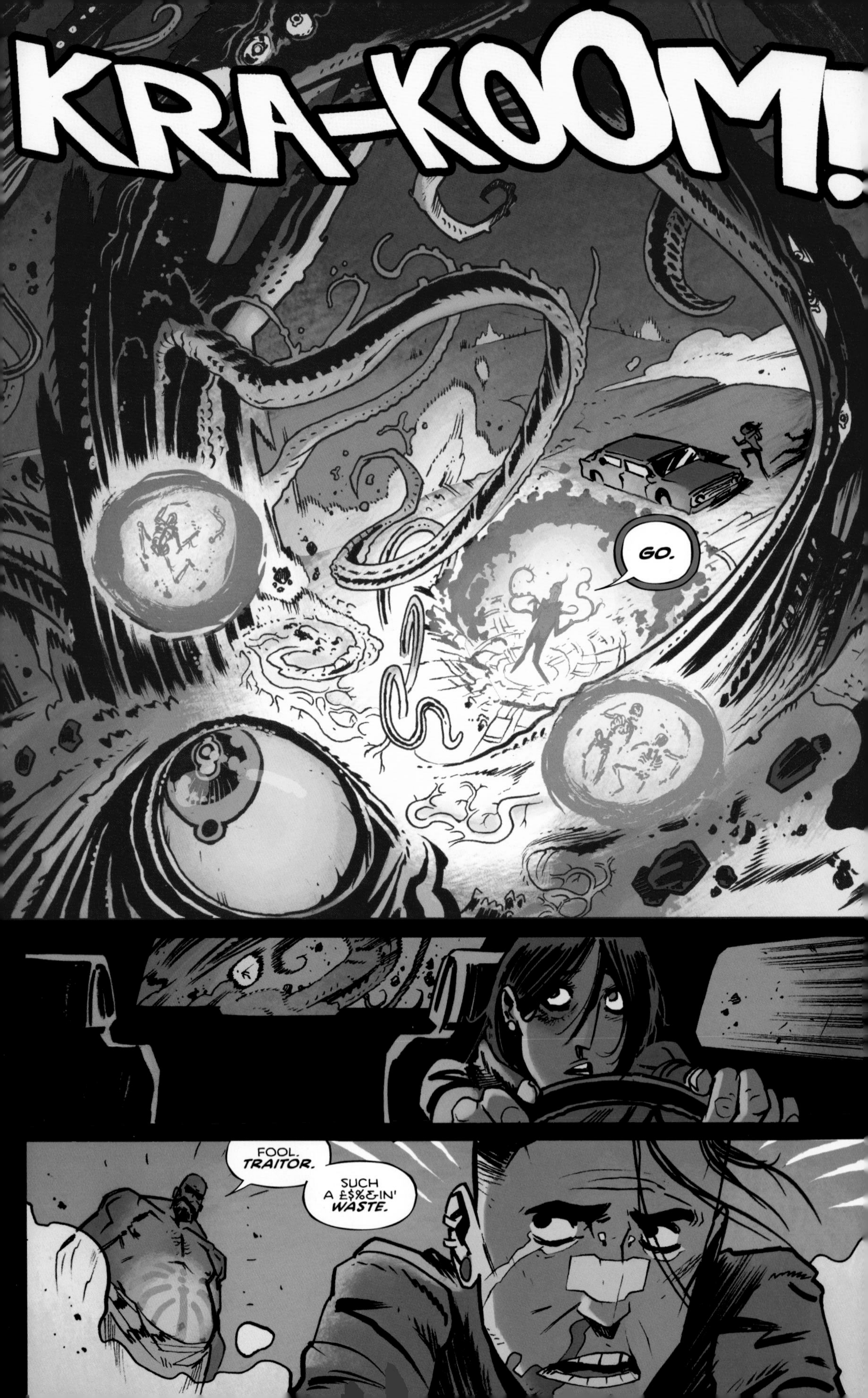
KRA-KOOM!
GO.
FOOL. TRAITOR.
SUCH A £$%&IN' WASTE.

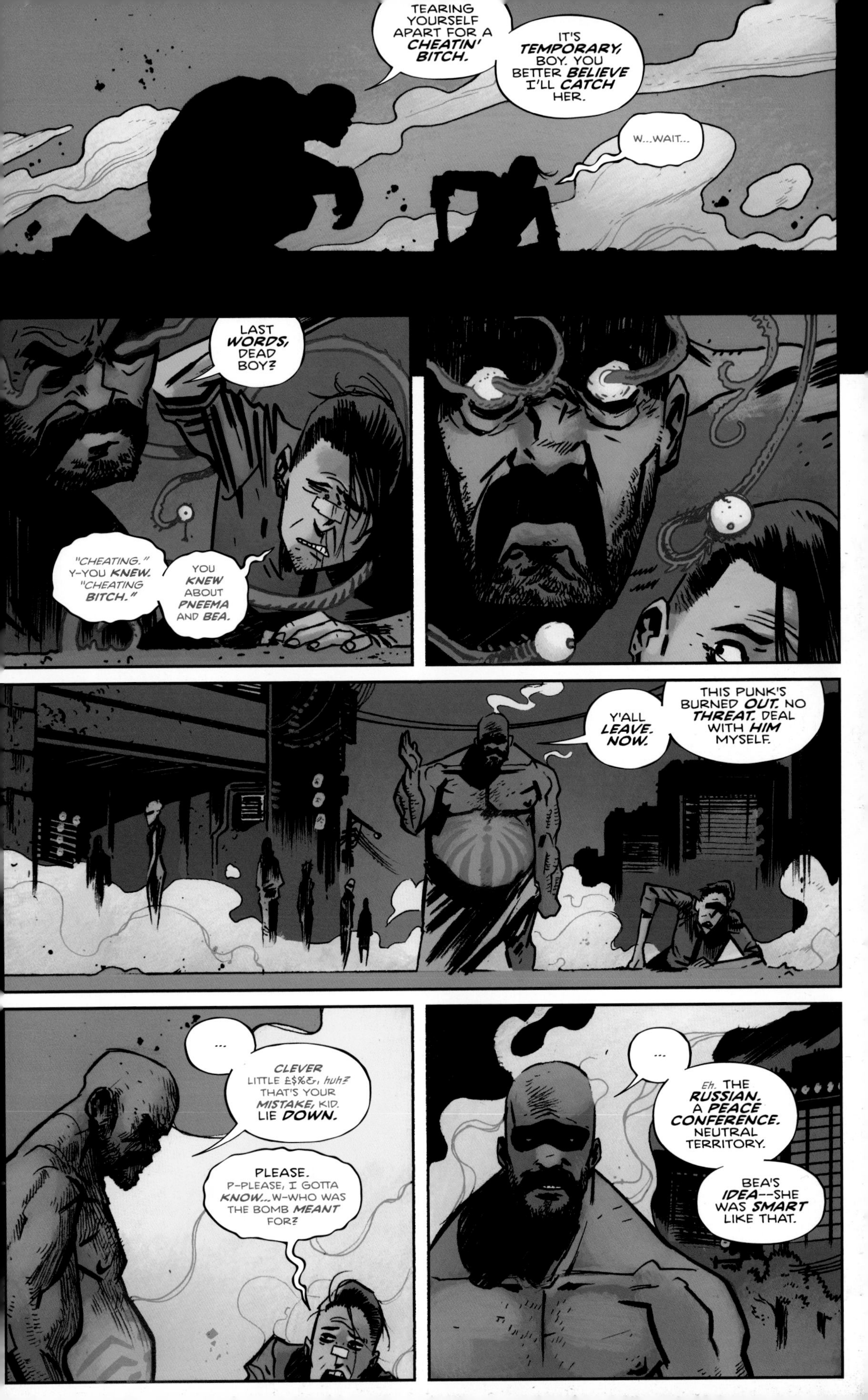
TEARING YOURSELF APART FOR A CHEATIN' BITCH.
IT'S TEMPORARY, BOY. YOU BETTER BELIEVE I'LL CATCH HER.
W...WAIT...
LAST WORDS, DEAD BOY?
"CHEATING." Y-YOU KNEW. "CHEATING BITCH."
YOU KNEW ABOUT PNEEMA AND BEA.
Y'ALL LEAVE. NOW.
THIS PUNK'S BURNED OUT. NO THREAT. DEAL WITH HIM MYSELF.
...
CLEVER LITTLE £$%&, huh? THAT'S YOUR MISTAKE, KID. LIE DOWN.
PLEASE. P-PLEASE, I GOTTA KNOW... W-WHO WAS THE BOMB MEANT FOR?
...
Eh. THE RUSSIAN. A PEACE CONFERENCE. NEUTRAL TERRITORY.
BEA'S IDEA--SHE WAS SMART LIKE THAT.

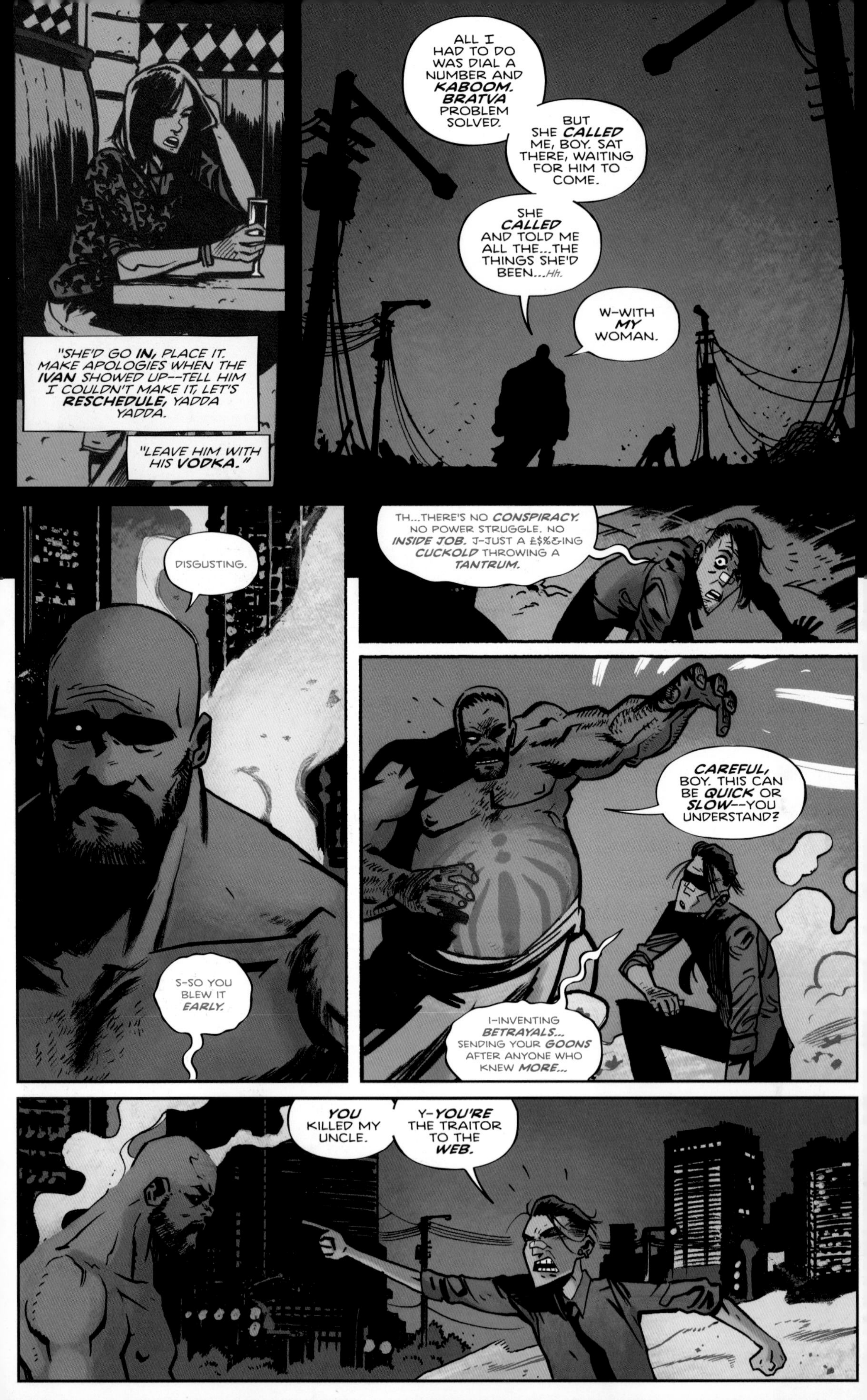
"SHE'D GO IN, PLACE IT. MAKE APOLOGIES WHEN THE IVAN SHOWED UP--TELL HIM I COULDN'T MAKE IT, LET'S RESCHEDULE, YADDA YADDA.
"LEAVE HIM WITH HIS VODKA."
ALL I HAD TO DO WAS DIAL A NUMBER AND KABOOM. BRATVA PROBLEM SOLVED.
BUT SHE CALLED ME, BOY. SAT THERE, WAITING FOR HIM TO COME.
SHE CALLED AND TOLD ME ALL THE...THE THINGS SHE'D BEEN...Hh.
W-WITH MY WOMAN.
DISGUSTING.
S-SO YOU BLEW IT EARLY.
TH...THERE'S NO CONSPIRACY. NO POWER STRUGGLE. NO INSIDE JOB. J-JUST A £$%&ING CUCKOLD THROWING A TANTRUM.
CAREFUL, BOY. THIS CAN BE QUICK OR SLOW--YOU UNDERSTAND?
I-INVENTING BETRAYALS... SENDING YOUR GOONS AFTER ANYONE WHO KNEW MORE...
YOU KILLED MY UNCLE.
Y-YOU'RE THE TRAITOR TO THE WEB.

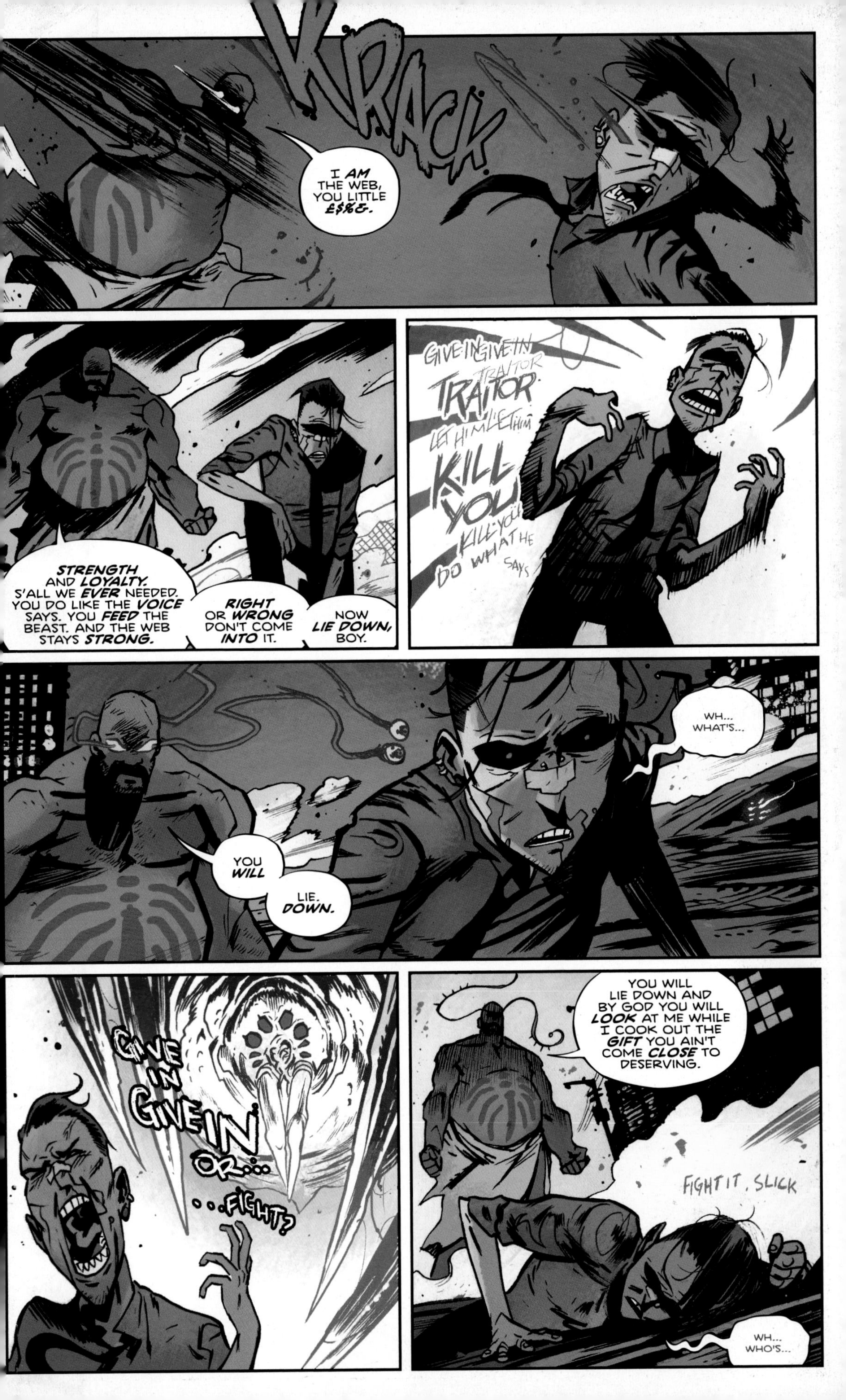
KRACK
I AM THE WEB, YOU LITTLE £$%&.
STRENGTH AND LOYALTY. S'ALL WE EVER NEEDED. YOU DO LIKE THE VOICE SAYS. YOU FEED THE BEAST. AND THE WEB STAYS STRONG.
RIGHT OR WRONG DON'T COME INTO IT.
NOW LIE DOWN, BOY.
GIVE IN GIVE IN
TRAITOR TRAITOR
LET HIM LET HIM
KILL YOU
KILL YOU
DO WHAT HE SAYS
WH... WHAT'S...
YOU WILL
LIE. DOWN.
GIVE IN
GIVE IN
OR...
...FIGHT?
YOU WILL LIE DOWN AND BY GOD YOU WILL LOOK AT ME WHILE I COOK OUT THE GIFT YOU AIN'T COME CLOSE TO DESERVING.
FIGHT IT, SLICK
WH... WHO'S...

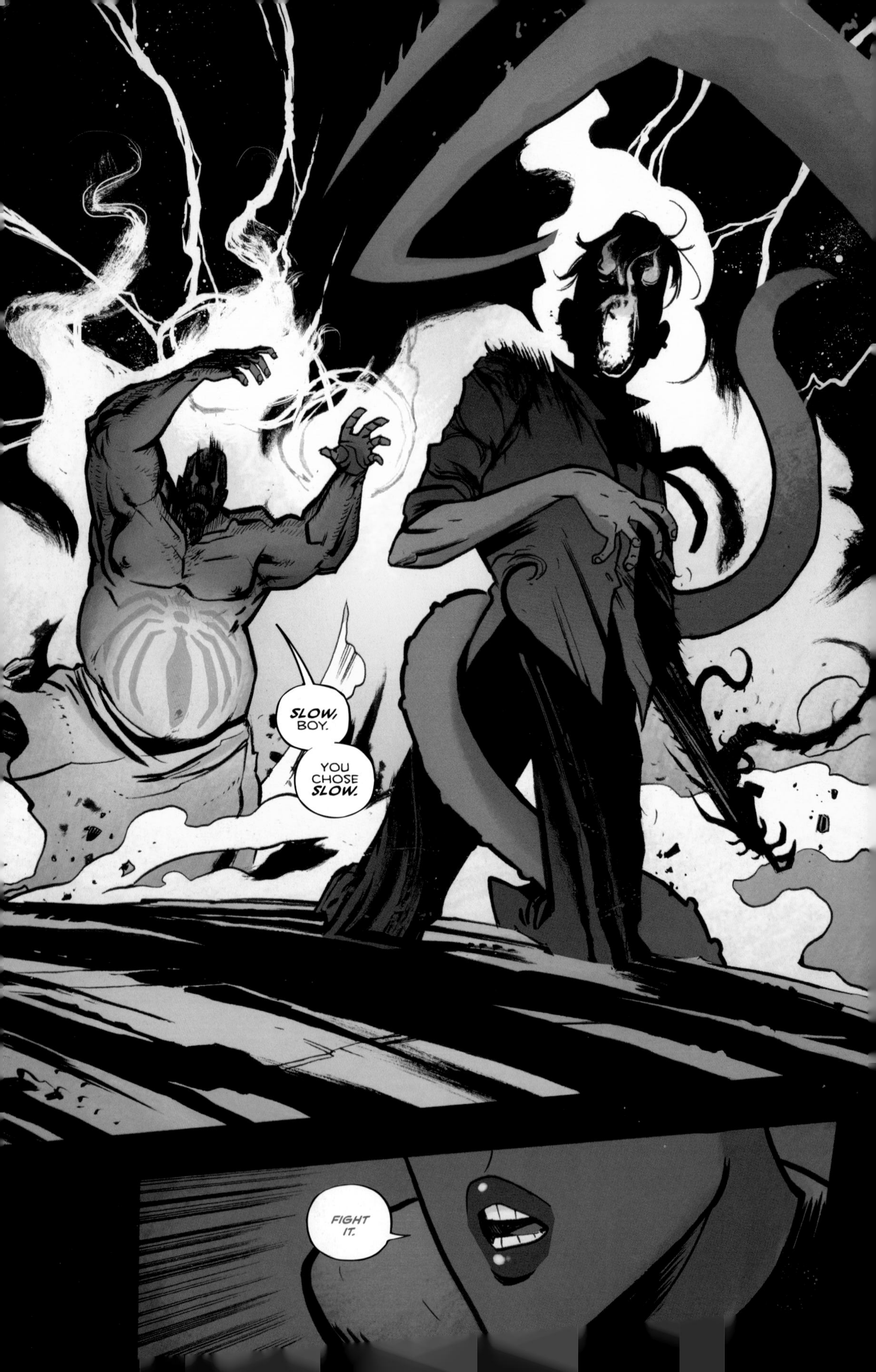
SLOW, BOY.
YOU CHOSE SLOW.
FIGHT IT.

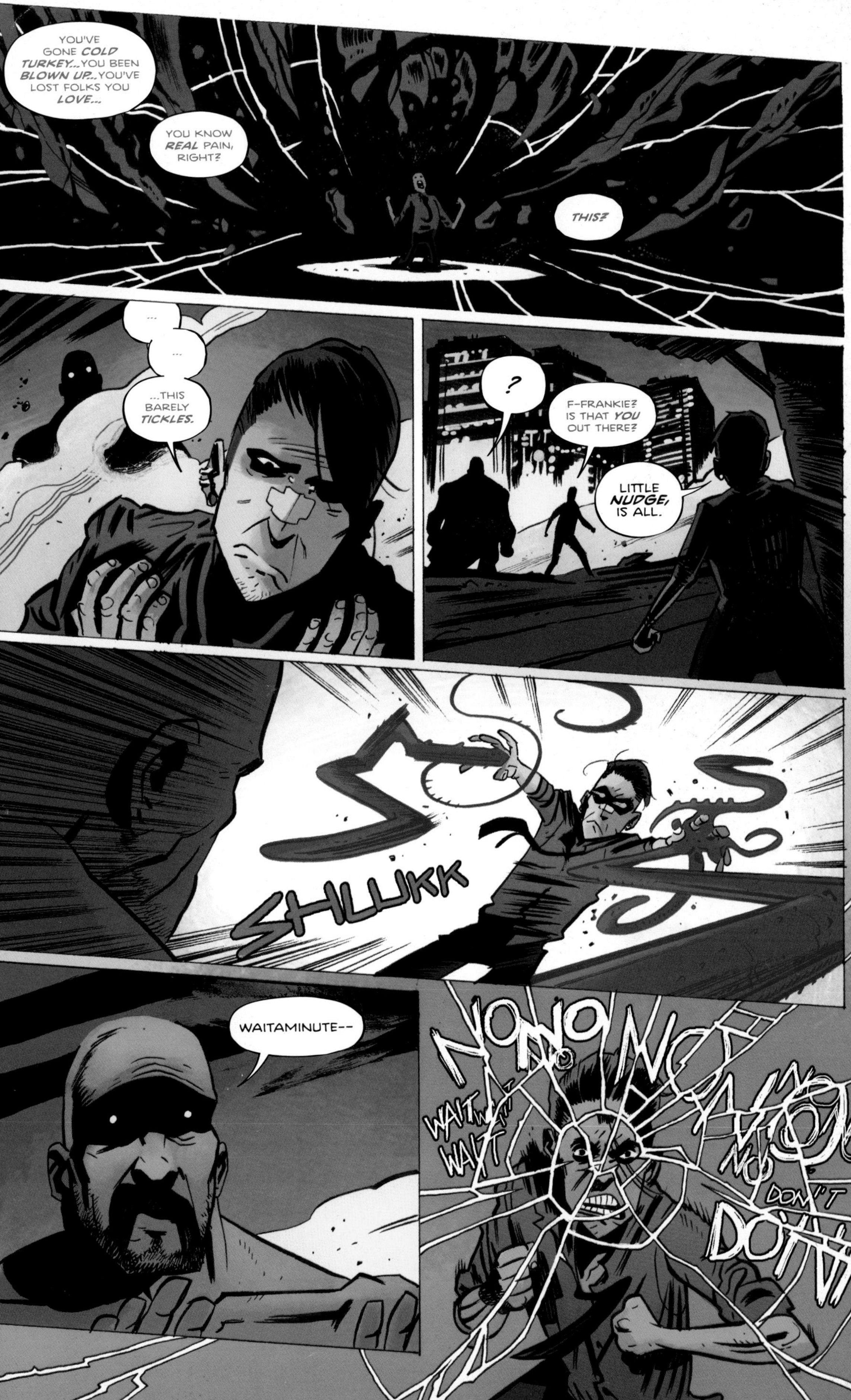
YOU'VE GONE COLD TURKEY... YOU BEEN BLOWN UP... YOU'VE LOST FOLKS YOU LOVE...
YOU KNOW REAL PAIN, RIGHT?
THIS?
...
...
...THIS BARELY TICKLES.
?
F-FRANKIE? IS THAT YOU OUT THERE?
LITTLE NUDGE, IS ALL.
SHLUKK
WAITAMINUTE--
NO NO NO NO
WAIT
WAIT
NO
DON'T

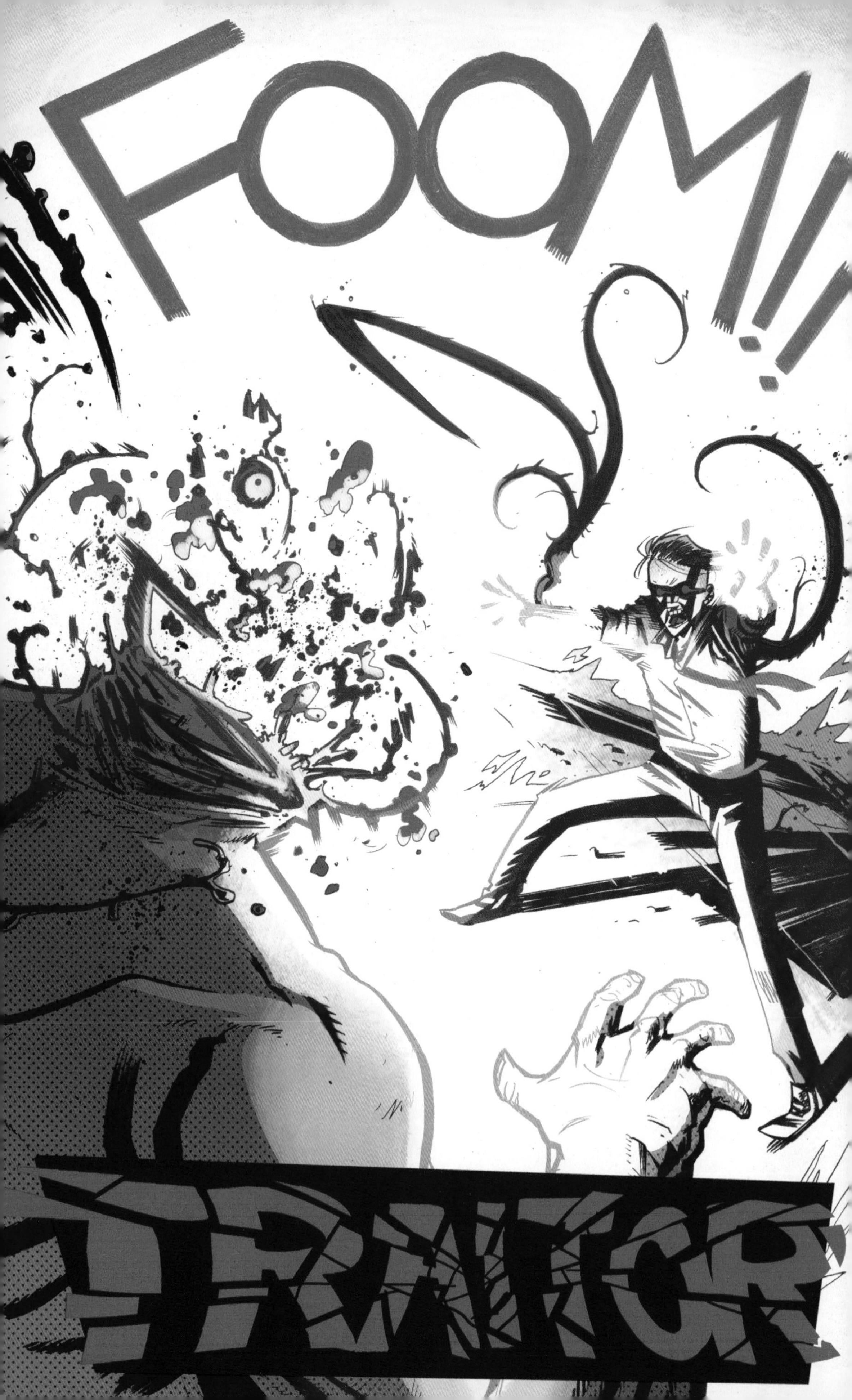
FOOM!!!

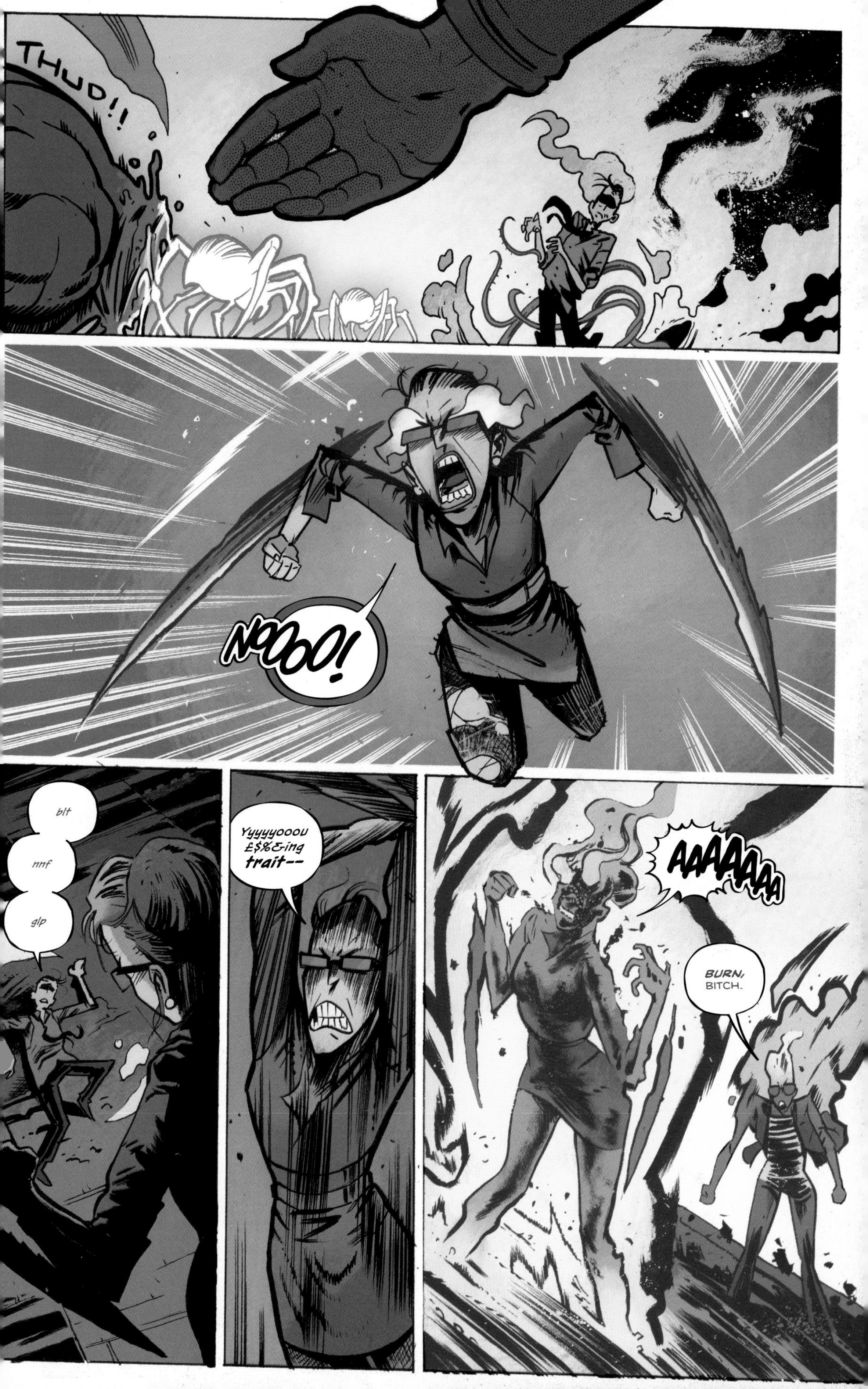
THUD!!
NOOOO!
blt
nnf
glp
Yyyyyooou £$%&-ing trait--
AAAAAAAA
BURN, BITCH.

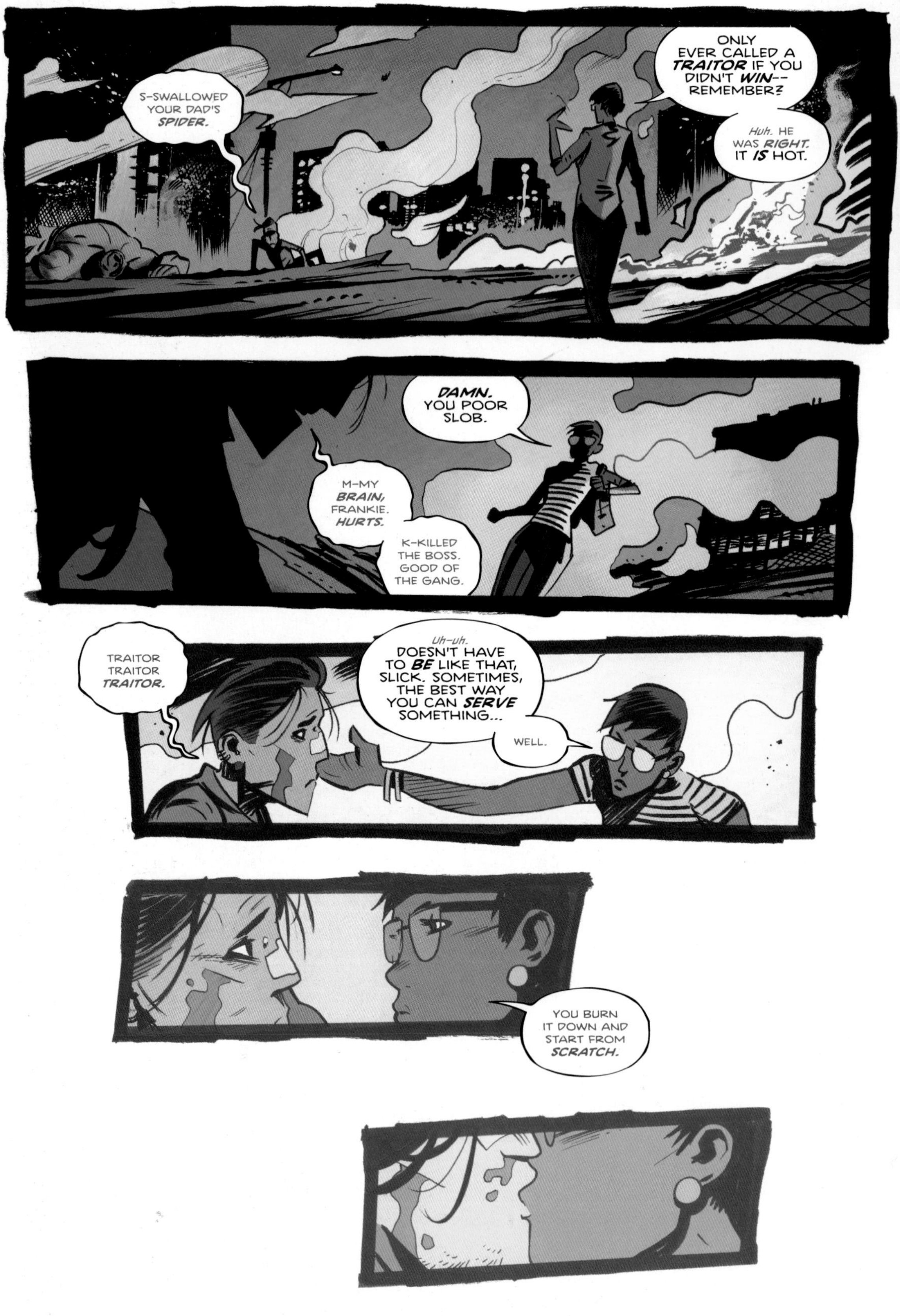
S-SWALLOWED YOUR DAD'S SPIDER.
ONLY EVER CALLED A TRAITOR IF YOU DIDN'T WIN-- REMEMBER?
Huh. HE WAS RIGHT. IT IS HOT.
DAMN. YOU POOR SLOB.
M-MY BRAIN, FRANKIE. HURTS.
K-KILLED THE BOSS. GOOD OF THE GANG.
TRAITOR TRAITOR TRAITOR.
Uh-uh. DOESN'T HAVE TO BE LIKE THAT, SLICK. SOMETIMES, THE BEST WAY YOU CAN SERVE SOMETHING...
WELL.
YOU BURN IT DOWN AND START FROM SCRATCH.

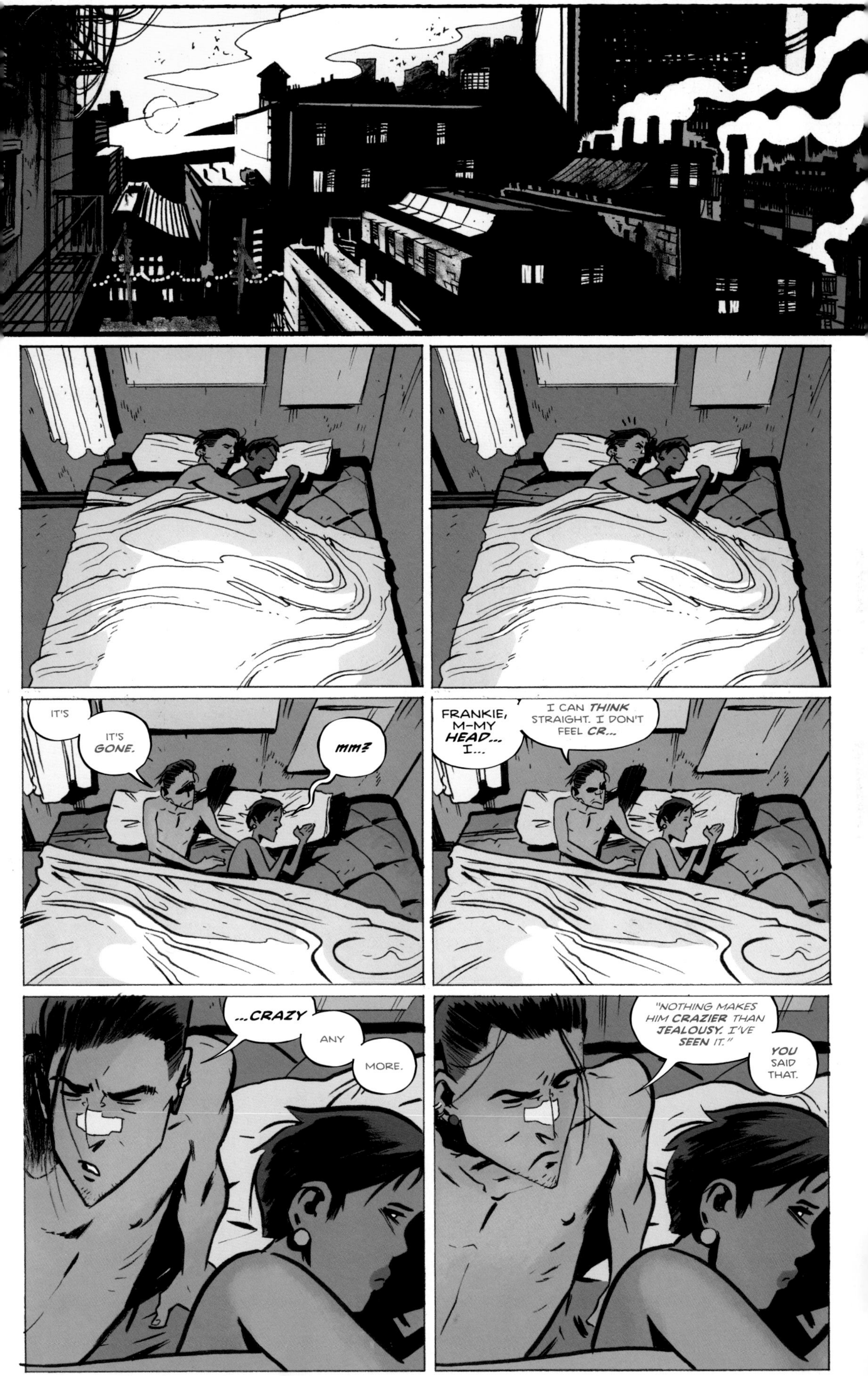
IT'S
IT'S GONE.
mm?
FRANKIE, M-MY HEAD... I...
I CAN THINK STRAIGHT. I DON'T FEEL CR...
...CRAZY
ANY
MORE.
"NOTHING MAKES HIM CRAZIER THAN JEALOUSY. I'VE SEEN IT."
YOU SAID THAT.

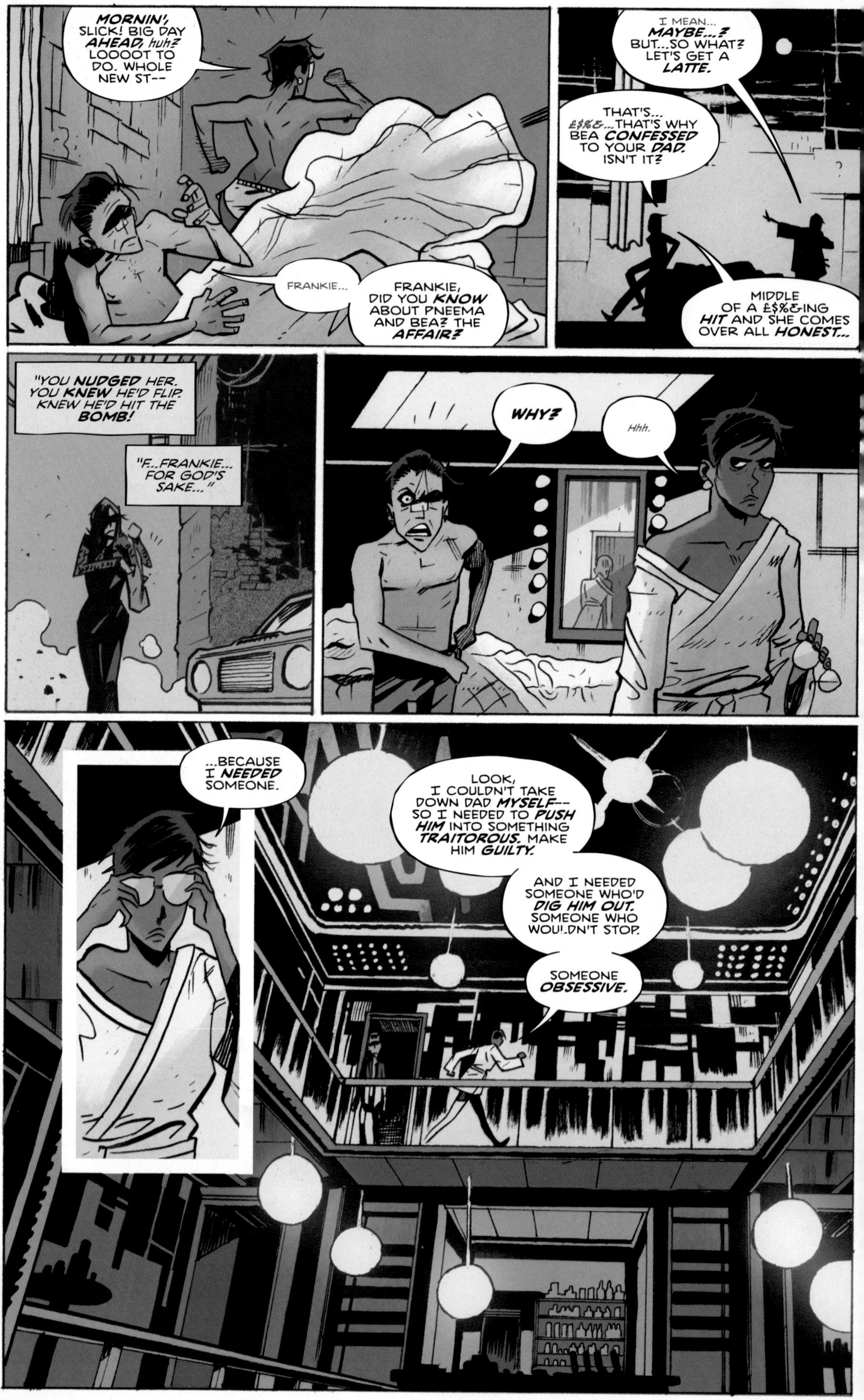
MORNIN', SLICK! BIG DAY AHEAD, huh? LOOOOT TO DO. WHOLE NEW ST--
FRANKIE...
FRANKIE, DID YOU KNOW ABOUT PNEEMA AND BEA? THE AFFAIR?
I MEAN... MAYBE...? BUT...SO WHAT? LET'S GET A LATTE.
THAT'S... £$%&...THAT'S WHY BEA CONFESSED TO YOUR DAD. ISN'T IT?
MIDDLE OF A £$%&ING HIT AND SHE COMES OVER ALL HONEST...
"YOU NUDGED HER. YOU KNEW HE'D FLIP. KNEW HE'D HIT THE BOMB!
"F...FRANKIE... FOR GOD'S SAKE..."
WHY?
Hhh.
...BECAUSE I NEEDED SOMEONE.
LOOK, I COULDN'T TAKE DOWN DAD MYSELF-- SO I NEEDED TO PUSH HIM INTO SOMETHING TRAITOROUS. MAKE HIM GUILTY.
AND I NEEDED SOMEONE WHO'D DIG HIM OUT. SOMEONE WHO WOULDN'T STOP.
SOMEONE OBSESSIVE.

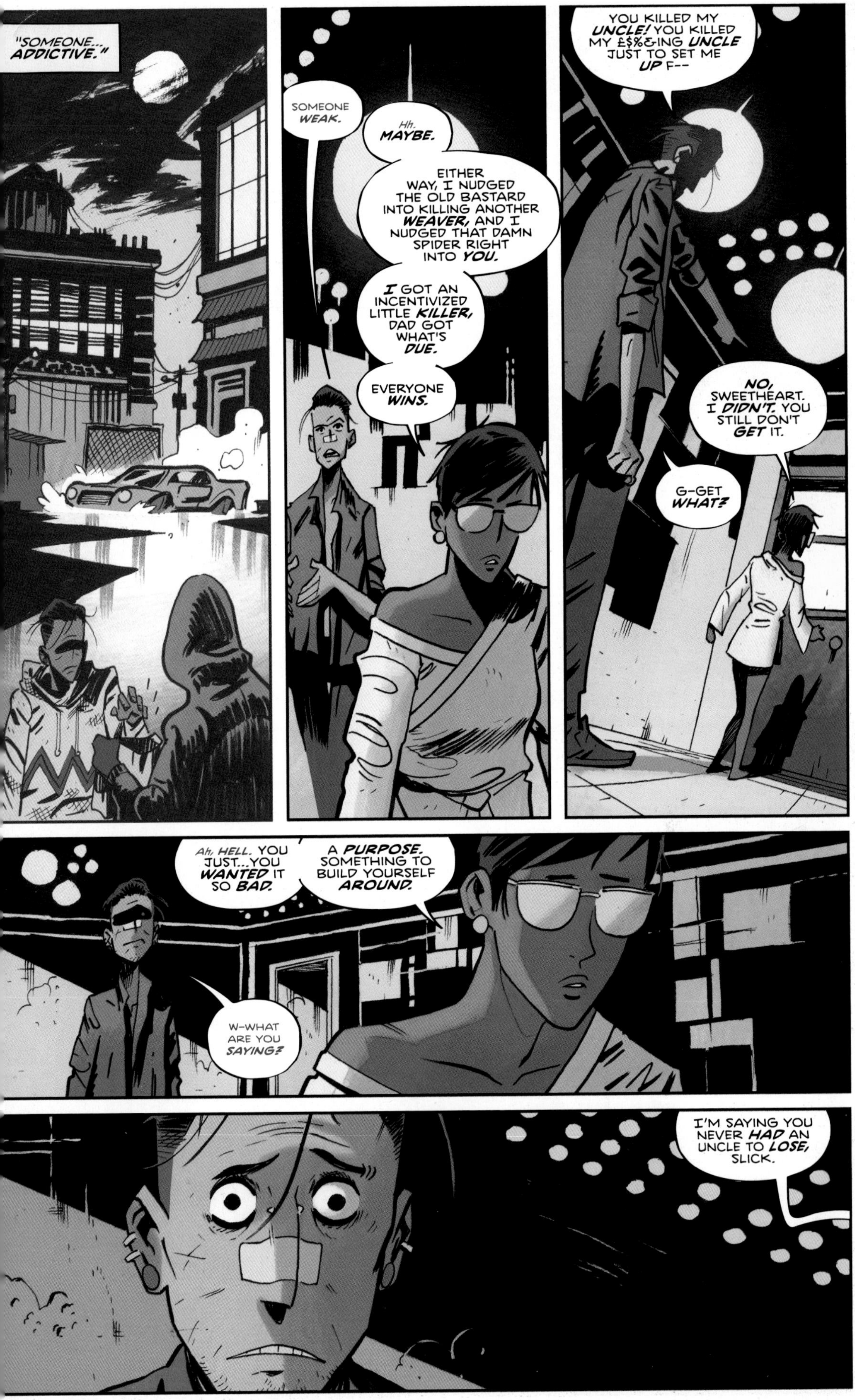
"SOMEONE... ADDICTIVE."
SOMEONE WEAK.
Hh. MAYBE.
EITHER WAY, I NUDGED THE OLD BASTARD INTO KILLING ANOTHER WEAVER, AND I NUDGED THAT DAMN SPIDER RIGHT INTO YOU.
I GOT AN INCENTIVIZED LITTLE KILLER, DAD GOT WHAT'S DUE.
EVERYONE WINS.
YOU KILLED MY UNCLE! YOU KILLED MY £$%&ING UNCLE JUST TO SET ME UP F--
NO, SWEETHEART. I DIDN'T. YOU STILL DON'T GET IT.
G-GET WHAT?
Ah, HELL. YOU JUST...YOU WANTED IT SO BAD.
A PURPOSE. SOMETHING TO BUILD YOURSELF AROUND.
W-WHAT ARE YOU SAYING?
I'M SAYING YOU NEVER HAD AN UNCLE TO LOSE, SLICK.

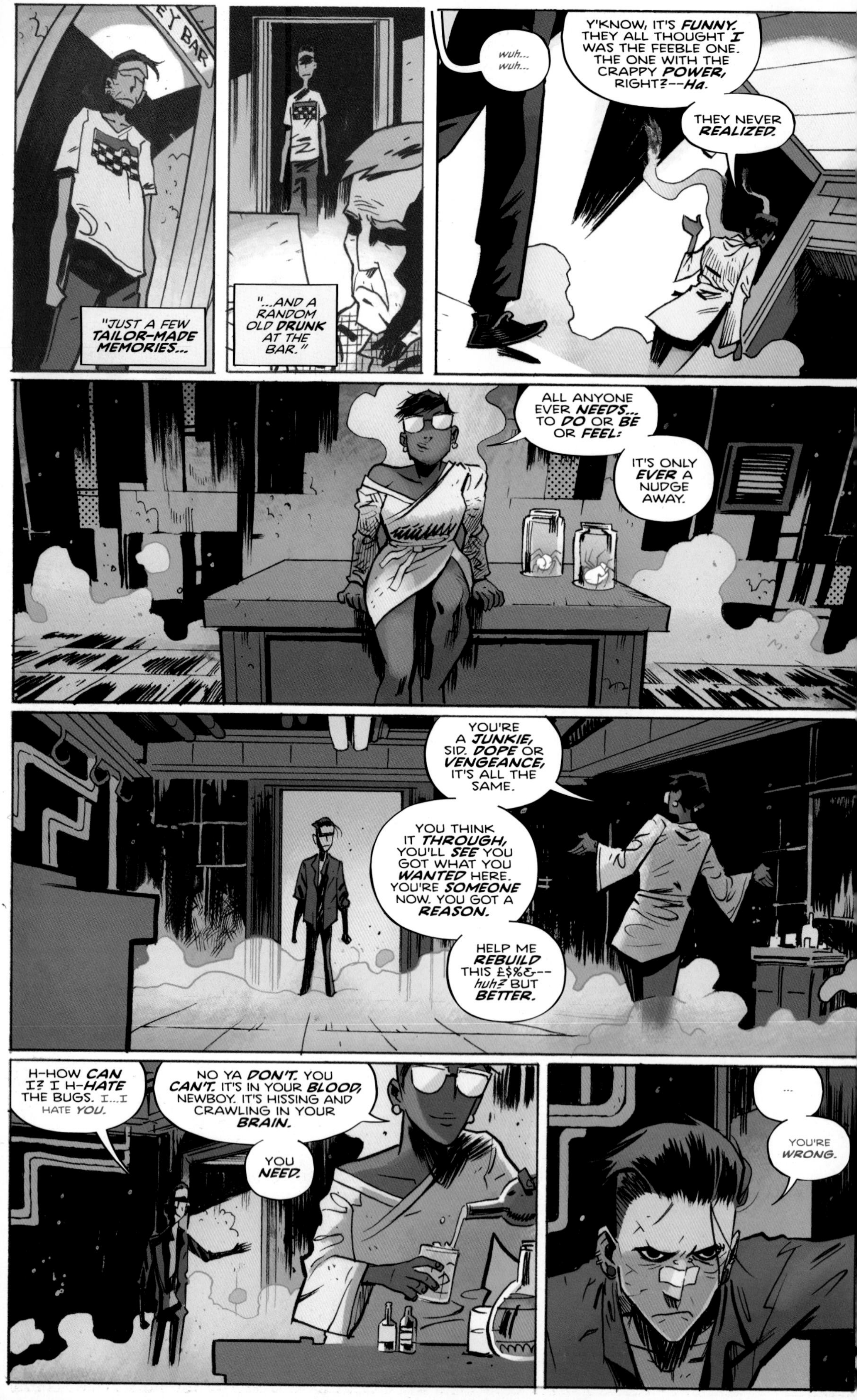
"JUST A FEW TAILOR-MADE MEMORIES...
"...AND A RANDOM OLD DRUNK AT THE BAR."
wuh... wuh...
Y'KNOW, IT'S FUNNY. THEY ALL THOUGHT I WAS THE FEEBLE ONE. THE ONE WITH THE CRAPPY POWER, RIGHT?--Ha.
THEY NEVER REALIZED.
ALL ANYONE EVER NEEDS... TO DO OR BE OR FEEL:
IT'S ONLY EVER A NUDGE AWAY.
YOU'RE A JUNKIE, SID. DOPE OR VENGEANCE, IT'S ALL THE SAME.
YOU THINK IT THROUGH, YOU'LL SEE YOU GOT WHAT YOU WANTED HERE. YOU'RE SOMEONE NOW. YOU GOT A REASON.
HELP ME REBUILD THIS £$%&-- huh? BUT BETTER.
H-HOW CAN I? I H-HATE THE BUGS. I...I HATE YOU.
NO YA DON'T. YOU CAN'T. IT'S IN YOUR BLOOD, NEWBOY. IT'S HISSING AND CRAWLING IN YOUR BRAIN.
YOU NEED.
...
YOU'RE WRONG.

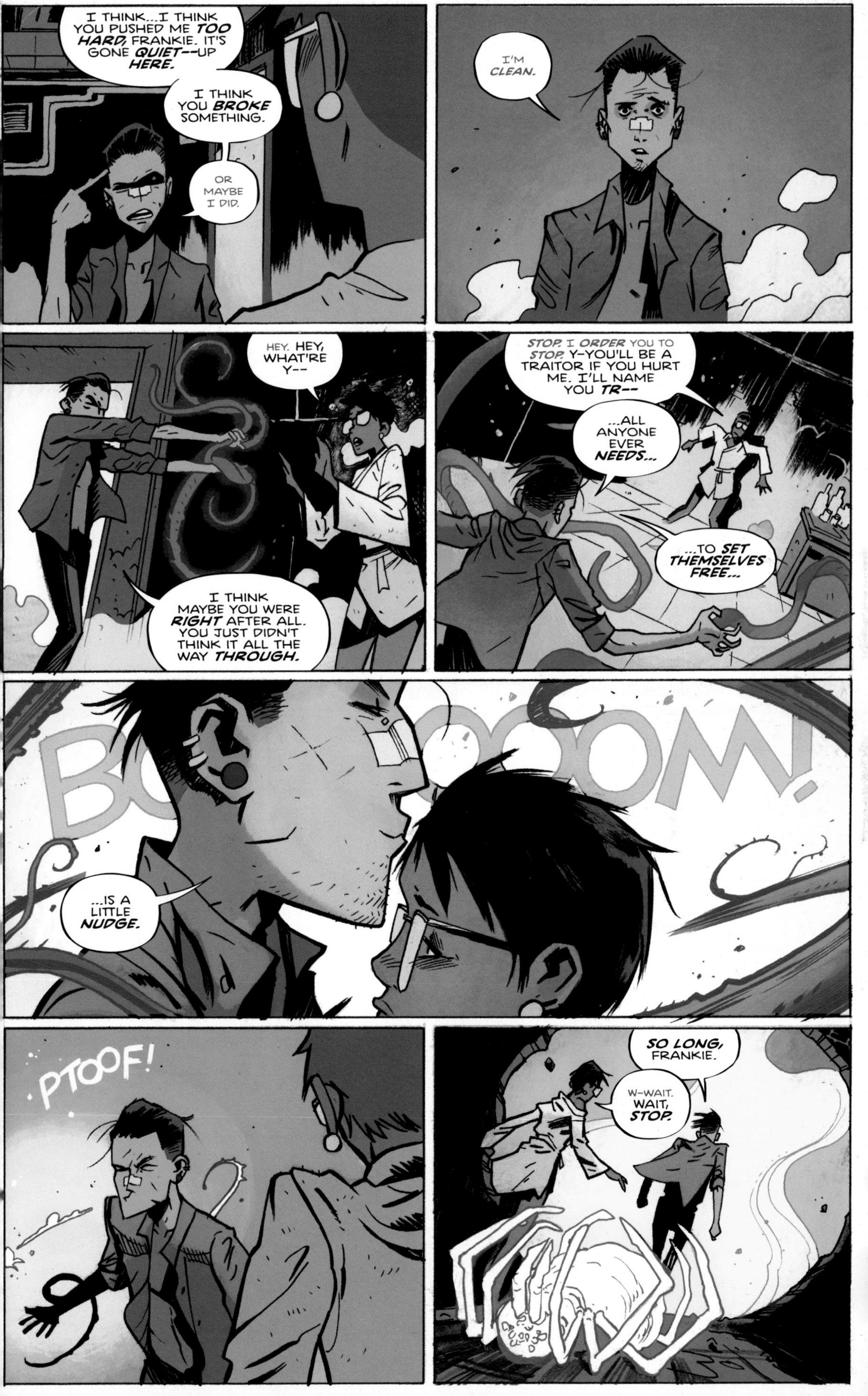
I THINK...I THINK YOU PUSHED ME TOO HARD, FRANKIE. IT'S GONE QUIET--UP HERE.
I THINK YOU BROKE SOMETHING.
OR MAYBE I DID.
I'M CLEAN.
HEY. HEY, WHAT'RE Y--
I THINK MAYBE YOU WERE RIGHT AFTER ALL. YOU JUST DIDN'T THINK IT ALL THE WAY THROUGH.
STOP. I ORDER YOU TO STOP. Y-YOU'LL BE A TRAITOR IF YOU HURT ME. I'LL NAME YOU TR--
...ALL ANYONE EVER NEEDS...
...TO SET THEMSELVES FREE...
...IS A LITTLE NUDGE.
PTOOF!
SO LONG, FRANKIE.
W-WAIT. WAIT, STOP.

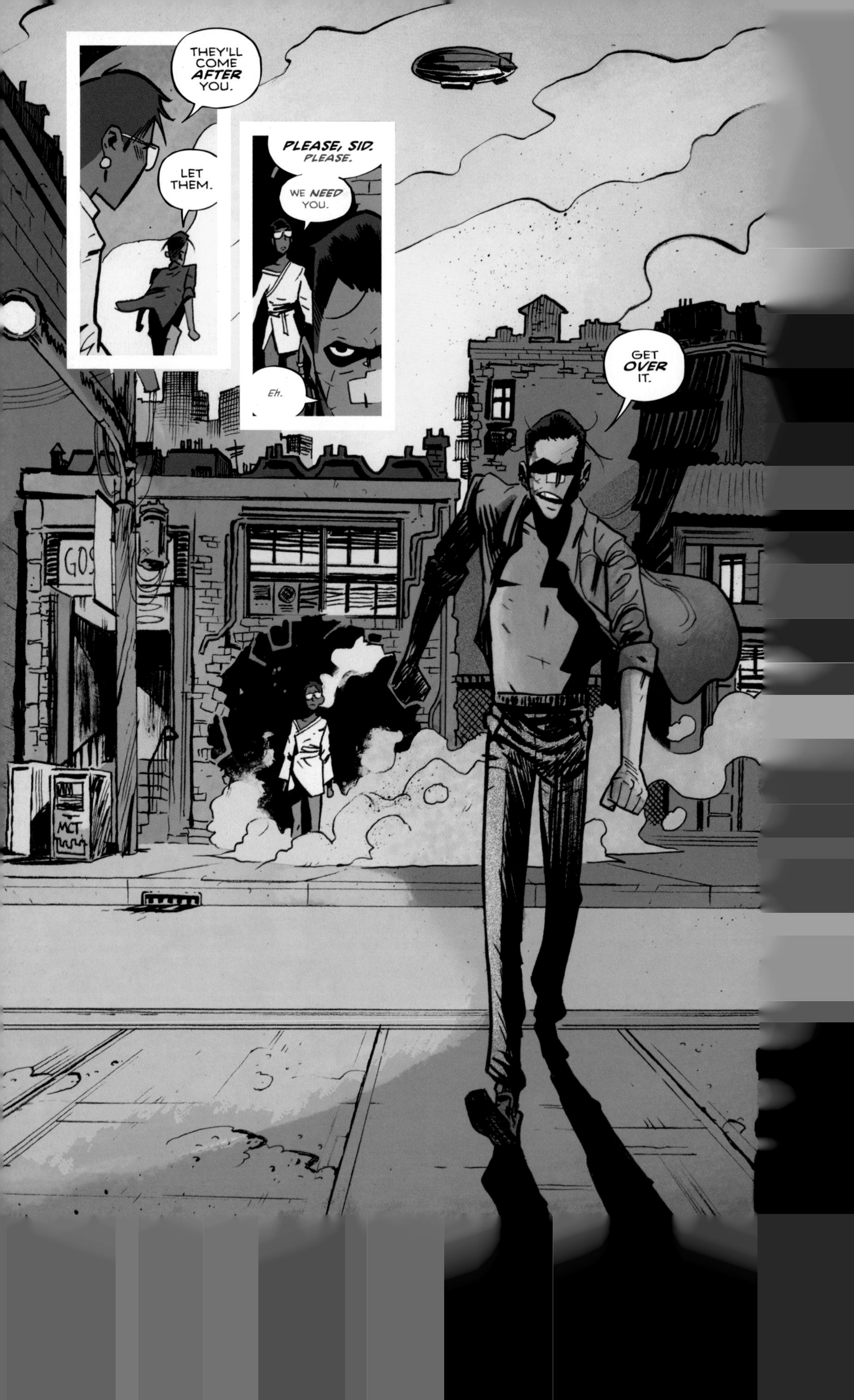
THEY'LL COME AFTER YOU.
LET THEM.
PLEASE, SID. PLEASE.
WE NEED YOU.
Eh.
GET OVER IT.

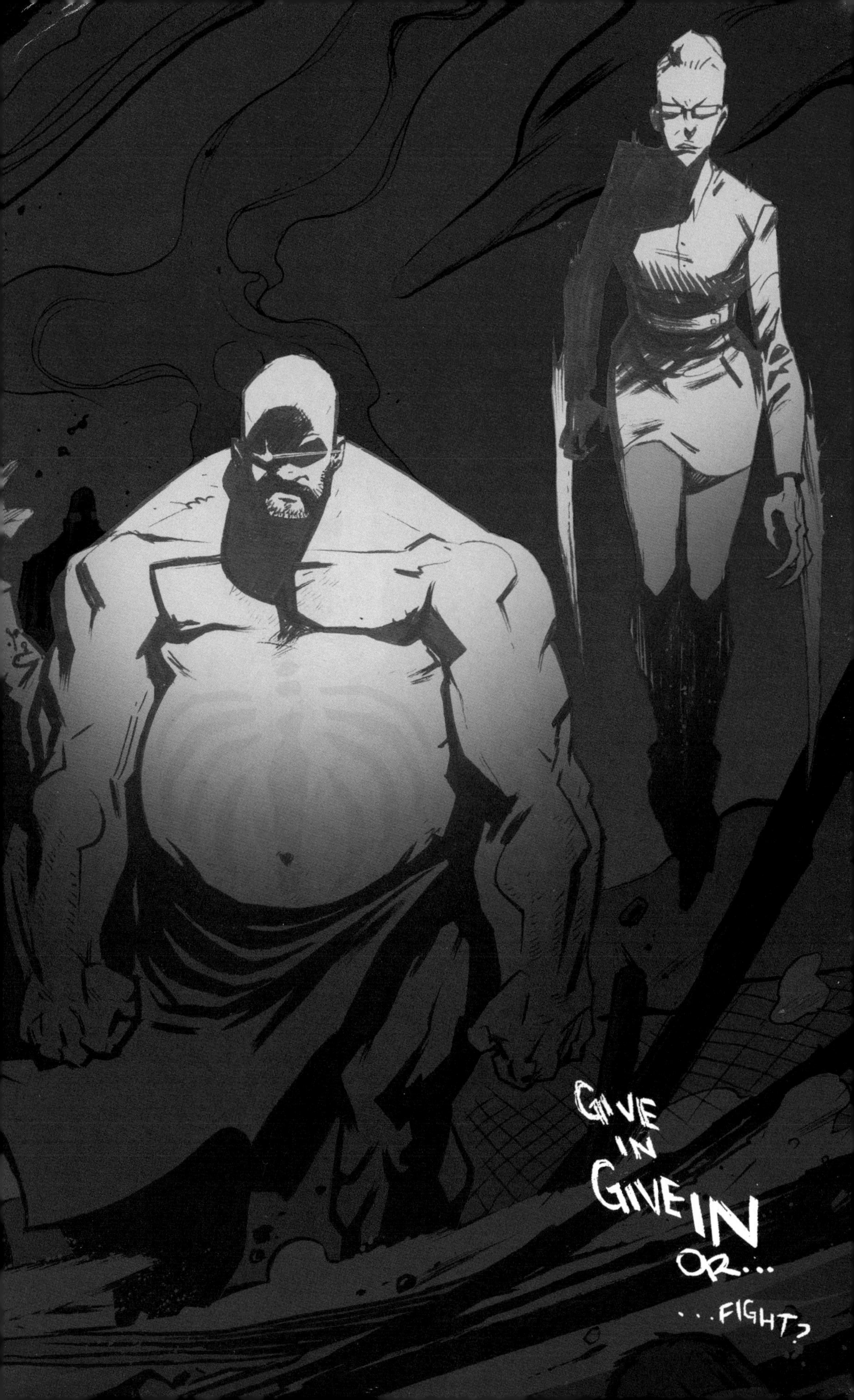
GIVE
IN
GIVE IN
OR...
...FIGHT?

COVER GALLERY

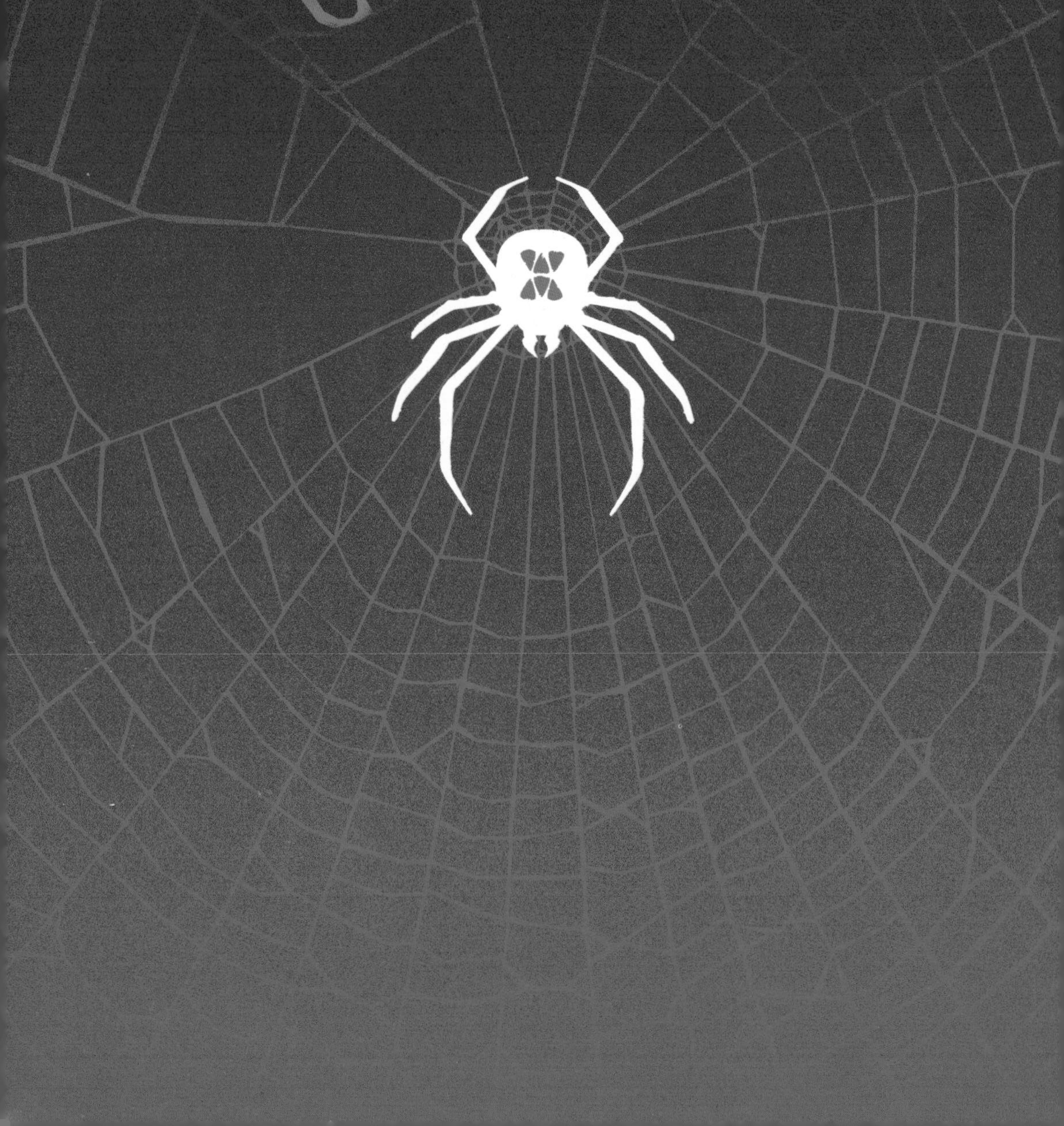

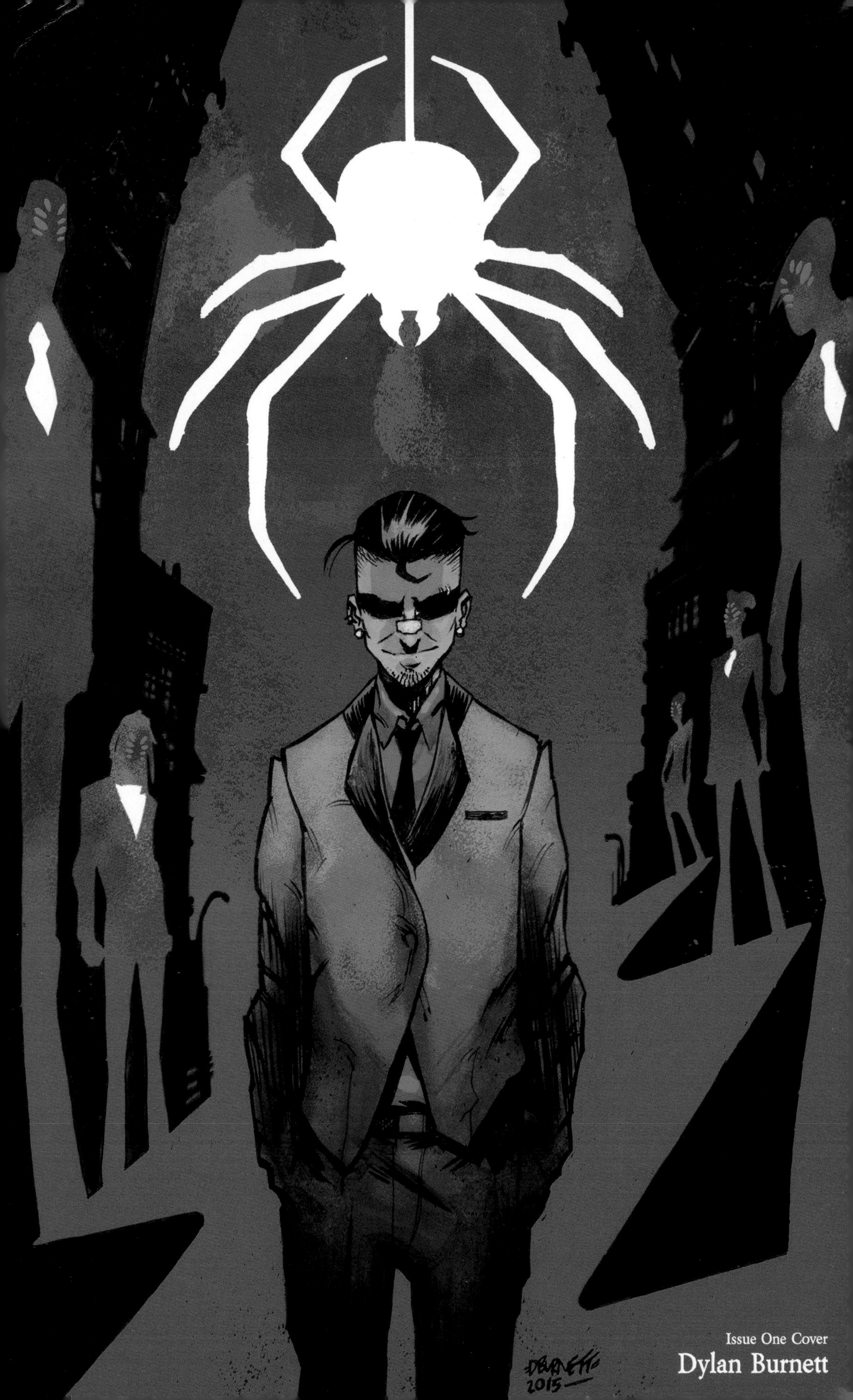
DBURNETT
2015

Issue One Cover

Dylan Burnett

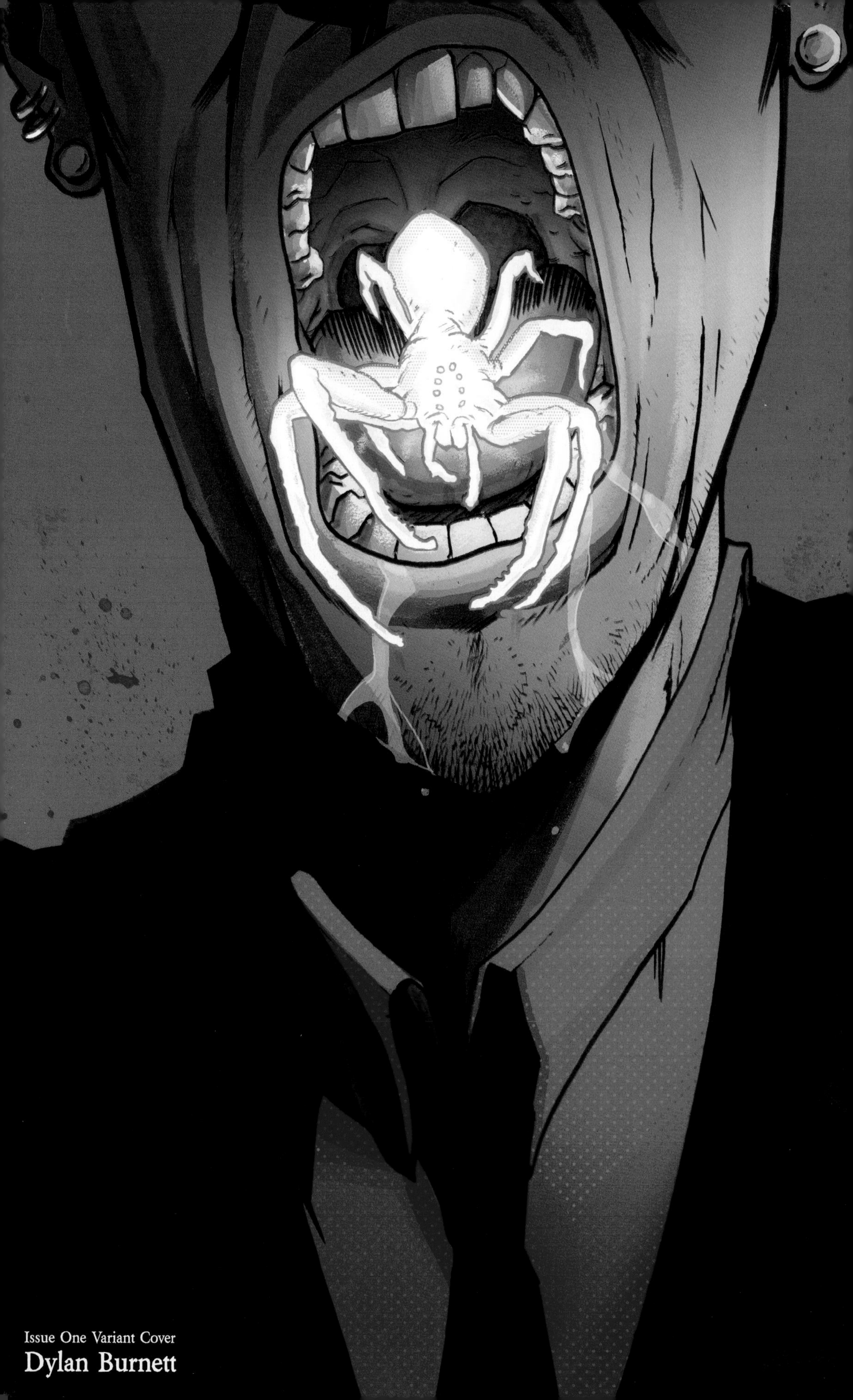

Issue One Variant Cover

Dylan Burnett

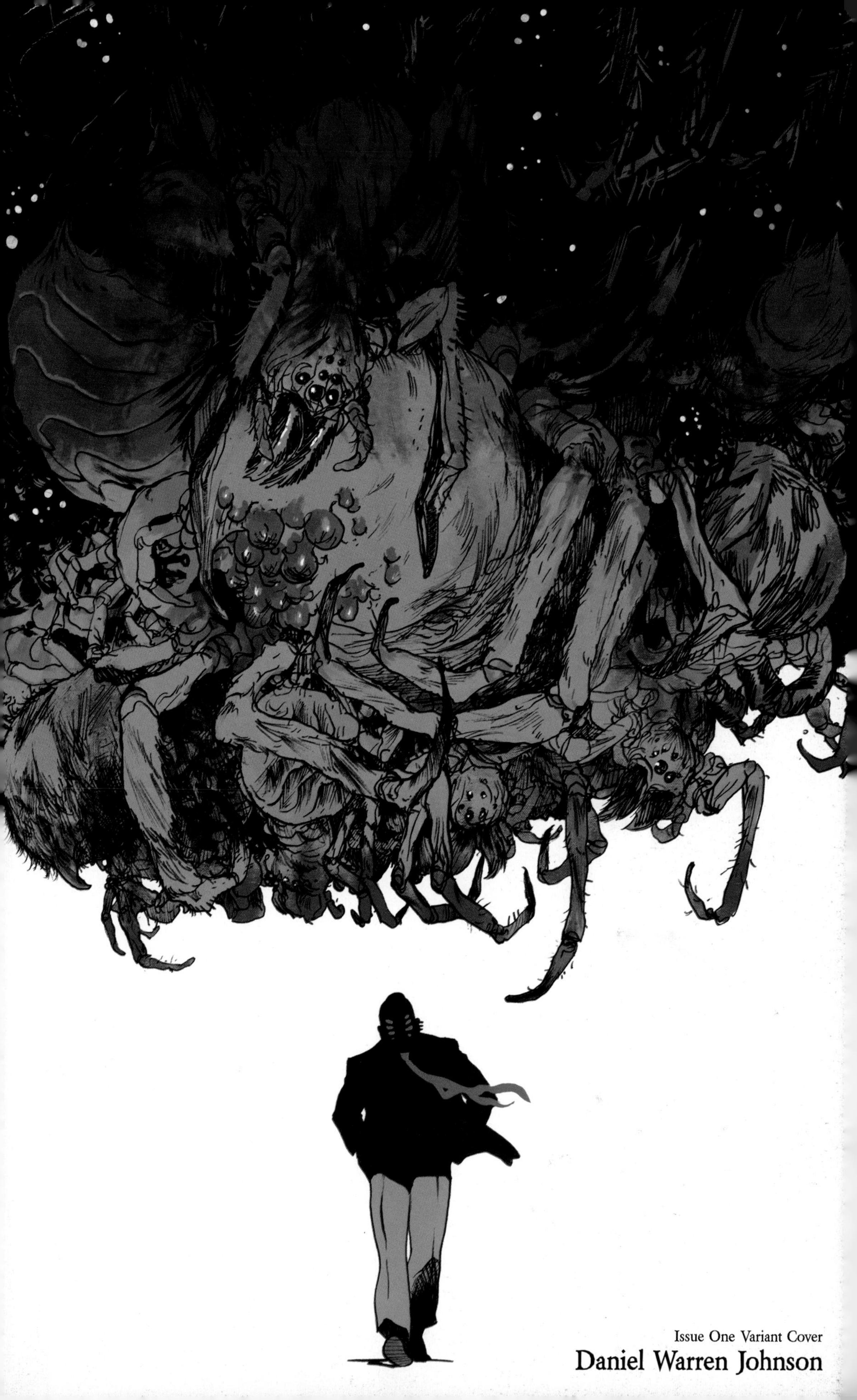

Issue One Variant Cover

Daniel Warren Johnson

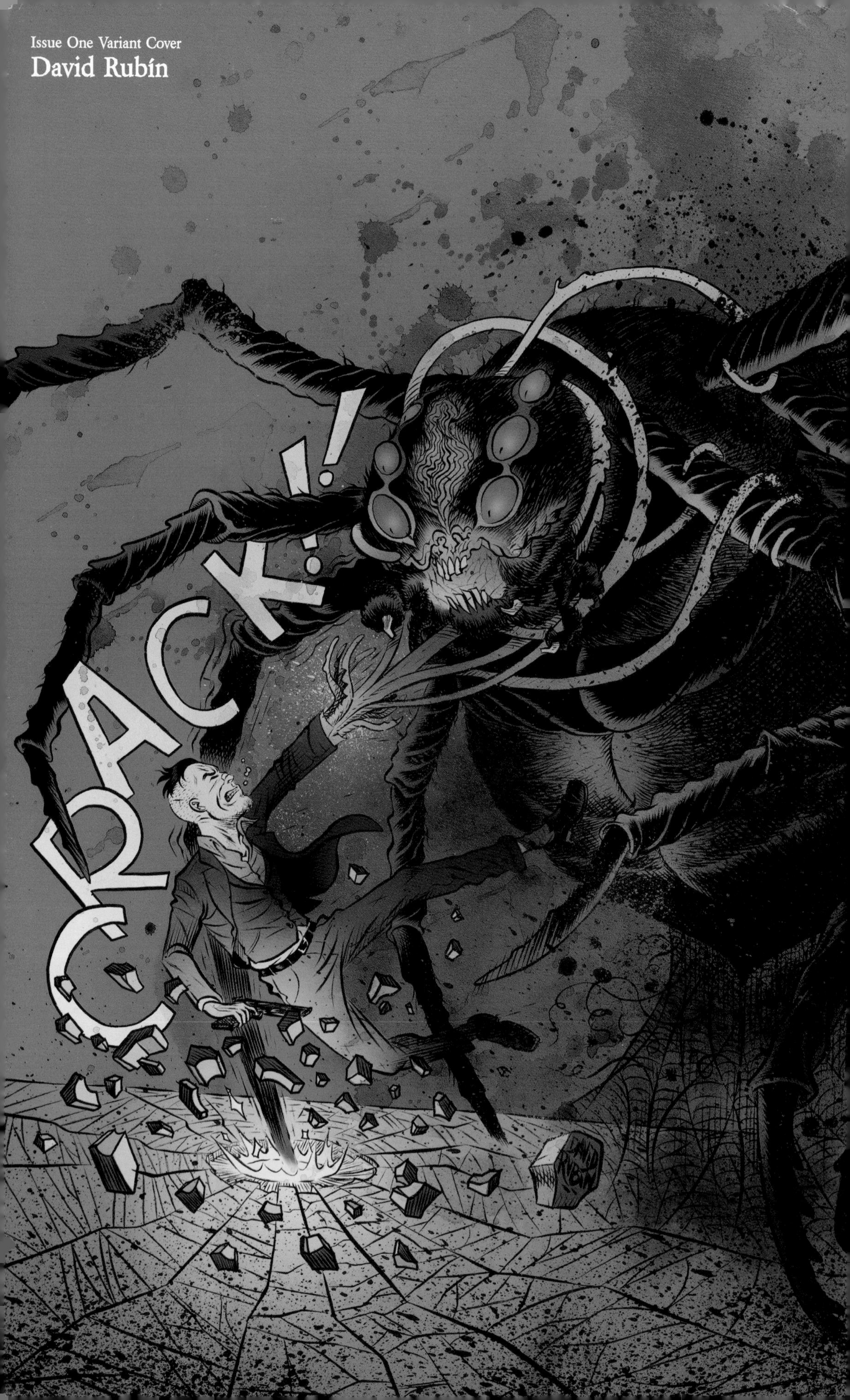
CRACK!!
Issue One Variant Cover

David Rubín

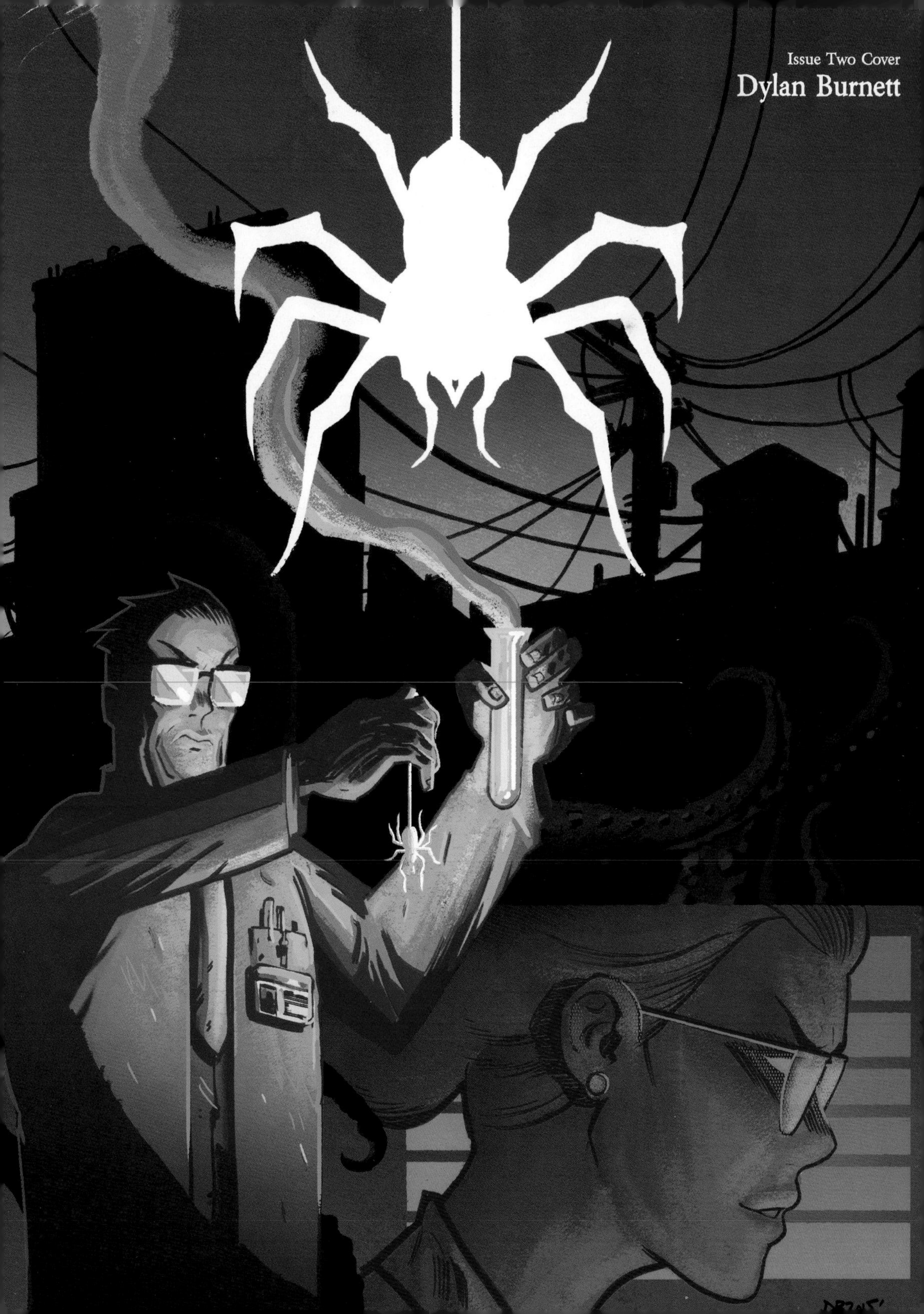

Issue Two Cover
Dylan Burnett

Issue Three Cover

Dylan Burnett

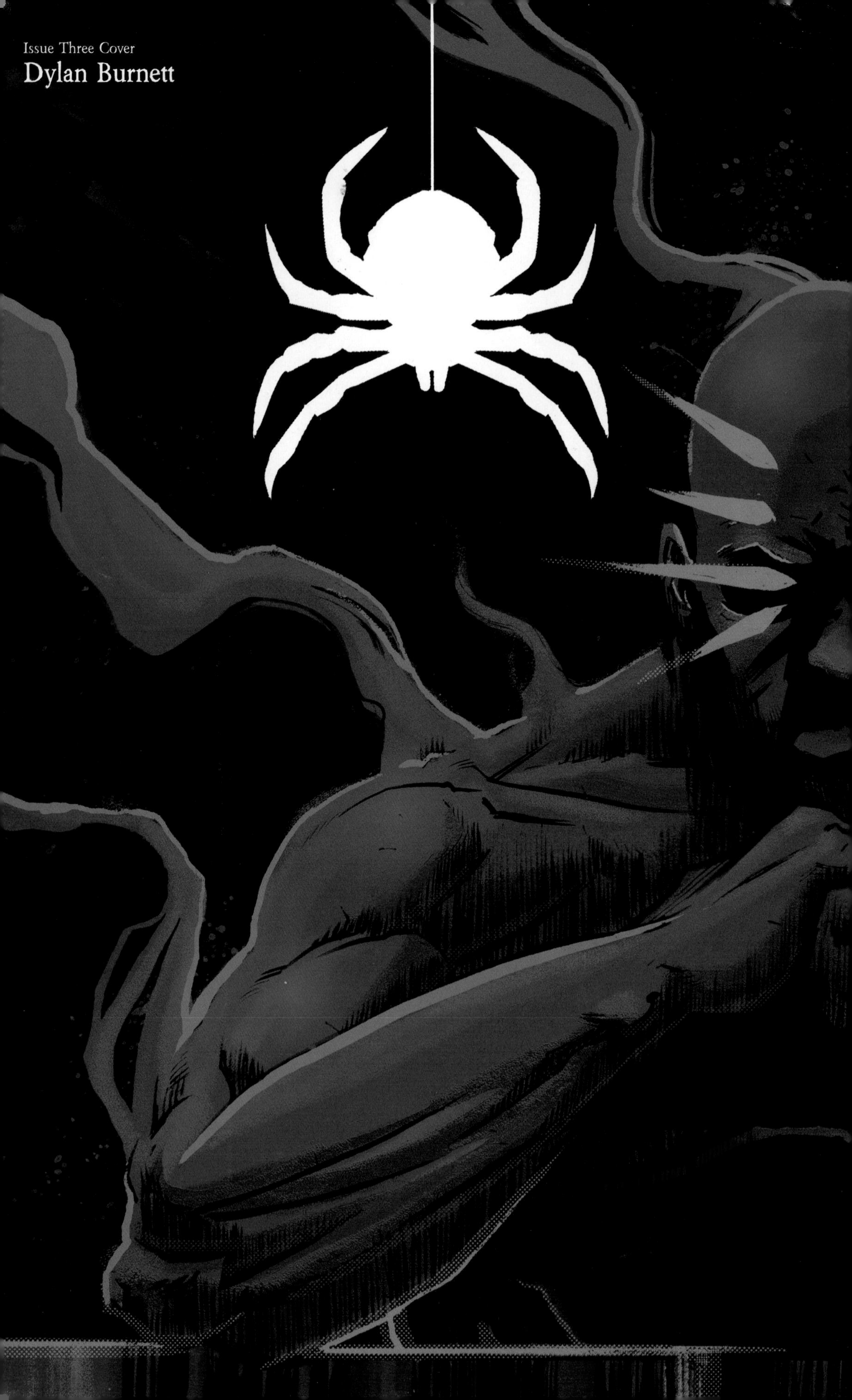

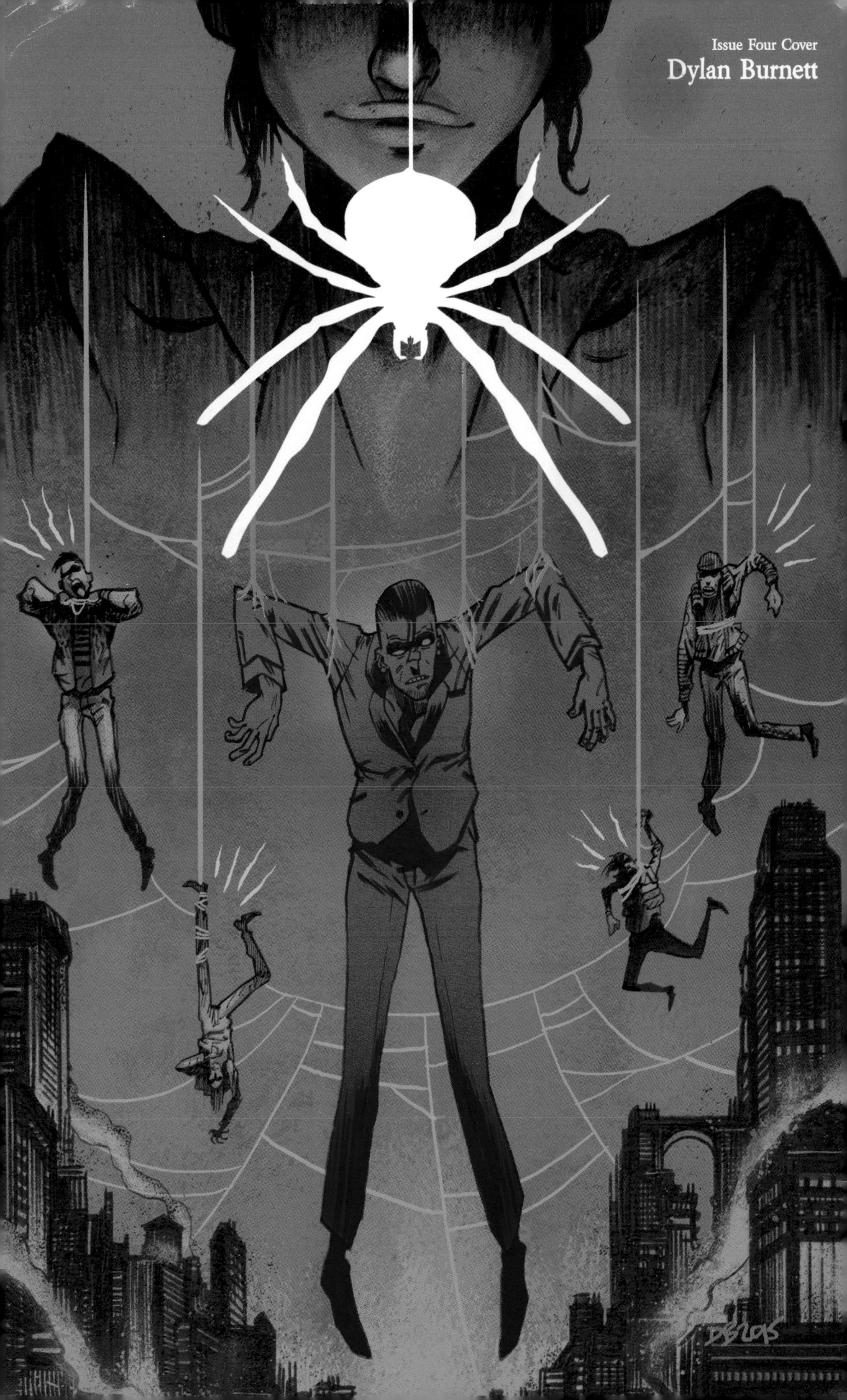

Issue Four Cover
Dylan Burnett

Issue Five Cover

Dylan Burnett

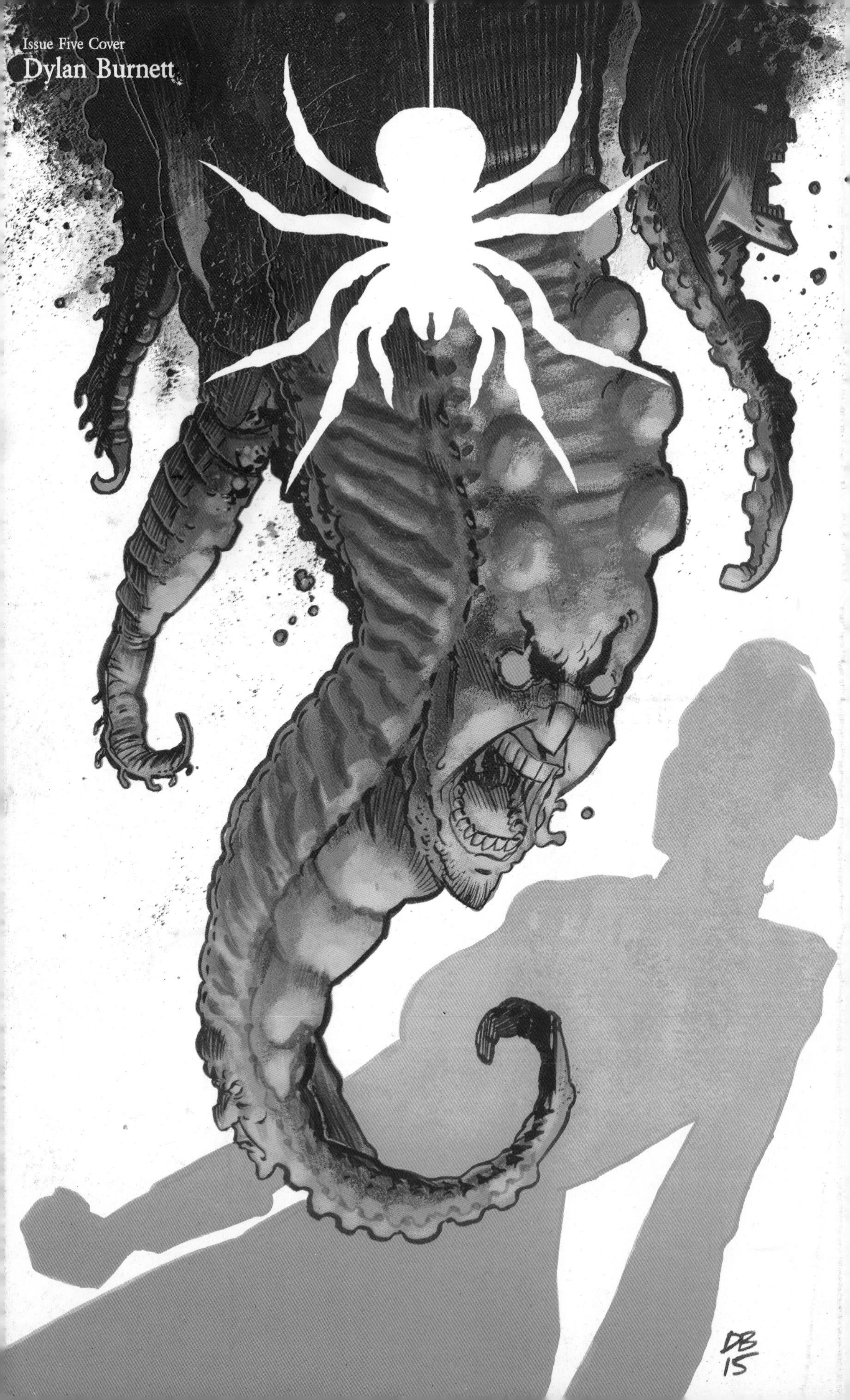
DB
15